Transforming the United Nations system

Transforming the United Nations system: Designs for a workable world

Joseph E. Schwartzberg

**United Nations
University Press**

TOKYO · NEW YORK · PARIS

United Nations University Press
United Nations University, 53-70, Jingumae 5-chome,
Shibuya-ku, Tokyo 150-8925, Japan
Tel: +81-3-5467-1212   Fax: +81-3-3406-7345
E-mail: sales@unu.edu   General enquiries: press@unu.edu
http://www.unu.edu

United Nations University Office at the United Nations, New York
2 United Nations Plaza, Room DC2-2062, New York, NY 10017, USA
Tel: +1-212-963-6387   Fax: +1-212-371-9454
E-mail: unuony@unu.edu

United Nations University Press is the publishing division of the United Nations University.

Cover design by Ian Youngs
Cover photograph by UN Photo/JC McIlwaine
Cover map by Philip Schwartzberg, Meridian Mapping, Minneapolis, MN

Printed in the United States of America for the Americas and Asia
Printed in the United Kingdom for Europe, Africa and the Middle East

ISBN 978-92-808-1230-5
e-ISBN 978-92-808-7199-9

Library of Congress Cataloging-in-Publication Data

Schwartzberg, Joseph E.
Transforming the United Nations system : designs for a workable world / Joseph E. Schwartzberg.
    pages   cm.
  Includes bibliographical references and index.
  ISBN 978-9280812305 (pbk.)—ISBN 978-9280871999 (e-ISBN)
  1. United Nations—Reorganization. 2. United Nations—Management. 3. International organization. I. Title.
JZ4984.5.S384   2013
352.3′672113—dc23   2013030110

Dedicated to the memory of
Stanley K. Platt, 1905–1997,
and
Martha Rugh Platt, 1907–2008,
indefatigable workers in the cause of peace and justice.

Endorsements

The first four endorsements below are from individuals who have had a major official tie to the United Nations. All subsequent statements are in alphabetical order, according to the surname of the endorser.

"This contribution of Professor Schwartzberg will be an essential reference work for all those who are concerned with the future of a new United Nations."
Boutros Boutros-Ghali, sixth Secretary-General of the United Nations

"Joseph Schwartzberg's important book aims at guiding the United Nations system into more productive and more workable patterns. His clear exposition and creative thinking will greatly stimulate and encourage those who tackle these formidable tasks."
Brian Urquhart, former Under-Secretary-General, United Nations

"It is a joy and a privilege to read a manuscript by Joseph Schwartzberg, replete with common sense approaches and pragmatic solutions. Anyone who reads him understands how obstacles can be overcome – one by one. United Nations reform is inescapable – not utopian. Indeed, world peace requires reform of global institutions and strengthening of the rule of law, nationally and internationally. A World Parliamentary Assembly with consultative functions would significantly advance this goal by giving greater legitimacy to global decisions through citizen input."

Alfred M. de Zayas, United Nations Independent Expert on the Promotion of a Democratic and Equitable International Order, and Professor of International Law, Geneva School of Diplomacy and International Relations

"This volume lucidly and intelligently presents a sweeping series of new, innovative ideas designed to reform the United Nations structure and performance. From weighted voting to the constructive use of regional representation, from new institutions to more effective use of existing ones, readers will find a rich mother lode to change and challenge current thinking. This book is a rare compendium of forward-looking ideas to structure closer world cooperation."

Thomas R. Pickering, former US Ambassador to the United Nations and former US Undersecretary of State for Political Affairs

"While coping with a changing world, the United Nations system is constantly changing. Schwartzberg enables readers to creatively develop a preferred vision of the future United Nations system, and develop policies for achieving this vision."

Chadwick Alger, Mershon Professor Emeritus of Political Science and Public Policy and former Director of the Mershon Center, Ohio State University

"The United Nations is the central but suboptimal piece of humanity's collective response to our increasing interdependence. Most proposals regarding the reform of the United Nations system are overly concerned about what is feasible, at the expense of what is ideal. Professor Schwartzberg's formidable work corrects that systemic bias, and shuttles between the feasible and the ideal, with elegance and rigor."

Hakan Altinay, Nonresident Senior Fellow of the Brookings Institution, Global Ethics Fellow of the Carnegie Council and President of the Global Civics Academy

"Authored by a renowned geographer, this challenging book brims with sensible and attainable proposals to strengthen the effectiveness of the United Nations and to promote international cooperation toward crucial objectives at a critical time."

Harm de Blij, Distinguished Professor Emeritus of Geography, Michigan State University, and former editor for ABC's *Good Morning America* television programme

"For believers in just governance, progressive democratization of the United Nations system is an essential process. The many innovative

proposals put forward in this wonderful book point the way to a better-governed world."
Johan Galtung, Professor of Peace Studies and founder of Transcend International

"*Transforming the United Nations System* by Joseph Schwartzberg, with its many well-reasoned and exhaustively documented specific recommendations, is a masterpiece and a necessary resource for anyone interested in a better future for humanity."
Ronald J. Glossop, Professor Emeritus of Philosophy, Southern Illinois University – Edwardsville

"Whether or not you agree with Professor Schwartzberg's specific proposals, this is a conscientious and thoughtful attempt to bring a needed dose of objectivity to the highly politicized issue of United Nations reform. It should be the starting point for anyone seriously interested in the topic."
Hurst Hannum, Professor of International Law, The Fletcher School of Law and Diplomacy, Tufts University

"Joe Schwartzberg is among the few who think creatively against the stream. His book provides a comprehensive United Nations reform agenda and should be studied carefully by those interested in and working towards a revitalized and strengthened United Nations system."
Klaus Hüfner, Honorary President, World Federation of United Nations Associations

"Building global institutions capable of coping with climate change, financial crises, nuclear proliferation and other global problems has become the central political concern in the twenty-first century. Professor Schwartzberg's book is, arguably, the most comprehensive attempt at combining the goal of a global democratic order and the realities of the existing international structure."
Fernando Iglesias, writer, journalist, member of Parliament of Mercosur, and Executive Secretary, Democracia Global

"Born of war, the nearly 70-year-old United Nations system lives on despite all the cries against its inadequacies. Joseph Schwartzberg's book is a refreshing call for retooling the present system of global governance to promote a more secure, dignified and happier world. The volume is a must-read for everyone who is concerned about the future."

Takashi Inoguchi, President and Chairman of the Board, University of Niigata Prefecture

"This book persuasively demonstrates that the political organization of the world requires a wide range of significant institutional innovations."
Lucio Levi, Professor of Political Science and Comparative Politics, University of Torino, and editor of *The Federalist Debate*

"From the preface to the appendices, Joe Schwartzberg has produced one of the most extraordinary books ever written on transforming the United Nations system. The vision, the proposals and breadth of the work are astounding. The maps, graphs and statistics alone are tremendous. And at issue is the survival of civilization."
William Pace, Executive Director of the World Federalist Movement – Institute for Global Policy and Convenor of the Coalition for the International Criminal Court

"My students are excited and inspired by Professor Schwartzberg's carefully crafted strategies for addressing the democratic deficits within the United Nations. His bold, concrete proposals stimulate in-depth classroom discussions as well as being popular essay topics. His practical, innovative models encourage students to move beyond a preoccupation with problems to focus on sophisticated yet practical solutions. This book should be on the syllabi of all courses on the United Nations."
Elizabeth Riddell-Dixon, Professor Emerita of Political Science, University of Western Ontario, Canada

"Joseph Schwartzberg is the preeminent expert on United Nations reform and *Transforming the United Nations System* is the culmination of his lifetime of research and practical engagement with the issue. Activists and scholars of transnational advocacy will welcome his compelling recommendations for enhancing the involvement and legitimacy of civil society actors in the United Nations system."
Kathryn Sikkink, Regents Professor of Political Science, University of Minnesota, and winner of the 2006 Gravemeyer Award for Ideas Improving World Order

"The product of formidable research, *Transforming the United Nations System* is a must read for those who want a knowledgeable analysis of the workings of the United Nations and its potential restructuring. Joe

Schwartzberg's magisterial publication is a great step toward better world government."

John E. Trent, Fellow, Centre on Governance, University of Ottawa, former Secretary General, International Political Science Association, and author of *Modernizing the United Nations System*

"Particularly promising among the many reform proposals in Professor Schwartzberg's work are his detailed recommendations for a universally representative, veto-free Security Council with objective, formula-based weighted voting."

Lucy Law Webster, Executive Director, Center for War/Peace Studies

"No one has thought longer or harder than Joe Schwartzberg about the challenges of designing a fairer and better world order. This book is an essential contribution to a long overdue conversation not only about United Nations reform but, more broadly, about what passes for our current system (or rather non-system) of global governance."

Thomas G. Weiss, Director, Ralph Bunche Institute for International Studies, City University of New York and past President of the Academic Council on the United Nations System and of the International Studies Association

Contents

List of figures and tables

About the author

Born in Brooklyn, New York in 1928, Joseph E. Schwartzberg received his PhD from the University of Wisconsin in 1960. He has since taught at the University of Pennsylvania (1960–1964 and summer 1965), the University of Minnesota (1964–2000) and Jawaharlal Nehru University in New Delhi (Fullbright Professor, 1979–1980). His academic specialities are the geography of South Asia, political geography and the history of cartography. His doctoral dissertation (1960) was published (1969) as monograph number 4 of the 1961 Census of India, with the title *Occupational Structure and Level of Economic Development in India: A Regional Analysis*. He has also done pioneering research on the geography of the Indian caste system during two years of fieldwork throughout India, and has published numerous works on the conflict in Kashmir. His monumental and highly innovative *Historical Atlas of South Asia* (University of Chicago Press, 1978 and Oxford University Press, 1992) won the Watumull Prize of the American Historical Association and a distinguished achievement award from the Association of American Geographers. He was the principal author and co-editor of two volumes of the projected 11-volume *History of Cartography*, writing on the indigenous cosmographic and cartographic traditions of South Asia, Southeast Asia and Greater Tibet. He has served on the editorial advisory board of the *Encyclopaedia Britannica* and as a consultant on South Asia to numerous publishers and several government agencies in the United States and India.

After 32 months of military service during the Korean War (final rank of first lieutenant), Schwartzberg spent an equal time living and backpacking in Europe, North Africa and Asia. He has since extended his travels considerably, having now visited more than a hundred countries. He has lived in India (four years), Germany, France and Spain, and is multilingual.

Schwartzberg served as chair of the University of Minnesota's Department of South Asian and Middle Eastern Studies, as a trustee and member of the Executive Council of the American Institute of Indian Studies and as an elected member and secretary of the US National Committee of the International Geographical Union. He participated in several Peace Corps training programmes (directing the first such programme for Ceylon), and for three years directed Minnesota Studies in International Development, an overseas internship programme.

A lifelong peace and justice activist, Schwartzberg has a particular interest in the UN system and has published numerous books and articles relating to global governance. Among his publications are *Revitalizing the United Nations: Reform through Weighted Voting* (Institute for Global Policy and World Federalist Movement, 2004) and *Creating a World Parliamentary Assembly: An Evolutionary Journey* (Committee for a Democratic UN, 2012).

Schwartzberg was a co-founder in 1996 of the Minnesota Alliance of Peacemakers, a consortium now including more than 80 peace and justice organizations. He served on the board of directors of the World Federalist Association (subsequently Citizens for Global Solutions and now GlobalSolutions.org), chaired its Policy and Resolutions Committee and for 14 years was president of its Minnesota Chapter. He is currently a member of the International Council of the World Federalist Movement as well as the Steering Committee of the World Federalist Institute (a think-tank). He was also in 1997 a founding member of another think-tank, the Kashmir Study Group, and a co-author of several of its publications. In 2009 the University of Minnesota's Office of International Programs bestowed on him its yearly Award for Global Engagement and the honorary title of Distinguished International Emeritus Professor.

Foreword

Ramesh Thakur

In a number of key meetings during and after the Second World War, visionary world leaders drew up rules to govern international behaviour and established a network of institutions, centred on the United Nations, to work together for the common good. Both the rules and the institutions – the system of global governance with the United Nations as its core – are showing their age, prompting scepticism over their capacity to cope with the growing numbers and complexity of pressing global challenges that must be addressed with some urgency.

The basis of world order, with the United Nations at the centre of the system of global governance, has come under increasing strain in recent years due to seven major disconnects. The first is the gap between the inflated expectations of what the United Nations can accomplish and the limited authority and modest resources given to it. A second is the growing disconnect between the threats to peace and security and the obstacles to economic development, lying increasingly within nations rather than in relations among and disputes between states. A third and related disconnect is the persistence of policy authority and the requisite resources for tackling problems being vested in states, while the source and scope of the problems are increasingly global and require the globalization of the process of policy-making. A fourth is the greater recognition given to individuals as both subjects and objects of international relations, reflecting an increasingly internationalized human conscience. A fifth is the growing gravity of threats rooted in non-state actors, including but not limited to terrorists. A sixth is the growing salience of weapons of mass destruction that, in their reach and destructiveness, challenge the very basis of the territorial state. And the seventh is the strategic disconnect between the distribution of military, political and economic power in the real world and the distribution of decision-making authority in the artificially constructed world of intergovernmental organizations. Especially as wealth, power and influence seep from the West to the global South, a global institutional rebalancing must accompany the shift of the geopolitical centre of gravity.

How can the United Nations be so restructured as to empower it to enforce global norms and UN Security Council resolutions against recalcitrant regimes like Syria's Bashar al Assad but not have the authority and capacity to take any action against Israel, or to stop Iran from acquiring nuclear weapons but not reverse Israel's nuclear-armed status? Unless and until this is done, will Washington recommit to the international organization? Conversely, if and when it is done, how many others will walk away from the world body, viewing it "not as an independent broker but as a glorified sub-contractor to the United States"?[1] Can the United Nations square this particular circle of the circumstances in which it is right and wrong to use force across (and, increasingly, within) borders in today's world? How true is it to say that "As a pre-cold-war organization operating in a post-cold-war world, the UN has struggled to be relevant and effective"?[2]

Over the past few years the organization has proven itself to be remarkably agile on some occasions, but not up to the task on many others. On the one hand it could be argued that the United Nations has promised much but accomplished little. Equally, however, one could argue that, on balance, the world has been a better and less bloody place with the United Nations in being than would have been the case without the organization's existence.

That existence in turn has been sustained by the UN's ability to manage change by implementing reforms. Set up to manage the world in the revolutionary conditions prevailing after a major world war, the organization has had simultaneously to reflect, regulate and respond to the changing circumstances all around it since 1945, and in particular since the end of the Cold War. When in 2003 George W. Bush, president of the organization's most powerful and influential member, threw down the gauntlet of relevance, the demands on the United Nations continued to be great and urgent, the expectations of it compelling and poignant. It was, after all, to the United Nations and the Europeans that Bush turned for "nation-building" in Afghanistan after the military defeat of the Taliban government; it was to the United Nations that he turned to buttress his campaign against Iraq; it is the United Nations that is left to face the unimaginable task of alleviating HIV/AIDS in Africa; it is the United

Nations that led the efforts at humanitarian relief operations after the devastating earthquake and tsunami that struck across the Indian Ocean at the end of 2004; and it is the United Nations that will be the forum for negotiating the successor to the much-lauded Millennium Development Goals when they expire in 2015.

There are two different ways of conceptualizing UN reform. In public perception, the United Nations is a collective entity. In reality, the organization is a collection of discrete entities, each with its own set of rules, members and interests. From a reform perspective, three distinctions are especially pertinent: between the UN Secretariat, of which the Secretary-General is the chief administrative officer; between the intergovernmental organs, which are served by UN officials and whose members are the political masters of the UN Secretariat; and in the interaction between the two. Kofi Annan's 1997 and 2002 reports[3] on reform focused mainly on those changes that lie within the purview of the Secretary-General. His successor Ban Ki-moon has continued the tradition of introducing various changes in how the administrative system works to service the needs, expectations and demands of member states.

A second way to conceptualize UN reforms also starts with public perceptions. For most people, the mention of the subject conjures up one of two scenarios: reforming the structure, composition and procedures of the UN Security Council; or eliminating waste, inefficiency, bureaucratic rigidity, costliness and so on associated with the world organization. Among governments in many Western countries, and ordinary people in many developing countries, the United Nations is often seen as a bloated, high-cost, junket-loving irrelevance to their real needs and concerns – little more than a talkfest. The failure of so many critics to distinguish the organization as an international civil service from the games governments play, often including their own governments, has long been a source of deep frustration to many UN officials and supporters.

The 2004 report of the High-level Panel on Threats, Challenges and Change cast its ambitions on a much bigger canvas than Annan's efforts to streamline the structure and operations of the UN Secretariat, proposing in addition several major normative, procedural and structural reforms.[4] But in 2005 the United Nations once again emerged largely reform-proof from the major effort invested in the exercise.

Efforts to emphasize reform as an ongoing process are reflected also in a number of reviews, initiatives and developments outside the UN Secretariat, by what scholars have described as the Third UN (the first two being UN officials and member states). The 2000 report of the Brahimi Panel,[5] for example, looked back on the half-century's experience of peacekeeping in order to bring it into line with the realities of the new century. Other reports, for example on Rwanda and Srebrenica,[6] have underlined the UN's new-found capacity and willingness to engage in serious introspection with regard to some painful episodes in its history and draw the necessary lessons from them. The "responsibility to protect" is a good example of policy innovation; the Peacebuilding Commission, of institutional adaptation; and the many reforms introduced in UN peace operations since the Brahimi Report, of organizational learning.

In his new book *The Great Convergence* (2013), the distinguished Asian public intellectual Kishore Mahbubani, twice the permanent representative of Singapore to the United Nations, comments on great-power machinations that keep the organization intentionally weak and ineffectual.[7] He argues that the major powers cannot tolerate any international organization that is both independent and powerful, and have a common interest in choosing a Secretary-General who is pliant and duly respectful, not independent-minded, bold and visionary. A couple of times in the past they have mistakenly chosen the latter type.

Mahbubani continues that Western-sourced middle-class values mean that the principles on which such governance advances must be built are democracy, power sharing, equity and accountability – as well as geopolitical realignments. But the West is proving singularly reluctant and obdurate in exporting democratic structures and procedures to international governance institutions, to ceding power in order to share it, to assuming equitable costs of managing the global commons, and in general to supporting a universal rules-based order in which one law applies to all.

As this suggests, often hidden in the details of reform proposals is the reality that the struggle for UN reform is a battle over policy and control, not just process nor even a simple management upgrade. In particular, should the United Nations be the forum of choice or of last resort for collective-action solutions to global problems: less or more environmental regulation, non-proliferation and disarmament or just non-proliferation, counterterrorism or human rights, a strong state that provides social protection and regulation or an unobtrusive state that lets capital and markets rule the roost, etc.? That is, it is a struggle between international Keynesianism and neoliberalism.

If we want multilateralism to be the preferred route, then strengthening the United Nations and making it more effective and relevant are imperative. For its performance has been patchy and variable. It has been neither uniform in its response nor consistent in the quality of services provided. Without the United Nations, in the last 50 years the world would have been a more, not less, dangerous place. Yet with the United Nations remaining essentially unchanged in structure, authority and powers, the world is unlikely to be a mainly free, healthy, prosperous and peaceful place in the next 50 years.

The legitimacy of the Security Council as the authoritative validator of international security action has been subject to a triple erosion: it has been perceived as being increasingly unrepresentative in composition, undemocratic in operation and ineffective in results. The industrialized and Western countries often chafe at the ineffectual performance legitimacy of the Security Council, and their desire to resist its role as the sole validator of the international use of force is the product of this dissatisfaction at its perceived sorry record. On the other hand, if the Security Council was to become increasingly activist, interventionist and effective, it is highly likely that the erosion of representational and procedural legitimacy would lead many developing and non-Western countries to question its authority even more forcefully.

If the organization fails to accommodate its structures, processes and agendas to the transformations sweeping the world, it will risk atrophy and fade into irrelevance, and the five permanent members of the Security Council along with the other 188 member states will be left gathering rosebuds of consolation at the death of an institution which gave them a status so exalted that they refused to dilute it by sharing it with the rising powers.

In addition to the valuable recommendations of the many blue-ribbon international panels, many individuals have invested heavily in labours of love in trying to understand what changes are necessary and desirable and how they might be implemented. Joe Schwartzberg is one such individual who has devoted decades to trying to come to grips with the challenge of proposals for reforming the United Nations by a combination of creative vision and political realism. He has concluded that what the organization needs is not mere reform but a wholesale transformation. He approaches his task as a political geographer, and his work is rich empirically more than theoretically. He notes the importance of such fundamental changes since the UN's inception in 1945, as the growing salience and role of international organizations, the proliferation and growing influence of non-governmental organizations, the march of globalization, the revolution of rising expectations and the folly of believing that the affluent one-sixth of humanity can retreat into globally gated communities. Rather, an inclusive global society demands a strengthening of international institutional machinery to manage the global commons on a fair and equitable basis as well as efficiently and effectively.

The United Nations as presently configured cannot play such a role and will instead fall into disrepute and desuetude. Believing that the design of decision-making institutions shapes the quality and legitimacy of their decisions, Schwartzberg outlines complex but interrelated changes in the design of the UN machinery in order to revitalize and greatly strengthen the UN system. He pays particular attention to the major political organs like the Security Council, the General Assembly, the Economic and Social Council and the Human Rights Council, but also foreshadows a World Parliamentary Assembly. Idealistic in conception, his ideas are nonetheless informed by realpolitik calculations of population size, economic weight, military power and other material drivers of the clout of international actors. This takes him inevitably into the contested notion of weighted voting.

The end result is a collection of analyses and a set of recommendations that are comprehensive, innovative, integrated and complex, befitting a machinery designed to address all the world's major collective-action problems. As Schwartzberg himself acknowledges, few are likely to be convinced by all of his analyses and persuaded of all his prescriptions for transforming the United Nations. Equally, however, few readers will leave this book without being much better informed about the UN machinery, the principles that animate it and the magnitude of the task confronting all who would rescue it from the prison of past power equations and realign it to the dreams and challenges of tomorrow.

Ramesh Thakur
Canberra, May 2013

Notes

1. Quoted in Thalif Deen, "UN Warned of Iraqi 'Deathtrap'", *Asia Times*, 13 May 2004.
2. Ivo Daalder and James Lindsay, "Divided on Being United", *Financial Times Weekend*, 6–7 November 2004.
3. Report of the Secretary-General, "Renewing the United Nations: A Programme for Reform", UN Doc. A/51/950, 1997; Report of the Secretary-General, "Strengthening of the United Nations: An Agenda for Further Change", UN Doc. A/57/387, 2002.
4. Report of the Secretary-General's High-level Panel on Threats, Challenges and Change, "A More Secure World: Our Shared Responsibility" UN Doc. A/59/565, 29 November 2004.
5. Report of the Panel on United Nations Peace Operations, "Comprehensive Review of the Whole Question of Peacekeeping Operations in All Their Aspects", UN Doc. A/55/305, 2000.
6. "Report of the Independent Inquiry into the Actions of the United Nations during the 1994 Genocide in Rwanda", UN Doc. S/1999/1257, 1999; Report of the Secretary-General Pursuant to General Assembly Resolution 53/35, "The Fall of Srebrenica", UN Doc. A/54/549, 1999.
7. Kishore Mahbubani, *The Great Convergence: Asia, the West, and the Logic of One World*, New York: Public Affairs, 2013.

Preface

The splitting of the atom has changed everything, save our mode of thinking, and thus we drift toward unparalleled catastrophe.

Henceforth, every nation's foreign policy must be judged at every point by one consideration: does it lead us to a world of law and order or does it lead us back to anarchy and death?
Albert Einstein

The correctness of Einstein's admonitions ought to be self-evident; but that is clearly not the case. Rather, most of the influential inhabitants of our planet prefer to live in a state of denial. Were that not so, they would sense the need to bestir themselves and try to correct glaring shortcomings in our system of global governance. And it is not only the threat of nuclear annihilation that is being denied. Comparable threats arise from other sources: global warming, loss of biodiversity, depletion of vital resources such as petroleum and fresh water, and the explosive potential inherent in the obscene gap between the world's haves and have-nots, to cite but a few. The reasons for inaction are many. But, among them, the inadequacies in the design of the institutional machinery of the UN system and the total absence of certain institutions that are urgently needed are especially noteworthy. This book puts forward numerous recommendations which, if adopted, would help remedy those deficiencies.

Let me here enunciate six fundamental propositions.
- We must find ways to supplant the law of force with the force of law in international affairs.

- Our planet is an exceedingly complex and interdependent organism; what nations do within their own borders often adversely affects other nations in unacceptable ways.
- Global problems require global solutions; there are many pressing problems that national governments cannot solve acting on their own.
- National sovereignty conveys to governments not only certain rights but also responsibilities; the foremost responsibility is the promotion of the security and welfare of the nation's citizens.
- All human beings are entitled to the enjoyment of political, civil, economic and social rights as set forth in the Universal Declaration of Human Rights and various treaties and covenants adopted in furtherance of that declaration.
- We are our brother's keeper; when nations fail egregiously to protect the rights of their citizens it becomes the responsibility of the international community to protect those rights.

Admittedly it is not now, nor will it soon be, within the power of the international system to act in full accordance with all of the above points. The world's imperfections are so numerous and widespread and its available human resources so limited that doing so would not be feasible. Nevertheless, the propositions put forward do suggest paths for movement towards global reform. As the institutional machinery of the UN system improves, the scope of its involvement should expand commensurately.

Since the founding of the United Nations in 1945, the world has undergone enormous changes. Among the many new developments, I here highlight only a few that are essentially extrinsic to the UN system in its present form, but whose increasing salience will require adjustments within the evolving system of global governance.

First, whereas global governance, such as it was in 1945, was generally perceived as the virtually exclusive preserve of sovereign states whose territorial integrity was inviolable, international organizations have come to be increasingly important. Apart from agencies functioning within the UN system, those with a more or less global scope include such entities as the World Trade Organization, the G-8 and G-20, and the Organisation for Economic Co-operation and Development. At a regional level the European Union plays an especially prominent role and serves as a model for further integration in other parts of the world. Organizations such as NATO and the Commonwealth of Nations have an increasingly widespread, if not quite global, reach.

The march of "globalization" over the last few decades has also resulted in a much greater role for non-state actors, especially giant multinational corporations (MNCs). The record of MNCs is decidedly mixed. Although they have unquestionably become powerful engines for economic growth, the benefits from that growth are very unevenly distributed and the methods of growth have entailed substantial and inadequately recognized negative consequences, most notably environmental deterioration, social and economic dislocation, and the subversion of local cultures. Not infrequently MNCs, often in concert with governments in the developed countries and with the blessing of the Bretton Woods institutions (which wealthy nations dominate), have been able to make inroads in the political and economic policies of relatively weak states, thereby calling their sovereignty into question. Future design for global governance must take the corporate sector into consideration.

Another important set of non-state actors are non-governmental organizations (NGOs), a key component of what is often termed "civil society". Their potential to play a major role in shaping public opinion and the thinking of policy-makers, especially in democratic polities, is enormous. NGOs have been especially active in promoting human rights, and the adoption of some of the relevant UN conventions and treaties would have been slower were it not for their involvement. It seems appropriate, therefore, for the United Nations to devise new governance mechanisms that would enable it better to draw upon NGO expertise and dedication.

Notwithstanding the recent global economic downturn, the past two generations, especially in the period since the end of the Cold War, have seen a widespread and continuing revolution of rising expectations. Where fatalistic acceptance of injustice was once the norm, voices demanding justice are increasingly raised. To the extent that those voices are ignored and denied participation in the political processes of their nations, some segment of the population will either resort to terrorism or lend support to others who do. Additionally, because of the revolution in communications technology, the possibility of forging common causes among the oppressed and dispossessed, in opposition to the privileged elements of the world's population, is greater than ever before.

At the global level, the affluent sixth of humanity has two choices. It can choose to live in what are, in effect, gated communities (as do many wealthy families within their own cities), protected from the "rabble" by whatever the state can provide in the way of military, police and surveillance apparatus. Or it can elect to ameliorate the situations that breed alienation and violence. The latter choice would require substantial strengthening of the institutional machinery of the international community. Though that would not be cheap, it should ultimately prove to be much less expensive than maintaining the unjust, phenomenally wasteful and dehumanizing status quo. This is not to assert that a wholesale redistribution of the world's wealth is necessary; but it is necessary to provide the world with a realistic sense of hope. That is certainly an attainable goal.

I did not come lightly to the conclusions expressed in the preceding paragraphs. Nor am I a recent convert to my current world-view. In 1949 or 1950, when working in Washington, DC, I first learned about a then new organization, the United World Federalists (UWF), as well as the international World Federalist Movement of which UWF was a part. Like many others in that relatively optimistic time, I was immediately convinced of the logic of the notion that a democratic world federation, modelled more or less along the lines of the US government, with a separation of powers between executive, legislative and judicial branches and a system of checks and balances among them, would provide the best possible antidote to future wars.[1] Since then I have continued to think, read and debate about questions of global governance in its broadest sense (even though the term "global governance" had not yet been coined).

Nearly three years of military service during the Korean War and an equal period of world travel immediately thereafter temporarily interrupted my involvement with world federalism, but contributed to my life-long commitment to causes within the global peace and justice movement. In any event, that war and the related rise of McCarthyism in America brought about a major setback to world federalist advocacy. Many of its supporters were seen, incorrectly, as crypto-communists; and organizational membership and financial support plummeted.[2]

After completing a PhD in geography in 1960, I embarked upon an academic career wherein my two principal foci were South Asia and political geography. The former of these specializations heightened my awareness of the necessity of considering the needs of the global South in devising plans relating to global governance; the latter taught me the importance of realpolitik. Both those perspectives are embodied in reform proposals throughout this work.

Over the past half-century or so, and especially since my retirement in 2000, I have presented my ideas on global governance to hundreds of lay and professional audiences. I have benefited greatly from critical feedback and occasionally modified my views accordingly. I have also had papers published in *Global Governance, Global Dialogue, The UN Chronicle, Political Geography, The Federalist Debate* and other scholarly journals; and authored chapters in several books as well as two monographs, *Revitalizing the United Nations System: Reform through Weighted Voting*[3] and *Creating a World Parliamentary Assembly: An Evolutionary Journey.*[4] These too have yielded useful feedback. Throughout my work, I have tried to strike an appropriate balance between the realist and the idealist perspectives.

I bring no special theoretical insights to the present work. Rather, my orientation has always been highly empirical. Additionally, I try to blend sound analysis with creative synthesis, to draw upon perspectives from a diversity of academic disciplines and to think independently and innovatively ("outside the box", to use an overworked cliché). Finally, my life experience, including travel in more than a hundred countries and associations with people of all economic classes and in many walks of life, has given me a catholicity of outlook and enhanced my ability to empathize with persons whose world-views vary markedly from my own.

It must be admitted that the record to date of attempts to reform the UN system provides little cause for optimism in regard to the prospects for the adoption of the reforms proposed in this work or, for that matter, any other far-reaching set of institutional reforms.[5] Changes for the better are by no means preordained, and humankind may indeed continue along paths that could lead to the demise of civilized society. The menu of perilous options available to our global society is ample. But so too is our menu of creative choices. Although I could be proven wrong, I believe that humankind will recognize the seriousness of the dangers on the horizon before they reach a phase that precludes their being adequately addressed, and that it will respond accordingly.

Nevertheless, overcoming the many obstacles in the path of needed reform will be a very tall order. Effecting major change will require much citizen education, creative political engagement from global civil society, the active involvement of highly respected and imaginative world leaders, political leadership from trusted progressive states within and outside the UN arena, intense global networking and, above all, the marshalling of human will on an unprecedented scale. Overcoming inertia to set the reform process into sustained motion will be especially difficult. As one well-informed wag put it, "The United Nations is notoriously the place where, in defiance of the laws of physics, inertia can develop momentum."[6]

Previous systemic changes in the architecture of global governance came about largely in the aftermath of major wars: the 1648 Treaty of Westphalia led to new notions of sovereignty following the Thirty Years War; the balance of power system within the so-called Concert of Europe emerged in the aftermath of the Napoleonic wars; the short-lived League of Nations followed the First World War; and an improved, though still seriously flawed, United Nations was spawned by the Second World War.

Obviously, no sane thinker would wish for yet another major conflagration, with the attendant risk of omnicide, as the catalytic event leading to further restructuring of global politics. But we face many other high-probability threats. Among these, the potentially devastating consequences of climate change are, perhaps, the most likely. A rise of sea level by only one or two metres brought about by progressive melting of the polar ice-caps would require tremendous capital outlays to enable the continued functioning of all of the world's major ports. It would inundate tens of thousands of square kilometres in deltaic lands, such as those of Bangladesh or Louisiana, displace hundreds of millions of people and could lead to the virtual disappearance of several small island states. Even sooner, humankind might be confronted with crippling shortages of petroleum and/or fresh water as a result of population growth and unchecked per capita demand. Even now atmospheric pollution in the burgeoning urban centres of developing countries such as China and India poses major public health hazards. To all of these we may add the dangers from new waves of terrorism, globalized crime, pandemics caused by previously unknown pathogens, and a variety of other hazards.

Whatever the eventual prods to effective action may be, when the human family finally awakens to the need to protect itself from itself, we may collectively summon the degree of will and focused intelligence required to fundamentally restructure the framework of global governance. The choice is ours. This book is intended to help make that choice easier than most people suppose.

Notes

1. A particularly influential work advocating world federalism in that period was Emery Reves, *The Anatomy of Peace*, New York: Harper & Brothers, 1945. The work was translated into several languages and millions of copies were sold worldwide. It called for a universal federal union and stood in contrast to Clarence Streit, *Union Now*, New York: Harper & Brothers, 1939, which advocated a federal "Atlantic Union" of Western democracies to face the threat then posed by the Axis powers. Among other works that were influential in the thinking of early world federalists, mention must be made of Committee to Frame a World Constitution (headed by Robert M. Hutchins), *Preliminary Draft of a World Constitution*, Chicago, IL: University of Chicago Press, 1948; Grenville Clark and Louis B. Sohn, *World Peace through World Law*, Cambridge, MA: Harvard University Press, 1958 (1st edn.) and 1964 (2nd edn., revised).
2. The best history of the movement is Joseph P. Baratta, *The Politics of World Federalism*, Westport, CT: Greenwood Publishing Group, 2003 (2 vols).
3. Joseph E. Schwartzberg, *Revitalizing the United Nations: Reform through Weighted Voting*, New York and The Hague: Institute for Global Policy, World Federalist Movement, 2004.
4. Joseph E. Schwartzberg, *Creating a World Parliamentary Assembly: An Evolutionary Journey*, Berlin: Committee for a Democratic UN, 2012.
5. Proposals for substantial reform of the system of global governance come along with surprising frequency. Some are comparable in scope to those put forward in this work; others would scrap or bypass the United Nations altogether and establish an essentially new "third-generation" global superstructure. The most widely discussed sets of proposals in recent years are the two put forward for the sixtieth anniversary global summit meeting of the General Assembly in 2005: "A More Secure World: Our Shared Responsibility", Report of the High-level Panel on Threats, Challenges and Change, UN GA Doc. A/59/565, 29 November 2004; Kofi Annan, "In Larger Freedom: Towards Development, Security and Human Rights for All", Report of the Secretary-General, UN GA

Doc. A/59/2005, 21 March 2005. A recent proposal more or less comparable in scope to my own, but differing greatly in its specifics, is Kemal Derviş and Ceren Ozer, *A Better Globalization: Legitimacy, Governance, and Reform*, Washington, DC: Brookings Institution Press, 2005. Recent proposals – by no means a complete list – that I would judge to be more ambitious than my own (though for the most part less detailed) are found in Maurice Bertrand, "Schematic Representation of the Current and Proposed Systems" and "Working Paper on the Establishment of a 'Charter-Objective' Project for a New World Organization", in Maurice Bertrand and Daniel Warner (eds), *A New Charter for a Worldwide Organization?*, The Hague: Kluwer Law International, 1997, pp. 39–44 and 45–66; Amitai Etzioni, *From Empire to Community, A New Approach to International Relations*, New York: Palgrave Macmillan, 2004; David Held, *Global Government, The Social Democratic Alternative to the Washington Consensus*, Cambridge: Polity, 2004; George Monbiot, *The Age of Consent: A Manifesto for a New World Order*, London: Flamingo, 2003; James A. Yunker, *Political Globalization: A New Vision of Federal World Government*, Lanham, MD: University Press of America, 2007.

6. Jeffrey Laurenti, "What 'Reinforcement' for the Security Council?", in Martin Ortega (ed.), *The European Union and the United Nations, Partners in Effective Multilateralism*, Chaillot Paper No. 78, Brussels: Institute for Security Studies, European Union, 2005, pp. 69–81, at p. 78.

Acknowledgements

Throughout my fairly long life, I have benefited from the guidance and example of many wise and compassionate mentors. While I cannot possibly list them all here, I do wish to express my gratitude to the collectivity of individuals who have contributed in ways large and small to the shaping of my thinking and the formation of my character. Two role models, however, the late Stanley and Martha Platt of Minneapolis, to whom this work is dedicated, must be individually recognized.

With respect to the book at hand, several persons call for special notice. First, I am deeply grateful to Ramesh Thakur for agreeing to write the incisive foreword, even when he was uncertain about what the work would include. My heartfelt thanks go also to my partner, Louise Pardee, for her forbearance of my long working hours, her discerning editorial assistance and her work on statistical spreadsheets (most of which do not appear here in printed form). My son, Philip, owner of Meridian Mapping, merits thanks for his meticulous execution of multiple incarnations of the maps and graphs that enliven my prose exposition. (Most of those illustrations appear in colour and larger size in previous publications.) My research assistants at the University of Minnesota, Ivan Bialostosky and Samuel Schueth, have earned my gratitude for conscientiously pursuing needed research materials and commenting critically on portions of my text. My gratitude goes also to secretaries in the Department of Geography of the University of Minnesota – Glen Powell, Bonnie Williams, Jodi Larson, Bryce Quesnel and Amber Kraemer – for a variety of technical assistance. Additionally, I thank the department for providing me with ample office space for so many years after my retirement in 2000.

For needed encouragement and advice as this work progressed I must single out Farooq Kathwari, chairman of the board of Ethan Allen, Inc.; William Pace, executive director of the World Federalist Movement – Institute for Global Policy; Don Kraus, executive director, GlobalSolutions.org; Lucy Webster and Myron Kronisch of the Center for War/Peace Studies; Andreas Bummel of the Committee for a Democratic UN; Ronald Glossop, emeritus professor of philosophy, University of Southern Illinois; Professor John Trent, Centre on Government, University of Ottawa; Professor Elizabeth Riddell-Dixon, Department of Political Science, University of Western Ontario; and Professor Thomas G. Weiss, Graduate Center, City University of New York.

For generous financial assistance in support of publishing, I am indebted to the Irfan Kathwari Foundation of Larchmont, NY.

Finally, may I express my gratitude to United Nations University Press for its decision to publish this work despite the author's many deviations from received wisdom in respect to the possibility of UN reform. In particular, I wish to note the contributions of Cherry Ekins, an independent contractor and copyeditor, for her meticulous reading of and many improvements in the text; Madge Walls, indexer; Marc Benger, senior sales and marketing coordinator; Adam Majoe, editor; Yoko Kojima, senior publications coordinator; Yoko Inoue, sales assistant; and Kae Sugawara, editor, whose diligence kept the publication project moving smoothly forward.

List of abbreviations

ASEAN	Association of Southeast Asian Nations
AU	African Union
CEB	Chief Executives Board for Coordination
CFC	chlorofluorocarbon
CHR	UN Commission on Human Rights
CIS	Commonwealth of Independent States
CONGO	Conference of Non-Governmental Organizations in Consultative Relationship with the United Nations
CSCC*	civil society coordinating council
DPKO	UN Department of Peacekeeping Operations
DPRK	Democratic People's Republic of Korea
EC*	WPA Electoral Commission
ECOSOC	UN Economic and Social Council
ECOWAS	Economic Community of West African States
EEZ	exclusive economic zone
EP	European Parliament
ESEC*	UN Economic, Social and Environmental Council
EU	European Union
FAO	UN Food and Agriculture Organization
G-77	Group of 77
GA	UN General Assembly
GC	UN Global Compact
GDP	gross domestic product
GHG	greenhouse gas
GNI	gross national income
GONGO	government-organized non-governmental organization

HRC	UN Human Rights Council
IBRD	International Bank for Reconstruction and Development (World Bank)
ICANN	Internet Corporation for Assigned Names and Numbers
ICAO	International Civil Aviation Organization
ICC	International Criminal Court
ICCPR	International Covenant on Civil and Political Rights
ICESCR	International Covenant on Economic, Social and Cultural Rights
ICISS	International Commission on Intervention and State Sovereignty
ICJ	International Court of Justice
ICSC	International Civil Service Commission
ICTR	International Criminal Tribunal for Rwanda
ICTY	International Criminal Tribunal for the Former Yugoslavia
IFAD	International Fund for Agricultural Development
IGO	intergovernmental organization
ILC	International Law Commission
ILO	International Labour Organization
IMF	International Monetary Fund
IMO	International Maritime Organization
INGO	international non-governmental organization
INTERPOL	International Criminal Police Organization
IO	international organization
ISAF	International Security Assistance Force
ITU	International Telecommunications Union
MDG	Millennium Development Goal
MNC	multinational corporation
MONUC	UN Organization Mission in the Democratic Republic of the Congo
MWP*	member of World Parliamentary Assembly
NAM	Non-Aligned Movement
NATO	North Atlantic Treaty Organization
NGO	non-governmental organization
NPT	Nuclear Non-Proliferation Treaty
OAS	Organization of American States
OECD	Organisation for Economic Co-operation and Development
OHCHR	Office of the High Commissioner for Human Rights
OPOV	one person – one vote
P-5	permanent five members of UN Security Council
PBC	Peacebuilding Commission
PCIJ	Permanent Court of International Justice
R2P	responsibility to protect
SAARC	South Asian Association for Regional Cooperation
SC	UN Security Council
SG	UN Secretary-General
SHIRBRIG	Standby High Readiness Brigade for UN Operations
UDHR	Universal Declaration of Human Rights
UN	United Nations

UNAA*	UN Administrative Academy
UNAMIR	UN Assistance Mission in Rwanda
UNARC*	UN Administrative Reserve Corps
UNCED	UN Conference on Environment and Development
UNCHC*	UN Common Heritage Council
UNCLOS	UN Convention on the Law of the Sea
UNCTAD	UN Conference on Trade and Development
UNDEF	UN Democracy Fund
UNDP	UN Development Programme
UNEF*	UN Emergency Force
UNEP	UN Environment Programme
UNESCO	UN Educational, Scientific and Cultural Organization
UNFCCC	UN Framework Convention on Climate Change
UNFPA	UN Fund for Population Activities
UNHCR	UN High Commissioner for Refugees
UNPC*	UN Peace Corps
UNRWA	UN Relief and Works Agency for Palestinian Refugees in the Near East
UNV	UN Volunteers
UPU	Universal Postal Union
USDP	US Department of Peace
UWF	United World Federalists
WFP	World Food Programme
WGIG	Working Group on Internet Governance
WHO	World Health Organization
WIPO	World Intellectual Property Organization
WMD	weapons of mass destruction
WMO	World Meteorological Organization
WPA*	World Parliamentary Assembly
WTO	World Trade Organization

* The entities whose acronyms are followed by an asterisk are proposed, but have not yet come into existence.

1

Introduction

Another world is not only possible; she is on her way. On a quiet day I can hear her breathing.
Arundhati Roy

One's destination is never a place, but a new way of looking at things.
Henry Miller

Hearken not to the voice, which petulantly tells you that the form of government recommended is impossible to accomplish.
James Madison, *The Federalist*, No. 14

Objectives

Global problems require global solutions. This dictum provides the motive for writing this book. The idea ought to be self-evident, but clearly is not. Our present system of global governance – if one can call anarchy a system – shows little evidence that the principal actors on the global stage have come to grips with the magnitude of the existential threats to a sustainable civilization. The world has thus far failed to put in place a set of agencies suitably empowered to deal with such long-standing threats as the war system and more recent threats, especially those posed by climate change and other forms of environmental degradation. Existing institutions, within and outside the UN system, must be strengthened and given broader mandates, and new agents of change must be created.

Transforming the United Nations system: Designs for a workable world, Schwartzberg,
United Nations University Press, 2013, ISBN 978-92-808-1230-5

The decisions they make must be recognized as legitimate. Time is short. Fundamental reforms in the near future are essential.

A simple, but key, premise underlying this work is that *the design of decision-making institutions has an important bearing on the quality and legitimacy of the decisions they make.* To the extent that this simple truth is recognized, society will be inclined to endow vital institutions with greater responsibility and provide them with greater resources. From this it follows that improved designs for existing institutions and, where needed, the creation of new, well-designed institutions can set in motion a virtuous cycle that will contribute significantly to the evolution of a more workable world.[1]

The workable world that I envisage centres on a revitalized and *substantially strengthened UN system.* While many of the essential institutions within that system are already in place, none is optimally constituted. In particular, their methods of allocating decision-making power bear little relationship to the actual power of global actors outside the arena of the UN itself. Consequently, their fairness and even their legitimacy are often called into question. Moreover, some institutions needed for an efficiently working UN system have yet to be created. Other agencies that have become obsolete or have failed to live up to the hopes and expectations of their creators should be eliminated. Finally, the entire system suffers from a serious democratic deficit. Institutions are needed by which to engage ordinary world citizens and civil society organizations in the work of global governance.

Among the multitude of existing and proposed components of the UN system that call for critical scrutiny, this work pays particular attention to the Security Council, the General Assembly, an Economic, Social and Environmental Council (to replace what is now the Economic and Social Council), a strengthened Human Rights Council (to replace the moribund Trusteeship Council), an eventual World Parliamentary Assembly, new civil society coordination councils and a standing UN Peace Corps. Other essential institutions, such as the International Court of Justice and International Criminal Court, will be more cursorily examined. Their chief shortcomings are not questions of design, but rather of neglect. Ways have to be found to ensure that they are used to a much greater extent than they have been to date.

While I will devote relatively little attention to the working methods – as opposed to the structure – of agencies within the UN system, several especially important functions do call for special scrutiny. These include fundraising and budgeting; recruitment and promotion of Secretariat staff; monitoring compliance with global laws, norms and standards; conflict resolution; administering failed and failing states; and integrating civil society and responsible entities within the corporate sector into the ongoing work of the United Nations.

Apart from my general advocacy of inclusiveness and fairness in the way decisions are made, this book is not about specific policies that the United Nations or its various affiliated agencies and programmes should follow. I am confident that reform of the decision-making processes will provide an adequate basis for forging wise and workable decisions and correcting mistakes that will, inevitably, be made from time to time.

Although my proposals are idealistic in conception, there is nothing utopian in what I shall be presenting. I do not foresee a world free from conflict, but rather one in which international warfare will become as inconceivable as war now is between member states within the United States or, for that matter, between member nations within the European Union. In such a world, conflict will be managed or contained with a minimum of violence, a maximum of reason and an acceptable degree of constructive UN engagement.

Nor do I envisage a world free from economic want and serious social and environmental stress. But I am convinced that humankind can, in as little as one or two generations, achieve and greatly surpass the well-publicized, but inadequately supported, Millennium Development Goals and thereby substantially narrow the obscene gulf separating the world's haves and have-nots. That achievement will greatly reduce the propensity for domestic violence and international terrorism, and free economic resources now allocated to the ill-conceived "war on terror" for the pursuit of more beneficent ends.

I have no illusions that any of what I shall propose will come about easily. Wealthy and relatively secure nations tend to support the status quo. Within the United Nations, the five permanent, veto-wielding members of the Security Council (the so-called P-5) will be particularly inclined to defend their anachronistic and unfair privileges, a situation derived from their being on the winning side in a war concluded two-thirds of a century ago. This is undoubtedly the greatest single reason why reform of the UN Charter has to date been so difficult and so seldom achieved. Additionally, in the absence of a reformed and strengthened United Nations, the United States in particular has for decades been inclined to rely on unilateralist initiatives or on self-appointed "coalitions of the willing" (under US leadership) to achieve its geopolitical objectives, often in defiance of international law and leading to tragic, even if unintended, consequences.

But medium and small powers are also inclined to pursue parochial and short-term interests. They too tend to resist any infringements on their precious sovereignty. Their leaders often fail to realize that promoting the good of the whole will generally also, in the long run, serve the good of their own nation. Nor would many acknowledge the remarkable extent to which their sovereignty has already been eroded by a multitude of intrusive forces, many of which may be subsumed under the general heading of "globalization". In short, vested interests, inertia and ignorance present powerful impediments to the realization of the agenda set forth in this work.

There are other serious problems as well. Greedy, overambitious and despotic leaders continue to bully their way on to the global political stage and stir up trouble in and beyond the areas they control. Serious tensions between cultures and individual nations persist. Severe ethnic and religious strife, mainly intra-national, remains endemic in much of the world. And major changes have emerged within the global ecosystem for which we are far from sufficiently prepared, and over which we will likely have little effective control.

Many problems within our astonishingly diverse and interconnected global society cannot be adequately dealt with by individual nations. Rather, they cry out for some measure of concerted regional and/or global oversight. Such oversight will necessitate the evolution or refinement of norms of international behaviour that not only establish the rights and responsibilities of nations but also codify and guarantee the rights and responsibilities of individual human beings. And individual citizens must be accorded a greater role in shaping their own destiny. The global democracy deficit must be progressively reduced. Our sense of global stewardship must be heightened.

Collectively, society will have to refine and accept fair and sustainable economic and environmental standards. This presupposes the existence of appropriately empowered institutions designed so that their decisions will be seen as legitimate, command broad international respect and receive political backing from the global community. This book discusses a number of such institutions and – in keeping with the dictum that *form follows function* – it will demonstrate why the designs proposed are appropriate for the functions to be performed.

I make no claim that any of the institutional designs put forward in this book are the only ones capable of promoting the objectives they address, and I recognize that many competing proposals have already been advanced for some of the institutions considered. But the ones presented here are those that I deem most promising, given my inevitably subjective assessments of the problems the institutions will have to address, the political and economic environment in which they will operate and the resources they are likely to command. Other worthy proposals will surely be forthcoming, each with its own pros and cons and likely costs and benefits; and nothing would please me more than to have my own formulations inspire others to advance alternative recommendations and have the merits of their respective ideas seriously debated.

Some of the proposals in this work would require amendment of the UN Charter. Others would not. Oddly, some of the most important proposed changes, for example the creation of an initially advisory World Parliamentary Assembly, would be in the latter category, in that Article 22 of the Charter authorizes the General Assembly to establish such "subsidiary organs" as it deems necessary for the proper performance of its functions. On the other hand, expanding the Security Council by even a single seat would require a Charter amendment. Other proposals might not require Charter amendment but would necessitate reinterpreting that document, as has already happened on numerous occasions, for example in regard to peacekeeping – a word of which the Charter makes no mention.

The timing for action on the changes proposed in this work would be flexible. There is no obviously optimal, much less necessary, sequencing for their adoption. While there are arguments favouring a gradual approach, adopting reforms one at a time, a strong case can also be made, on grounds of synergy, for adopting multiple changes as parts of one or more integrated reform packages. For example, the creation of a UN Peace Corps in tandem with the establishment of a UN Administrative Reserve Corps would give each of those agencies a greater chance of being effective than if either were to be established without the other. There is also the possibility of adopting the proposed reforms by means of a single grand constitutional process, commencing with a comprehensive review conference under the terms of Article 109 of the Charter. All things considered, a relatively gradual, piecemeal approach seems more promising at the outset. But that could well change as trust in the efficacy of a reformed UN system is generated.

Questions of perspective

Many recommendations in this work are predicated on the eventual acceptance of a political paradigm that interprets the term "sovereign equality of nations" quite differently from the way it is presently understood within the UN system. The current increasingly dysfunctional legal fiction in respect to sovereignty, originating with the 1648 Treaty of Westphalia, is enshrined in the "one-nation-one-vote" principle followed in the UN General Assembly and most other UN agencies. However, while nations pay lip service to the principle, they ignore it in practice when doing so suits their purposes and they believe they can do so with impunity. *The presumption of equality is, in fact, so glaringly at variance with the perceptions and behaviour of nations outside the arena of the United Nations itself that the disjuncture seriously compromises the credibility and legitimacy of the entire UN system.*

Yet the Security Council, the one UN organ whose decisions are meant to be binding, makes a mockery of the pretence of equality. Within the Council, five permanent members wield the veto and are therefore free from the fear that they will be adversely affected by any resolution of which they seriously disapprove. Another 10 elected members enjoy an enhanced diplomatic status, but only for a two-year, non-renewable term. And the 178 remaining nations are effectively denied the franchise. The vaunted sovereign equality principle simply does not apply.

To appreciate the absurdity of this principle as it works in the General Assembly, consider Figure 1.1, comparing the population of China, the UN's most populous member with roughly 1.35 billion inhabitants, with that of Nauru, the organization's least populous member, with a population of only 9,300. The ratio between China's population and that of Nauru is nearly 150,000:1; yet Nauru's vote is equal to that of China in the General Assembly. And, as we shall see in our discussion of reform of the General Assembly, there are so many other states with small populations (e.g. Tuvalu with 11,000) that it is theoretically possible for 129 nations, with a combined population of only 8 per cent of the world's total, to command the two-thirds majority needed to win a General Assembly vote on a substantive issue. Even more absurd is the theoretical possibility that 65 nations (one-third of the total membership), with a combined population below 1 per cent of the world total, can block passage of a substantive resolution.

The enormous disparities among nations, however, are not only demographic. They are also evident along other major dimensions: economic, military, performance in respect to human rights, stability of government and so forth. To comprehend this point in economic terms, imagine a graphic comparison of the gross national incomes (GNIs) of the microstate of Tuvalu and the United States similar to the one for population in Figure 1.1. If we were to keep the dot size for Tuvalu the same as that of Nauru in Figure 1.1, we would require a circle nearly four times as large as the one for China to depict properly the ratio between the two GNIs (roughly 560,000:1). Is it any wonder, then, that the UN Charter does not empower the General Assembly to make binding decisions?

While many works on UN reform do note the existence of substantial disparities among nations, most say little or nothing about their actual extent.[2] Readers, then, might understandably assume that they fall within some manageable range and are not much greater than, let us say, the disparities among states within the United States. However, the ratio between the populations of California and Wyoming, the most and least

Does this make sense?

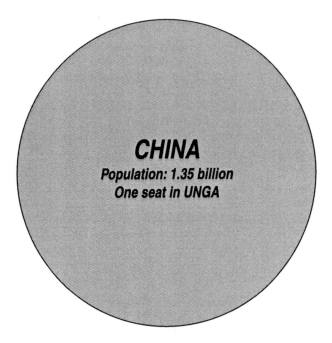

CHINA
Population: 1.35 billion
One seat in UNGA

NAURU ·←— *Population: 9,300*
One seat in UNGA

Figure 1.1 Comparison of populations of most and least populous UN members

populous states respectively in 2010, is a mere 66:1. This is an altogether different situation than the 145,000:1 ratio between China and Nauru.

To deal with the disparities and power differentials among nations, sensible decision-making rules should embody some principle of appropriately *weighted voting*.[3] However, deciding on the most appropriate bases for weighting will depend on the tasks that particular institutions are expected to perform. The institutional designs put forward in this work – in contrast to virtually all others – are predicated on this general functional principle. And the reasoning behind each specific decision will be made explicit. The proposed designs entail simple, objective mathematical formulae, the logic of which derives from the issues they address, with due regard for the often-divergent interests of shareholders and stakeholders within the UN system.

Although the preamble of the UN Charter propounds a number of lofty goals, the primary focus of that document was national security. The drafters of the Charter looked backward for much of their inspiration, and failed to anticipate the profound changes that would occur in the world over ensuing generations.[4] Apart from the differentiations between major powers (the P-5) and other independent states, and between independent states and dependencies, no distinctions among states were made on the basis of population, economic capability, degree of democratic governance or other criteria relevant for effective global governance.

Developments unanticipated by the UN's founders include the Cold War; the development of nuclear and other weapons of mass destruction; the profound regime changes in mainland China; the collapse of the Soviet Union; the rising fortunes of Japan and Germany relative to those of the United Kingdom, France and Russia, and the even more striking economic rise of China and India; the remarkable swiftness of decolonization and the concomitant proliferation of independent (but generally weak and penurious) nations; the proliferation, over most of the world, of regional institutions, most notably the European Union; the dramatic increases in economic and cultural globalization; the burgeoning of civil society institutions; the economic ascendancy of multinational megacorporations; the spread of global crime syndicates and terrorist networks; the looming threats posed by resource depletion, environmental degradation and, above all, climate change; and the revolutionary developments in transportation and electronic communication. The Charter provides little guidance on how to deal with any of these issues. But they are far too important not to be provided for in twenty-first-century institutions of global governance.[5]

Over time parts of the Charter, such as the references to "enemy states", the specification of the now-moribund Trusteeship Council as one of the UN's principal organs, the provisions relating to the never-functional Military Staff Committee and the specification of the USSR as a "permanent" member, have become anachronistic. In the case of the USSR, however, a bit of diplomatic legerdemain recognized the Russian Federation as the legal successor to that entity. But, all things considered, the Charter has proved to be a woefully myopic and inflexible document. Sensitivity to the need for flexibility in the design of institutions is, I would claim, one of the distinguishing characteristics of the present work.[6]

Organization of the book

Chapters 2–13 are essentially prescriptive, focusing mainly on how to improve the design of institutions within and on the periphery of the UN system. Where appropriate, these chapters provide an introductory historical account of efforts to date to deal with specific institutions comprising the UN system or with subjects of particular global importance. They then pay especial attention to devising simple mathematical formulae for more rational and just decision-making in respect to the subjects they discuss. The following paragraphs relate mainly to the recommendations put forward in this work.

Chapters 2–7 relate to agencies that already are, or ought to be, core bodies within the UN system. Two such bodies, the General Assembly (GA), discussed in Chapter 2, and a proposed World Parliamentary Assembly (WPA), discussed in Chapter 3, might in time evolve into the two chambers of a global legislature, respectively representing states and people (i.e. ordinary citizens). Initially they would have only consultative and recommendatory powers, but would gradually assume an increasing role in the crafting of binding legislation. For the GA, a system of weighted voting is recommended that would take into consideration not only the presumed sovereign equality of nations but also their population and contributions to the UN budget. For the WPA, several sequentially ordered schemes for apportioning seats are presented.

The much – and justifiably – criticized Security Council forms the focus of Chapter 4. Although there are literally dozens of proposals for its expansion (including several by the present author), this chapter proposes two versions of a universally representative council with 12 regional seats (of which three would be held by single nations: the United States, China and India), and weighted regional voting. In one version, nations could belong to one region only; in the other, dual regional memberships would be permitted.

Chapter 5 relates to the Economic and Social Council (ECOSOC), a body whose achievements have fallen far short of what many UN backers had envisioned. This work advocates a radical restructuring of ECOSOC and a change of its name to Economic, Social and Environmental Council (ESEC). It also recommends a hybrid decision-making system, with some council members appointed by individual major states and most elected by regions.

The expansion and protection of human rights form an increasingly salient part of the global agenda. Presently, the Human Rights Council is under the General Assembly and composed, in large part, of nations with weak human rights records. Chapter 6 proposes that the council's future membership be merit-based, its mandate enlarged, its decision-making system reformed and the body elevated to the position of a core UN agency.

The judicial components of the UN system, especially the International Court of Justice, are woefully underutilized. Chapter 7 suggests several ways of correcting this deficiency and forging more coherent relationships between judicial bodies at the global and regional levels, as well as with more specialized tribunals such as the International Criminal Court and the World Maritime Court.

Little heralded, but enormously important, are the UN Secretariat and the specialized agencies, funds and programmes which that body assists. Chapter 8 discusses how best to promote coherence and eliminate redundancy among these agencies.

Recruitment and retention of competent staff are a perennial problem throughout the UN system. Especially problematic is the promotion of gender equity and fair regional representation. Recommendations for dealing with these problems are put forward in Chapter 9.

The idea that the United Nations should be exclusively a collectivity of nations is increasingly open to challenge in a democratizing world. Apart from the proposed WPA (Chapter 3), there is need for a regularized system whereby expert input from the burgeoning assemblage of civil society organizations can contribute to the decision-making of various UN agencies. Chapter 10 suggests how such a system might be organized.

Adequate and reliable funding is a *sine qua non* for the realization and maintenance of most of the functional institutions proposed in this work. Chapter 11 sets forth a number of possible ways for raising needed funds and advocates, *inter alia*, that assessments for the regular budget be a uniform but very low (and easily affordable) percentage of the GNI of all member nations.

Chapter 12 focuses on questions of security. It promotes a number of new, sometimes radical, perspectives on the highly controversial question of UN peacekeeping and the incipient field of "peacebuilding". Among its recommendations are the establishment of a standing, all-volunteer, elite UN Peace Force, the institution of a UN Administrative Reserve Corps (UNARC) and the creation of a UN Administrative Academy for the training of UNARC personnel. Ways of minimizing threats from weapons of mass destruction, especially nuclear threats, and dealing with terrorism are also discussed.

In recent decades environmental concerns and economic and ecological sustainability have emerged as issues of existential importance. Dealing effectively with these concerns demands coordinated efforts on a global scale and recognition of many components of our shared environment as "global commons". New regimes for managing these commons so they may serve the entire human family, as well as other life forms, and protecting the environment in general are considered in Chapter 13.

If implemented, the reforms suggested in Chapters 2–13 would result in a configuration for the system of global governance that is substantially different from the one that presently exists. While many possible futures are conceivable, Chapter 14, "A new global governance architecture", argues that the optimal choice will be *a constitutional system of democratic, federal world governance*. It highlights the key differences between that preferred future system and the present state-centric United Nations. It anticipates that the new system would operate simultaneously on multiple levels in accordance with the principle of subsidiarity. (Such a multitiered system has proved effective for the European Union and is implicit in every well-functioning federal system.) The proposed new system would also differ from the old in terms of the sweeping range of actors who would enjoy a constitutionally recognized right to participate as agents in global decision-making: states, regional intergovernmental organizations, popularly elected members of a WPA and representatives of civil society operating through a system of coordinating councils. The new system would also be marked by a more equitable gender balance as well as equitable representation from both rich and poor nations.

Most of the major changes suggested in this work will not be possible in the absence of UN Charter reform, or even of the drafting of a completely new global constitution. Charter amendment, however, has until now proved so difficult that many observers have concluded that meaningful reform cannot be achieved. While I do not agree, I do recognize in Chapter 15, "Getting there", that effecting a major transformation of the present system will require a multipronged, long-term strategy. It will necessitate changing the political climate in key UN member nations, establishing a system of *global education*, fostering a *cosmopolitan ethos*, creating effective *civil society networks* to spearhead reform campaigns and forging *new alliances* between civil society, foundations, progressive governments and other change agents. It is unlikely that major transformations will come about early in the reform process. Rather, a few key and highly noticeable reforms – in regard to funding, decision-making and/or peacekeeping – might become *internal* catalysts for further change. Since fundamental changes are most likely in the wake of major catastrophes, additional *external* and more potent catalysts will likely include horrific acts of terrorism or any of a wide range of possible natural crises brought about by global warming, population growth or other causes.

Notes

1. Of particular relevance in the evaluation of the proposals put forward in this work is a special number of *International Organization* in autumn 2001. The introductory essay by the issue editors presents an explicit theoretical framework (based primarily on rational choice theory) for analysing the design of international institutions: Barbara Koremenos, Charles Lipson and Duncan Snidel, "The Rational Design of International Institutions", *International Organization* 55(4), pp. 761–789. The theoretical concerns of the present work regarding UN reform do, by and large, address that essay's suggestions as to what

contributes to a rational institutional design. Another excellent study analysing and evaluating attempts at reform is Edward C. Luck, "Reforming the United Nations: Lessons from a History in Progress", International Relations Studies and United Nations Occasional Paper No. 1, Academic Council on the United Nations System, New Haven, CT, 2003.

2. Kemal Derviş, an economist and former head of the UN Development Programme, provides a noteworthy exception: Kemal Derviş, *A Better Globalization: Legitimacy, Governance, and Reform*, Washington, DC: Center for Global Development, 2005.

3. The case for and the problems and use of weighted voting are analysed by Paul C. Szasz, *Alternative Voting Systems in International Organizations and the Binding Triad Proposal to Improve U.N. General Assembly Decision-Taking*, Monograph No. 17, Wayne, NJ: Center for UN Reform Education, 2001. A good theoretical discussion appears in Carole Barrett and Hannah Newcombe, "Weighted Voting and International Organizations", *Peace Research Reviews* 2(2), special issue, published by the Canadian Peace Research Institute, Oakville, ON, April 1968. Other relevant works are cited in Chapter 2.

4. The perspectives of the major players in drafting the charter are admirably set forth in Stephen C. Schlesinger, *Act of Creation, The Founding of the United Nations: A Story of Superpowers, Secret Agents, Wartime Allies and Enemies, and Their Quest for a Peaceful World*, Boulder, CO: Westview Press, 2003.

5. A good general account of changes in the world system will be found in Strobe Talbott, *The Great Experiment: The Story of Ancient Empires, Modern States, and the Quest for a Global Nation*, New York: Simon & Schuster, 2008.

6. A thorough decade-by-decade review of attempts to reform various components of the UN system is found in Klaus Hüfner and Jens Martens, *UNO-Reform zwischen Utopie und Realität, Vorschläge zum Wirtschafts- und Sozialbereich der Vereinten Nationen*, published as Vol. 6 of *Internationale Beziehungen*, Frankfurt-am-Main: Peter Lang, 2000. Supplementing this work and more complete in respect to political matters is a topically organized compilation: Paul Taylor, Sam Daws and Ute Adamczick-Gerteis (eds), *Documents on Reform of the United Nations*, Aldershot: Dartmouth, 1997. A more critical insider's detailed review of UN activities and reform efforts is Maurice Bertrand, *The United Nations: Past, Present and Future*, The Hague: Kluwer Law International, 1997. See also Luck, note 1 above; Thomas G. Weiss and Sam Daws (eds), *The Oxford Handbook on the United Nations*, Oxford and New York: Oxford University Press, 2007.

2

Reform of the General Assembly

I believe at some future day, the nations of the earth will agree on some sort of congress which will take cognizance of international questions of difficulty and whose decisions will be as binding as the decisions of our Supreme Court are upon us.
Ulysses S. Grant, US president, 1869–1877.

Introduction

In their respective reports to the UN General Assembly (GA) in anticipation of its 2005 Millennium Review summit session, both the High-level Panel on Threats, Challenges and Change and Secretary-General Kofi Annan noted the "unique legitimacy" and potential importance of that universally representative body.[1] But each also lamented the fact that the GA suffered from serious deficiencies. The panel observed that its "norm-making capacity is often squandered on debates about minutiae", noted that its relevance was undermined by its "inability to reach closure on issues" and suggested that the keys to reform "are focus and structure".[2] The Secretary-General (SG) went even further. He took note of the concern of many member states about "the decline in the Assembly's prestige and its diminishing contribution to the organization's activities", and agreed with the widely held perception that that the body "needs to streamline its procedures and structures". To correct these shortcomings, Annan called for "bold measures to rationalize its work".[3] However, neither the panel nor the SG spelled out what changes would be required.

Transforming the United Nations system: Designs for a workable world, Schwartzberg, United Nations University Press, 2013, ISBN 978-92-808-1230-5

The key problem limiting the GA's capacity to make binding decisions is its one-nation-one-vote system of decision-making. Yet this issue was simply not addressed. This system renders the Assembly incapable of devising broadly acceptable ways of dealing with pressing and increasingly serious global and regional problems. *Despite the universality of its membership, the present allocation of power in the Assembly utterly fails to reflect the distribution of power in the world outside the United Nations itself.* Under such circumstances many GA deliberations are little more than exercises in political posturing. Non-binding GA resolutions are accorded little respect and routinely flouted. A more rational, realistic decision-making system is urgently needed. For decades during the Cold War any attempt to institute significant reforms would almost surely have been futile, and would-be reformers outside the UN system were generally ignored by those within it. But times have changed. In the current era global statespersons, in alliance with civil society, should, had they the will to do so, be able to effect the needed changes.

The reforms I envision would entail a system of weighted voting based on principles that are at once reasonably fair yet politically acceptable. Additionally, to make the outcome worthy of the effort that change would require, a way must be found to ensure that Assembly resolutions on issues of truly global concern will be regarded not merely as recommendations but as binding obligations.

Given the enormous power disparities among UN member nations, no proposal for reallocating decision-making power will be deemed optimal by all concerned parties. Nevertheless, from a global perspective, a broadly acceptable system would be attainable. Most of this chapter will be devoted to presenting and analysing a weighted voting proposal that would facilitate the adoption of binding resolutions and provide a platform from which necessary additional reforms could be launched. The generally salutary short-term impacts of the proposal on future GA negotiations will be indicated, with particular reference to blocs of nations – large and small, wealthy and poor, free and not free – that would gain or lose in voting weight from its adoption.

Although this chapter's thrust is on GA decision-making, I do not suggest that GA-related reform should be confined to that issue. Of particular importance is the possibility (discussed in Chapter 3) of establishing – alongside the GA – a World Parliamentary Assembly to give the world's *people*, not merely UN member *nations*, a voice in global governance. Subsequent chapters will explore reforming the relationship between the GA and other entities within and outside the UN system, and will also consider how budgetary reform would enhance the GA's ability to carry out its mandate.

The growing need for voting reform

The profound changes in the General Assembly since the founding of the United Nations were clearly not anticipated by those who drafted its Charter. Today's United Nations is a virtually universal body, whose members account for 99.6 per cent of the world's people. The number of member nations has almost quadrupled, rising from the original 51 to the present total of 193 (Figure 2.1).

While originally composed solely of nations that had declared war on the Axis powers and their allies prior to the end of the Second World War, the expanded United Nations ultimately included every one of those former enemy states. Also contributing to the swelling membership was the proliferation of states resulting from the disintegration of the Soviet Union, Yugoslavia and Czechoslovakia. But the main reason for the organization's growth was the wave of decolonization that swept across Africa, much of Asia and the Pacific, and the Caribbean region.

The change in the distribution of UN members was profound. Africa, accounting for a mere four members in 1945 (7.8 per cent of the total), now has 55 members (28.5 per cent). Asia, too, has greatly increased its proportion of the total membership. In the Caribbean region alone, 13 new states were added, all former British and Dutch dependencies (only two of them, Jamaica and Trinidad & Tobago, have populations exceeding a million). This group of states, admitted over the period 1962–1983, collectively contains scarcely 0.1 per cent of the world's population, yet accounts for 6.7 per cent of all GA votes. Similarly anomalous are the dozen small island member nations of the western Pacific.

Expanded membership brought important changes in the political orientation of the GA and increasingly polarized decision-making, first of East versus West, then of North versus South.[4] The former problem, presaged even as the Charter was being drafted, persisted throughout the Cold War. The latter became salient only with the decolonization of most of Africa in the 1960s, and still continues. Because the global East and South often made common cause in confronting the West – on issues bearing on colonialism, racism (especially apartheid), Zionism, economic development and international trade – the comfortable majority initially enjoyed by the United States, in league with other economically advanced democracies (and their respective client states), was steadily eroded.[5]

States that had been dependencies prior to the Second World War, in concert with countries of Latin America that gradually weaned themselves away from unwavering political allegiance to the West, became a new "third world" bloc. Within and outside the United Nations they have

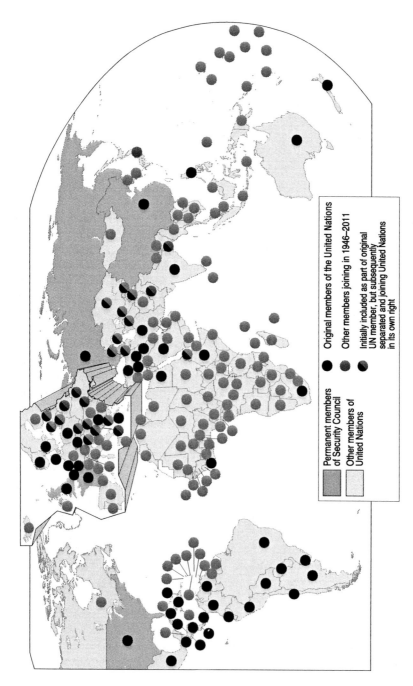

Figure 2.1 Members of the United Nations, 2011

come together in two largely congruent entities: an informal caucus known as the Non-Aligned Movement (NAM), focusing mainly on political affairs, and the so-called Group of 77 (G-77), whose principal concerns tend to be economic.[6] The former of these was established in Belgrade in 1961, with leadership provided by five charismatic personalities: Gamal Abdel Nasser of Egypt, Kwame Nkrumah of Ghana, Jawaharlal Nehru of India, Achmed Sukarno of Indonesia and Josip Broz Tito of Yugoslavia. Currently the NAM has 118 members. The G-77, established within the UN Conference on Trade and Development (UNCTAD) in 1964, presently comprises 131 nations if one includes China (discussed below).[7] Because it has become the more influential of the two caucuses, especially since the end of the Cold War, I shall throughout this work refer mainly to the G-77 when discussing nations of the "global South", with the understanding that its positions on most contentious issues coming before the GA were also endorsed by the NAM.

While China has never formally applied for membership in the G-77, it has actively participated in the group's deliberations since the early 1990s and is often counted among its members. Given China's power, it is accorded a special status; it is not uncommon to see media references to "the G-77 and China". The same would not apply to the NAM, with which China has never been politically associated.

With or without support from China and other formerly communist countries, the G-77 was often able to command the required two-thirds majority to win GA votes on a wide range of issues; even after the Soviet Union's collapse, it can easily muster large majorities. But the veto power in the Security Council (SC), on which the Soviet Union formerly relied so heavily, came to be increasingly exercised by the United States and, less often, by the United Kingdom and France. This practice effectively nullified the recommendations of many GA decisions, transforming them into virtually meaningless pyrrhic rhetorical victories for the global South.[8] Consequently, the fact that GA decisions are merely recommendatory is widely perceived in the North as a good thing. Until such time as the United Nations adopts a system of weighted voting that realistically reflects the actual global distribution of power, it seems doubtful that any major state will willingly grant the GA, the most representative organ within the UN system, the authority to make binding decisions.

Concomitants of GA expansion were a slight reduction in the average member's population (despite a tripling of world population since 1945) and dramatic decreases in the average member's area and percentage contributions to the UN budget (see Table 2.1). Even more dramatic were declines in the median population, area and level of UN contributions.

Table 2.1 Mean, median, maximum and minimum population, area, GNI and assessed contribution to regular budget of UN member nations, 1946 and 2010

	1946 (51 nations)	**2010** (192 nations)
Population		
a Mean	6.3 m (1.96%)	35.4 m (0.521%)
b Median	Australia, 7.3 m (0.39%)	Tajikistan and Serbia, average 7.18 m (0.106%)
c Maximum	China, 512 m (27.4%)	China, 1.34 bn (19.7%)
d Minimum	Luxembourg, 286,000 (0.01%)	Nauru, 9,300 (0.00015%)
e Ratio of c to d	1,770:1	134,000:1 **(76 × 1946 ratio)**
Area (square km)		
a Mean	1.823 m (1.96%)	0.493 m. (0.521%)
b Median	Poland, 314,000 (0.34%)	Honduras and Democratic People's Republic of Korea, average 116,000 (0.052%)
c Maximum	USSR, 21.6 m (23.2%)	Russia, 17.1 m (18.4%)
d Minimum	Luxembourg, 2,586 (0.028%)	Monaco, 1.95 (0.0000001%)
e Ratio of c to d	8,350:1	8.4 m:1 **(1,005 × 1946 ratio)**
Gross national income (US$)		
a Mean	n.a.	319 m (0.521%)
b Median	n.a.	Jordan and Democratic People's Republic of Korea, average 26.0 bn (0.042%)
c Maximum	n.a.	United States, 14,601 m (23.8%)
d Minimum	n.a.	Tuvalu, 26 (0.00000004%)
e Ratio of c to d	n.a.	562,000:1
Assessed share of regular UN budget		
a Mean	1.96%	0.521%
b Median	Yugoslavia, 0.34%	Average for 4 nations: 0.013%
c Maximum	United States, 39.87%	United States, 22.00%
d Minimum	6 nations, 0.04% each	39 nations, 0.001% each
e Ratio of c to d	997:1	22,000:1 **(22 × 1946 ratio)**

Notes:
1. Figures in parentheses in lines *a–d* are percentages of 1946 and 2010 totals for all UN member nations. Ratios are rounded off to two or three significant figures.
2. 1946 population figures are estimates.
3. China data are *de facto* rather than *de jure*; they include data for Hong Kong and Macao, but not for Taiwan in the year 2010.
4. USSR area figures for 1946 exclude Ukraine and White Russia, each of which had its own UN seat.
5. m = million, bn = billion, n.a. = not available.

Sources: Population data for 1946 were estimated by the author extrapolating backward from earliest data provided in *UN Demographic Yearbook, 1979, Historical Supplement*; area data for 1946 are from *Statesman's Yearbook, 1946*; data on UN assessments up to 2006 are from personal communications from Mark E. Gilpin and Mya M. Than of the UN Contribution Service. Data for 2010 on population, area and GNP are from *Encyclopaedia Britannica Book of the Year, 2011*; data for UN assessments as of 2010 are from UN Secretariat, ST/ADM/SER. B/789, 24 December 2009.

Thus the United Nations has evolved into an incongruous organization with a relatively small number of major states, a considerably larger number of medium-level actors and a substantial majority of members with little individual international significance.

Especially striking are the enormous disparities between the largest and smallest member nations in regard to all four variables in Table 2.1. The steady decline in the population of the smallest member states is documented in Table 2.2.[9] Even in 1946, disparities between the largest and smallest nations were vastly greater than those among the primary administrative divisions (e.g. states in the United States and India, provinces in China and *Länder* in Germany) of any present or former nation-state. Nevertheless, the disparities have increased by several orders of magnitude since the UN's founding.[10]

At the founding of the United Nations, its 51 nations (26 per cent of the present total) already accounted for roughly 70 per cent of the world's population. Since then, voting power has been skewed more or less steadily towards states that are relatively inconsequential players on the global stage. As early as 1961 the proportion of the world's people living in UN member states, then numbering 104, had risen to approximately 91 per cent (if we include the people of mainland China, then supposedly represented by the government on Taiwan). The subsequent incorporation of 89 additional members (46 per cent of the total) increased the proportion of the world's population within the United Nations by less than 9 per cent. Particularly noteworthy is the proliferation of membership by microstates. This trend seems likely to continue, assuming that many of the world's remaining dependencies eventually attain their independence. No fewer than 39 current members have less than a million inhabitants each, and 13 have fewer than 100,000, including two with populations of roughly 10,000.

Table 2.2 Least populous members of the United Nations, 1945–2012

Period	Nation	Population (000s) at time of UN admission
1945–1946	Luxembourg	285
1946–1965	Iceland	132
1965–1974	Maldives	97 (increasing to 125 by 1974)
1974–1976	Grenada	104
1976–1983	Seychelles	64
1983–1992	St Kitts & Nevis	46
1992–1994	San Marino	23
1994–1999	Palau	16
1999–2012	Nauru	12 (decreasing since to 9)

The 65 least populous members – enough to block a two-thirds majority vote – comprise not quite 1 per cent of the total population of all member nations! And, in theory, the 128 least populous members, enough to provide the two-thirds majority needed to pass a substantive resolution, account for not quite 8.5 per cent (1/12) of humanity. Even worse is the situation regarding contributions to the UN budget. As of 2010, some 39 nations paid the arbitrary minimum of 0.001 per cent each; and the 65 smallest contributors, paying from 0.001 to 0.004 per cent each, collectively contributed only 0.110 per cent of the total. A two-thirds majority could be constituted from 128 members, each assessed from 0.001 to 0.046 per cent, who collectively pay a mere 1.271 per cent of the total UN budget! (Appendix 1 provides figures for all member nations.)

It may be objected that the hypothetical worst-case scenarios indicated in the preceding paragraph are unlikely to come to pass. After all, the world's smaller nations seldom, if ever, vote as a coherent bloc in cases where the GA does not adopt resolutions by consensus. (Apart from size, Monaco and Nauru have little in common.) Although this is undoubtedly true, there are far more than enough small nations, in terms of both population and assessed contributions, to facilitate dominance within the GA of a wholly unrepresentative minority of the world's people. If one is to oppose – quite rightly – the undemocratic veto by any one of the five strong nations with permanent membership in the SC, one should also oppose unwarranted exercises of political power by GA coalitions of the very weak. Moreover, absurd as the present situation is, the prospect is that it will become worse in the future, because a number of the world's several dozen remaining dependencies will eventually attain their independence, increasing the ranks of microstates, and also because of the probable break-up (as happened recently in Sudan) of a number of strife-ridden multiethnic states.

Given the inordinate degree of voting power conferred on the weak by what has been called the "immoral egalitarianism" of the one-nation-one-vote rule,[11] it is hardly surprising that on issues affecting the vital interests of the major world powers, those states will often resort to political tactics of dubious propriety, by either bribery or the use of threats, to purchase or otherwise influence the votes of the numerically preponderant weak. Such practices, common during the period of the Cold War, subvert the political process. Recent – and largely successful – heavy-handed American efforts to block UN support for the International Criminal Court (ICC) are a case in point.[12] While the degree to which malpractices have influenced the outcome of important GA votes is debatable, one may reasonably suppose that a well-designed system of weighted voting would substantially mitigate the problem.

A realistic basis for weighted voting[13]

Assuming acceptance of the necessity of weighted voting in the UN GA, several questions arise.

- On what variable(s) should the weighting be based?
- What measuring system (e.g. absolute values, percentages of UN totals, ranks) should be employed in respect to the selected variable(s)?
- If more than one variable is chosen, in what way should they be combined?
- What are acceptable limits within which differences in weight will be permitted?

While none of these questions has a simple or obvious answer, one may suggest a set of conditions that would provide a basis for an effective weighted voting system. The following are desiderata for an effective voting system in the UN GA.

- *It should be based on clear and valid principles.*
- *It should be relatively simple.*
- *It should be objectively determined.*
- *It should be applied equally to all members.*
- *It should be flexible* (easily adjustable for future demographic and economic changes as well as change in the number of UN members).
- *It should be nuanced* (i.e. a small change in one of the determining factors should not result in a large change in voting power; nor should a large change in any determining factor result in only a small change in voting power).
- *It should be "realistic"* (i.e. the distribution of voting power in the GA must have a meaningful and broadly acceptable relationship to the distribution of power outside the UN arena).

These considerations, of which the last is arguably of the greatest practical importance, may be used in judging the acceptability of dozens of proposals for weighted voting that have already been put forward, as well as others likely to be advanced in the years ahead.[14] Regrettably, virtually all published proposals are seriously flawed in at least one respect; and only a few have enjoyed, even if briefly, significant support among UN reform activists. In this context, an admonition of the High-level Panel on Threats, Challenges and Change is especially pertinent:

In approaching the issue of United Nations reform. It is as important today as it was in 1945 to combine power with principle. Recommendations that ignore underlying power realities will be doomed to failure or irrelevance, but recommendations that simply reflect raw distributions of power and make no effort to bolster international principles are unlikely to gain the widespread support required to shift international behavior.[15]

A weighted voting system

Fundamentals

I here propose a voting system assigning equal importance to each of three basic principles:
- the *democratic/demographic principle*, in which population is the determining factor
- the *economic/capacity to be effective principle*, represented by contributions to the UN budget
- the *legal/sovereign equality of nations principle*, according to which all nations are counted equally.

Whether any one of these principles may be judged to be more important than the others is moot. The answer depends on the values attached by various actors to morality, legality and political and economic practicality. It thus seems wisest initially to combine the three as if they were all of equal relevance. This may be accomplished by means of the following simple formula:

$$W = (P + C + M)/3$$

in which W represents the weight that would be given to a nation's vote in the GA; P represents that nation's population as a percentage of the total population of all UN members; C represents the nation's assessed and paid financial contribution to the United Nations over a specified period (say the previous five years) as a percentage of the total contributions over the same period; and M represents the nation's unit share of the total membership (1/192 or 0.5214 per cent as of 2010). Data for all UN member nations are provided in Appendix 1.

The population and membership terms of the allocation equation pose no problems; the contributions term, however, requires discussion. The present UN scale of country assessments is determined by a fairly complex set of rules (discussed in Chapter 11). By and large, assessments are related to the gross national income (GNI) of each member state, though with progressive adjustments: downward for the poorer nations and upward for those that are relatively affluent.[16] The principal exception to this practice is in the assessment of the United States, which was recently reduced from 25 to 22 per cent, even though the US share of the of the world's total gross product (in 2009) came to 24.7 per cent (a significant decline from previous years). But, as previously argued, formulae for weighted voting should treat all countries equally. For this reason (and others discussed in Chapter 11), I propose that future contributions to the UN budget be strictly proportional to GNI, but set at a level that even the poorest nation can afford, say at an initial rate of 0.1 per cent.

Based on GNI data for 2009, an assumed assessment level of 0.1 per cent would have yielded UN revenues of approximately $58 billion, well over twice the total current expenditures for the entire UN system.[17] Of this amount, the US pro rata share would come to $14.5 billion, far more than it presently pays; but in return its GA votes would count for more than those of any other nation. At the low end of the assessment spectrum would be Tuvalu, which has the smallest economy of any nation in the United Nations. Its annual assessment would come to a mere $27,000 (compared to the roughly $18,000 that it now pays, given the minimum assessment level of 0.001 per cent); but its vote would not be different from the 0.174 per cent that would be allocated to 10 other microstates.

With an assessment system based on GNI, most countries in the world would pay significantly more in UN dues than they presently do. However, the totals would in no case be onerous. On the contrary, the benefits flowing from a substantially strengthened UN system would greatly exceed the modest expenditures entailed.

To illustrate how the formula would work, assuming continuation of the present system of assessments, I provide the following examples.

- *For the United States:* W would be $(4.558 + 24.728 + 0.521)/3$. This comes to 29.807/3 or 9.936.
- *For China:* W would be $(19.783 + 8.616 + 0.521)/3$. This comes to 28.920/3 or 9.640.
- *For the smallest microstates*, with negligible (n) populations and negligible (n) contributions to the UN budget (each less than 0.0005 per cent): W would be $(n + n + 0.521/3)$ or 0.174.

The ratio between the United States, the country with the greatest weight, and the smallest microstates would thus be roughly 54:1.[18]

Outcomes

Appendix 1 indicates GA voting weights for all countries of the world based on the proposed formula, and provides data on current assessment rates and GNI. Figure 2.2 shows the global distribution of voting power based on the use of assessments proportional to GNI in the weighted voting formula. The circles on the map, representing each of the 192 member nations (in 2010), are scaled in proportion to each country's weight. Within the circles of 31 nations with weights above the world average of 0.521 per cent, voting weights are indicated to the nearest 0.1 per cent.

Of nations losing strength, relative to their equal unit weight under the present system some (e.g. Belgium, Colombia, Democratic Republic of

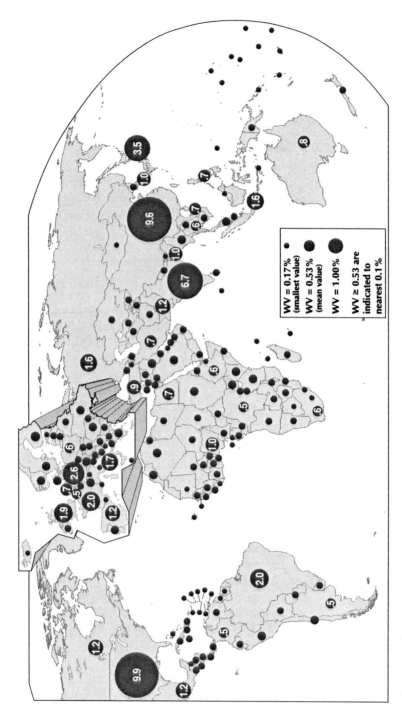

Figure 2.2 Proposed distribution of weighted votes in UN General Assembly
Note: WV = weighted vote.

the Congo) would be only marginally affected. And in no case could any country, however small or weak, lose more than two-thirds of its present 0.521 per cent of the total.

Table 2.3 indicates country weights for the top 17 countries in rank order, using both the current level of UN assessments and GNI for the contribution term in the weighting formula. As one would expect, under both methods of computation all nations in the P-5 group would gain substantially, though the gain for Russia would be substantially less than that for China, the United Kingdom and France. No less noteworthy, both lists include a substantial number of developing nations (seven in the first and eight in the second), along with those of the economically powerful West/North that have traditionally dominated global politics. Additionally, a formula using GNI would result in generally higher scores for developing nations (e.g. 9.640 per cent versus 7.831 per cent for China), while generally lowering the scores of those that are wealthy (e.g. 3.541 per cent versus 4.974 per cent for Japan). The major exception to this rule would be the United States, whose current assessment rate of 22 per cent represents a special departure from the system of calculating assessments used for the rest of the world.

Table 2.3 Weighted votes of leading nations using current UN assessments and assessments proportional to GNI (2009) in weighted voting formula

Weighting with current assessments		Weighting in proportion to GNI	
Nation	Weight	Nation	Weight
United States	9.026	United States	9.936
China	7.831	China	9.640
Japan	6.100	India	6.700
India	4.974	Japan	3.541
Germany	3.246	Germany	2.553
United Kingdom	2.680	France	2.045
France	2,522	Brazil	2.005
Italy	2.136	United Kingdom	1.937
Brazil	1.698	Italy	1.670
Mexico	1.490	Russia	1.624
Spain	1.461	Indonesia	1.605
Canada	1.410	Mexico	1.249
Russia	1.403	Spain	1.233
Indonesia	1.392	Pakistan	1.175
Republic of Korea	1.168	Canada	1.149
Pakistan	1.105	Nigeria	1.049
Nigeria	0.975	Bangladesh	1.002
Total for group	50.617	Total for group	50.104

A legislative concomitant of the proposed system of weighted voting

As this work repeatedly notes, global problems require global solutions. In our highly interdependent world there are numerous problems that individual nations cannot adequately deal with acting on their own. In light of this irrefutable fact, *the time has come to endow the GA with a limited capacity to pass legally binding resolutions* rather than restricting it solely to a recommendatory role (except for a few matters such as establishing the UN budget, electing members of the SC and other major UN organs, and approving top-level personnel appointments). So long as the competence of the GA remains as it is now, the gains realized from weighted voting, while not insignificant, would be less meaningful than they should ideally be. Therefore, in matters that cannot be adequately addressed at the national or lower levels of governance, the GA should, as early as possible, be authorized to make binding legislative decisions. In time, should a UN Parliamentary (People's) Assembly be established, the GA would share legislative competence with that body, as discussed in Chapter 3.

The ability to create new international law would, however, have to be carefully circumscribed. At the outset, it should apply to a limited range of important substantive issues. Just what those issues might be would be a matter for negotiation. How to deal with this question was addressed by the late Paul C. Szasz in a study of *Alternative Voting Systems in International Organizations*, published by the Center for UN Reform Education.[19] Szasz, whose career included more than 40 years of service to the United Nations and related agencies, asserted that the scope of legislative authority for the GA would best be limited to matters with an obvious "international dimension", especially those deemed to be "global" or "worldwide" in nature, and also "general", as opposed to matters relating to a specific contentious issue, such as for example a boundary dispute. Barred from legislation would be matters "essentially within the jurisdiction of any state". It would also be appropriate to draw up a list of specific "preclusions" (matters not subject to GA legislation) in addition to the list of admissible issues. In the admissible category Szasz suggested that the GA might be empowered to legislate with respect to:

> the high seas, Antarctica, outer space, weapons of mass destruction, the international trade in weapons, international trade and commerce, transboundary environmental matters, human rights (though that might be considered too broad a subject), and humanitarian rules of warfare...[20]

In regard to human rights, I would suggest that only egregious offences such as genocide and ethnic cleansing should initially be subject to binding resolutions made in concert with the SC and a reformed Human Rights Council. A more controversial set of topics, in Szasz's view, would include "refugees and stateless persons, narcotic drugs, international terrorism and related crimes". Szasz's list of preclusions included such issues as "immigration and naturalization, education, health (except in transboundary aspects), [and] domestic taxation".[21]

For GA resolutions to be binding, I would suggest – on legal, pragmatic and moral grounds – that three conditions be met: first, that they fall within the admissible range of issues for GA legislation; second, that they be approved by a group of nations with a combined weight accounting for at least two-thirds of the total weights of all the members present and voting; and third, that in the interests of democracy, the concurring nations must also account for a simple majority (not two-thirds) of the total population of all UN member nations present and voting. Such relatively democratic decisions would then have the character of international law, and would therefore be applicable to all UN member nations and also subject to enforcement action by the SC should the latter body see fit to take such action.[22] (Some provisions noted in this and the following paragraph would likely require modification when, and if, a World Parliamentary Assembly comes into being and is granted legislative competence.)

Apart from the above provisions, it would be in order to require more demanding super-majorities – say as much as 75 per cent of all weighted votes as well as approval by nations with at least three-fifths, or even two-thirds, of the total population of all UN members – for a limited range of issues. These might include proposals for Charter revision, recommendations to the SC to impose sanctions on nations in serious breach of international law and requests to the SC to dispatch armed peacekeepers to deal with serious threats to the peace.

Authorizing the GA to enact binding legislation has the potential, in some circumstances, to create tension between it and the SC. In such an eventuality, Clause 1 of Article 12 of the UN Charter would provide an important and legitimate check. It reads:

While the Security Council is exercising in respect to any dispute or situation the functions assigned to it in the present Charter, the GA shall not make any recommendations with regard to that dispute or situation unless the Security Council so requests.

Benefits of a change to weighted voting

Obviously, the enhanced capability of the GA, together with a more realistic reconfiguration of power relationships within that body, will strengthen the UN's credibility, make it much more democratic and create a new political dynamic, especially in respect to truly global problems.[23] Here I examine some of the reasons why that dynamic should work for the betterment of the UN system and the world as a whole.

Tables 2.4–2.6 indicate the strength of various groups of member nations with respect to a number of important demographic, economic and human rights variables. The figures relating to values using the weighting formula are, in all cases, those derived using GNI data in the weighting equation.

The groups considered in Table 2.4 are nations that would be relative gainers and losers in changing from a one-nation-one-vote system to a weighted voting system (assuming that system were in place in the year 2010).

Particularly striking is the fact that the three principal gainers (the United States, China and India) presently have only 1.6 per cent of the votes in the GA, despite accounting for 41.6 per cent of the world's people and 35.7 per cent of the total UN budget. Under the proposed weighted voting system their combined weights would come to 26.3 per cent, a more than 16-fold increase. The 28 additional nations that would become relative gainers account for 14.6 per cent of the votes, yet have 36.1 per cent of the world's people and provide 50.1 per cent of the UN's budget. Under the proposed system their share of votes would come to a much more reasonable 33.6 per cent. It is thus evident that *nations with roughly 78 per cent of the world's population and contributing almost 86 per cent of the total UN budget would see themselves as better off with weighted voting – with roughly 60 per cent of the total weight* (as against only 14.6 per cent under the present one-nation-one-vote system). Those are very powerful majorities.

Table 2.4 Strength of groups of nations that would gain or lose voting weight from a change to a system of weighted voting

	Gainers			Losers
	Weights >6.0%	Weights 0.521%–6.0%	Total	Weights <0.521%
Number of member nations (and unweighted votes)	3	28	31	161
% of all nations (and unweighted votes) in UN	1.6	14.6	16.1	83.9
% of total population in UN	41.6	36.1	77.7	22.3
% of total budgetary contributions	35.7	50.1	85.8	14.3
% of total weighted votes	26.3	33.6	59.9	40.1

While many of the 161 nations that might initially see themselves as worse off may be expected for a time to oppose a change to weighted voting, the fact that they enjoy only negligible power, economically or otherwise, outside the UN arena weakens their bargaining strength and would subject them to pressure to accede to the proposed reform should a majority of the economically more powerful and/or populous nations eventually support it. Yet the reduction in voting strength for the weaker states – from roughly 84 per cent to 40 per cent – would still leave those states in a highly favoured position given their relatively small aggregate population and limited economic capability. Thus *the proposed new system would remain strongly biased in favour of the weak,* though not nearly to the absurd degree characterizing the present system. In brief, most would soon recognize that 40 per cent of *something* – an empowered GA that can respond effectively to the needs of the weak – would be a great deal more favourable to their long-term interests than their present 84 per cent of the votes in what might, in practical terms, be regarded as virtually *nothing.*

Important changes in the GA's balance of power would occur also in the economic domain. These are evident in Table 2.5, which indicates the strength of major economic blocs, the G-77 and the Organisation for Economic Co-operation and Development (OECD), under the present and proposed voting systems. (The nations constituting each of these blocs are indicated in Appendix 1.)

Presently, the 130 relatively poor nations of the G-77 command roughly 68 per cent of all GA votes, slightly more than enough for the two-thirds majority needed to pass a substantive resolution, while the 33 relatively affluent nations comprising the OECD account for 17 per cent of the votes, with the balance being made up from nations of the former Soviet bloc and other once socialist states, plus a scattered group of small states (mostly microstates in Europe and the Pacific that have not associated themselves with either of the former two groups). Under the proposed

Table 2.5 Strength in General Assembly of major economic blocs under one-nation-one-vote and weighted voting systems

	OECD (33 nations)	G-77 (including China) (130 nations)	Others (29 nations)
% of votes under present system	17.2	67.7	15.1
% of total weighted votes	35.9	56.4	7.9

Note: Chile, a member of both the G-77 and the OECD, is counted only with the latter bloc.

weighted voting system the strength of the G-77 would decline to 56.4 per cent, while that of the OECD would be raised to 35.9 per cent. Of the remaining 7.9 per cent of weighted votes, most are held by Russia and other nations whose economic orientations are, on the whole, moving towards those of the OECD bloc. A key point in this context is that neither of the two major economic blocs can independently marshal the two-thirds majority needed to win a vote on a substantive proposal in the GA. Thus instead of passing a plethora of meaningless resolutions favoured by the G-77 (averaging nearly one per working day since 1946 and increasing over time), many of which the world's wealthier nations then largely ignore, *each economic bloc would necessarily have to listen to and try to understand the concerns of the other and then enter into creative compromises* if the GA is to craft needed economic or environmental resolutions.[24] On balance, this would be a very salutary development.

No less important than the altered balance of voting strength between the major economic blocs is the fact that the proposed weighting system would substantially augment the voting weight of the world's free and democratic nations, as indicated (though with appropriate caveats) in the annual ratings of Freedom House.[25] Table 2.6 shows the relative power under the present and proposed systems of groups of countries ranked as free, partly free and not free. (The scores of all countries are given in Appendix 1.)

The most important information in the table is that the 84 nations in the "free" cohort would have their combined share of the total vote raised from the present 43.7 per cent to 54.8 per cent, a substantial jump. Although the 46 nations in the "not free" group would also see a slight increase in their combined average strength, from 24.0 to 24.8 per cent, that change is not nearly sufficient to offset the gains to the world's relatively free nations. Today, virtually all of the world's relatively wealthy states have more or less free and democratic regimes. They, together with a number of poorer – but also democratic – states, should be able to forge a strong and generally cohesive voting bloc with enormous potential for advancing democratic governance, protecting and promoting basic human rights, and furthering other objectives in the interest of the global community.

Table 2.6 Strength in General Assembly of nations grouped by Freedom House designations under one-nation-one-vote and weighted voting systems

	Free (84 nations)	Partly free (52 nations)	Not free (46 nations)
% of votes under present system	43.7	32.3	24.0
% of total weighted votes	54.8	20.3	24.8

Adapting to future changes

Among the desiderata for a system of weighted voting was the need for
flexibility. Obviously, the weighted votes of member nations will have to
be periodically adjusted – sometimes markedly – according to fluctuations in
their relative population sizes and economic fortunes, as well as changes
in the total number of UN member nations. This will necessitate periodic
reallocation of national weights. The frequency of such reallocation –
whether every decade, as with legislatures in the United States, or more
often – should not be a major concern and would be negotiable; but there
is no compelling reason why more frequent adjustments – say every fifth
year – should not be made. The modalities for determining each nation's
weighted vote would most appropriately be entrusted to a neutral agency
within the UN Secretariat, subject to approval by the GA, just as budget
assessments are currently determined.

   In addition to the routine types of change referred to in the preceding
paragraph, it would be wise to facilitate adjustments to the system based
on changes in the political map and also in prevailing global opinion in
respect to the relative importance of the three elements integrated within
the weighting system. Since the political map of the world is forever in
flux, all recommendations for UN reform should anticipate and be adapt-
able to future changes. Up to now, when states have merged (e.g. West
and East Germany, North and South Yemen, and Egypt and Syria – albeit
briefly – in the United Arab Republic) their two GA votes became but
one. The opposite was true with respect to countries created on the disintegration of certain states (Pakistan out of India, Bangladesh out of Pakistan, Eritrea out of Ethiopia and a host of states out of the Soviet Union,
Yugoslavia and Czechoslovakia). In all such cases the newly independent
nations soon became members of the United Nations. It seems perverse,
however, to reward state failure by conveying extra voting strength to the
region in which that failure occurred (e.g. six nations and six votes in
what was formerly Yugoslavia) and, conversely, to penalize voluntary national integration. This problem, however, would be substantially mitigated under the proposed system, in that statehood *per se* is but one
among three factors determining each nation's voting weight.

   But what of future federal unions? Though it is certainly not imminent,
the most likely of these appears to be a truly federal European Union.
Should the constituents of such a federation – which would likely comprise more than 30 formerly independent states – be penalized for having
the good sense to integrate economically and politically, by losing out in
the membership term of the weighting equation? A compromise on this
issue would be in order. So as not greatly to discourage beneficial future
unions, one might stipulate that for a specified period (again, say up to 15

years) following the creation of a union, the federating units would retain their individuality for purposes of representation in the GA (and also other UN bodies). The allocation of three GA seats to the Soviet Union (including seats for the Ukraine and White Russia) up to the time of its disintegration provides a precedent for such an arrangement. During the transitional period, one would hope, the economic gains derived from new union would suffice to compensate for any political loss in a progressively less confrontational UN political arena.

Whatever the pragmatic merits of the proposed system may be, the idea of giving equal weight to three factors – population, budgetary contributions and membership – is bound to meet with disapproval in certain quarters. So too would endowing the GA with legislative powers. Most nations still guard their sovereignty zealously and resist its being encroached upon by external actors, including the United Nations. Nevertheless, the sovereignty of individual states in an age of growing global interdependence is becoming increasingly problematic and often dysfunctional. Many observers would therefore conclude that the weight of the membership term in the weighting formula should be diminished with the passage of time. Others, especially those with a pronounced democratic bent, will recoil from the idea that wealth (as represented by assessed UN contributions) should be weighted as heavily as population, not recognizing that without this condition the more affluent nations of the world would have insufficient incentive to agree to meaningful UN reform. However, with the world's steady, even if fitful, evolution towards more democratic governance – a process that would receive considerable impetus from a reformed and more effective UN system – the wealthy nations' fear of being outvoted on certain issues by poorer, but more populous, nations in transition to becoming full-fledged democracies should gradually diminish.

In light of these considerations, it would be wise to require reconsideration (but not necessarily change) of the weighting formula after a specified period. Again, 15 years might be appropriate. If at that time, in the collective wisdom of the GA as expressed in a requisite two-thirds vote, a change is deemed to be in order, it could be enacted. If the Charter amendment originally establishing a weighted voting system were appropriately worded, no additional amendment would be necessary. Thus 15 years or so after the original amendment takes effect, the weighted voting formula $W = (P + C + M)/3$ might be changed to $W = (2P + 2C + M)/5$. This would significantly augment the relative weight of both the population and contributions terms of the equation and correspondingly reduce the original formula's bias favouring small states. In another 15 or so years, assuming further democratization, another change might be made, making the formula $W = (3P + 2C + M)/6$, whereby population would become the principal determinant of voting weight.

By the time the changes envisaged above are effected, however, the proposed World Parliamentary Assembly (Chapter 3), comprising representatives elected either by the parliaments of the UN member states or, in the fullness of time, by popular elections, might be in place and functioning alongside the appointive GA. *Charters are not written in stone, and the process of democratic reform should continue as long and as far as the global community deems necessary.*

Notes

1. "A More Secure World: Our Shared Responsibility", Report of the High-level Panel on Threats, Challenges and Change, UN GA Doc. A/59/565, 29 November 2004, paras 240–243; Kofi Annan, "In Larger Freedom: Towards Development, Security and Human Rights for All", Report of the Secretary-General, UN GA Doc. A/59/2005, 21 March 2005, paras 158–161.
2. High-level Panel, ibid., paras 240–241.
3. Kofi Annan, note 1 above, paras 159–160.
4. For a chronological summary of how different groups of nations voted on salient issues coming before the GA see M. J. Peterson, *The UN General Assembly*, London and New York: Routledge, 2005, pp. 9–40.
5. Numerous studies of changing voting patterns within the GA have been published. The definitive work is Miguel Marín-Bosch, *Votes in the United Nations General Assembly*, The Hague: Kluwer Law International, 1998.
6. For a discussion of the relationship between the two groups see Lydia Swart and Jakob Lund, *The Group of 77: Perspectives on Its Role in the General Assembly*, New York: Center for UN Reform Education, 2010.
7. Membership in the G-77, once as high as 132, has fluctuated over time. Many new countries were admitted on gaining independence, while other countries left on joining the OECD (e.g. Mexico in 1994 and the Republic of Korea in 1996) or the European Union (e.g. Cyprus and Malta in 2004 and Romania in 2007). Chile joined the OECD in 2010, but has yet to give up membership in the G-77. However, it will be treated solely as an OECD member in the balance of this work. The NAM membership has undergone fluctuations similar to those of the G-77.
8. For data on 240 SC vetoes between February 1946 and August 1997 see Sidney D. Bailey and Sam Daws, *The Procedure of the UN Security Council*, 3rd edn, Oxford: Oxford University Press, 1998, pp. 231–239.
9. Data derived from the *UN Demographic Yearbook*, various years.
10. In contrast to the United Nations, the League of Nations never accepted the membership applications of any country less populous than Luxembourg, which at the time of its admission in 1920 had a population of approximately 260,000.
11. The characterization, cited by Marcus Franda in *The United Nations in the Twenty-first Century, Management and Reform in a Troubled Organization*, Lanham, MD: Rowman & Littlefield, 2006, p. 96, was put forward in an editorial, "Too Many Undemocratic Countries Flout Their Obligations to Peace", *Ottawa Citizen*, 23 September 2003, p. A16. The editorial opined that the one-nation-one-vote rule allowed the GA to be "hijacked

by undemocratic nations that use the organization for their own dubious purposes". Chapter 4 of Franda's work provides an excellent critique of GA voting.

12. Although the GA was not directly involved in creating the ICC, the position of its members in respect to the court has a bearing on their political relations with the United States. In pursuance of the American Servicemembers' Protection Act of 2002, the United States cut off various types of foreign aid to 35 countries that became states parties to the ICC, and by May 2005 had negotiated "bilateral immunity treaties" with 100 nations, including both states parties and non-states parties, stipulating that they will not press charges before the ICC against American military or civilian personnel for crimes committed on their territory that are within the court's purview.

13. An excellent discussion of weighted voting, not only as it might be applied in the United Nations but also as it has been used in other organizations, is in Carol Barrett and Hannah Newcombe, "Weighted Voting in International Organizations", a special number of *Peace Research Reviews* 2(2), 1968, published by the Canadian Peace Research Institute, Dundas, ON. Despite the relatively early date of this work, the theoretical portions remain valid.

14. Probably no student of weighted voting has probed the matter more deeply than the late Hannah Newcombe, founder and long-time director of the Canadian Peace Research Institute. Her many relevant publications include Barrett and Newcombe, ibid.; Hannah Newcombe, "Voting Systems in the United Nations", *Bulletin of Peace Proposals* 1, 1970, pp. 70–80; Hannah Newcombe, *Design for a Better World*, Lanham, MD: University Press of America, 1983. Additional analytic studies include Walter Hoffman (ed.), *A New World Order: Can It Bring Peace to the World's People? Essays on Restructuring the United Nations*, Washington, DC, World Federalist Association, 1991; Robert K. Morrow, *Proposals for a More Equitable General Assembly Voting Structure*, Monograph No. 5, Washington, DC: Center for UN Reform Education, 1989; Paul C. Szasz, *Alternative Voting Systems in International Organizations and the Binding Triad Proposal to Improve U.N. General Assembly Decision-Taking*, Monograph No. 17, Wayne, NJ: Center for UN Reform Education, 2001. Prescriptive works of particular note include John F. Banzhof, "Weighted Voting Doesn't Work: A Mathematical Analysis", *Rutgers Law Review* 19, 1965, pp. 317–343; Grenville Clark and Louis B. Sohn, *World Peace through World Law*, Cambridge, MA: Harvard University Press, 1958 (1st edn) and 1964 (2nd edn); Richard Hudson, "Time for Mutations in the United Nations", *Bulletin of the Atomic Scientists* 32(9), 1976, pp. 39–43; Richard Hudson, *The World Needs a Way to Make Up Its Mind*, Special Study No. 5, New York: Center for War/Peace Studies, 1981; Lionel S. Penrose, "The Elementary Statistics of Majority Voting", *Journal of the Royal Statistical Society* 109(1), 1946, pp. 53–57; L. S. Penrose, "Equitable Voting in the United Nations", *Proceedings of the Medical Association for the Prevention of War* 4, July 1966, pp. 12–19; Joseph E. Schwartzberg, "More on 'The Geography of Representation in the United Nations': An Alternative to the Morrill Proposal", *Professional Geographer* 25(3), 1973, pp. 205–211; Joseph E. Schwartzberg, *Revitalizing the United Nations: Reform through Weighted Voting*, New York and The Hague: Institute for Global Policy/ World Federalist Movement, 2004.

15. High-level Panel, note 1 above, Part 4, "A More Effective United Nations for the Twenty-first Century, Synopsis", p. 64.

16. Several previous works by the author referred to gross national product, rather than GNI, as a possible term in the weighted voting formula. The practical effects of changing to GNI are, however, negligible.

17. The reason for using population data for 2010 and GNI data for 2009 is that assessments in a given year would be made retrospectively, based on GNI levels for one or more preceding years. In actual practice one would probably consider the total GNI of

the preceding three to five years; but, for the sake of simplicity, this work uses data for only one.

18. Coincidentally, this is remarkably close to the range in number of congressmen in the US House of Representatives, varying from 53 for California to one for each of eight states.

19. Paul C. Szasz, note 14 above, pp. 44–47.

20. Ibid., pp. 46–47.

21. Ibid., p. 47.

22. The idea of empowering the General Assembly to make binding decisions has been persuasively argued by Richard Hudson in many publications of the New York-based Center for War/Peace Studies.

23. Support for the political realism of my proposal comes from a digression on GA reform within a review by Hannah Newcombe focusing on my work on Security Council reform: Hannah Newcombe, "Rational Scheme for a Reformed UN Security Council", *Science for Peace Bulletin* 24(1), 2005, available at http://scienceforpeace.sa.utoronto.ca/ Essays_Briefs/Newcombe/NewcombeSecurityCouncil(2005).htm. Newcombe writes: "There is ... some similarity [between it and] ... Richard Hudson's 'Binding Triad,' in the three factors chosen and in making GA votes binding. However, Hudson's scheme requires simultaneous 2/3 majorities on population, GNP and UN membership, a requirement that would be difficult for any resolution to achieve. The Schwartzberg scheme is more permissive ... My own [Newcombe's] scheme based on population and GNP (only two factors) is not as good as Schwartzberg's, a humble statement for an author to make."

24. According to figures compiled by Franda (note 11 above), the total number of resolutions passed since 1946 reached 12,000 in 2004, averaging 220 per year. The annual average increased from 119 during the first five years of the UN's existence to a high of 320 during the 1992–1997 quinquennium. A study by Marín-Bosch (note 5 above) indicates that 55 per cent of GA resolutions were passed without a vote, 15 per cent by an unrecorded vote and only 30 per cent by a recorded vote. Moreover, during the period 1946–1997, 73 per cent of all GA resolutions were passed "without objection", signifying that there was either no vote or no negative votes. A similar, more up-to-date set of yearly data (through the GA's fifty-eighth session, 2003–2004) is provided in Peterson, note 4 above, pp. 75–77.

25. Ratings are provided at www.freedomhouse.org/research/index.htm. The methodology of ranking is also explained. Because of the highly subjective nature of judgements as to what constitutes a democracy (discussed in Chapter 7), I have not ventured to estimate the aggregate weighted votes of the world's democracies.

3

A World Parliamentary Assembly

The will of the people shall be the basis of the authority of government; this will shall be expressed in periodic and genuine elections which shall be by universal and equal suffrage and shall be held by secret vote or by equivalent free voting procedures.
Universal Declaration of Human Rights, Article 21, Clause 3

A United Nations Parliamentary Assembly – a global body of elected representatives – could invigorate our institutions of global governance with unprecedented democratic legitimacy, transparency and accountability.
Boutros Boutros-Ghali

Man's capacity for justice makes democracy possible; but man's inclination to injustice makes democracy necessary.
Reinhold Niebuhr

Introduction

The UN Charter begins on a deceptively promising note. "We the peoples" are its opening words. One will seek in vain, however, for any clause in the document that specifies a means by which ordinary people can play a role in the organization's deliberations and decision-making. The United Nations is presently an organization of *states*, not of *persons*. Its democratic deficit is profound. How best to progressively minimize that deficit forms the subject of this chapter.

What are the implications for the United Nations of Article 21 of the Universal Declaration of Human Rights, cited above? Since it clearly

Transforming the United Nations system: Designs for a workable world, Schwartzberg, *United Nations University Press, 2013, ISBN 978-92-808-1230-5*

stipulates that "The will of the people shall be the basis of the authority of *government*" (emphasis added), some will argue that the article is simply not relevant. The United Nations, after all, was not intended to be a world government. Nevertheless, there can be no denying that many decisions taken by entities comprising the UN system, whether or not they are regarded as binding, contribute to the governance of masses of citizens of the UN's 193 member states. Whatever the intentions of the UN's founders may have been, governance decisions taken within the organization over the decades since its creation have significantly impacted the lives of virtually the whole of humanity; and they are certain to do so increasingly in the decades ahead. Thus a powerful case can be made for greater citizen input into the UN decision-making process.[1]

In fact, advocacy for some form of citizen input in the making of decisions relative to global governance has assumed diverse forms over the past few generations. Not all recommended innovations entail working under the umbrella of the UN system.[2] While various systems for ascertaining citizens' views outside the United Nations are certainly feasible in the near term, I firmly believe that a World Parliamentary Assembly (WPA) – difficult though its creation would be – would be the optimal vehicle for achieving this objective and imparting to the United Nations the "unprecedented democratic legitimacy, transparency and accountability" which former Secretary-General Boutros Boutros-Ghali, among many other forward-thinkers, believes it should have.[3] Hence the recommendations put forward here relate solely to the UN-based option.

With or without a WPA, the time has come – as argued in Chapter 2 – for the General Assembly to be accorded a greater role in making binding decisions in respect to a limited range of matters of truly global concern. In short, the GA should evolve from what many believe to be a generally ineffectual "talk-shop" into a viable legislative body. And if there were to be a UN legislature, its decisions would be much more acceptable if it represented *people* as well as *states*. The democratic deficit can and should be overcome. A more democratic United Nations will inevitably be a stronger and more legitimate organization.

Establishing a WPA will not be easy. The obstacles to be overcome are many. Of particular note are the large number of states (presently 193) to be represented, the exceedingly skewed distribution of their population, the diversity of their languages and cultures, the exceptionally large number of constituents that would have to be represented by individual parliamentarians if the total number of parliamentarians is to be kept within reason, and the wide variation among nations in respect to their past experience and current practices relating to democratic governance. None of these problems, however, is insurmountable.

The approach adopted in this chapter is essentially evolutionary, envisaging three stages of development: first, a WPA with only advisory power and comprising parliamentarians (MWPs) appointed or elected by their respective governments – a less than ideal, but politically feasible, arrangement; second, a popularly elected body with gradually increasing legislative competence (exercised in conjunction with the GA), with parliamentarians selected on a national basis and greatly varying numbers of constituents per MWP from one country to the next; and third (well into the future), a maximally democratic system in which country boundaries are often ignored and the number of constituents per MWP is relatively similar everywhere. Since the transition from stage one to stage two will be fraught with difficulty, a rather detailed discussion of fundamental desiderata and needed institutional arrangements is provided.

Stage one: An advisory body with MWPs chosen by national governments

Preparatory measures

Obtaining agreement within the United Nations that a WPA is necessary is unlikely to come about without substantial and persistent pressure by civil society on the governments of progressive member nations. Those nations in turn would have to take the lead in promoting the WPA idea within the GA, whose assent by a two-thirds majority would be essential. Fortunately, Article 22 of the UN Charter stipulates: "The General Assembly may establish such subsidiary organs as it deems necessary for the performance of its functions." The WPA could thus be declared such an organ. A GA vote calling for its establishment could not be blocked by a Security Council veto. Nevertheless, a campaign for a WPA, once seriously launched, would – despite the growing need and demand – presumably require at least a few years to come to fruition.

Once the requisite GA resolution is adopted, devising the WPA architecture would necessitate considerable diplomatic finesse and would benefit from the input of administrative experts from most, if not all, major regions and cultures of the world. Absent such input, the legitimacy of any future WPA would be called into question. What appears to be needed, then, is some sort of expert panel analogous to the High-level Panel on Threats, Challenges and Change, established under Kofi Annan in 2003 to deal with UN reform in general prior to the 2005 GA summit. But the proposed group should have a more focused mandate than that of the high-level panel and more time for concentrated deliberation.[4] This should enable the crafting of a broadly acceptable proposal to present to the GA for approval and the necessary funding.

Method of apportionment

Taking into consideration the conservative attitudes of most UN member nations in matters relating to UN reform, the organizational problems that establishing a WPA would entail, lingering doubts about the need for such a body and the lessons imparted by the sometimes negative parliamentary experience of the European Union, the WPA should be endowed initially with only advisory and consultative powers and be composed of parliamentarians elected by the legislatures of their respective states, or – where a legislature is lacking or dysfunctional – of individuals selected by the national executive.

But what would be the manner of representation? In principle, many would argue, democracy demands adherence to the concept of "one person – one vote" (OPOV).[5] This would suggest that the number of representatives from China would vastly exceed that of any other nation apart from India, and be more than four times as great as that of the United States. However, China is not yet a democracy. The great mass of its people have no voice in determining the country's policies; and it is presently inconceivable that the United States would consent to membership in a body in which it would be so greatly outvoted by China or, for that matter, even by a democratic India. Nor can one imagine that other wealthy democracies of the global North would consent to a WPA wherein their collective votes would be far fewer than those of parliamentarians from nations that are desperately poor or ruled by authoritarian regimes, or both. Finally, there is no reason to suppose that demographically small – and for the most part poor – nations, which account for a great majority of the UN's membership, would voluntarily surrender to a handful of demographic giants the political clout they presently enjoy under the UN's current one-nation-one-vote system. In short, the practical political arguments in opposition to this OPOV position, at least at the outset of the WPA's existence, are essentially the same as those noted in Chapter 2 in respect to weighted voting in the GA.[6] A politically expedient *near-term* solution to the representation problem should be along similar lines. It would employ objective mathematical formulae that embody a compromise among three relevant principles: the demographic/democratic principle, the economic/contributions principle and the legal principle of the sovereign equality of nations. Applying this reasoning to the present situation, two simple formulae are here proposed.

The first formula is the one proposed for determining country weights in voting on substantive matters in the UN GA, namely:

$$W = (P + C + M)/3$$

Here W, a nation's weight, would be the average of three terms: P, its population as a percentage of the total for all member nations; C, its contributions (counting only those paid on time) to the regular UN budget (here assumed to be in strict proportion to its gross national income) as a percentage of the total; and M, its membership as a percentage of the total membership (1/192 or 0.5208 per cent as of 2010).[7]

The second formula provides a simple means of translating individual national weights into integer values to specify the number of WPA seats to which each nation will be entitled:

$$S = W/D$$

In this formula, S signifies the number of seats for a given nation, rounded off to the nearest integer; W represents the national weight as determined by the previous formula; and D is a lowest common denominator, namely the minimum weight of any UN member nation, which presently is 0.1738 per cent, the weight registered by both Tuvalu and Nauru. In short, the number of seats to which each UN member would be entitled would be its weight as a multiple of that of Tuvalu rounded to the nearest integer. All nations with weights up to 0.2607 per cent (1.5 times 0.1738 per cent) would have one seat. For a nation to have two seats, its weight would be in the range 0.2608–0.4345 per cent (i.e. 1.5–2.5 times Tuvalu's weight). For three seats the inclusive weights would be 0.4346–0.6083 per cent. And so forth.

This method of apportionment would, as of 2010, result in a global total of 564 seats, distributed by nations as shown in Figure 3.1. Of these, 57 (10.1 per cent of the total) would go to the United States, 55 to China, 39 to India, 20 to Japan, 15 to Germany, etc. Country and world totals would, of course, be periodically adjusted in light of changing demographic and economic realities. Summary data for the year 2010 are presented in Table 3.1.

A striking feature of Table 3.1 is that no fewer than 114 nations (59.4 per cent of the total membership) would have only one seat. But the system would, nevertheless, be strongly biased in their favour. Collectively, those nations contain only 6.8 per cent of the total world population, yet would account for a total of 20.2 per cent of all the seats. In general, the less populous the state the greater the bias in its favour, and vice versa.[8] China, for example, with 19.8 per cent of the world's people, would (if the system were presently in place) be given only 9.8 per cent of all seats.[9] And its 55 MWPs would on average each represent some 24.5 million constituents. At the opposite extreme, the delegate from Nauru would represent a mere 9,300!

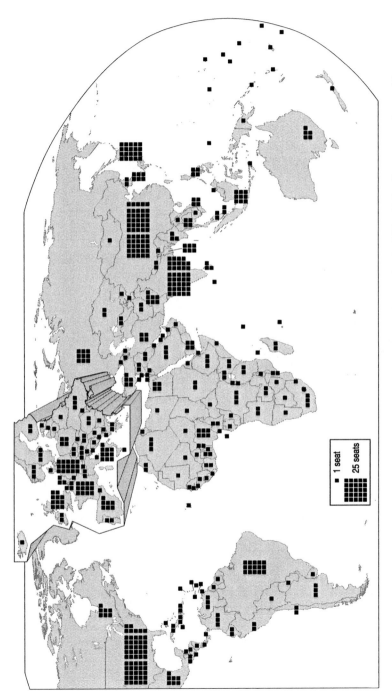

Figure 3.1 Proposed apportionment of seats in stage one of hypothetical World Parliamentary Assembly

41

Table 3.1 Shares of UN member nations, seats and population (2010) in a World Parliamentary Assembly with selection of parliamentarians by national governments

Seats per nation	Nations Number (%)		Seats Number (%)		Population Millions	(%)	Average population per seat Millions
1	114	(59.4)	114	(20.2)	462.8	(6.8)	5.509
2–3	51	(26.6)	117	(20.7)	1,253.1	(18.4)	10.710
4–7	16	(8.3)	84	(14.9)	1,295.4	(19.0)	15.421
9–15	7	(3.6)	78	(13.8)	835.8	(12.3)	10.703
20–57	4	(2.1)	171	(30.3)	2,956.2	(43.5)	17.288
Total	192	(100.0)	564	(100.0)	6,802	(100.0)	12.061

Apart from the bias in favour of demographically small states, including the contributions term in the weighting equation would also result in a bias favouring wealthy nations, whatever their size. The pragmatic justification for this – though only in stage one – is that without this formulation, wealthy nations would have insufficient incentive to take part in the system and poor nations would be denied the benefits to which a more inclusive WPA would lead.

In considering power within a WPA, one should recognize that influence derives not only from the number of seats to which individual countries or blocs of nations are entitled, but also from the soft power of example and ideas. The testimony of MWPs representing exemplary states will generally carry greater weight than declarations from failed or failing states. Similarly, MWPs recognized for their high moral standing, charisma, oratorical skill or issue-based expertise would, irrespective of their home state, be able to exercise influence out of proportion to their single vote.[10] This would be especially true in an assembly in which MWPs are expected to act independently and follow the dictates of their own conscience.

Functioning

In filling WPA seats the legislatures of the UN members with more than one seat would (following the example of the European Parliament – EP) be enjoined to assign seats, to the extent feasible, in proportion to the breakdown by parties within the legislatures themselves. Thus for nations with two seats, the ruling and the leading opposition party would each be likely to have one seat. (In some situations, however, the ruling party might enjoy so wide a margin as to be entitled to a monopoly of the nation's allotted seats.) For the United States, with its strongly entrenched two-party system, there would typically be an approximation of equality between Democrats and Republicans. For countries with numerous significant parties, the breakdown would be more complex. For example, given the party breakdown following the 2009 elections to the German Bundestag, six of that nation's 15 seats would go to Christian Democrats, three to Social Democrats and two each to the Free Democrats, Left Bloc and Green Alliance.[11] Apart from party proportionality, parliaments in populous countries would also be urged to allocate WPA seats on a *regionally fair* basis and with due regard to *gender balance* so as to increase the overall sense of WPA inclusiveness.

Although the *number* of seats would be assigned by nations, the actual *seating* of delegates in the WPA would be by party, more or less along the left-to-right spectrum, in accordance with the custom in the European Union and many other parliaments. Thus social democrats (going by various names in different countries) would sit as a bloc, as would conservatives, liberals and so forth. Given the comparatively minor ideological distinctions between most Democrats and most Republicans in the United States, it is likely that MWPs from both those parties would occupy adjoining banks of seats in the WPA, somewhat to the right of centre.

From the perspective of liberal democracies, the greatest problem in the proposed system, as has already been suggested, is likely to be the anticipated monolithic representation from China (were it to participate), which for all practical purposes remains a one-party state (though that problem will likely be significantly mitigated by the time a WPA actually comes into being).[12] Also objectionable from a liberal democratic perspective would be the substantial representation of other more or less authoritarian states, very likely including Russia, with nine seats. Cumulatively, however, the total of such questionably allocated seats would not be especially great (probably less than a fourth of the total). In any event, since the WPA would serve initially only in an *advisory* capacity and would presumably employ open voting, the GA, to which it would report, would be aware of the sources and political context of particular WPA votes and treat them with appropriate circumspection. So, too, would well-informed – and increasingly influential – members of civil society.

Among the *positive* aspects of the proposed system, one should recognize the potential importance of engaging all parties in WPA discussions and exposing MWPs from non-democratic regimes, as well as from fledgling democracies, to dialogues on issues of global importance, thereby providing them with a template of how democratic government might be applied domestically. This would promote democracy in states where it is presently lacking and hasten transition to a more liberal system. Additionally, to the extent that WPA debates would be publicized by the mass media, they would play an educative role, exposing concerned citizens worldwide to the viewpoints of spokespersons from countries other than their own.

The manner of choosing MWPs would be left to each participating nation, and nations would be free *not* to join if that was their wish. Terms of office (perhaps three years), however, would be uniform. So, too, would be the salaries (preferably modest), working conditions and official perquisites. Provisions would be made for support from a secretariat, including simultaneous translations in each of the UN's six official languages. There would also be payments for staff assistance in the home country of each MWP to manage the anticipated two-way flow of information and opinion between representatives and their constituents: ordinary citizens and civil society activists. Basic expenses for the WPA should be borne by the United Nations, rather than by individual countries, though there would be no bar to supplemental *logistical* (not personal) support from official or private sources, subject to strict requirements for public disclosure of payments wherever applicable.

Once well established, the WPA would normally meet for a period of, say, two or three weeks at the United Nations immediately prior to and possibly overlapping the beginning of GA sessions in September. At the outset it would elect its president and one or more vice-presidents and form needed committees. If the president were selected from a country of the global North, it would be understood that the (first) vice-president would be selected from the global South, and vice versa. Additionally, the WPA's opening plenary session would be used to decide its agenda for the year ahead and engage in general discussion of matters brought to its attention by the GA and other components of the UN system. To encourage maximum freedom of discussion there would be a UN guarantee of sanctuary, if needed, in some friendly nation for MWPs who had the temerity to speak in ways deemed politically unacceptable to the nations they represented.

Since it is likely that little of substance would be settled in the brief period of WPA plenary sessions, much of its work would be handled by committees. While the number and scope of committees would be determined by the WPA itself, one might anticipate such foci as human rights, security, disarmament, international trade, finance, economic development, the environment, democratization, international migration, etc. In forming committees due regard would be paid to regional and gender balance. Each MWP would be expected to belong to at least one committee, and there would be no bar to holding multiple memberships. Each committee would elect a *core group* of MWPs, including a chair, charged with establishing the committee's agenda and working methods, especially during the period when the WPA was not in session. An elected vice-chair would assume the chair's responsibilities should the need arise. Core members would remain at UN Headquarters, in either New York or Geneva, for as long as necessary following the close of the WPA plenary sessions and could reconvene, at UN expense, if and when necessary.

Whether MWPs should be eligible for re-election is moot. While much may be said in favour of continuity, the exceedingly large number of constituents represented per MWP, together with the political, economic, social and cultural diversity that would characterize most constituencies, suggest a need for limited terms. This would facilitate a broader range of representation over time by various interest groups, heighten the sense of WPA inclusiveness and undergird the WPA's legitimacy. On the other hand, there is a need to maintain institutional memory since debate on many issues would carry over from one WPA term to another. A compromise solution would allow re-electing up to one-half of the core group within each WPA committee, but only for a second term. These measures, along with modest but adequate salary structures, would minimize the likelihood of self-serving MWP careerism and reduce susceptibility to corrupt practices.

During the initial WPA period, MWPs from around the world – a significant number of whom are likely to be relative newcomers to politics – would learn how to work cooperatively in a substantially more democratic milieu than that of the present GA. It is even conceivable during this period that some reform-minded national parliaments would authorize the *popular* election of their nation's MWPs, rather than retaining that privilege for themselves. Outside the United Nations, the WPA's formative phase would, as previously noted, also likely witness the diffusion of democratic institutions to countries presently subject to authoritarian regimes. Should these suppositions prove correct, the stage would gradually be set for a new phase in the WPA's development – a phase in which all MWPs are popularly elected and the WPA is accorded increasing legislative authority.

After a predetermined and clearly stipulated period (not to exceed 25 years), the WPA, in conjunction with the General Assembly, would be legally obliged to devise a plan for a more democratic, popularly elected successor body. But some transitional arrangement will be necessary.

Transitional arrangements

Desiderata

The following desiderata should guide the transition from stage one to stage two of the WPA.

- A set of clear rules should be established to determine eligibility for representation.
- The WPA must be open to participation by representatives from *all* countries, including dependencies.
- No country should be *required* to participate in the WPA if it deems that doing so would not be in its best interest.
- An adequately resourced Election Commission (described below), led by highly respected public figures, should ascertain whether election rules have been followed and recommend corrective action where they have been breached.
- The number of WPA seats should be great enough to provide a voice for all significant political ideologies, parties and factions, yet small enough to be manageable.
- If MWPs cast votes of equal weight, country-wise differences in the number of constituents per representative should, over time, be progressively diminished.
- If MWPs cast weighted votes, the weight of such votes should reflect the relative numbers of their constituents.
- Elections should, to the extent feasible, be conducted according to some system of proportional representation within a system of electoral fields, each of which would elect multiple MWPs.
- The system should incorporate appropriate checks and balances.
- Representatives must *be* and *feel* able to express their views freely and without fear of retribution from their home government or any other government for opinions deemed politically unacceptable.
- Transparency and accountability in decision-making should be maximized.
- Simultaneous translation and other provisions should be made to facilitate comprehension of debates and reports in languages different from the mother tongues of individual parliamentarians.
- Substantive decisions should require varying qualified super-majorities, depending on the subject being deliberated.
- The WPA should determine its own procedural rules and create a system of committees in support of its work.
- The WPA must receive adequate financial and logistical support from the UN Secretariat and also have its own secretariat.
- MWPs should be given staff support while resident among their respective constituencies, with additional logistic assistance to ensure ongoing communication between parliamentarians and constituents.
- Provision must be made to facilitate continuity of debate and programmes from one parliamentary session to the next.

The foregoing list will strike some readers as excessively detailed and overambitious; but there is no reason why all of its provisions cannot be adopted, even if perfect compliance will not always prove possible. But as the WPA assumes a genuine law-making role, the bar of compliance would have to be raised. Since no country would be obliged to participate, it should not be too much to expect that, once that decision is freely made, playing by fair and uniformly applied rules would become a country's moral and diplomatic obligation.

Electoral Commission

To ensure that WPA elections are carried out, to the maximum possible extent, on a level playing field, it will be essential to establish an impartial, expert, internationally recruited, professional Election Commission (EC), which would serve the following functions:
- certify the number of seats per country according to objective, uniformly applied criteria
- recommend – subject to WPA approval – rules of fairness regarding who may run for office, acceptable electoral practices and funding, eligibility for voting, etc.
- *prior to* scheduled WPA elections, receive and evaluate detailed protocols from all participating countries indicating their proposed measures to ensure that elections will be fairly conducted; and, *following* the elections, receive reports demonstrating that the elections were, in fact, fairly carried out
- be authorized to determine *in advance* whether fairness criteria were actually being met and foreclose polling where they were being seriously compromised or ignored
- determine, *subsequent to* polling, whether elections were fairly conducted and, in cases of egregious rule violation, recommend to the WPA nullification and/or rescheduling of fraudulent elections.[13]

The EC would be guided by the following *rules of fairness.*
- The franchise will be universal and may not be abridged on the basis of gender, sexual orientation, age (above a stipulated minimum), property qualifications, wealth, literacy or education, previous condition of servitude, race, language, religion, place of birth, ideology or political affiliation.
- The criteria for voting eligibility will also apply to eligibility to run for political office, subject only to the limitation indicated immediately below.
- To be eligible to run for office one would have to obtain a stipulated minimum number of signatures to establish that one is a seriously regarded candidate. A reasonable figure might be 25,000 or 1 per cent of the electorate, whichever is lower.
- For an election to be deemed fair, it would have to be *genuinely contested* by two or more candidates.
- Strict – and modest – limits on election financing would be mandatory.

- In countries with only one WPA seat, the winning candidate would have to receive an *absolute majority* of all valid votes. This implies use of *ranked preference* ballots and the instant run-off method of determining a winner.
- Use of intentionally libellous campaign rhetoric or literature could disqualify a WPA candidate at the EC's discretion.
- In countries allotted more than a single WPA seat, elections would be held on the basis of *proportional representation* (discussed below).
- To preclude elections being determined by small elite groups, no election would be regarded as valid if fewer than a specified percentage of the electorate cast ballots. This might initially be set as low as 10 or 15 per cent, and could be increased over time.
- A reasonable and more or less uniform time period for campaigning would be required between the selection of candidates and the date of elections. For logistical reasons, given the broad territorial extent of many constituencies, campaigning would likely be mainly via the internet or by UN-subsidized TV.
- Balloting by mail and electronic methods would be encouraged, but not to the exclusion of more traditional means.
- Elections would be held within a narrow time frame – say one or two weeks – worldwide, preferably in the northern hemisphere spring. This would give successful candidates several months in which to prepare themselves for their new duties in September. To preclude early returns influencing voting in areas with relatively late polling dates, counting ballots and announcing results would not be permitted until all voting had ended.
- To ensure that candidates and MWPs could act without fear of political reprisal for expressing politically unpopular views, countries holding WPA elections would have to grant all contestants immunity from punishment for whatever they might say in seeking or holding office. Additionally, since immunity could not be ensured in the event of a change of national regime, such individuals should be guaranteed the right of political asylum should the need arise.

Despite much lofty rhetoric relating to gender equity and nearly universal accession to the UN Convention on the Elimination of All Forms of Discrimination against Women, women are still woefully underrepresented in virtually all national legislative bodies. Correcting this bias should be high on the world's social agenda. The WPA would provide an excellent venue for addressing the problem. The following gender-neutral recommendations are offered.

To ensure better gender balance among WPA candidates and elected MWPs, political parties contesting two or more seats in a given country should be obliged, when drawing up slates of nominees, to ensure that not less than one-third nor more than two-thirds of the candidates on the party slate be either male or female. Further, in ranked party lists of WPA candidates in electoral fields comprising three or more seats, neither male nor female candidates could be listed in three consecutive ranks.

Stage two: A popularly elected WPA with increasing legislative competence

Background

In its second stage the WPA would be gradually empowered to participate, in conjunction with the GA, in framing *binding global legislation in important matters of unquestionably global or wide international concern.* What would be considered an admissible issue for legislative action would evolve over time; and the acceptance of each incremental power would – as discussed in Chapter 2 – undoubtedly be subject to vigorous debate.

The manner of representation would remain a crucial question. The possibilities are numerous (in fact theoretically infinite). A key factor in judging the desirability of a given method is the degree to which one subscribes, on the one hand, to the democratic principle of OPOV, as for example in the US House of Representatives, or, on the other hand, whether one favours the politically more expedient principle of "degressive proportionality", whereby the average number of constituents per parliamentarian increases progressively with increasingly large national populations, as is generally the case in the EP.[14]

In a monograph published in 2012 by the Committee for a Democratic UN, I illustrated four apportionment models for a WPA.[15] Of these, one was the stage one system presented in Figure 3.1. Another was the stage three OPOV system illustrated in Figure 3.2. For the intermediate stage I described and illustrated two systems, both entailing progressive proportionality. One was a more nuanced, but relatively complicated, variant of the EP system; the other was based on the so-called Penrose method described below.[16] Given the spatial constraints of the present work, I here limit the discussion to a variant of the latter system.

A stage two apportionment system

An argument advanced by many game theorists, including not a few academics, is that the voting power of each nation in a world assembly should be in accordance with the *square root* of each nation's population in millions.[17] The logic underlying this counterintuitive proposition – that of the "Penrose method" – calls for analysis. The basis for supporting it lies in the valid recognition that, in a wide variety of decision-making settings (weighted voting games, board meetings of shareholding directors of many corporations and in a handful of US state legislatures in which the representatives of counties cast weighted votes based on their county's population), the ratio between the *actual voting powers* of any two participants – i.e. their ability to become part of a winning combination of players or voters or, conversely, of a blocking coalition to prevent undesired decisions – is not directly proportional to the weight of their votes, as classic democratic theory would have us believe. Rather, that capability increases disproportionately as differences in voting power increase. Thus, it is argued, fairness demands reduction in the assigned weight of the more powerful (in our case, populous) players.

From a mathematical perspective the most appropriate reduction, allegedly, would result from weighting in accordance with the *square root* of the relevant variable (population in millions, number of shares of stock held, etc.).[18] For the WPA this figure would be called the "seat determinant". Rounding such figures off to the nearest integer would indicate the number of seats. Were the Penrose method to be adopted for a WPA today, it would apportion seats as follows: 37 for China, 34 for India, 18 for the United States, 15 for Indonesia, 14 each for Brazil and Pakistan, 13 each for Nigeria and Bangladesh, 12 for Russia, 11 for Japan and so forth. The United Kingdom and France, both P-5 powers, would each have eight seats. To take some examples from among relatively small but influential states, Switzerland, with a population of 7.807 million (square root = 2.794), would be given an integer weight of 3, while Norway, with a population of 4.888 million (square root = 2.211), would have a weight of 2. The threshold population separating countries with two seats from those with only one would be 2.25 million (1.5 squared). All 56 UN member nations with populations below that figure (using 2010 data) would be apportioned one seat each.

Conceived and promoted essentially on theoretical grounds, the Penrose method pays insufficient heed, arguably, to the actual distribution of political power among nations. Its advocates have failed to present persuasive empirical evidence indicating why one should use the *square* root of the population in millions, rather than, let us say, the 1.8th root or any other root, in apportioning weights and/or seats. Further, the basic argument underlying the method is valid only to the extent that MWPs from a single country vote *en bloc*. But, to the extent that they act as *independent decision-makers*, the logic for the system is diminished. To be sure, occasions would undoubtedly arise when all, or virtually all, MWPs from a given populous nation would choose to vote *en bloc*; but there is no reason why that would be the norm.

Notwithstanding my reservations, I believe that the reasoning underlying the Penrose method does have considerable validity and one could employ square roots to arrive at a workable system, provided that one then assigns *politically acceptable weights* to the votes of each seat holder. Obviously, any number of weighting formulae may be devised, and each participating nation would be inclined to support a formula deemed most favourable to its own interests. The demographically largest nations would argue, citing traditional democratic principles, for the closest possible approach to an OPOV system, weighting the vote of each seat holder by the total number of his/her constituents. Most small nations, on the other hand, would support a formula embodying minimal weighting coefficients, or preferably no weighting at all. Experiments with numerous possibilities between these extreme positions suggest that a workable *via media* could be negotiated.

Table 3.2 indicates the distribution of *seats* (not *weighted votes*) according to the Penrose method.[19] It indicates a total of 758 seats (assuming universal participation), which should be a manageable number and sufficient for the representation of all globally significant political ideologies. (This number would change periodically in response to demographic changes, but would probably never exceed 1,000 given the facts that representation would continue to be based on the square root of population rather than on total numbers, which increase at a much faster rate, and that global population will likely peak late in the present century.) The seat distribution is skewed, however, in favour of relatively small nations. At one extreme, the 56 nations with only one seat each, accounting for only 0.6 per cent of the world's population, would occupy 7.4 per cent of the seats. At the other extreme, China and India, with a combined 37.0 per cent of the world's population, would be given only 9.4 per cent of the seats.

Table 3.2 Shares of UN member nations, seats and population (2010) in a popularly elected World Parliamentary Assembly with seat apportionment according to square root of each nation's population

Seats per nation	Nations Number (%)		Seats Number (%)		Population Millions (%)		Average per seat Millions
1	56	(29.2)	56	(7.4)	44.1	(0.6)	0.788
2–3	65	(33.9)	160	(21.1)	425.0	(6.2)	2.656
4–7	48	(25.0)	247	(32.6)	1,311.3	(19.3)	5.309
8–18	21	(10.9)	224	(29.6)	2,507.8	(36.9)	10.951
34–37	2	(1.0)	71	(9.4)	2,518.0	(37.0)	35.465
Total	192	(100.0)	758	(100.0)	6,802.2	(100.0)	8.974

There are many possible ways of arriving at weighted votes to make the system politically acceptable to the demographically larger powers: by arithmetic, geometric (exponential) or logarithmic progression; by square or other roots; by arbitrarily established population tiers; and so forth. None is an obviously correct choice; the final determination will have to be diplomatically negotiated. Nevertheless, I here present one possible and reasonable solution.

The proposal is to take the square root of the seat determinant as a weighting coefficient, which we shall call the "weight determinant". It indicates the weight that would be assigned to the vote cast by each seat holder from a given country. (For the 39 countries with populations less than a million, however, a minimum weight of 1.0 would be assigned.) In the case of China, the weighting determinant would be $\sqrt{36.7}$ or 6.06; for India $\sqrt{34.3}$ or 5.85; for the United States $\sqrt{17.6}$ or 4.20; and so forth. National weights would then be the product of the weight determinant multiplied by the number of seats. Table 3.3 illustrates the system as it would apply to a small sample of nations.[20] The global distribution of seats, by weight ranges, is shown in Figure 3.2.

From a political perspective the ratio of Chinese to American votes will loom as a key factor in determining US willingness to accept the pro-

Table 3.3 Seats and weighted votes for selected nations and world in hypothetical World Parliamentary Assembly

	China	USA	South Africa	Sweden	Bahrain	World
Population (P: millions)	1,346.0	310.1	50.0	9.4	1.0	6,802.0
Seat determinant (SD: $\sqrt{P}$)	36.7	17.6	7.0	3.1	1.1	
Seats (S: SD to nearest integer)	37	18	7	3	1	758
Weight determinant (WD: $\sqrt{SD}$)	6.06	4.20	2.66	1.75	1.10	
Total votes (V: SD × WD)	222.2	73.9	18.8	5.9	1.2	2,053.0
Population per seat (P/S: millions)	36.4	17.2	7.1	3.1	1.2	9.4
Population per vote (P/V: millions)	6.1	4.2	2.7	1.8	1.1	3.4
Votes as % of world total	10.80	3.60	0.92	0.15	0.05	100.00
% of world's population	19.70	4.60	0.74	0.14	<0.01	100.00

Note: Assumptions are that the system was in use in 2010, and data are as of that year; and that membership is universal.

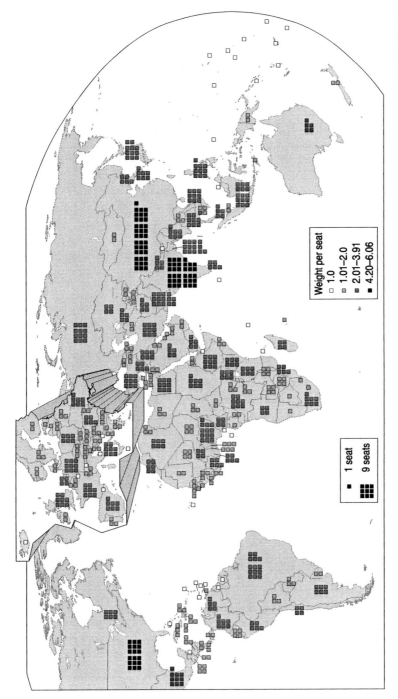

Figure 3.2 Proposed apportionment of seats and seat weights in stage two of hypothetical World Parliamentary Assembly in which members of parliament cast weighted votes

Weight per seat
☐ 1.0
▨ 1.01–2.0
▦ 2.01–3.91
■ 4.20–6.06

■ 1 seat

▦ 9 seats

53

posed stage two WPA. Several factors, however, should mitigate America's concerns. First, China's participation would be contingent on its prior agreement to play by the stipulated democratic rules – which it would have ample reason to do – thereby contributing to a more politically just world order. Second, UN legislation would require the concurrence of both the WPA and the GA, in which the United States would be a relatively more powerful player. Third, the 3:1 voting ratio between China and the United States is not nearly as great as the 4.3:1 ration between their populations. Finally, the voting ratio will be progressively diminished because, for the foreseeable future, the role of population growth in the United States will be much higher than in China, where population decline is expected to set in around the year 2030.[21]

Comparison of the last two lines of Table 3.3 makes clear that the proposed system conforms to the principle of degressive proportionality: the lower a nation's population rank, the more favoured it is in the allocation of voting power. A full array of national data reveals that only countries ranked 1 through 18 (Turkey being the eighteenth) would have fewer votes proportionally than their share of the world's population. Russia, Japan and Germany would fall in this group, but other relatively important powers such as France, the United Kingdom and Italy (ranking 21, 22 and 23 respectively) would not. South Africa (ranking 25) would be slightly more favoured than Italy, and the sampled nations of Sweden and Bahrain would be even more advantaged. Towards the bottom of the population spectrum would be the 39 nations with fewer than a million inhabitants. Each of these, no matter how small, would be accorded one seat with a voting weight of 1.0.

Proportional representation

In the proposed stage two system, 136 nations would have two or more seats. Those countries would be enjoined to allocate their seats by political parties, using a system of proportional representation. But whereas stage one allocations would reflect the distribution of seats in the respective national *parliaments*, those of stage two would be in accordance with *popular voting* in WPA elections. Such a system would substantially increase the probability that minority views and interests would be fairly represented. It would not matter whether a particular minority was ideological, occupational, racial, religious, linguistic or otherwise defined. The essential point is that democratic governance should seek to ensure that all significant factions have a reasonably good chance of being heard and playing meaningful roles in governance.

The argument against geographically delimited *single-member electoral districts* may best be made with reference to the hypothetical case of India.

There, as of the census of 2001, 16.2 per cent of the population were members of "scheduled castes" (politically marginalized ex-untouchables), 8.2 per cent "scheduled tribes" (indigenous peoples), 13.4 per cent Muslims and 6.1 per cent of other religious minorities.[22] Although there is some overlap among these groups (for example, many tribals are Christians), their combined population in 2010 came to approximately 475 million.[23] Nevertheless, with single-member constituencies, it is conceivable that not one member of these minorities would be elected to a WPA. With proportional representation, however, they should collectively be able to elect substantial proportions of India's total cohort of MWPs in any election, and would fare much better than under a first-past-the-post system with single-member constituencies.

Although electoral opportunities comparable to those noted for India might not be available to the largely indigenous populations of relatively small countries such as Guatemala or Laos, one may assume that indigenous MWPs from more populous countries, such as Mexico or India, would be sympathetic to their concerns in WPA debates. Similarly, a Green MWP from Germany, let us say, would tend to promote the interests of otherwise unrepresented "greens" wherever they might reside. And a Conservative from the United Kingdom might champion causes advocated by otherwise unrepresented conservatives in other parts of the world. This sort of advocacy would not be forthcoming in single-member constituencies, especially those in which candidates backed by economic power and a well-entrenched political base would enjoy an inordinately great advantage in a first-past-the-post system.

In countries with up to 8, 9 or even 10 WPA seats, a single nationwide slate of candidates might be presented to the voters. Such a system would eliminate substantial costs and political haggling required for the territorial delimitation of single-member constituencies. Additionally, it would preclude the pernicious practice of electoral gerrymandering. Each political party in a given race would be entitled to nominate as many candidates as there are seats to be filled, subject to the stipulated rules of fairness.

But in most countries projected to have eight or more seats, a single slate of candidates would confront many voters with an excessively difficult set of choices. In such cases, the country could be divided into two or more broad regions, or "electoral fields", each accounting for no fewer than 4 and no more than 10 seats, and each with its own party slates of candidates. Wherever 11 or more seats were to be filled, division into two or more electoral fields would become *mandatory*. In all some 24 countries might be affected if these recommendations were in effect. The number of fields would vary from one apportionment system to another, and would be fewer under the recommended stage two system than under other possible dispensations. For example, for China's 37 seats there would have to be no fewer than four fields and no more than nine (as opposed to 22 and 53 fields respectively for its hypothetical 213 seats – out of a hypothetical 1,000 – in an OPOV system). Of the 24 nations that might elect to establish electoral fields, only 10, with 11 or more seats, would be *required* to do so under the proposed stage two rules. Territorial delimitation of electoral fields would be the responsibility of nations participating in WPA elections.

Assembly procedures and qualified majority voting

Most of the procedural recommendations relating to a stage one WPA would also be applicable for the larger stage two assembly. The main difference, apart from holding popular elections, would be the gradually increasing role that the WPA might play, in conjunction with the GA, in framing legislation.

The pace, nature and extent of change would be negotiable, but early budgetary oversight would be appropriate. Later, in keeping with the need for checks and balances, it would be desirable to provide for a WPA check against questionable decisions in the SC, the GA and other UN agencies. This accountability measure would, in effect, establish the principle of a non-binding, though politically potent, *people's veto*. Whether such a veto could eventually be made legally binding is a matter for future debate.

As in the EP, the WPA would function best through a system with "qualified majority" voting, requiring specified super-majorities depending on the issue of concern. Votes on *procedural* issues would require no more than a simple majority. Other votes, those with no more than an *advisory* intent, might also be passed by simple majorities. Though non-binding, they could potentially exercise considerable political and moral influence. On some *substantive* issues two-thirds majorities would be in order; and decisions so taken – concurrently in both the WPA and the GA – should be legally binding and enforceable. Another set of issues – for example imposing economic sanctions – might require a three-fourths majority. Finally, a vote to nullify SC decisions (which could be authorized only through major Charter revision) might require a four-fifths majority. Detailed recommendations on these contentious issues are beyond the purview of this work.

Institutional process

To launch and legitimize the second stage of the WPA it would be necessary to obtain prior UN agreement on an *institutional process*. This agreement might include the following conditions (though all the numbers in square brackets would be negotiable).

a. At least [50] per cent of the UN's member *nations* would have to agree to the conditions established for the WPA. This group of nations would have to include UN members from at least [four] continents.

b. The participating nations would have to account for at least [50] per cent of the world's *population.*

c. The participating nations would have to account for at least [50] per cent of the regular UN *budget.* Stage two would not commence until [10] years after the date when the previously noted conditions were met. Additional nations would undoubtedly elect to accede to the WPA accord during this period. No nation, however, would be *required* to accede.

d. Within a period of [10] years, beginning with the date of a country's declaration of intent to join the WPA, the country would have to provide credible evidence of its ability to fulfil the conditions for participation, including holding at least two successive national parliamentary elections judged to be fair by the EC.

e. A nation would be declared eligible to elect members to the WPA immediately on certification that it had met the specified conditions, and could, within a year of its eligibility, elect the number of representatives to which it was entitled under the apportionment system then in use.

f. The requisite funding would have to be sanctioned by the UN GA.

Several of the above conditions might require modification if a substantial proportion of the countries acceding to the WPA were to do so as members of future *federal unions.*

One may anticipate that, once the accession thresholds for launching a stage two WPA are in place, popular movements in many initially reluctant but democratic nations would, acting largely through non-governmental organizations, pressure their respective governments to participate, and that many additional nations would do so in order not to be excluded from a key component of the emerging global decision-making process. Further, once the utility of the WPA were to be demonstrated, the accession process would inevitably gain momentum. Thus the period from the initial establishment of a stage two system to one with near-universal membership might prove much shorter than most advocates of radical reform now believe possible.

Costs

By UN standards, establishing and maintaining a viable WPA would at the outset appear rather expensive, and costs would increase significantly in changing from a stage one to a stage two system. Among anticipated expenses are the following.

- Designing, building and maintaining the physical facilities for annual meetings in New York. (Building costs, however, might be amortized over a period of up to 50 years.)
- MWP salaries, travel costs and *per diem* expenses.
- Costs for offices and other infrastructure for MWPs in their home bases. (It would be reasonable, however, to pass these costs on to the participating national governments.)
- Salaries for support staff, including the WPA Secretariat in New York and aides (at least two per MWP and more for core committee members) in their home bases.
- Support for WPA Secretariat and UN Secretariat staff functions (simultaneous translation, recording and printing of debates and position papers – even if limited to "executive summaries" – etc.).
- Support for the proposed EC, including needed administrative and investigatory staff.

Assuming universal WPA membership, it is hard to imagine its being maintained for less than $0.5 billion per year (in constant US dollars, as of 2010). While that figure might seem high in relationship to the current regular UN budget (roughly $1.8 billion per year), it is actually remarkably low in comparison to the budgets for the legislatures of a number of the world's leading democracies, and probably less than that of one or more states within the United States.[24] Putting the matter in a different perspective, if one assumes for the sake of argument that the WPA were functioning today, with an annual budget of US$700 million to serve a world with some 7 billion inhabitants, its cost would come to only 10 cents per person! Expensive? Hardly.

Stage three: Institutionalizing worldwide electoral fields and the one-person-one-vote principle

Although, as noted, it is possible on grounds of political expediency to justify the great differences in the number of constituents per MWP from one country to another in stages one and two of the proposed WPA, those inequities violate a basic tenet of representative democracy, the OPOV principle, according to which the franchise of all voters should carry more or less equal weight. That the 9,300 citizens of Nauru should be entitled to one WPA seat while a Chinese MWP would be expected to represent, on average, 36.3 million in our stage two model is hardly just. In a hypothetical WPA with 1,000 seats and a future world maximum population of 10 billion, a truly democratic allocation would be one in which each seat represented some approximation of the average of 10 million constituents.

In a WPA purporting to represent *people* (and their political *parties*), rather than *nations*, there should then come a stage three system that would provide representation wherein national boundaries are frequently ignored in the interests of greater and more universal voting equity. Thus assuming continuing global diversity in political perspectives, there will be need for an assembly in which the entire world would be divided into a set of "electoral fields", each with four to 10 popularly elected seats filled in accordance with some agreed-upon system of proportional representation. Many of these fields would consist of portions of given nations (analogous to US congressional districts), while others would combine a number of small neighbouring nations (as, for example, in Central America). Figure 3.3 illustrates for the Americas how such a system might be territorially organized. Whether or not it can be established before the end of the present century is moot. I here omit the suggested details of its organization – for a fuller analysis interested readers may consult my previously cited WPA monograph.[25]

Conclusions

Creating a World Parliamentary Assembly would be a feasible, though difficult, undertaking, and there are multiple ways of reaching that goal. My preference is for a WPA evolving along a path similar to that followed by the European Union, then going further towards a more empowered legislative body, and eventually towards acceptance of the one-person-one-vote ideal, transcending existing international borders.[26]

This chapter has gone into considerable detail in discussing what a WPA would require in stages one and two of its development because many advocates of such a body suppose – naively in my opinion – that once the logic of popular representation at the global level is widely accepted, everything else will fall easily into place. Hence they cavalierly ignore many practical problems that creating such an institution would entail. Others will grant that the idea appears desirable in theory, but then assert that the act of creation would be too complex, costly and politically sensitive to implement. In the absence of concrete blueprints, advocacy of a WPA will continue to be derided by sceptics as hopelessly utopian.

Future generations will cease to accept the UN's glaring democratic deficit and its attendant lack of transparency and accountability. A democratically constituted WPA could greatly mitigate these deficiencies and do much to promote more legitimate governance at both *national* and *international* levels. With a WPA and other reforms in place, we can expect a world in which people of different nations will be more inclined to

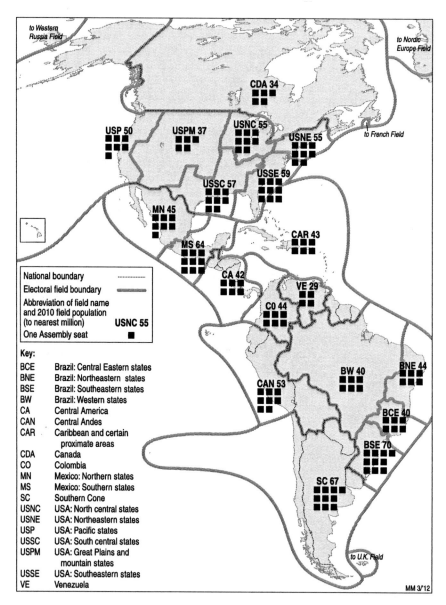

Figure 3.3 Hypothetical apportionment of seats for the Americas in proposed 1,000-seat Parliamentary Assembly, by electoral fields

listen to and learn from one another, in which states will be less prone to violent conflict and in which a revitalized United Nations will be better able to address the needs of all of Earth's inhabitants. Providing the diverse strands of humankind, in whose interests the United Nations was founded, with a meaningful voice in making the decisions that will shape their destiny will do more to legitimize the global organization than any other reform that I can envisage.

Acknowledgement

This chapter is a substantial abridgement and reworking of Joseph E. Schwartzberg, *Creating a World Parliamentary Assembly: An Evolutionary Journey*, Berlin: Committee for a Democratic UN, 2012.

Notes

1. Seminal monographs are Dieter Heinrich, *The Case for a United Nations Parliamentary Assembly*, Amsterdam and New York: World Federalist Movement, 1992; Andreas Bummel, *Internationale Demokratie entwickeln: Für eine Parlamentarische Versammlung bei den Vereinten Nationen* (*Developing International Democracy: For a Parliamentary Assembly at the United Nations*), Stuttgart: Committee for a Democratic UN, 2005.
2. A diverse set of proposals is found in Saul H. Mendlovitz and Barbara Walker (eds), *A Reader on Second Assembly & Parliamentary Proposals*, Wayne, NJ: Center for UN Reform Education, 2003. Comparative analyses of multiple proposals are in Carol Barrett and Hannah Newcombe, "Weighted Voting in International Organizations", *Peace Research Reviews* 2(2), special number, 1968; Hannah Newcombe, "Voting Systems in the United Nations", *Bulletin of Peace Proposals* 1, 1970, pp. 70–80; Hannah Newcombe, *Design for a Better World*, Lanham, MD: University Press of America, 1983; Andreas Bummel, *The Composition of a Parliamentary Assembly at the United Nations*, Berlin: Committee for a Democratic UN, 2010; Joseph E. Schwartzberg, *Creating a World Parliamentary Assembly: An Evolutionary Journey*, Berlin: Committee for a Democratic UN, 2012. Other noteworthy works advocating or illustrating a specific proposal or approach include an anthology of essays by Richard Falk and Andrew Strauss, *A Global Parliament: Essays and Articles*, with a foreword by Boutros Boutros-Ghali, Berlin: Committee for a Democratic UN, 2001; David C. Huckabee, *The House of Representatives Apportionment Formula: An Analysis of Proposals for Change and Their Impact on States*, Washington, DC: Congressional Research Service, Library of Congress, 2001; Robert Johansen, "The E-Parliament: Global Governance to Serve the Human Interest", *Widener Law Review* 13, 2007, pp. 319–345; Lionel S. Penrose, "The Elementary Statistics of Majority Voting", *Journal of the Royal Statistical Society* 109(1), 1946, 53–57; Lionel S. Penrose, "Equitable Voting in the United Nations", *Proceedings of the Medical Association for the Prevention of War* 4, July 1966, pp. 12–19.
3. Much of the relevant literature uses the term UN Parliamentary Assembly rather than World Parliamentary Assembly (WPA), as in this chapter. My preference for WPA stems from its de-emphasis of "nations" and, by implication, its greater emphasis on people(s).

4. The high-level panel met as a group over five sessions totalling only 18 meeting days. Additionally, there were 18 regional sessions and issue workshops conducted over a period of 87 days.

5. Literature on the subject still adheres, for the most part, to "one *man* – one vote", but this work alters the phrase to a gender-neutral form.

6. A more extended analysis appears in Joseph E. Schwartzberg, *Revitalizing the United Nations: Reform through Weighted Voting*, New York and The Hague: Institute for Global Policy, World Federalist Movement, 2004, pp. 13–16.

7. As the analyses in this work were carried out prior to South Sudan's independence, that country is not considered in this chapter.

8. An exception exists for nations in the 9 to 15 seat range, which have fewer constituents per seat holder than those in the 4 to 7 range. This is explained by the fact that the former group happens to be, on average, much wealthier than the latter, thereby driving up its average seat total.

9. However, assuming the system were in place, China might pull ahead of the United States within the next decade.

10. Examples of diplomats from tiny countries exercising an enduring influence on UN thinking and the development of world law are provided by the careers of Ambassador Arvid Pardo of Malta, in respect to establishing the "common heritage of mankind" principle relating to the seabed and ocean floor beyond the limits of national jurisdiction, and subsequently by Ambassador Tommy Koh of Singapore in negotiations leading to the UN Comprehensive Law of the Sea Treaty.

11. German Bundestag official website, www.bundestag.de/htdoc_e/. Proportional party allocations for 16 selected countries, based on their latest elections and using four different allocation scenarios, are provided by Bummel, note 2 above, pp. 45–48.

12. Harbingers of political change in China are legion, despite official government repression of dissent. Of particular importance is the influence of the internet. This issue is reviewed in Guobin Yang, "Technology and Its Contents: Issues in the Study of the Chinese Internet", *Journal of Asian Studies* 70(4), 2011, pp. 1043–1050.

13. This provision would undoubtedly be costly, but it follows a precedent established and not infrequently employed by the Electoral Commission of the Republic of India in respect to elections for the lower house of the Indian parliament as well as the legislative assemblies of India's states. It should also be noted that the United Nations already has considerable experience in facilitating and monitoring elections, beginning with the organization of the first elections held in Namibia in 1989. Since 1992 its electoral activities have been carried out mainly under the aegis of the Electoral Assistance Division established that year within the Secretariat by General Assembly Resolution A/Res/46/137. Between 1989 and 2005 the United Nations received 363 requests for electoral assistance, and responded positively to most of them.

14. National representation in the EP is diplomatically negotiated, rather than determined by a mathematical formula. At the two extremes, as of 2009 the six MEPs from Luxembourg represented on average 76,667 constituents each (slightly less than the 80,800 for Malta's five MEPs), while France's 72 MEPs represented an average of 873,417 (slightly more than the 832,606 for the 99 MEPs from Germany), a maximum ratio of 11.4:1. By way of contrast, in the US House of Representatives the extremes were 495,000 and 905,000 for the single representatives from Wyoming and Montana respectively, a ratio of 1.8:1.

15. Schwartzberg, note 2 above. See also Joseph E. Schwartzberg, "Creating a World Parliamentary Assembly", *The Federalist Debate* XV(3), 2002, New Series, pp. 10–16. This study was anthologized, with some editing, in Mendlovitz and Walker, note 2 above,

pp. 80–92, under the title "Overcoming Practical Difficulties in Creating a World Parliamentary Assembly (WPA)".

16. Penrose, 1946, 1966, note 2 above. See also John F. Banzhaf, "Multi-Member Electoral Districts: Do They Violate the 'One Man, One Vote' Principle?", *Yale Law Journal* 75(8), 2005, pp. 1309–1338.

17. Penrose, 1946, 1966, note 2 above.

18. The literature on the subject is substantial, and the mathematics underlying the arguments is complicated. The methods followed yield various indices of the probability of determining an outcome. The most widely used measure, the so-called Banzhaf power index (or Penrose-Banzhaf index), is explained in, *inter alia*, John F. Banzhaf, "Weighted Voting Doesn't Work: A Mathematical Analysis", *Rutgers Law Review* 19, 1965, pp. 317–343. The power of the index is greatest in voting systems that require only simple majorities, and declines in systems requiring super-majorities. Additionally, the power of the index is greatest in systems with relatively few players and declines as the number of players increases. In a body as large as the WPA would be, it seems doubtful that the Penrose method, in its pure form, would add much to the fairness of decision-making.

19. The seat numbers *apportioned* (as opposed to those actually *held*) would be the same whether or not certain nations chose to participate in the WPA. Laggard nations would simply assume their predetermined seat entitlements whenever they decided to enter into the system.

20. Complete data for all 192 UN member nations as of 2010 are provided in Schwartzberg, note 2 above, pp. 115–120.

21. About that time India is expected to overtake China as the world's most populous country.

22. Wikipedia, "Demographics of India", http://en.wikipedia.org/wiki/Demographics_of_India. Relevant data from the 2011 census were not yet available at this writing.

23. Author's estimate.

24. For example, based on data on the website of the California state legislature, the annual budget for that state in 2009–2010 should have come to well above $500 million (author's estimate). Details are provided in Schwartzberg, note 2 above, p. 80.

25. Schwartzberg, ibid., pp. 90–94.

26. Erskine Childers and Brian Urquhart, *Renewing the United Nations System*, Uppsala: Dag Hammarsköld Foundation, 1994, provide two very useful tables in this regard, comparing the European experience with what might eventuate in the creation of a WPA: "Development of a UN Parliamentary Assembly", p. 178, and "Functioning of a UN Parliamentary Assembly in relation to the existing UN structure", p. 179.

4

Reform of the Security Council

The proposed system of comprehensive security will become operative to the extent that the United Nations, its Security Council and other international institutions and mechanisms function effectively. A decisive increase is required in the authority and role of the United Nations.
Soviet General Secretary Mikhail Gorbachev, address to United Nations, September 1987

Introduction

Among the many components of the UN system none is more consequential than the Security Council, whose actions – or failures to act – often seriously affect the welfare of much, if not all, of humankind. Presently, the SC is the only UN organ whose decisions are legally binding. Yet its very legitimacy, dominated as it is by the five permanent, veto-wielding members who happened to be on the winning side in the Second World War, is increasingly called into question. It is hardly surprising, then, that this anachronistic and insufficiently representative body has been the object of more recommendations for reform than any other UN entity.[1]

SC reform has, in fact, has been under continuous review within the UN General Assembly ever since the GA's establishment in 1993 of the Open-Ended Working Group on the Question of Equitable Representation on and Increase in the Membership of the Security Council. Literally scores of reform recommendations have been put forward since that date

Transforming the United Nations system: Designs for a workable world, Schwartzberg, *United Nations University Press, 2013, ISBN 978-92-808-1230-5*

from countries, independent scholars and think-tanks in all quarters of our planet.[2] Especially important were the two formulations put forward in 2004 by the prestigious High-level Panel on Threats, Challenges and Change appointed by Secretary-General Kofi Annan the previous year. Although these formulations were warmly endorsed by Annan, they, like all previous and subsequent formulae, were deemed to have serious flaws from the perspective of significant blocs of nations and failed to be adopted.[3]

The launching platform for this chapter's discussion of SC reform is an analysis of the decreasing representativeness and legitimacy of the present system with the passage of time. The special and anachronistic privileges of the P-5 powers receive particular scrutiny. I then suggest desiderata for SC membership that would be widely regarded as logical, politically realistic, representative, flexible and fair. With these in mind, I propose replacing the current system with a council composed of representatives of 12 regions, including all UN member nations, in which each regional representative casts an objective mathematically determined weighted vote. Additionally, I explain how SC delegates would be more democratically elected than at present, why the proposed method would conduce to greater meritocracy and legitimacy, how the business of the SC might efficiently be conducted and why the new system would promote greater regional cooperation outside the United Nations. I also discuss a variant of the proposed new system in which UN member nations could, if they chose, be represented simultaneously in two of the 12 regions established.

The penultimate section of the chapter takes up the seemingly intractable question of the veto. It suggests ways by which its use can be circumscribed and even phased out altogether. The conclusion briefly recapitulates the merits of the proposal.

Declining representativeness of the present system[4]

Originally, the UN Charter established a Security Council of 11 members, five of which – China, France, the Soviet Union, the United Kingdom and the United States – were designated as "permanent". Another six elected members served staggered, non-renewable two-year terms, three being elected every year, with "due regard being paid in the first instance to the contribution of Members to the maintenance of international peace and security and to the other purposes of the Organization, and also to equitable geographical distribution".[5] Thus more than a fifth of the original 51 UN members were represented on the SC when it first convened. In 1946 the population of the 11 initial SC members collectively comprised

63 per cent of the total population of all the then member nations (nearly 56 per cent being accounted for by the five permanent members), while the combined population of the six non-permanent members comprised only a sixth of the total population of the 46 states from which that group was selected.

As new nations were accepted into the organization, the representativeness of the SC's membership declined substantially (even if one ignores the dramatic decrease occasioned by the fact that mainland China was not truly represented during the period 1950–1971 when Taiwan held the permanent seat reserved for "the Republic of China"). This expansion led, inevitably, to a demand to expand the SC's membership. Although the GA voted in 1963 to increase the membership to 15, it was not until 1965 that the requisite ratifications of the enabling Charter amendment were obtained. When the expanded SC, newly containing a total of 10 non-permanent members, convened in January 1966 the proportion of SC members to total members rose from 9.9 to 13.5 per cent; but with further UN expansion that proportion immediately began again to decline, sinking by the year 2011 to only 7.9 per cent. It is thus hardly surprising there is now almost universal agreement that the time has come to enlarge the SC yet again, by anywhere from two to 15 new members.

Figures 4.1 and 4.2 respectively provide a geographic and a historical perspective on the representativeness of the SC. Figure 4.1 shows, for all countries of the world, the number of terms served on the SC from 1946, when that body first met, to the year 2010, and distinguishes between terms served before and after SC expansion in 1966.[6] It also indicates, as of 2011, the number of years of each country's SC service as a proportion of the number of years of eligibility, which is dependent on its date of admission to the United Nations (as indicated in Appendix 1).[7] For non-permanent members, the range in years served varies from zero for 72 states, and one for Liberia (one of three nations serving one half-term in 1946), to as many as 20 for Brazil and Japan. But as Brazil is a Charter member of the United Nations, while Japan joined only in 1956, Japan has had a higher frequency of membership, 36 per cent, compared to 30 per cent for Brazil. The only other countries serving for more than 20 per cent of the total years of eligibility were Germany (29 per cent),[8] Argentina (24 per cent) and Italy (21 per cent). Another seven served more than 15 per cent.

Figure 4.1 reveals many puzzling anomalies. For example, the small island nation of Mauritius, with a population of only 1.2 million, has served four years, only two fewer than Indonesia, which with 233 million people (in 2010) ranks as the world's fourth most populous state. Similarly Panama, with a population less than a thirtieth that of Mexico, has served ten years compared to Mexico's seven.[9] But one must consider the varying fervour with which individual countries lobby for SC seats. Whereas many nations vie keenly with others in their region to be elected, Mexico appears to have concluded, at times, that the SC selection process is excessively dominated by the permanent members, especially the United States, and that the prize of membership was simply not worth the effort of courting GA votes.[10] In any event, the politicization of the selection process and the insufficient role played therein by merit cannot be seriously questioned.

The 72 nations that have never served at all on the SC are, for the most part, rather small. But the list does include Myanmar, Afghanistan and Saudi Arabia. Israel is another conspicuous omission.[11] South Africa and Viet Nam (with a population of roughly 90 million) were admitted for the first time only in 2007 and 2008 respectively. In all the named cases, the nations in question are (or were) widely viewed as pariah states, a fact that virtually precluded their selection. Other states also suffered, presumably, from negative perceptions or determined opposition from one or more of the P-5 powers. This likely explains why Iran, for example, never served after its initial term in 1955–1956. Also noteworthy is the number of very small states that have held SC seats, including Bahrain, Cape Verde, Djibouti, Gabon, The Gambia, Guinea-Bissau, Guyana, Malta (the least populous), Mauritius, Qatar and Trinidad & Tobago, all with between 0.4 million and 1.8 million inhabitants (as of 2011).

The regional differences revealed by Figure 4.1 indicate that attention to "equitable geographical distribution" – whatever that might mean – has often been given precedence over representation based on "contribution[s] ... to the maintenance of international peace and security", the aforementioned *primary* principle set forth in the UN Charter. Until 1966 the six non-permanent seats were generally allocated as follows: two seats for Latin America, and one seat each to Western Europe, Eastern Europe, Southwest Asia/North Africa and the diverse group of nations comprising the older members of the (British) Commonwealth.[12] This arbitrary formula not only left a growing number of countries, including such important states as Japan and Indonesia, without a clear regional affiliation, but also failed utterly to allow for adjustments in representation in response to the membership explosion within Africa south of the Sahara and, to a lesser degree, within Asia as well. Although the formula was not always strictly followed, Latin America and Eastern Europe, many would argue, received substantially more than their due (largely for reasons relating to the Cold War), while Africa and Asia received significantly less. For example, Indonesia, though admitted to the United Nations as early as 1950, did not serve on the SC until 1973–1974.

Since 1966 a new, but still arbitrary, regional allocation scheme has been in effect. Five of the 10 non-permanent seats are now allocated to

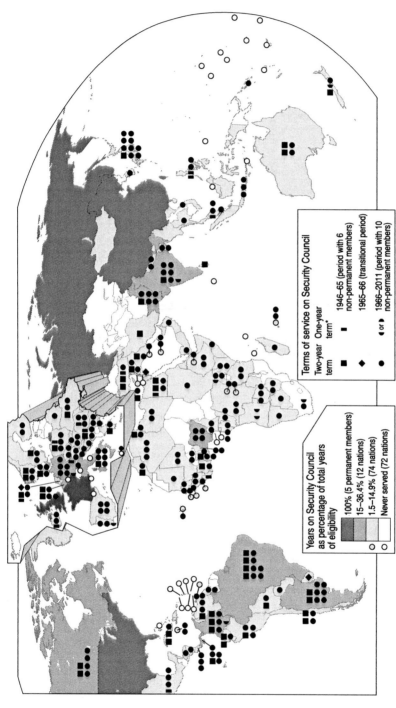

Figure 4.1 Frequency of representation in Security Council, 1946–2011

Note: Russia, Serbia and the Czech Republic are here considered as the successors of the Soviet Union, Yugoslavia and Czecho-slovakia respectively; the Federal Republic of Germany is considered as the successor to both West and East Germany.

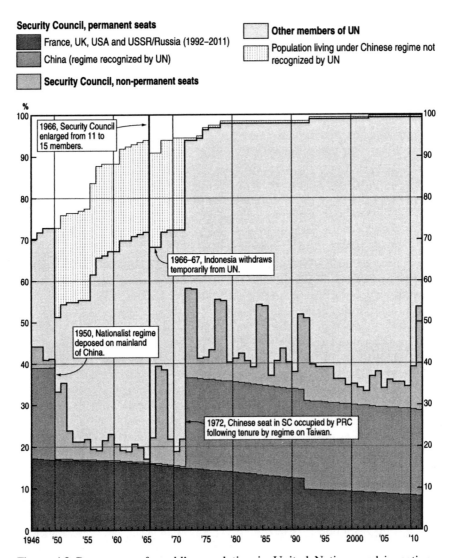

Security Council, permanent seats

France, UK, USA and USSR/Russia (1992–2011)

China (regime recognized by UN)

Security Council, non-permanent seats

Other members of UN

Population living under Chinese regime not recognized by UN

1966, Security Council enlarged from 11 to 15 members.

1966–67, Indonesia withdraws temporarily from UN.

1950, Nationalist regime deposed on mainland of China.

1972, Chinese seat in SC occupied by PRC following tenure by regime on Taiwan.

Figure 4.2 Percentage of world's population in United Nations and in nations with seats in Security Council, 1946–2011
Note: Populations shown are mid-year estimates.

Africa and Asia combined, two to Latin America and the Caribbean, two to "Western Europe and Other" and one to Eastern Europe. Although this does represent some gain for the Afro-Asian bloc, examination of population and economic data, as well as the number of member countries from those two continents, leads one to question whether the reform has been sufficient. The 104 member nations from Africa and Asia (excluding China) have a combined population (as of 2010) of approximately 3.85 billion out of a total of 4.95 billion (roughly 78 per cent) for the 187 UN members other than the P-5; yet they are allotted only half of the 10 non-permanent seats and only one permanent seat, that of China, out of a total of five. Latin America and Eastern Europe remain relatively advantaged regions. So too does the amorphous "Western Europe and Other" bloc, especially when one considers the ties of most of its members to the permanently seated France, United Kingdom and United States.

The populations of the permanent and non-permanent SC members relative to those of all UN members combined and of the world as a whole are depicted, year by year, in Figure 4.2.[13] (National data are presented in Appendix 1.) Analysis of this presentation leads to interesting conclusions. Most striking, perhaps, is that the share of the P-5 in the total population of both UN members and the world as a whole has declined more or less steadily (if one ignores the period when the government on Taiwan held the Chinese seat), from an initial high of 39 per cent of the world total, and 63 per cent of the UN total, to the present share of roughly 28 per cent for both the United Nations and the world as a whole. The explanation lies not only in the expansion of the UN's membership, but also in the differential demographic trends in various parts of the world, with slow – sometimes negative – growth rates in most economically developed countries and relatively rapid growth in those less affluent. Yet there has been no commensurate diminution in the P-5's institutional power.

The relative shares of the population held by China and the four other P-5 powers are also of interest. The overwhelming demographic predominance of China is striking for most of the period since the UN's founding. However, the period 1950–1971, when the rump government on Taiwan held the permanent Chinese seat, represented a strange and contentious departure from this pattern. Less dramatic, but also important, is the decline in the population represented when Russia assumed the former permanent seat of the Soviet Union.

The share of the ever-changing composition of the cohort of non-permanent members in the population represented on the SC and also in the world as a whole has fluctuated greatly and in a seemingly random manner. In 1965, for example, the then six non-permanent members – the Netherlands, Malaysia, Bolivia, Côte d'Ivoire, Uruguay and Jordan, in that order of population size – collectively accounted for a mere 1 per cent of the world's total population, less than that of any *one* of the P-5. Only two years later, in the expanded SC, the cohort of 10 non-permanent members were, again in descending order of population, India, Japan,

Brazil, Nigeria, Ethiopia, Canada, Argentina, Bulgaria, Denmark and Mali. These nations accounted for almost a fourth of humanity. That share was not reached again until 2011, when the non-permanent group consisted (in order of demographic rank) of India, Brazil, Nigeria, Germany, South Africa, Colombia, Portugal, Lebanon, Bosnia & Herzegovina and Gabon. Not surprisingly, all seven of the non-permanent peak periods shown in Figure 4.2 are accounted for by the six-and-a-half terms (13 years) when India served as an SC member, since India alone has more than a sixth of the world's population. Those same years were the only ones in which the population of the SC was more than half that of the United Nations as whole, and in nine of those years more than half of humankind.

Oddly, the increase in non-permanent members from 6 to 10 had little effect on their share of the number of people living in UN member nations. The average for the cohort of 6 in the period 1946–1965 was approximately 8.5 per cent, while that for the cohort of 10 over the period since 1966 rose to only 9.5 per cent. However, since the proportion of the UN members' population living in countries other than the P-5 steadily increased, the average share of the non-permanent SC members relative to the group of nations from which they were elected actually declined substantially in the post-1965 period.

Finally, one may ask to what degree non-permanent SC members ostensibly representing a particular region of the world actually bother to determine the wishes of other countries in that region before voting on substantive issues, rather than being guided by what they perceive to be in their own *national* interest. Would Mauritius, for example, seek the opinion of the government of Guinea-Bissau? Would Pakistan consult Bhutan? Not likely. What, then, in such cases is the real meaning of the euphemism "representation"?

Additional shortcomings of the present system and of leading reform proposals[14]

Compounding the anachronistic permanency accorded to the P-5 members of the SC is the fact that they alone possess the power of the veto, thereby effectively immunizing them from any meaningful form of UN censure for acts detrimental to others in the global community or offences within their own borders. This special status of the P-5 flies in the face of contemporary power realities and should be terminated. Germany and Japan have surpassed France, the United Kingdom and Russia in economic power, and countries such as India and Brazil are expected to do so shortly. Since nothing that humans create can be said to be permanent, the very word "permanent" should be expunged from the UN Charter. Additionally, the double standard inherent in the P-5 veto privilege diminishes the UN's moral legitimacy and is increasingly questioned by virtually all non-P-5 nations.

Apart from the inequity between the P-5 and other nations, there is inequity within the P-5 itself. A major source of dissatisfaction is the degree to which the present system has privileged first the mainly capitalistic "West" and then the developed global "North". Currently four of the P-5 members are developed nations while only one, China, is still – despite its phenomenal recent growth – a developing power.

The Charter's inflexibility in respect to the P-5 raises important questions relating to possible changes in the political map of the world. When the Soviet Union imploded, the Russian Federation claimed to have inherited its legal mantle and, with it, its SC seat.[15] But what if the ethnically diverse Russian state should itself implode? At what point would a rump P-5 state become too inconsequential to merit permanent SC status? This question applies also to the United Kingdom. Suppose Scotland, Wales and Northern Ireland were to secede; would one then – following the USSR/Russia precedent – assign an SC seat to England, the UK's largest remnant?

Alternatively, what if both the United Kingdom and France become parts of a future European federation? How would they or the federation then be represented in the SC? Would other potential federations – in Africa, Latin America, Southeast Asia, the Middle East or elsewhere – become legitimate claimants to an SC seat if Europe's claim were recognized?

The process of selecting non-permanent SC members leaves much to be desired. While subject to a formal vote in the GA, there is typically only one candidate from a given "region" or exactly as many candidates as there are seats to be filled, the candidate nations having been chosen through diplomatic manoeuvring in the corridors of the United Nations or other convenient venues. For candidates from Africa, gentlemen's agreements provide for loose rotation among willing nations, with little regard for their respective qualifications. And in no regional caucus is there any explicit quantitative basis for choosing among aspiring nominees. To their credit, the Latin American and "Western European and Other" caucuses do, not infrequently, put up more candidates than there are seats to be filled. But even if none of them is viewed favourably by nations from other regions, there is no politically acceptable way to preclude their election.

The unrealistic power distribution within the SC is a perennial shortcoming of the present system. I have already discussed the special privileges of the P-5; but, paradoxically, small powers may also exert power out of proportion to their weight in the world beyond the United Nations. In 1984, for example, when SC membership simultaneously included both Malta, with a then population of a quarter of a million (the lowest of any nation in the SC's history), and India, with its then population of more than 725 million, both nations cast the same unitary vote. Further, in non-veto situations the votes of each non-permanent SC member equalled those of any of the P-5.[16]

Despite abundant evidence of the shortcomings of the existing SC system, leading attempts to improve it focus mainly on two questions: which nations are sufficiently important to merit a permanent seat or rotating "semi-permanent" seat (an oxymoron); and whether new permanent members shall enjoy the power of the veto. They ignore the facts that even with as many as 10 new seat holders, almost four-fifths of the world's nations and a substantial share of the world's population would remain unrepresented. They fail to consider that for every new permanent member there would be one or more disgruntled "wannabes" or nay-sayers: Pakistan in regard to India, China in respect to Japan, Italy in respect to Germany, Argentina and Mexico regarding Brazil, and South Africa and Egypt in respect to Nigeria (should the latter be anointed). They offer no critique of the ill-considered regional division of the world for purposes of choosing representatives. Finally, no proposal has the temerity to call for an end to the unjust entrenched privilege that the veto conveys.

Universal weighted regional representation[17]

I have noted the incongruity – one might even say absurdity – of a Security Council in which the vote of a very small state such as Malta had the same capability in shaping decisions as India, its fellow non-permanent seat holder in 1984. I have also noted the small size and limited diplomatic capacity of many UN members, 72 (38 per cent) of which had by 2010 yet to serve a single year on the SC. With these considerations in mind, I devised a series of scenarios providing a more rational system of representation. While I regard all of them as superior to the present system, space constraints require that I present here only the two that strike me as the most promising.[18]

Both call for a *universally* representative SC with 12 regional seats, each carrying a mathematically determined weighted vote.[19] Up to four of the regions could be composed of but a single powerful nation, provided that the region meets accepted objective criteria for recognition. The remainder would be assemblages of more or less similar, but not necessarily contiguous, states. Each multinational region would nominate slates of two to five candidates – through processes described below –

and from each such slate SC representatives would be elected by the GA. Additionally, each region would devise its own set of decision-making rules by which its representatives would be guided. Two similar proposals are presented, the first allowing nations to be members of only one region, and the second allowing nations to enjoy simultaneous membership in two.

Guiding considerations

The proposed system is predicated on the following considerations.

- Given the incapacity of many small nations to function effectively within the contemporary world and frequent SC failure to take note of the views of many nations in its decision-making processes, a system of representation by *major world regions* would offer many advantages not otherwise attainable.
- The regions established for representational purposes would be alterable as need arises.
- Regions should have a population, territorial extent and/or degree of economic importance such that the legitimacy of their representation in the SC will not be seriously questioned.
- The ensemble of regions must be such as to maximize internal regional homogeneity with regard to multiple factors: culture, religion, language, economic interests and shared historical experience. This will facilitate the region's speaking with a single majority voice.
- To the extent practicable, the make-up of any given region should avoid co-membership therein of long-standing antagonists.
- Each multinational region shall establish its own rules of procedure for determining regional policies and guiding its representatives in the SC. Ideally, these rules would include a system of *internal* weighted voting for the region's member nations.
- Ideally, no single nation within a multinational region should have a greater voting weight than that of all the other member nations combined. (Possible exceptions are discussed below.)
- Individual nations should have the right to request that their membership be transferred to another region if that better suits their interest, though without any guarantee that such a request will be honoured.

Initial regional framework and weighting

With the above considerations in mind, the entire world would be divided for purposes of SC representation into 12 regions. Those depicted in Figure 4.3 represent my best judgement as to what would prove optimal. This map reflects, to a remarkable degree, regional organizations – e.g.

the European Union (EU), the Arab League, the Association of Southeast Asian Nations (ASEAN), etc. – that already exist. Nevertheless, it is merely suggestive; the actual determination would be entrusted to a committee of the UN General Assembly. From time to time, should need arise, the GA would be empowered to recommend alterations in the regional boundaries without resort to amending the UN Charter.[20]

Up to four regions might consist of a single nation, provided that it met some predetermined eligibility criterion or criteria. I would suggest that eligibility be contingent on the nation's having the sum of its percentages of the world's population and of contributions to the UN budget exceed a threshold of 12 per cent. Should more than four nations exceed this threshold, only the top four would qualify. Given the *present scale of assessments*, the qualifying nations would be the United States, China, India and Japan, in that order. But if, as recommended, *assessments were in strict proportion to GNI*, Japan would no longer qualify.

Although the GA would establish the initial framework for multinational regions, individual nations would subsequently be allowed to request transfer from one region to another subject to the approval of the region within which membership is sought. Additionally, under the second of my two proposals, they would be allowed to request simultaneous representation in two regions (subject to provisions noted below).

Each regional seat holder would cast a weighted SC vote (W) based on the average of three terms, as indicated in the following equation:

$$W = \frac{P + C + 8.33\%}{3}$$

wherein P represents the region's *population* as a percentage of the total population of all UN member nations, C represents the region's total paid *contributions* to the UN budget as a percentage of the total budget over a specific period (say of five years) and 8.33 per cent is a *constant* signifying that the global perspective of each of the 12 regions is equally worthy of respect.[21]

The validity of the population and contributions terms of the equation is intuitively obvious and has been discussed in relation to recommended reform of the GA. The arguments need not be repeated here. But it is worth recalling that, from a pragmatic perspective, the world's wealthier countries would have little incentive to accept the proposed new system if there were to be no counterweight to the population term, which privileges populous but relatively poor nations such as China (despite its recent economic surge) and India. An additional pragmatic consideration is that linking voting strength to actually *paid* contributions, rather than to assessments, ensures that nations would pay what they owe, in that failure

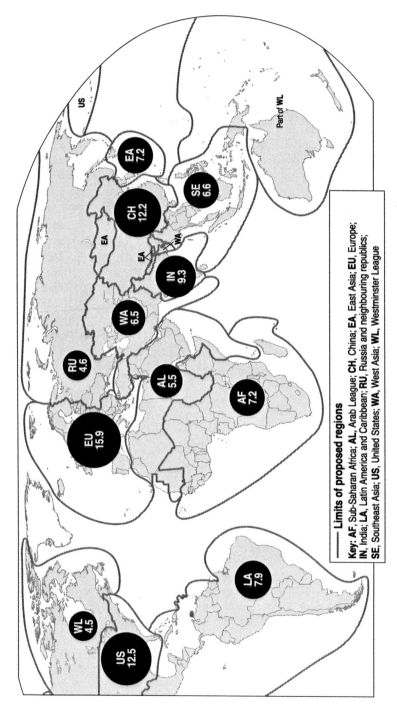

Figure 4.3 Weighted votes of 12 member regions of hypothetical Security Council

to do so would automatically impose on them a future penalty in the form of reduced voting weight. This would eliminate economic blackmail via the withholding of assessed dues that certain countries (most notably the United States) have occasionally resorted to for political purposes.

The constant, 8.33 per cent (one-twelfth), calls for comment. It signifies the presumed equal worth of each region's global perspective. This presumption would, in effect, serve as a pragmatic legal fiction. Although the proposition of equal worth can be neither proved nor disproved, it is akin to the widely accepted legal fiction positing the sovereign equality of nations. An important effect of using the constant is that it narrows the gulf between the weights of the most and least powerful regions and would, presumably, enhance the political acceptability of the system.

Required majorities in respect to *procedural* matters would require total weighted votes exceeding 50 per cent, while decisions on *substantive* matters would require a two-thirds majority (66.7 per cent) and concurrent approval by regions whose combined populations exceeded 50 per cent of the world's total.

Table 4.1 provides relevant data for each of the 12 regions depicted in Figure 4.3, including number of member countries, which does not enter into the weighting equation but is nevertheless of interest. The weighted regional votes indicated in the last column appear to reflect reasonably the real-world disparities in power and capability from one region to another. The range is from 15.86 per cent for Europe to 4.49 per cent for the Westminster League, a ratio of roughly 3.5:1. Without the constant,

Table 4.1 Regions to be represented in proposed UN Security Council

Region	No. of UN members	Population (%)	Total GNI (%)	Weighted vote (%)
Africa South of the Sahara	43	11.68	1.47	7.16
Arab League	21	5.21	2.81	5.45
China	1	19.79	8.61	12.24
East Asia	6	3.43	9.95	7.24
Europe	41	7.97	31.27	15.86
India	1	17.25	2.33	9.30
Latin America and Caribbean	33	8.46	6.92	7.90
Russia and Neighbours	6	3.07	2.62	4.67
Southeast Asia	12	8.97	2.53	6.61
United States	1	4.56	24.71	12.53
West Asia	12	8.62	2.51	6.49
Westminster League	15	1.02	4.27	4.54
Total	192	100.00	100.00	100.00

8.33 per cent, in the equation, the range would have been from 19.62 to 2.58 per cent, yielding a ratio of 7.6:1, which would probably prove politically unacceptable to some of the weaker regions.

A fairer, more workable allocation of power

An important consequence of applying the proposed weighted voting formula is that it would establish an SC with a reasonable balance between five regions predominantly within the developed North (i.e. Europe, the United States, East Asia, Russia and the Westminster League), with a combined weight of 45.3 per cent, and seven remaining regions mainly of the global South (roughly the G-77 plus China), with a combined weight of 54.7 per cent. Since binding votes on substantive matters would require a two-thirds majority, the practical effect of this is that on issues on which there is a North-South division of opinion it would be necessary to engage in genuine dialogue between the two cohorts to forge workable compromises. The resultant compromise would have greater legitimacy in the eyes of the global community than many decisions rammed through the present SC at the insistence of one or more of the predominantly Northern P-5.

In Chapter 2 I noted the propensity of great powers to resort to bribery and coercion to influence the votes of weak nations in both the GA and the SC. This problem would be obviated with a system of regional voting, in that it would be virtually impossible to bribe or coerce a multinational region. By reducing the present enormous power disparities among actors on the UN stage, the proposed system would enhance the ability of the weak to resist inappropriate pressure from the strong, to be guided by the merits of individual cases and to contribute to the crafting of legitimate resolutions.

I comment briefly below on the three single-nation regions and then on the nine multinational regions in descending order of their voting strength. In discussing the latter group, I consider each region's inclusiveness and coherence, and suggest why certain of its constituent nations might support and others oppose the proposed system.[22]

The three single-nation regions

Were the proposed system in place (as of 2010), those countries and their voting weights would be the United States (12.52 per cent), China (12.24 per cent) and India (9.30 per cent). Barring the creation of a single federal entity in Europe, changes in this set of qualifying countries are unlikely for the foreseeable future in that Japan, the fourth-ranking power, has for some time been on a declining demographic and economic trajectory relative to the world as a whole.

In the present SC the United States and China now each cast but one vote out of 15 (6.67 per cent of the total), the same as any other SC member, however weak that member might otherwise be. Thus their greatly enhanced voting strength under the proposed system might prove a sufficiently attractive trade-off to induce them to give up the veto. For India, the relative gain would be even greater.

Europe (15.86 per cent)

In the present proposal Europe includes all the current EU members, as well as a number of Eastern European countries presently slated to join or likely to become eligible in the near future, four microstates that are in the United Nations but not full EU members, and Israel. It excludes several former republics of the Soviet Union that are grouped with Russia, as well as Turkey. The region is already highly integrated in many respects, and its procedures for consultation and policy formulation might serve as models for other regions.

Europe, excluding Russia, usually holds four or five seats on the SC as presently constituted, including the permanent seats of the United Kingdom and France. Arguably, then, Europe has been since the UN's inception the most overrepresented of all continents. Thus its voting strength as a proportion of the SC total would be reduced considerably under the proposed system. (But that would also be true in virtually all other SC reform proposals put forward in recent years.) Also, as frequently happens, when the European members of the SC vote on different sides of a particular issue, thereby cancelling each other out, the *net* result is that Europe's power in the SC may come to little or nothing. (This was the case in voting on the failed SC resolution to take military action against Iraq in 2003.) If, on the other hand, Europe were to speak with a united voice, its power would exceed that of any other region. No other part of the world could so effectively serve as a counterweight to the United States, should the need arise.

Latin America and the Caribbean (7.90 per cent)

This region includes all the countries of the Americas to the south of the United States. All of its members belong to the Organization of American States, with the exception of Cuba (whose membership is presently suspended); all have had a long colonial past (mainly ending in the nineteenth century); and a great majority of the region's population speak one of the Romance languages and adhere to Roman Catholicism.

The region typically holds two SC seats, and several of its more frequently included member nations would probably initially oppose the relative reduction in power under the proposed system. Brazil might be particularly reluctant to see its hopes for a permanent SC seat thwarted. Nevertheless, as with Europe, the potential for Latin America's speaking to the traditional great powers with a united voice would likely enhance the region's ability to play a significant role in world affairs.

East Asia (7.24 per cent)

This region would be one of several in which a single member nation, in this case Japan, would have a greater population and economic power than all the others (the Republic of Korea and Democratic People's Republic of Korea (DPRK), Mongolia, Nepal and Bhutan) combined. It would also be troubled by long-standing grievances between the two Koreas, as well as between both those nations and Japan. The DPRK, however, would be "an odd-man-out" in any regional group that one can envisage (assuming that China has a seat to itself). And the Republic of Korea and Japan, despite past animosity, carry out extensive two-way trade and, by and large, now live as good neighbours. As for landlocked Mongolia, Nepal and Bhutan – each wedged in geographically between two great powers – regional placement is inevitably problematic. But the fact that each must live within the shadow of China, plus one additional relative political giant, gives them a certain commonality of concern. Finally, all six states of the region have histories in which various forms of Buddhism have been and remain a powerful cultural force. For the region to cohere and function efficiently, it will have to be especially attentive to diplomatic protocol and intra-regional compromise. While the DPRK will probably maintain its policies of political intransigence, Japan, which would presumably be the regional seat holder more often than not, would probably find it advisable not to play too heavy-handed a role in the affairs of the region.

Africa South of the Sahara (7.16 per cent)

Comprising the 43 nations of Africa that are not members of the Arab League, this region would have the largest number of member states of any of the proposed regions. It would also have the smallest gross regional income. Its members all belong to the African Union, a presently weak body, but one that seeks to emulate the integrative experience of the European Union. The region's world-view has been strongly shaped by shared historical experience, first with colonialism and then neocolonialism, and their attendant racism and rampant economic exploitation.

Given Africa's leading share of the UN membership, some proponents of an enlarged SC have suggested that Africa as a whole be awarded one-fourth or more of the seats, including two permanent seats. It would thus not be easy to persuade African nations (especially Nigeria and South

Africa, both aspirants to permanent seats) to settle for a much smaller share of SC voting power. However, questions of prestige aside, if Africa's nations reflect on their present negligible effectiveness in framing SC decisions to date and their susceptibility to pressures applied by external powers, they might conclude that they would be able to exert greater influence speaking with a common voice than through the voices of a few mainly weak states, each guided by its own political agenda.

Southeast Asia (6.61 per cent)

This relatively populous region is, arguably, the most culturally and politically diverse of the 12 proposed. Within it are mingled peoples practising Hinayana and Mahayana Buddhism, Confucianism, Islam, Christianity, Hinduism and numerous tribal religions as well as states with remarkably diverse political and economic traditions derived from European, American and Asian colonial powers. Its constituent nations include several present or recent autocracies, among which are the military oligarchy of Burma/Myanmar (recently relaxing its draconian rule) and the nominally communistic regime of Viet Nam; a number of fledgling democracies, several of which have been especially susceptible to *coups d'état* (e.g. the Philippines); and a paternalistic welfare state (Singapore) that is like no other in the world. The region, however, is far less diverse than Asia as a whole, which the United Nations now uncritically considers a region (sometimes along with and sometimes without Africa) for purposes of representation in the SC and other UN organs. In both area and population, the region is made up mainly by the 10 members of the remarkably successful ASEAN, plus outlying Sri Lanka and the recently independent Timor-Leste.

The region has been perennially underrepresented in the SC, usually having either one or no representatives in a given year. (Indonesia's minimal representation has been especially problematic.) Thus Southeast Asia would likely see itself as an immediate gainer under the proposed new system and, given its strong growth trajectory, might anticipate even greater gains in future decades.

West Asia (6.49 per cent)

Grouped within West Asia are 12 predominantly Muslim, but non-Arab, nations of Asia from Turkey eastward as far as Bangladesh. Other members include Pakistan and Iran, six former republics of the Soviet Union and the Republic of Maldives. Despite the region's common faith, its level of political integration is minimal and the modern political antecedents of its constituent nations vary greatly. While all the suggested members are among the 57 states forming the Organization of Islamic Cooperation (formerly the Organization of the Islamic Conference), there is no organization akin to the Arab League or ASEAN that covers an area corresponding to the whole or a greater part of the region.

Save for Pakistan, the region has thus far been poorly represented in the SC, in many years lacking even a single member. Thus its constituent nations would presumably look favourably on the proposed system.

Arab League (5.45 per cent)

This strategically situated region is coterminous with the present League of Arab States and is marked by a relatively high degree of linguistic, religious and cultural homogeneity. It also shares a legacy of having been subjected to Ottoman and/or Western imperialism. It has from time to time acted in concert on political issues (especially concerning Israel), and for the foreseeable future will have great strategic importance because it accounts for a major share of the world's production and reserves of petroleum and natural gas.

One Arab state normally occupies an SC seat. While the region's relative power might be seen as being slightly diminished under the proposed system, the loss should not be enough to elicit strenuous objection to change.

Russia and Neighbours (4.67 per cent)

This region comprises the present Russian Federation and five neighbouring republics that are, or were, participants in the Commonwealth of Independent States and are culturally – though not in all cases geographically – European, namely Armenia, Belarus, Georgia, Moldova and Ukraine. A special problem in this grouping is that the political, economic and military power of Russia within it is much greater than that of all the other members combined.

Despite the dissolution of the USSR, the subsequent kleptocratic turn of the Russian economy and the nation's remarkable demographic decline, Russia retains a permanent SC seat and remains an important player on the global stage. It seems likely, therefore, that it would not be receptive to major changes in the SC's composition, though other states within the region might well be. But Russia's attitude might change in the future as its economic recovery continues, thanks to its vast resource endowment in regard to petroleum, natural gas and other strategic minerals, and, most important, its well-educated population.

Westminster League (4.54 per cent)

The term "Westminster League" was coined by the author to relate to Canada, Australia, New Zealand and 12 small island nations of the western Pacific. All but a few of these are parliamentary democracies within the Commonwealth of Nations, established by the 1931 Statute of Westminster, and all but Canada are members of the Pacific Islands Forum. The region's three principal nations have similar histories of mainly European settlement, primarily English-speaking populations, advanced free-market economies and active and constructive engagement with the United Nations. They also cooperate closely in many global endeavours. While the small West Pacific island nations are culturally quite distinct, they too are mainly Westminster-style democracies, use English as a *lingua franca* and are under the political tutelage of Australia, New Zealand or the United States. Though sparsely populated and accounting for only 1 per cent of the world's population (with Canada having not quite half that total), the region collectively accounts for 4.27 per cent of the world's GNI (more than each of six other regions). Moreover, it coves a seventh of the world's land area and therefore bears substantial responsibility in preserving global biodiversity and a healthy global ecosystem.

Collectively, the region's members have served a total of 27 years on the Security Council. There is ample reason to suppose that it would see itself as benefiting substantially from the proposed new system of SC representation.

Concluding observations

Despite divergent aspirations and perspectives, most nations should view favourably the SC reforms proposed here, while others, especially those aspiring to gain permanent or semi-permanent seats (with the notable exception of India), will not. Although certain regions that might appear to be losing relative strength in the SC (e.g. Africa or Latin America) would likely *initially* oppose the proposed change, dispassionate reflection on the inadequacies of the present system should eventually lead most of their constituent nations to a different view. The vast majority of nations would realize that *in most years they are not represented at all*, since seat holders predictably act almost exclusively in the interests of their respective home *nations* rather than in the interests of the *regions* from which they were selected. Further, nations would realize that, at any given time, some of the 10 non-permanent members that now ostensibly represent them are strongly constrained by considerations of political expediency and reluctant to give offence to great powers on whose good will they largely depend. Thus the collective effectiveness of the non-permanent members tends to be substantially less than it might ideally be. However, under the proposed system of *universal* representation, every nation would have some voice in the formulation of regional policy and in deciding how to vote on specific issues.

Finally, should restructuring the SC form part of a larger package of UN reforms, it would likely be accompanied by measures to strengthen the UN's overall competence so that its ability to be of use to nations of the global South would be greatly enhanced. Surrendering a bit of power in a relatively ineffectual body in anticipation of deriving substantial benefits from a revitalized organization should strike most world leaders as an eminently sensible trade-off.

Means of selection, terms and functioning of representatives and alternates

The process of selecting SC delegates and alternates under a system of universal regional representation would be somewhat different for single-nation regions and those with multiple members. Each nation in the former set would simply nominate its representative by whatever method its government prescribed (as is the current practice). Multinational regions would, by methods of their own devising, be allowed to nominate between two and five candidates, but with no two from the same country. Additionally, neither males nor females could constitute less than a third or more than two-thirds of the slate of nominees. From these slates, ranked-choice votes of the General Assembly would make the final selections. If no candidate had an absolute majority of the weighted votes cast, the candidate with the lowest total would be eliminated and his/her second-place votes would be reassigned to the remaining candidates. The process would continue until one candidate obtained an absolute majority. The candidate with the second-highest total at that point would be designated as the region's alternate representative and serve in the representative's stead when needed.

Rather than choosing all representatives for concurrent three-year terms, they would serve overlapping three-year terms, with four regional members being chosen each year. Nominations from multinational regions would be made in May or June, to allow time for campaigning up to the actual election in September. (Lobbying for support occurs even now as nations seek the few seats that are actually contested.[23]) Terms would commence on the first working day of January in the year following election.

Once elected, representatives would be expected to act in the SC on behalf of the entire group of nations they represent. This presumes regular consultation – whether face to face or, more routinely, by electronic means – among the foreign ministries and UN delegates of all the region's members so as to work out common approaches in regard to issues coming before the SC, as well as frequent and full reporting by representatives to all the constituent nations. Egregious failure to meet these expectations would probably lead to defections from the region and/or rejection of the representative by the region during the next triennial caucus period. Alternatively, the representative might be recalled even earlier by some previously agreed procedure and replaced by his/her alternate.

Not long ago the policy formulation procedure just described would have been logistically unworkable; but electronic communication technology can greatly mitigate remaining difficulties, even in regions with as many national members as Africa South of the Sahara or as spatially dispersed as the hypothesized Westminster League. Nevertheless, while much deliberation of SC issues would be handled via the internet, it would serve a region's general interests to institute periodic face-to-face summit meetings to formulate general regional policies.

Some regions, especially those with large national disparities in GNI, might adopt a formula for national weights similar to the one by which regional weights were determined in respect to the SC, namely:

$$W = \frac{P + G + M}{3}$$

where W signifies the nation's weighted vote, P the nation's population, G the nation's GNI and M the nation's unit membership, all expressed as percentages of the regional total.

But there are important differences between the situation within regions and that within the world as a whole. First, per capita income disparities *within* regions are generally much less than those *between* regions. Second, although nations pay annual assessments to the United Nations, there would be no comparable assessments levied against nations within multinational regions. Thus a preferable regional formula might exclude an economic term in the weighting equation. A more democratic and reasonable intra-regional formula might be:

$$W = \frac{P + M}{2}$$

wherein W, P and M have the same meaning as in the previous formula and the G term is omitted. This might be prescribed by the GA as a *default formula* in the event that another cannot be agreed upon within a stipulated period after the new system goes into effect.

An important consideration favouring the default formula is that its adoption would prevent the domination of decision-making in certain regions by their most powerful nations. For example, within the Westminster League Canada has not quite half the population and a significantly greater GNI than all the other members combined. Similar findings would obtain if the default formula were to be applied to Japan and the five other members of the East Asia region. Within Russia and Neighbours the predominance of Russia's population and GNI – 68.0 and 86.6 per cent of the regional totals respectively – would be even greater. If the proposed default formula were applied, the national weighted votes of the region's members would be Russia 42.4 per cent, Ukraine 19.4 per cent, Belarus 10.6 per cent, Georgia 9.4 per cent, Moldova 9.3 per cent and Armenia 9.1 per cent.[24]

Devising formulae for *intra-regional* weighted voting in multinational regions and establishing procedural rules to guide SC representatives and alternates would be left to the regions themselves. While these exercises would undoubtedly be marked by tough political bargaining, relatively large powers would have to consider that failure to agree upon an equitable formula would likely result in defections from the region and losses in its voting weight.

The rules guiding the votes of multiregional seat holders might call for simple intra-regional majorities on procedural matters, two-thirds majorities on most substantive matters and three-fourths majorities in regard to resolutions calling for armed intervention in a given area. If such rules and the default voting formula were in place, they would permit Russia, with 42.4 per cent of the regional total, to have veto power within its own six-nation region, yet not so much power as to be able to make unilateral decisions.

Consultation among members of multinational regions would presumably not be limited to issues likely to come before the SC; they would also probably extend to matters falling under the purview of the GA and other organs of the UN system, including its affiliated agencies. In general, formation of a united political front would enhance a region's bargaining capability. Members would probably also use such meetings to discuss matters for which the United Nations bears relatively little responsibility (e.g. multinational river basin development, educational exchanges, rules governing migration, tariff policies, etc.). The system of regional representation would, then, lead to fruitful consultation and cooperation on a variety of important matters and promote healthy regional integration.

In discussing the make-up of the suggested multinational regions it was noted that some contained politically anomalous states (e.g. the DPRK), which would often be out of tune with most, or all, other members of their respective regions and see themselves as permanent minorities. But that is what they already are. In any event, they would receive a better hearing in the councils of their region, among neighbours with which they are most likely to interact, than they would as odd-men-out in the United

Nations as a whole. If they choose not to take advantage of that opportunity, the onus for their lack of influence would fall entirely on them.

Additionally, we must note that transnational consultation and cooperation would not be limited to the regions established for purposes of SC representation. There is no reason, for example, why the nations of NAFTA (the North American Free Trade Area) or SAARC (the South Asian Association for Regional Cooperation) should not continue to carry out all their present functions even though their member states lie in two or more regions established for SC representation. Nor should there be any bar to prevent the members of any region from inviting participation from extra-regional states in deliberating questions of mutual concern, even if the invited parties are not given a vote in determining the region's position when it comes down to SC decision-making.

Further, the system would conduce to meritocracy. Rather than nominating some political hack or crony of a nation's leader as a possible regional representative, each member of a multinational caucus would seek to promote the candidacy of an individual of commanding stature and relatively high international visibility, in hopes that its caucus would include that individual in its slate of SC candidates and, once nominated, he/she would then be chosen in the GA balloting.

Finally, the proposed system would heighten a sense of democratic participation in the UN system as a whole. It would give GA representatives a meaningful role in selecting individuals entrusted with the well-being of the planet. It would promote cultures of accountability, not only to one's own region but also to the world as a whole.

Representation with overlapping regional membership

To this point, the discussion has presumed that each of the world's nations would have membership in only one of the 12 proposed regions. But numerous nations have significant ties to more than one of the regions outlined in Figure 4.3. Turkey, for example, aspires to be an EU member, but presumably would also wish to strengthen its voice in the affairs of the West Asian region. Similarly the United Kingdom, while among the most important members of the European Union, might also wish to associate itself with the Westminster League. Additionally, many small, English-speaking parliamentary democracies – especially those in the Caribbean region – might wish to accede in whole or part to the Westminster League in the belief that their concerns would be taken more seriously in that region and their political clout there would be greater than if they were to remain wholly within the weightier region of Latin America and the Caribbean. Or, to choose a final example, the 10

African nations that account for more than half the strength of the Arab League might wish to reinforce their current bond with the 43 other nations of Africa.

Table 4.2 indicates the areas of the world most likely to wish to belong to two regions for purposes of representation in the SC, assuming that a workable system for doing so were in place. Alternatively, some of the countries named might wish to transfer completely from one region to another. It seems unlikely, however, that every one of the 45 countries noted in the table would actually take advantage of the opportunity to alter their assigned status.

Although a system allowing national affiliations with only one region would be simpler than one in which nations could simultaneously belong to two regions, there is no reason in principle why the latter could not be established. The key to devising a just and workable system would be to establish rules whereby a country choosing membership in two regions would have its weight in decision-making divided between the two so

Table 4.2 Likely areas of overlap between proposed Security Council regions or of changes in regional affiliation

From	To	Likely applicants
Africa	Westminster League	Mauritius, Seychelles
Arab League	Africa	Ten Arab League members in northern and eastern Africa; non-Arab areas (e.g. South Sudan) seceding from Arab League states
Arab League	West Asia	Iraq or part thereof in the event of partition of the country
East Asia	Southeast Asia	Nepal, Bhutan
Europe	Westminster League	United Kingdom, Ireland, Malta, Cyprus
Latin America and Caribbean	Westminster League	Eleven small former British dependencies in Caribbean region; Guyana, Suriname
Russia and Neighbours	Europe	Armenia, Azerbaijan, Belarus, Georgia, Moldova, Ukraine
West Asia	Europe	Turkey
West Asia	Russia and Neighbours	Azerbaijan, Kazakhstan; less likely Kyrgyzstan, Tajikistan, Turkmenistan, Uzbekistan
West Asia	Southeast Asia	Bangladesh
West Asia	Westminster League	Maldives

that its overall contribution to SC decision-making would be the same as if it were in only one region.

The weighted votes of regions would obviously be affected if they were to include one or more nations with dual regional membership. To illustrate how the adjustments might be made, consider the hypothetical case of Turkey. Were Turkey to opt for membership in both West Asia, the area to which it was originally assigned, and Europe, which it aspires to join, its population and UN budgetary contributions – 1.074 and 0.903 per cent respectively of the UN totals – would be divided evenly between the two regions in calculating the weighted votes of each, thereby diminishing the weight of the former and adding to that of the latter. In the case of the United Kingdom, originally assigned to the European region, suppose that it also wished to enjoy membership in the Westminster League, within which it might play a leading role. In that case, the population and GNI terms of the weighting equation, 0.915 and 4.374 per cent respectively, would be divided equally between the two regions in computing their regional weights. Corresponding adjustments would be made for all other transfers.

There is no way of knowing a priori which set of countries would opt for dual regional membership or transfer from one region to another. But if those options were liberally utilized, I would anticipate significant increases in the weighted votes of Africa and the Westminster League; a modest increase for Southeast Asia; modest losses for Latin America and the Caribbean, Russia and Neighbours, Europe and West Asia; and a significant decrease for the Arab League.

A final stipulation in respect to any nation with overlapping regional memberships would be that it could be elected to the Security Council as a representative from either of the two regions to which it belonged, but not simultaneously from both.

Eliminating the veto

As previously emphasized, the anachronistic, morally indefensible veto power in the SC should be terminated, whatever the changes might be in respect to representation. Although an overwhelming majority of UN member nations would presumably support such a reform, its implementation would most likely be forestalled for a time by one or more P-5 powers. Surrender of the veto would require a substantial *quid pro quo*. In Chapter 2 a workable trade-off was suggested, establishing a veto-free SC in exchange for enhanced voting weights for the P-5 in a reformed and more empowered GA. But there should also be another powerful inducement, namely the certainty that a fairer voting system in both the

GA and the SC would enhance the legitimacy of UN decisions and contribute substantially to promoting a more lawful, just and orderly world. If, in a reformed United Nations, all or a great majority of nations were to be meaningfully represented, fewer individuals would conclude that resort to terrorism or revolution was the only effective means of bringing about political change; and those who did, nevertheless, actually engage in violence would find few supporters.

But suppose that a bargain cannot be struck to do away with the veto by a single bold act. It might still be eliminated in stages, over a transitional period of, say, up to 15 years. This process could be effected, in part, by gradually increasing the number of P-5 nations whose dissenting votes would suffice to block resolutions that an otherwise qualifying SC majority favoured. Thus one might require two negative P-5 votes for a veto in the first five years of the reform period, three in the following five-year period and so forth.

Additionally, there might be a phased narrowing in the range of subjects to which the veto might apply. The first step in this process would be to prohibit a veto by any of the P-5 in a case in which that member was itself a principal party. Subsequently, one might proscribe vetoes regarding egregious violations of human rights conventions, especially regarding genocide and ethnic cleansing.[25] Then one might preclude vetoes of resolutions calling for the use of inspection teams or monitors in situations deemed to present a threat to the peace. Vetoes of resolutions calling for economic sanctions against offending states might be permitted for a somewhat longer period. The last category of resolution on which the veto may be allowed might be resolutions calling for armed intervention in an area of actual or impending military conflict. Finally, any P-5 nation choosing to exercise its veto power over a specific issue should be required to submit to the GA a detailed legal explanation of its reasons for doing so.[26]

Summary and conclusions

That the Security Council is unfairly constituted is almost universally acknowledged. Although scores of reform proposals have been put forward, most fail to address adequately the principal defects of the present system: the anachronistic special privileges of the P-5 (permanent membership and the power of the veto), and the SC's insufficient representativeness.

The proposed SC with 12 regional seats, each with a weighted vote, squarely addresses these shortcomings. It employs a simple mathematical formula that would greatly reduce politically arbitrary factors in the selection of SC representatives. The proposal would allow a small, objectively determined number of powerful nations (presently the United States, China and India) to hold SC seats in their own right. The remaining seats would be allocated to multinational regions. The proposal would have two variants, one in which member nations could belong to only one region, and another in which simultaneous membership in two regions would be permissible. In either model, transfer of nations from one region to another would be allowed.

Additional reforms would include phasing out the veto and establishing new rules for decision-making utilizing not only the elected SC representatives but also the foreign ministries of all of member nations.

Reform will not be easy; but if the United Nations is to rise to the challenges it will confront in the century ahead, it will have to muster the will to correct its most glaring deficiencies.

Notes

1. A good overview of the issues involved in respect to the Security Council, along with relevant abstracts from the text of several key documents, is provided by Paul Taylor, Sam Daws and Ute Adamczick-Gerteis (eds), *Documents on Reform of the United Nations*, Part VI, "The Reform of the Security Council", London: Dartmouth Publishing, 1997, pp. 415–458. Similar terrain is traversed by W. Andy Knight, "The Future of the UN Security Council: Questions of Legitimacy and Representation in Multilateral Governance", in Andrew F. Cooper, John English and Ramesh Thurkur (eds), *Enhancing Global Governance: Towards a New Diplomacy?*, Tokyo: United Nations University Press, 2002, pp. 19–38. A perspective rooted in international law, but focusing more on process than on structure, is provided by Benjamin B. Ferencz, *New Legal Foundations for Global Survival: Security Through the Security Council*, Dobbs Ferry, NY: Oceana Publications, 1994. Also valuable from a legal perspective is Walter Hoffmann, *United Nations Security Council Reform and Restructuring*, Monograph No. 14, Livingston, NJ: Center for UN Reform Education, 1994. For thoughtful cautionary notes see Edward C. Luck, "How Not to Reform the United Nations", *Global Governance* 11(4), 2005, pp. 407–414.
2. Capsule summaries of 73 proposals for SC reform over the period 1945–2005 are presented in Manuel Fröhlich, Klaus Hüfner and Alfredo Märker, *Reform des UN-Sicherheitsrats: Modelle, Kriterien und Kennziffern*, Blaue Reihe Nr. 94, Berlin: Deutsche Gesellschaft für die Vereinten Nationen, 2005, pp. 19–40. Forty-nine proposals in this listing, which makes no claim to completeness, date from the period 1993–2005. For detailed, regular summaries of the work of the open-ended committee see the website of the Center for UN Reform Education, http://centerforunreform.org.
3. For a well-balanced discussion of the history of attempts to reform the SC, with particular attention to current debates, see Bardo Fassbender, "Pressure for Security Council Reform", in David M. Malone (ed.), *The UN Security Council: From the Cold War to the 21st Century*, Boulder, CO and London: Lynne Rienner, 2004, pp. 341–355. A more detailed analysis, written from a legal perspective, is provided by Ingo Winkelmann, "Bringing the Security Council into a New Era", *Max Planck Yearbook of United Nations Law* 1, Heidelberg: Max Planck Institute, 1997, pp. 35–90. Although Winkelmann's

review may at first appear dated, the recent positions of the more vocal national delegations essentially recapitulate views put forward during the intense debates of the 1990s.

4. The quantitative analyses in this chapter exclude South Sudan.

5. UN Charter, Article 23, paragraph 1.

6. I am grateful to Rolando Gomez of the Office of the Spokesman for the Secretary-
   General for sending me data for this map, up to the year 2003, via fax, 21 January 1997,
   and for several later communications. Data by regions up to 1997 are also provided by
   Sydney D. Bailey and Sam Daws, *The Procedure of the UN Security Council*, Oxford:
   Clarendon Press, 1998, pp. 148–151. Data for years subsequent to 2003 were obtained
   from the UN website.

7. Specific membership years for all SC member nations from 1945 to 2003, as well as the
   relative frequency of membership, are provided in Joseph E. Schwartzberg, *Revitalizing the United Nations: Reform through Weighted Voting*, New York and The Hague:
   Institute for Global Policy, World Federalist Movement, 2004, Appendix IV. For the
   years 2004–2011 data may be derived from the website of the UN Security Council,
   www.un.org/en/sc/members, which provides a complete record of membership. The G4
   proposal may be accessed as GA Doc. A/59/L.64, 6 July 2005. The Uniting for Consensus proposal is accessible as GA Doc. GA/10371, 26 July 2005. A fuller account of the
   author's critique of the high-level panel's report, as well as the G4 proposal, will be
   found in Joseph E. Schwartzberg, "Getting It Wrong on Security Council Reform",
   paper presented at annual meeting of Academic Council on the United Nations System,
   Ottawa, 16–18 June 2005, unpublished (available by request to schwa004@umn.edu).

8. The German figure includes four years of membership by West Germany and two by
   East Germany prior to their unification in 1990, and five additional years thereafter.

9. The repeated US backing of the SC candidacy of Panama (prior and subsequent to
   Manuel Noriega's tenure as Panama's president) helps explain this anomaly.

10. David Malone, "Eyes on the Prize: The Quest for Nonpermanent Seats on the UN Se-
    curity Council", *Global Governance* 5(1), 2000, pp. 3–23.

11. Israel was not in any electoral group for purposes of SC membership until 2001, when it
    was admitted into the "Western European and Other" group.

12. For an excellent review of the history of representation by regions see Sam Daws, "The
    Origins and Development of UN Electoral Groups", in Ramesh Thakur (ed.), *What Is
    Equitable Geographic Representation in the Twenty-first Century?*, Tokyo: United Nations
    University Press, 1999, pp. 11–29.

13. The year-by-year population estimates from which Figure 4.1 was created, up to the
    year 2003, were derived from various annual volumes of the *UN Demographic Year-
    book*, with abundant interpolation by the author, and are indicated in Schwartzberg,
    Revitalizing, note 7 above, Appendix V. For the years 2004–2011 data were derived *The
    Encyclopaedia Britannica Book of the Year*, Chicago, IL: Encyclopaedia Britannica,
    2004–2011.

14. Schwartzberg, "Getting It Wrong", note 7 above, provides a detailed discussion.

15. Interestingly, the GA merely "acquiesced" in the post-Soviet assumption of power by
    the Russian Federation, but at no time took a vote legitimizing it. More tenuously one
    may assert that the "People's Republic of China" is not the same nation as the "Repub-
    lic of China", designated as one of the P-5.

16. There has, however, not been a single case in the history of the SC when any combina-
    tion of its non-permanent members has succeeded in blocking a vote on an issue on
    which the P-5 concurred.

17. Supporting the post-Westphalian approach adopted in this section is Luk Van Langen-
    hove, "Towards a Regional World Order", *UN Chronicle* 3, 2004, pp. 12–13 and 33. It
    asserts (p. 33) the need for a "global forum based on international law that allows world

regions to interact with each other and settle their disputes", and that "The Security Council needs to become a hybrid forum composed of nations that can be considered to be global actors, together with regional organizations that group the other nations into global actors."

18. For two systems of representation based in large part on self-formed blocs of states see Schwartzberg, *Revitalizing*, note 7 above. In both proposals the number of SC seats would be 18 and the proportion of the world's population represented in any given year would likely exceed 90 per cent.

19. Among works proposing SC representation by regions or critiquing such proposals are Volker Weyel (ed.), "The Quest for Regional Representation: Reforming the United Nations Security Council", *Critical Currents* 4, May 2008, special number (published by the Dag Hammarskjöld Foundation); Kennedy Graham and Tania Felicio, *Regional Security and Global Governance: A Study of Interaction between Regional Agencies and the UN Security Council, with a Proposal for a Regional-Global Security Mechanism*, Brussels: Brussels University Press, 2006; Kennedy Graham, "Towards a Coherent Regional Institutional Landscape in the United Nations? Implications for Europe", Bruges Regional Integration & Global Governance Papers No. 1, UNU/College of Europe, Bruges, 2008.

20. For example, with the creation of South Sudan, an area unlikely to seek membership in the Arab League, the area of the Arab League region would be diminished and that of Africa South of the Sahara increased. But as the map relates to the year 2010, it does not reflect this change.

21. The author experimented with numerous formulae before concluding that the one presented here would yield an optimal set of weights. Regional data for six of these formulae (apart from those calling for equal regional votes) are provided in Joseph E. Schwartzberg, "Regional Representation as a Basis for Security Council Reform", unpublished draft, November 2004 (available by request to schwa004@umn.edu).

22. The judgements that follow may fruitfully be compared with those of many authors represented in Mary Farrell, Björn Hettne and Luk Van Langenhove (eds), *Global Politics of Regionalism: Theory and Practice*, London and Ann Arbor, MI: Pluto Press, 2005.

23. Malone, note 10 above, *passim*.

24. These percentages were calculated by the author using data in Appendix 1.

25. Ariela Blätter, "The Responsibility Not to Veto", *Minerva* 37, November 2010, pp. 47–53, available at www.globalsolutions.org, and published by Citizens for Global Solutions in shortened form in *The Global Citizen*, Fall 2010, pp. 6–7.

26. Paolo Bargiacchi, "Strengthening the Rule of Law as a Means of Reforming the UN Security Council", in Giovanni Finizio and Ernesto Gallo (eds), *Democracy at the United Nations: UN Reform in the Age of Globalisation*, Brussels: Peter Lang, 2013, pp. 275–288.

5

From ECOSOC to ESEC

The economy, even if globalized, must always be integrated into the overall fabric of social relations, of which it forms an important, but not exclusive, component.
Pope John Paul II

Existing global economic and social governance structures are woefully inadequate for the challenges ahead ... Rarely are environmental concerns factored into security, development or humanitarian strategies.
High-level Panel on Threats, Challenges and Change

Introduction

No component of the UN system has been the object of more widely divergent criticisms and recommendations than the Economic and Social Council (ECOSOC).[1] There are, on the one hand, harsh critics, mainly from the global North, who would do away with it altogether. On the other hand, many engaged observers, primarily but by no means exclusively from the global South, would, despite ECOSOC's largely disappointing record, strengthen the body substantially and broaden its mandate.[2] There are those who see it as much too large to function efficiently, and others who decry its democratic deficit and argue that its membership – like that of the General Assembly – should be universal.

Notwithstanding ECOSOC's many and obvious shortcomings, this chapter makes a case for strengthening that body, especially in respect to

Transforming the United Nations system: Designs for a workable world, Schwartzberg, *United Nations University Press, 2013, ISBN 978-92-808-1230-5*

its traditional role in facilitating the coordination of development policy throughout the UN system; for adding environmental oversight to its core functions and changing its name to the Economic, Social and Environmental Council (ESEC); for enlarging its membership from 54 nations to 60; and for instituting a hybrid, regionally based system of partially weighted voting, guaranteeing the individual representation of all of the world's leading nations while simultaneously enabling smaller nations to have a meaningful voice in shaping and guiding global policies.

How ECOSOC functions

The problems that have contributed to ECOSOC's inadequate performance stem largely from its ambiguous relationship with the GA. This problem is inherent in the UN Charter.[3] Article 60 of Chapter IX, "International Economic and Social Cooperation", states:

> Responsibility for the discharge of the functions of the Organization set forth in this Chapter shall be vested in the General Assembly and, under the authority of the General Assembly, in the Economic and Social Council, which shall have for this purpose the powers set forth in Chapter X.

While this formulation casts ECOSOC in a clearly subordinate role, Article 65 (Chapter X) stipulates: "The Economic and Social Council may furnish information to the Security Council and assist the Security Council upon its request." There is no suggestion here that action by ECOSOC is to be mediated through the GA. Other clauses in Chapter X also call for or allow ECOSOC to deal, in its own right, with other entities of the UN system (e.g. various specialized agencies and the five regional economic commissions), individual member nations and non-governmental organizations (NGOs). These provisions confirm ECOSOC's status as a "principal organ" of the system (so specified in Article 7) on a par with, rather than subordinate to, the GA. Further confounding the matter is Article 13, which calls on the General Assembly to

> initiate studies and make recommendations for the purpose of ... promoting international co-operation in the economic, social, cultural, educational and health fields and assisting in the realization of human rights and fundamental freedoms for all.

These GA functions overlap, virtually in their entirety, those assigned to ECOSOC in Article 62, Clause 1, which reads as follows:

The Economic and Social Council may make or initiate studies and reports
with respect to international economic, social, cultural, educational, health, and
related matters and may make recommendations with respect to any such matters to the General Assembly, to the Members of the United Nations, and to
the specialized agencies concerned.

It is not surprising, therefore, that following a promising beginning –
and contrary to the hopes of many – ECOSOC has functioned increasingly in the shadow of the GA and settled largely into the role of a
conduit of information rather than an initiator or proactive coordinator
of meaningful action.[4] Further, to the extent that it does make prescriptive recommendations, ECOSOC (like the GA) lacks the authority to
make them legally binding and has no enforcement capability.

ECOSOC operates largely through subsidiary bodies. Among these are
nine "functional commissions", whose memberships range from 24 to 53
nations; two *ad hoc,* open-ended working groups, both with universal
membership of the 54 nations in ECOSOC; seven "expert bodies" (of
which two are composed of government experts and five of individuals
working in their personal capacity); three "standing committees"; and
two other "related bodies", one dealing with the advancement of women,
the other focusing on narcotics.[5] There is considerable overlap among
these entities (e.g. between the Functional Commission on Narcotic
Drugs and the International Narcotics Control Board). Yet nowhere does
there appear to be any entity dealing with the environment in general or
such specific problems as climate change, pollution, loss of biodiversity or
water scarcity. In this respect, ECOSOC's agenda seems to be seriously in
need of updating.

ECOSOC cannot function effectively without serious high-level review
and analysis of environmental issues. A strong case, then, can be made for
expanding its mandate and changing its name to the UN Economic,
Social and Environmental Council. A desirable concomitant change would
be the institutionalization of a deeper and more systematic relationship
between ECOSOC and the myriad NGOs accredited to it, as well as
strengthening ECOSOC's links to other influential non-state actors.

Rationalization of ECOSOC's functions should entail not only broad-
ening its mandate but also shedding non-core functions. In this respect,
the decision at the UN's 2005 World Summit to replace ECOSOC's Commission on Human Rights with a Human Rights Council (HRC) under
the aegis of the UN GA appears warranted.

Apart from its dubious relationship with the GA, ECOSOC's economic
effectiveness is diminished by its unrealistic one-nation-one-vote system
of decision-making. As with the GA, this diminishes its credibility, especially among developed countries. To the extent that more affluent na-

tions attempt to act collectively – or with a modicum of harmony – on economic matters of global scope, such as finance, world trade, energy policy and economic sustainability, they typically prefer to bypass ECOSOC and work through other, more flexible agencies. Foremost among these are the powerful Bretton Woods institutions, which do have systems of weighted voting based on financial contributions.[6] Additionally, the major actors have turned at times to the OECD, comprising some 34 nations with advanced economies. In the interests of diplomatic efficiency, however, the great powers have increasingly worked through smaller consultative bodies, the so-called G-6, G-7, G-8 and, most recently, G-20. Created in 1975, the G-6 was made up of France, Germany, Italy, Japan, the United Kingdom and the United States. Canada joined that group the following year, turning it into the G-7; and with the addition of Russia in 1997, it became the G-8.

But a chorus of voices from the economically emerging powers of the previously excluded global South (e.g. Brazil, China, India, Mexico and South Africa) resulted in the formation in 1999 of the G-20, a much more inclusive – but unelected and still informal – body which seeks to determine policy through periodic meetings of finance ministers and also, especially since 2008, heads of state or government.[7] Collectively, the G-20 accounts for roughly 85 per cent of the gross world product, 80 per cent of world trade and about two-thirds of the world's population. Although its membership is problematic, it does include at least one nation from every major world region and – unlike the G-6, G-7 and G-8 – has a semblance of balance between developed and developing nations. Not surprisingly, the G-20 has been widely criticized, not only for its exclusivity and lack of transparency, but also for its alleged role in undermining the authority of the United Nations and the Bretton Woods institutions. A stinging rebuke – with which I concur – came from Norwegian Foreign Minister Jonas Gahr Støre, who declared:

> The G-20 is a self-appointed group. Its composition is determined by the major countries and powers. It may be more representative than the G-7 or the G-8, in which only the richest countries are represented, but it is still arbitrary. We no longer live in the 19th century, a time when the major powers met and redrew the map of the world. Nobody needs a new Congress of Vienna.[8]

Despite such criticism, the G-20's global influence has steadily increased. At its 2009 summit meeting in Pittsburgh it was agreed that it would thenceforth replace the G-8. This suggests that the only way by which a reformed ECOSOC/ESEC could regain significant global influence in economic matters would be for it to become *universally inclusive* and adopt some uniformly applicable system of *weighted voting*, based at least in part on relative economic power as well as on population. The realities of economic and demographic power simply cannot be ignored. Nor, however, should one ignore the sensitivities of the vast majority of UN member nations excluded from the deliberations of both the G-20 and, in any given year, ECOSOC in its present form.

A final impediment to ECOSOC effectiveness is the brevity of its sessions. ECOSOC usually meets in two sessions per year – in New York in the spring and Geneva in the summer – for a total of not more than 40 working days, during which time delegates are expected to read, digest and discuss literally thousands of pages of reports from its own subsidiary bodies, as well as from NGOs and other agencies with which it works.[9] Its mission is impossible to perform effectively, especially so for some delegates for whom neither English nor French is a mother tongue. If ECOSOC/ESEC is to become truly effective, it will have to extend its working calendar considerably and possibly even become a year-round functioning body, as is the Security Council.

Representativeness of ECOSOC

ECOSOC's membership as a share of the UN total has fluctuated substantially.[10] As the membership of the United Nations expanded, the share in ECOSOC steadily declined. But that share has also been twice substantially increased as a result of Charter reform, first by enlargement from 18 to 27 members in 1965 and then by a second increase, to 54 members, in 1972.[11] Table 5.1 indicates ECOSOC's share of the total UN membership in selected years.

Seats in ECOSOC are for staggered three-year terms, one-third of the total membership being elected each year. Immediate re-election is permissible and there is no limit to the number of consecutive terms that a member may serve. Thus, while no nations are so designated, some nations have been "permanent" (or almost permanent) seat holders. As

Table 5.1 Inclusiveness of UN member nations in ECOSOC at selected dates

Date	Membership of UN	Membership of ECOSOC	% of UN total in ECOSOC
1945	51	18	35.3
1965	116	18	14.5
1966	121	27	22.3
1971	131	27	20.6
1972	134	54	40.3
2012	193	54	28.0

with the SC, seats in ECOSOC are differentially allocated to five regional caucuses. The distribution assigns 14 seats to Africa, 11 to Asia, 6 to Eastern Europe, 10 to Latin America and the Caribbean and 13 to Western European and other states.[12] This regional division is an anachronistic relic of the Cold War period, especially in the overrepresentation of Eastern Europe. It makes little sense in other respects as well. The allocation is predicated more on the *number of UN members* within each of the five regions specified than on the *number of people* to be served or the members' *contributions* to the UN budget. It bears little relationship to the distribution of power in the contemporary world, especially so in regard to Asia. Nor does it adequately reflect the world's major political and cultural divisions.

Although ECOSOC membership never exceeded approximately 40 per cent of the total UN membership, that figure provides an erroneous sense of ECOSOC's inclusiveness, in that most of the world's more populous and economically important nations have served simultaneously since its enlargement in 1972. There have been few years – perhaps none – since then in which less than half of the earth's population was represented. Additionally, members have since 1972 always accounted for a substantial majority of the gross world product and contributions to the UN budget.

Roughly a score of countries have served more than 60 per cent of their years of eligibility in ECOSOC. Leading this group were the P-5 powers, all of which have served continuously since the United Nations was founded, as well as the Republic of Korea, the only additional country to have served without a break since joining the United Nations. Close behind were Brazil, Germany and Japan, each having served every year but one of its period of UN membership.

The political dynamics underlying election to ECOSOC are not easily explained. As with other UN agencies, the process appears highly politicized. Political pressure exerted by major powers on behalf of specific candidates undoubtedly plays a role; and expedient political trade-offs – e.g. "we'll support your candidate for an ECOSOC seat if you'll support ours for a seat on the Human Rights Commission" – are allegedly commonplace.

A study by the author in 2009 of seating in ECOSOC over the period since 1972, when membership was increased to 54, raises numerous questions.[13] Why, for example, did Pakistan serve for 84 per cent of the years considered and India only 74 per cent? What explains the 47 per cent representation rate for Belarus (a country whose human rights record is so dismal that it is denied membership in the Council of Europe), as compared to only 32 per cent for its neighbour, Ukraine, with a population almost five times as large? Why was the participation rate for the

Democratic Republic of the Congo (74 per cent) – highest by far in Africa – so much greater than that of Nigeria (53 per cent), the continent's most populous state? By what logic can one explain the election of Somalia as a seat holder for five separate terms, including the years 1991–1993 and 2007–2009, despite that nation's having been a failed state continuously since 1991? And what accounts for the exceptionally strong showing of Romania (71 per cent), Colombia (71 per cent) and Venezuela (63 per cent)?

In contrast to the SC, relatively minor states, especially from Africa and the Caribbean region, have quite often succeeded in gaining election to ECOSOC. As of 2009, Rwanda had served on it for 39 per cent of the study period, Lesotho for 32 per cent, Djibouti for 24 per cent and Guinea-Bissau for 20 per cent. Among Caribbean states, Jamaica led with 50 per cent, but five additional nations had representation rates above 20 per cent.[14] The data suggest candidacies based on intra-regional gentlemen's agreements and frequent adherence to a rotational system of selection among aspiring states. The Asian caucus, on the other hand, seldom advanced the candidacy of minor nations.

Finally, comments are warranted regarding countries having never served a single term on ECOSOC. Among them, for reasons unknown, are such wealthy and influential states as Switzerland and Singapore; and a number of states widely regarded as pariahs in the international community, such as the DPRK, Myanmar and Israel (South Africa became a member for the first time only after terminating its apartheid regime).

No study, as far as I know, has attempted systematically to explain these peculiarities. While some of the regional bias in allocation would favour an East European country such as Romania or Belarus, national preferences must also play a role. Some countries apparently attach greater importance to ECOSOC than others and campaign actively for election, perhaps expecting thereby to enhance their visibility in the economic arena, in lieu of doing so in the political arenas of the SC and GA. Other nations may be so lacking in respect for ECOSOC that they do not feel the demands of membership are worth the bother of engagement.

Despite ECOSOC's being a far more representative body than the SC or the G-20, its pattern of membership is highly problematic. While the arbitrary composition of the G-20 has rightly been criticized, that of ECOSOC borders on bizarre. It does not reflect the real distribution of world power; nor is it merit-based. Had ECOSOC been given a chance in recent decades to play a major role in global affairs, it seems unlikely that its idiosyncratic allocation of decision-making authority would be tolerated. But if a revitalized ECOSOC/ESEC is to become an important player on the global stage, substantial changes in its representation system will be necessary.

A proposed new structure

The considerations in reforming the structure of the SC are, in large part, applicable for ECOSOC as well. However, the major difference in the size of the two bodies – now 15 versus 54 members – suggests a need for different approaches in allocating and filling ECOSOC seats. That the SC is frequently called on to make expeditious decisions during political crises argues strongly for keeping its membership small (this work suggesting 12). ECOSOC, on the other hand, is a body whose deliberations ought not to be hasty. The issues it addresses have multiple dimensions and must be approached from diverse political, economic, social and ethical perspectives. Moreover, they are manifested differently in different world regions. These considerations suggest a need for a larger body than the SC, though not seats for all member nations. Given the number of commissions and other subsidiary bodies to be staffed by ECOSOC members, a decision to change to universal seat holding would needlessly strain the diplomatic resources of many of the world's smaller nations. While there is no obviously optimal number of seats, I recommend only a modest increment, from the present 54 to a new total of 60. That comes to about 31 per cent of the present UN membership, roughly in the middle of the historical range indicated in Table 5.1.[15]

A more consequential issue is how to achieve a realistic allocation of decision-making authority that is at once regionally representative and capable of ensuring a fair hearing for the views of small nations while also ensuring adequate recognition for those that are relatively powerful. These goals can be met through a hybrid system that provides *differentially weighted* votes and guaranteed seats for nations that wield substantial power and *uniformly weighted* votes for a more numerous elected group of smaller nations.[16] As in my recommendations relating to the GA and SC, I propose objective mathematical formulae for determining voting weights for specific nations. I also recommend a regional framework similar to the one presented in respect to universal representation in the SC.

The proposed approach would require amending Article 61 of Chapter X of the UN Charter. It might begin as follows:

The Economic and Social Council [or the Economic, Social and Environmental Council] shall consist of sixty Members of the United Nations elected by the General Assembly in accordance with procedures to be established by a duly constituted committee of the General Assembly. The General Assembly will elect Members of the Council in the first instance, on the basis of their ability to make a contribution to the work of the Council and more generally to the work of the Organization, and also to equitable geographical distribution.

Up to one-third of Council seats may be allocated to individual Members who will be entitled to cast differentially weighted votes in accordance with one or more predetermined formulae taking into consideration the Members' population and paid contributions to the UN budget. The remaining seat holders will be elected from regionally nominated slates of candidates and all will cast votes with a lesser uniform weight.

The foregoing text would be followed (as at present) by several clauses specifying the rules relating to term length, with a change from three to two years, and staggered elections, with one half of the membership being chosen each year.[17] As at present, renewable terms would be permitted. The article would then require a concluding clause, which might read as follows:

The General Assembly may at intervals of not less than fifteen years [or some other agreed-upon period] amend the formulae and other rules according to which seats on the Economic and Social Council are filled and according to which voting weights are assigned.

The purpose of amending along the lines indicated would be to ensure flexibility and the ability of ECOSOC/ESEC to change in accordance with the demographic and economic fortunes of member states as well as unanticipated political eventualities (e.g. the creation of new federal unions, or the demise of certain member nations) without resort to further Charter amendment.

Applying the above recommendations, I propose a multistep process for allocating and filling ESEC seats on a regional basis and determining the weight of the votes to be cast by each seat holder. The following paragraphs, together with Table 5.2 and Figure 5.1, indicate how the process would unfold if the proposed system were in effect as of 2010.

The allocation process would begin by determining the set of nations that are entitled to an individual ESEC seat by virtue of having a national weight in excess of a specified threshold based on the GA formula proposed in Chapter 3:

$$W = (P + C + M)/3$$

in which W = the nation's voting weight, P = its percentage share of the total population of all UN members, C = its percentage share of all contributions to the regular UN budget[18] and M = its percentage share of the total UN membership (1/192 or 0.52 per cent). I recommend a threshold of 1 per cent. This would yield a cohort of 17 nations (mapped in Figure 5.1). In descending order of weights (see Appendix 1) they are the United States, China, India, Japan, Germany, France, Brazil, United Kingdom,

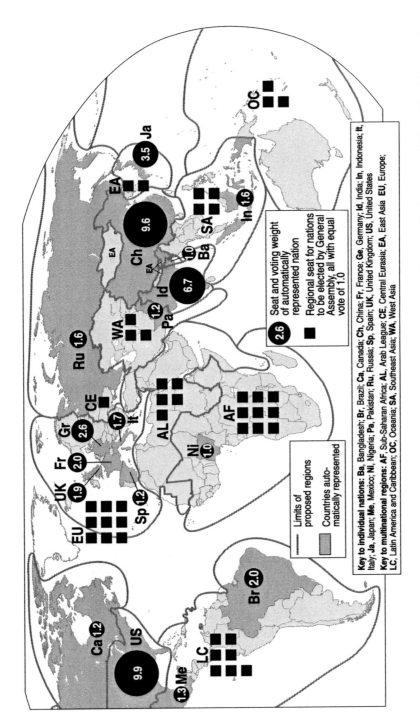

Figure 5.1 Composition of proposed regionally organized 60-seat Economic, Social and Environmental Council with partially weighted voting

Key to Individual nations: **Ba**, Bangladesh; **Br**, Brazil; **Ca**, Canada; **Ch**, China; **Fr**, France; **Ge**, Germany; **Id**, India; **In**, Indonesia; **It**, Italy; **Ja**, Japan; **Me**, Mexico; **Ni**, Nigeria; **Pa**, Pakistan; **Ru**, Russia; **Sp**, Spain; **UK**, United Kingdom; **US**, United States
Key to multinational regions: **AF**, Sub-Saharan Africa; **AL**, Arab League; **CE**, Central Eurasia; **EA**, East Asia; **EU**, Europe; **LC**, Latin America and Caribbean; **OC**, Oceania; **SA**, Southeast Asia; **WA**, West Asia

Limits of proposed regions
Countries automatically represented

2.6 Seat and voting weight of automatically represented nation

■ Regional seat for nations to be elected by General Assembly, all with equal vote of 1.0

Italy, Russia, Indonesia, Mexico, Spain, Pakistan, Canada, Nigeria and Bangladesh. Collectively, these 17 nations would have a total weight of 50.124, 69.9 per cent of the world's total population and 77.1 per cent of the world's total GNI.

All remaining UN member nations would then be grouped by regional caucuses, ideally similar to those used in determining seats for the SC (Figure 4.3) in the model calling for universal weighted regional membership. Nine such regions are identified in Figure 5.1.[19]

The remaining seats would then be proportionally allocated among the regions based on the respective totals of their national weights. These regional weights (indicated in column c of Table 5.2) would range from a high of 10.799 for Africa (excluding Nigeria, which would be automatically seated) to a low of 1.313 for Central Eurasia (a group of five former Soviet republics).

Each regional weight would then be adjusted by dividing it by 1.160 (1/43 of the remainder of 49.876, after deducting the total of 50.124 for the 17 top-ranking states from 100). The adjusted weights appear in column d.

The adjusted weights would then be rounded to the nearest integer to determine the number of seats, as shown in column e.[20]

Each regional caucus would, by methods of its own choosing, put forward a slate of national candidates for its allocated number of seats, sub-

Table 5.2 Framework for allocating 43 seats among nine multinational regions within a reformed ECOSOC/ESEC

Region	Number of member nations	Aggregate regional weight	Weight divided by 1.160	Number of seats
a	b	c	d	e
Africa South of the Sahara	42	10.799	9.309	9
Arab League	21	6.319	5.448	5
Central Eurasia	5	1.313	1.132	1
East Asia	5	1.961	1.691	2
Europe	36	10.763	9.278	9
Latin America & Caribbean	31	7.573	6.528	7
Oceania	14	3.220	2.776	3
Southeast Asia	11	4.312	3.717	4
West Asia	9	3.615	3.117	3
Total	175	49.876	42.997	43

Notes:
1. This presentation assumes the proposed system was in place as of 2010.
2. The divisor, 1.160, in column d represents the average weight per seat, derived by dividing the nine-region total weight of 49.876 by the number of seats, 43.

ject to a requirement – to ensure truly competitive elections and promote meritocracy – that the number of candidate nations be at least one-and-a-half times the number of seats to be filled. The GA would then elect its preferred candidates. Rankings, weights and regional boundaries would, of course, vary over time, and ESEC membership and weights would change accordingly.

Although it is impossible to make definitive comparisons between the proposed and present systems, in that ECOSOC membership changes annually, one may confidently assert that the proposed system would yield a more representative and inclusive body, in regard to both proportion of humanity represented and members' total contribution to the UN budget. The former would likely regularly exceed 80 per cent and the latter could well pass 90 per cent in any given year. Additionally, the system would provide an objective, fairer, more culturally sensitive regional distribution of voting power than does the present crude and increasingly anachronistic state-centric system. It would also give a better, more nuanced reflection of national and regional power. Giving nations a stake commensurate with their global influence and strengthening ECOSOC's global role should incline political actors to take that body (hopefully reformed as ESEC) more seriously than they have done in recent decades.

It is also appropriate to compare the proposal to the G-20 mechanism for addressing global economic issues. As one would expect, most of the 17 nations automatically seated in the proposed system are also members of the G-20 (which has only 19 national members, the twentieth being the European Union), the exceptions being Bangladesh, Nigeria, Pakistan and – if one ignores the European Union – Spain. Of the G-20, Argentina, Australia, Saudi Arabia, South Africa and the Republic of Korea would not be among the 17 automatic members of the proposed ESEC. The major difference between the two entities is that the G-20 excludes the vast majority of UN member nations (especially those of the global South) from its decision-making process. While it may thereby gain in efficiency, it does so at the cost of legitimacy and international resentment. Moreover, as the G-20 has no formal voting mechanism, it is subject to falling under the political sway of a handful of major economic powers projecting their own economic agenda on to the rest of the world.

The role of regional caucuses

Although the proposed 60-seat ESEC should provide a reliable representation of the viewpoints of virtually all parts of the world, it would not obviate the need for intra-regional consultation on matters of common concern. In the discussion in Chapter 4 of a system of regional representation in the SC I noted the value of frequent regional meetings of heads of state or government and of foreign ministers to formulate, to the extent possible, common regional policies. Similar meetings would, presumably, take place in regard to matters addressed by ESEC, and delegates would be guided accordingly. Most regional matters could probably be dealt with via electronic media at the ministerial level, but key decisions would be reserved for regional summit conferences once or twice a year. The requisite logistical infrastructure is already largely in place.

There would be no need for all regions to adopt identical calendars, working methods or rules for internal decision-making. Each multistate region – optionally including nations holding seats in their own right – would function in ways that it deems most appropriate. Each would decide on the frequency of meetings and its own rules of protocol. Within parameters set forth by the GA committee dealing with ESEC membership, each region would decide upon its method for putting forward candidates to fill open seats. Each would determine the rules in regard to number of successive terms that elected seat holders might serve, and specify the minimum number of years (if any) between terms. Some regional caucuses might wish to establish weighted voting procedures for their internal decision-making, while others might choose to retain an intra-regional one-nation-one-vote system. Finally, each region could establish rules as to how much freedom of action its elected delegates would enjoy.

The proposed system of representation would presumably contribute substantially to regional and global integration and promote fruitful exchanges in matters beyond the UN's purview. Global discussions originating on matters within ESEC's purview might be fruitfully extended to other matters of concern only to one or a few regions. Overall, deliberations would be characterized by a high degree of transparency. Additionally, they would provide opportunities for promising young diplomats to gain international exposure and recognition, and groom them for more prominent roles on regional and global stages. They would also enhance the ability of weak nations, especially those of the global South, to stand up *collectively* to inappropriate political pressures from the global North and put forward reasoned cases for greater global equity.

Summary and conclusions

ECOSOC suffers from numerous structural and functional deficiencies that have greatly limited its effectiveness. These shortcomings, however, are correctable. To minimize functional redundancy within ECOSOC and the GA, a reformed body, ESEC, should be given greater responsibility in respect to economic, social and environmental matters. Devising optimal lines of authority and efficient organizational relationships will inevitably require considerable experimentation. But reforms along lines set forth in this chapter should substantially promote the legitimacy and effectiveness of the system.

Whatever form a future ECOSOC/ESEC may take, it should be able to integrate the findings of and lessons learned by all the governmental and non-state agencies with which it interacts and devise coherent action programmes for addressing them. Its programmatic recommendations should be forwarded to the GA and the proposed WPA (should that body be established). When matters involve threats to the peace, reports to the SC will also be needed.

The problem of allocating power in ECOSOC/ESEC can best be addressed by a system in which the world's major and middle-level powers (17 as of 2010) are automatically represented with differentially weighted votes and a cohort of relatively small, but highly regarded, nations are also elected to seats, with an equal unit vote. Weighted votes would be determined by objective mathematical formulae devised by a duly authorized GA committee, with the understanding that the formulae could be modified as needed. The nations with weighted votes would collectively account for more than two-thirds of the world's population and more than three-fourths of its GNI, while most of the world's nations would be grouped within multinational regional caucuses allotted anywhere from one to nine seats each.

Ideally, ECOSOC/ESEC governance caucuses – including most countries with an automatic seat entitlement – would be similar to, if not identical with, those proposed for electing delegates to the SC. Once established, the caucus system should lead to regular interaction and cooperation among their respective member nations and facilitate implementation of UN-sponsored programmes as well as cooperative ventures outside the ambit of the United Nations.

Notes

1. A thorough discussion of ECOSOC's functioning and proposals for its reform is that of Gert Rosenthal (a former president of ECOSOC and Guatemala's permanent representative to the United Nations), "The Economic and Social Council of the United Nations: An Issues Paper", Dialogue on Globalization Occasional Paper No. 15, Friedrich Ebert Stiftung, New York, 2005. The bibliography accompanying this essay will guide the reader to numerous original documents dealing with reform proposals. A general discussion appears in Gert Rosenthal, "Economic and Social Council", in Thomas G. Weiss and Sam Daws (eds), *The Oxford Handbook on the United Nations*, Oxford: Oxford University Press, 2007, pp. 136–148. Comments are made by Edward C. Luck,

"Principal Organs", in Thomas G. Weiss and Sam Daws (eds), *The Oxford Handbook on the United Nations*, Oxford: Oxford University Press, 2007, pp. 665–668. More scathing than the reviews by Rosenthal is the trenchant account by Marcus Franda, *The United Nations in the Twenty-first Century: Management and Reform Processes in a Troubled Organization*, Lanham, MD: Rowman & Littlefield, 2006, pp. 157–186.

2. Among those recommending the dissolution of ECOSOC was the prestigious Commission on Global Governance, which advocated replacing it with an "Economic Security Council". Commission on Global Governance, *Our Global Neighbourhood*, Oxford: Oxford University Press, 1995, pp. 236–302. The Nordic countries, on the other hand, supported the prevalent Southern perspective in a series of reports published over the period 1991–1996 and argued for a stronger ECOSOC role as a coordinator of efforts by various parts of the UN system, a view that was essentially echoed by the South Centre in 1996 (studies cited by Rosenthal, "Economic and Social Council", ibid., pp. 142–143 and 147). Similar views were expressed, *inter alia*, in High-level Panel on Threats, Challenges and Change, "A More Secure World: Our Shared Responsibility", UN Doc. A/59/565, 2004, pp. 68–71; Kofi Annan, "In Larger Freedom: Towards Development, Security and Human Rights for All", UN GA Doc. A/59/2005, 2005. In chronological order, the most detailed reform recommendations, apart from those already mentioned, are Maurice Bertrand, "Some Reflections on Reform of the United Nations", UN GAOR Joint Inspection Unit, 40th Session, Agenda Item 120, UN Doc. A/40/988/Add. 1, 1985 (calling for total ECOSOC restructuring and renovation); "Report of the Independent Working Group on the Future of the United Nations", Ford Foundation, New York, 1994, www.library.yale.eduu/un/unle3f.htm (calling for the creation of separate Economic and Social Councils); Erskine Childers and Brian Urquhart, *Renewing the United Nations System*, New York and Uppsala: Ford Foundation/Dag Hammarskjöld Foundation, 1994 (calling, *inter alia*, for ECOSOC representation within an overarching "UN System Consultative Board"); Klaus Dicke and Manuel Fröhlich, "Reform of the UN", in Helmut Volger (ed.), *A Concise Encyclopedia of the United Nations*, 2nd edn, Leiden and Boston, MA: Martinus Nijhoff, 2010, pp. 587–582 (arguing, counter to Childers and Urquhart, in defence of a decentralized system); Klaus Hüfner, "UN System", in Helmut Volger (ed.), *A Concise Encyclopedia of the United Nations*, 2nd edn, Leiden and Boston, MA: Martinus Nijhoff, 2010, pp. 827–850 (advocating a middle position, with centralized coordination and monitoring and decentralized execution of functions); Boutros Boutros-Ghali, *An Agenda for Development*, New York: United Nations, 1995 (an appeal for greater UN commitment); Kemal Derviş, *A Better Globalization: Legitimacy, Governance, and Reform*, Washington, DC: Center for Global Development, 2005 (proposing a regionally organized Economic Security Council with 14 seats and weighted voting).

3. The discussion of these ambiguities is based primarily on Rosenthal, "Economic and Social Council", note 1 above, pp. 138–141.

4. Childers and Urquhart (note 2 above, p. 134) report, for example, that in two more or less typical ECOSOC sessions totalling 35 working days in 1983 the delegates "were expected to digest mentally, discuss substantively, and use for effective coordinating conclusions, some 50 reports of 2,000 pages".

5. Rosenthal, "Economic and Social Council", note 1 above, p. 137, Table 7.1. Numerous examples of ECOSOC's functional overlap with other agencies are also provided by Franda, note 1 above, pp. 164–167.

6. Rosenthal, "Economic and Social Council", note 1 above, p. 144; Luck, note 1 above, p. 666. World Bank country-wise weights are indicated in Derviş, note 2 above, pp. 164–167.

7. A good account of the organization and history of the G-20 and various critiques of its operation will be found in Wikipedia, "G-20 Major Economies", http://en.wikipedia.org/wiki/g-20.major_economies.

8. "Norway Takes Aim at G-20, 'One of the Greatest Setbacks Since World War II'", interview in *Der Spiegel*, 22 June 2010, www.spiegel.de/international/europe0,1518702104,00. html (cited in Wikipedia, ibid., p. 7).

9. Franda, note 1 above, p. 166.

10. Data relating to ECOSOC membership were derived from its website, www.un.org/en/ ecosoc.

11. ECOSOC is the only UN organ that has been the object of two Charter amendments.

12. For critical observations on the size and regional composition of ECOSOC membership see Jens Martens, "The Reform of the UN Economic and Social Council (ECOSOC): A Never-ending Story?", 14 November 2006, Global Policy Forum, New York, gpf@globalpolicy.org.

13. Joseph E. Schwartzberg, "Reforming ECOSOC Decision-Making within a Regional Context", unpublished paper presented at annual meeting of Academic Council on the United Nations System, Trinidad, June 2009; available on request to schwa004@umn.edu and via www/josephschwartzberg.org.

14. In 2009 St Lucia, Barbados and St Kitts & Nevis – with a combined population of roughly 0.6 million – were *simultaneously* serving. Could anyone regard this as an optimal contribution to the 10-member representation for the nearly 600 million people of the Latin American and Caribbean region, or to the mission of ECOSOC as a whole?

15. The recommended 11 per cent increase in membership (from 54 to 60) is greater than the 6 per cent increase over the period 1972–2009 in the proportion of the world's people within UN member nations, from roughly 94 per cent to the present 99.6 per cent, but much less than the 77 per cent increase in the number of UN members (from 109 to 193).

16. The Turkish economist Kemal Derviş, a former senior official of the World Bank and a former director of the UN Development Programme, is, to the best of my knowledge, the only other author to recommend a hybrid system of weighted representation with both regional and national membership. His system for a proposed "Economic and Social Security Council" is based on a formula with three terms (contribution to global public goods, population and GDP) and envisages six "permanent" seats (for the European Union, United States, Japan, China, India and Russia) and eight rotating seats assigned by regions. Voting weights per seat would range from 25.7 per cent for the European Union and 17.8 per cent for the United States down to a minimum of 2.2 for "Other Europe". This is a substantially greater proportional spread than that advocated in this chapter. Derviş, note 2 above, pp. 96–104.

17. Conversion to two-year terms would heighten the probability of election of small nations.

18. Taken in direct proportion to GNI, rather than the current rates of assessments, for reasons discussed in Chapter 3.

19. There is no reason, in principle, why somewhat differing groupings of nations could not be used. The regions would be proposed by the GA, with the understanding that any nation dissatisfied with its placement would be allowed to apply to another region for membership (but with no guarantee that its bid would be accepted by the members of that region). Nor is there any reason why some nations (e.g. Turkey) could not form part of two regions, as described in Chapter 4 in respect to the SC.

20. The weights for individual nations should be taken as absolute numbers rather than percentages; and, taken together with the equal unit weights (1.0) for regionally allocated seats, weights will not add up to 100. In principle, there is no reason why a total weight of 100 (or any other round number) is needed.

6

A credible human rights system

We hold these truths to be self-evident, that all men are created equal, that they are endowed by their Creator with certain unalienable Rights, that among these are Life, Liberty and the pursuit of Happiness.
US Declaration of Independence

... recognition of the inherent dignity and of the equal and inalienable rights of all members of the human family is the foundation of freedom, justice and peace in the world...
Universal Declaration of Human Rights

... the ideal of free human beings enjoying freedom from fear and want can only be achieved if conditions are created whereby everyone may enjoy his economic, social and cultural rights, as well as his civil and political rights...
International Covenant on Economic, Social and Cultural Rights

Introduction

Towards the end of the eighteenth century the American and French Revolutions set in motion an inexorable process of expansion of what are held to be inalienable human rights. Despite occasional setbacks, that process has since spread to all parts of the world, substantially deepened in scope and, especially since the end of the Second World War, accelerated in its pace. It has been highlighted by the unanimous adoption in

Transforming the United Nations system: Designs for a workable world, Schwartzberg, United Nations University Press, 2013, ISBN 978-92-808-1230-5

1948 of the Universal Declaration of Human Rights (UDHR) by the UN General Assembly;[1] by the subsequent drafting of the wide-ranging International Covenants on Civil and Political Rights and on Economic, Social and Cultural Rights; and by the passage in the United Nations of a host of more specific human rights covenants and treaties, many of which have already received the requisite number of ratifications to become parts of the body of binding international law.

Innumerable additional actions have been taken at the global, regional, national and local levels to increase further the salience of human rights in world affairs. Human rights courts have been established, enabling citizens to bring suit against governments for infringement of their rights and – in the European Union – even allowing a citizen of one nation to bring a suit against the government of another. Following the precedent set by the Nuremberg and Tokyo war crimes tribunals, the International Criminal Court and several *ad hoc* tribunals were created to deal with perpetrators of genocide, ethnic cleansing, crimes against humanity and war crimes. Human rights commissions and ombudspersons have been instituted in many nations to monitor adherence to constitutionally guaranteed human rights norms and specific human rights legislation. Outside governments, hundreds, if not yet thousands, of human rights NGOs have been created, even including some in repressive states, to advance the broad human rights agenda.[2] Many of these NGOs have been granted consultative status with the United Nations.

Thus one may now speak of the existence of a complex global human rights system. Though still inchoate and seriously flawed, that system will continue to expand and become of increasing concern to the UN system, within which it is partially embedded. It would therefore be in order, as the process of UN reform moves forward, to pay greater attention to human rights concerns. This chapter sets forth several ways of doing so. Specifically, I propose elevating the Human Rights Council (HRC) from its present subordinate position within the GA to that of a principal organ of the United Nations on a par with the GA or SC. I also recommend several major departures from established practices: that HRC members be chosen primarily on the basis of their *individual* merits, rather than as representatives of the countries from which they happen to come; that there be mandatory greater gender balance in HRC membership; and that members include representatives from the hitherto unrepresented indigenous peoples. Additionally, I recommend enhanced, universal human rights monitoring; more regular and more detailed reporting on human rights by regional organizations, individual nations and NGOs; greater use of legal systems to adjudicate human rights disputes; increased resort to UN-mandated sanctions against egregious violators of human rights law; and in extreme situations – and *as a last resort* – application of the use of force in keeping with the new norm of the "responsibility to protect".

The UN record to date[3]

Promotion of human rights was among the original concerns of the UN Charter. While various UN organs were charged with specific human rights responsibilities, the onus fell mainly on ECOSOC.[4] At its inaugural session in 1946 ECOSOC created the Commission on Human Rights (CHR) and charged that it establish a set of fundamental human rights standards or norms. The path-setting major outcome of this mandate was the 1948 UDHR. The same year witnessed adoption of the Convention on Genocide. Numerous additional covenants and conventions followed: the most wide-ranging and important were the International Covenant on Civil and Political Rights (ICCPR) and the International Covenant on Economic, Social and Cultural Rights (ICESCR). These two covenants, adopted in 1966 and ratified by 1976, along with the UDHR are commonly referred to as the International Bill of Human Rights.

Although human rights are officially regarded as being universal and indivisible, the fact that there are two basic covenants, rather than one, was and remains fraught with political significance.[5] Nations most favourably disposed to the ICCPR were the Western democracies, led by the United States, while those inclined to stress the ICESCR were nations of the Soviet-led Eastern bloc, along with most of the recently decolonized states in Asia, Africa and the Caribbean and Pacific regions. The human rights set forth in the two covenants were fundamentally different in nature and in their practical implications. Those of the ICCPR prevent states from abridging the freedom of their citizens in respect to such matters as speech, religion, assembly, voting and so forth. In general, one can easily ascertain whether or not specific rights are being honoured. The rights set forth in the ICESCR, however, may be regarded essentially as "programmatic aspirations".[6] Governmental behaviour in regard to such rights (for example, the right to development or a minimal standard of living) cannot easily be evaluated.

Throughout the Cold War, UN initiatives to promote the human rights enunciated in the two major covenants were rare. Failure to achieve particular aspirations may not indicate lack of governmental volition, but rather lack of capability. Hence, some observers believe that responsibility for securing human rights implies a moral obligation on the part of developed nations to support efforts by underresourced countries to provide for the needs of their own populations. Recognizing this, the United Nations adopted, in the year 2000, a set of Millennium Development Goals. The near-universal commitment to these goals signals a significant departure from previous practice. But it is not evident that the good intentions proclaimed at the Millennium Summit session will be translated into practice.

The machinery established to monitor and promote human rights observance is complex and scattered among agencies in New York, Geneva, The Hague, Paris, Vienna and Washington.[7] Many of the relevant bureaucracies were initially established within the CHR, operating from its headquarters in Geneva under the aegis of ECOSOC. At its inception this commission had a membership of 18 nations. As the United Nations grew in size, CHR membership was periodically increased, reaching a total of 53 in 1992.[8] A number of its constituent agencies were carried over to its successor organization, the slightly smaller HRC, a 47-member body established in 2006; and oversight of the body was transferred from ECOSOC to the GA. Additionally, seven human rights "treaty bodies" reporting directly to ECOSOC were formed to monitor and promote compliance with major human rights covenants and conventions.[9]

The proliferation of the human rights bureaucracy, like that of the United Nations in general, has resulted in numerous inefficiencies and substantial waste, and given rise to a widespread concern to achieve "system coherence". It also contributed to the establishment in 1993 of the Office of the High Commissioner for Human Rights (OHCHR), an extension of the good offices of the UN Secretary-General. This important office served/serves as the secretariat of the CHR/HRC and provides a focal entity for the entire human rights system. Among its functions are to provide early warnings of impending human rights emergencies and advise the Secretary-General on when to deal with them; analyse relevant reports; call for action by elements of the UN human rights system; monitor compliance with treaty obligations; facilitate technical assistance; report periodically on the state of human rights worldwide; and help coordinate the work of the human rights system.[10]

Aiding the CHR, and subsequently the HRC, were/are scores of unpaid volunteer rapporteurs and independent experts working through the OHCHR. As with the working groups, their mandates relate(d) either to specific problematic countries or, in several dozen cases, to thematic issues (e.g. the right to education, the right to food, the rights of migrants, violence against women and torture). While there was much overlap between the functions of the working groups and those of the volunteer experts, the latter generally offered the advantage of being independent, whereas the views of working group members were typically politically tinged by the official positions of the countries they represented. An additional check against politicized decision-making was the HRC's establishment in 2007 of an advisory committee of 18 independent experts to serve as its "think-tank" on thematic issues. As with the HRC itself, it is arguably still too early to evaluate its work; but the fact that the committee lacks decision-making authority inevitably hinders its effectiveness.

Monitoring human rights observance by individual countries under the CHR was neither uniform, comprehensive nor systematic. It often failed to expose the shortcomings of serious offenders.[11] Although most major human rights treaties call for periodic reports on compliance by the states party to them, such reports are typically filed late, if at all; and, with few exceptions (e.g. sanctions against South Africa for its policy of apartheid), there have been no penalties for non-compliance. The HRC hopes to correct this deficiency through a universal periodic review system, calling for staggered, comprehensive and compulsory four-year reviews of all UN member nations. Reviews received to date, however, have been excessively lenient, bestowing praise on states even when little was merited, because of the practice of allowing countries under review to secure friendly comments from their allies, rather than being subjected to objective scrutiny.[12] A depoliticized system is sorely needed.

While modest improvements have occurred in the UN's core human rights agency, there is a long way to go to achieve a desirable level of legitimacy and credibility. The current electoral system in the HRC remains essentially the same as it was in the CHR. Membership is allocated regionally, rather than on merit. Terms are for three years and staggered. The number of countries per region – rather than the regional population, its economic capability or the human rights record of its constituent countries – is the chief factor in the allocation process.

The five regional caucuses from which HRC delegates are chosen are those used in selecting members of the SC and ECOSOC, anachronistic groupings evolving as artefacts of the Cold War. They persist only because bureaucratic inertia prevents formulation of more sensible alternatives. The present seat allocation is Africa 13; Asia and Pacific 13; Eastern Europe 6; Latin America and Caribbean 8; and Western Europe and Other States 7.[13]

Some of the most egregious human rights offenders served multiple successive terms on the CHR, thereby protecting themselves from serious scrutiny. This was possible because elections were seldom contested and required only a simple majority, rather than the two-thirds recommended by some critics.[14] Other powerful states served continuously, or almost so, since the CHR was established.[15] Yet (as of 2010) 55 out of 192 UN member nations never served even a single year on the CHR.

In the 2004 report of the High-level Panel on Threats, Challenges and Change, the CHR came in for substantial criticism. Among the panel's comments was the following:

In recent years, the Commission's capacity to perform ... [its designated] tasks has been undermined by eroding credibility and professionalism. Standard-setting to reinforce human rights cannot be performed by States that lack a demonstrated commitment to their promotion and protection. We are concerned that in recent years States have sought membership on the Commission not to strengthen human rights but to protect themselves against criticism or to criticize others. The Commission cannot be credible if it is seen to be maintaining double standards in addressing human rights concerns.[16]

Not specifically mentioned in the panel's report was the striking contrast between the persistent criticism (much of it deserved) relating to human rights abuses allegedly committed by Israel in the West Bank and Gaza and the blind eye turned by the CHR (along with other UN agencies) to comparable abuses by numerous other regimes. This was undoubtedly among the reasons for the panel's censure, and also for widespread disenchantment with the United Nations in the United States and other Western democracies.[17]

Notwithstanding the central roles assigned to the OHCHR and CHR/ HRC, the GA as a whole as well as the SC have, particularly since the end of the Cold War, also elected to deal with human rights issues, especially in situations deemed to present threats to the peace. Their record in handling such matters is mixed. Some peacekeeping missions necessitated by gross violations of human rights did meet with considerable success. Others, while failing to bring about a durable peace, prevented a local descent into anarchy or civil war. Often, however, missions were inadequately staffed, insufficiently funded and/or, as in Somalia, ill executed; and SC failure to maintain close liaison with key human rights agencies in the UN system and NGOs in the field hindered the functioning of many missions.[18] Moreover, use of the veto by one or two P-5 powers often prevented decisive action in times of urgent need. Thus many decisions – or failures to reach decisions – have been based more on power politics than on principle. Especially egregious were the failures to prevent genocide in Rwanda and Darfur, to prevent the premeditated slaughter of thousands of Bosniak Muslims in Srebenica and – as of this writing in 2012 – to contain the violence wracking Syria, Yemen and Bahrain.

All too often the United Nations has turned a blind eye to the offences of tyrants, especially those ruling over small and strategically unimportant states. Conversely, given the P-5 veto privilege, glaring offences by major powers – in Tibet, Chechnya, Iraq and elsewhere – do not incur UN censure or sanction and may not even find a place on the SC agenda.

The UN's minimal engagement in Darfur is particularly noteworthy in light of the GA's adoption, at its summit meeting in September 2005, of the potentially epochal *responsibility to protect* (R2P) principle and the endorsement of that principle by the SC the following year.[19] Contrary to previous diplomatic norms, yet supported by the leaders of roughly 150 nations, the R2P principle does not provide a state with licence to act however it pleases within its own borders. Rather, it asserts the state's responsibility to safeguard the most basic human rights of its own citizens. Further, when a state fails egregiously in this responsibility by abetting or allowing on its territory genocide, ethnic cleansing, war crimes or crimes against humanity, it becomes the responsibility of the international community, acting through the United Nations, to protect the victims of such acts. Regrettably, notwithstanding the widely proclaimed "Never again!" sentiment that marked the passage of the R2P resolution, 10 years after the Rwandan genocide the SC failed to take effective action to avert or stem human rights catastrophes in Darfur and elsewhere.[20]

In addition to the GA and SC, we must take passing note of the Trusteeship Council, established as a principal organ of the United Nations in accordance with Chapter XII of the UN Charter. The task assigned to that body was to supervise the international trusteeship system, whereby a number of territories formerly under German, Italian and Japanese rule were to be governed by designated Allied powers until such time as they could be granted their independence. In 1984, with the independence of the last such trust territory, the tiny Pacific island state of Palau, the work of the Trusteeship Council was effectively concluded. Yet, lacking Charter amendment, the council still exists. Amending the Charter to eliminate this pointless anachronism is long overdue.[21]

Apart from their treatment by the principal organs of the United Nations, human rights issues form part of the concern of many other bodies within the UN system. The findings and recommendations of many UN specialized agencies (e.g. the World Health Organization, the International Labour Organization and UNESCO – the UN Educational, Scientific and Cultural Organization) often incorporate a human rights dimension.[22] Human rights promotion figures prominently in field operations of the UN Development Programme. Even the Bretton Woods institutions now factor the need to honour human rights into many of their investment decisions. The International Court of Justice, surprisingly, has handled few cases focusing on human rights. On the other hand, the International Criminal Court – not technically part of the UN system, but working closely with it since its establishment in 2002 – seems destined to play a major role in prosecuting egregious violators of fundamental human rights.

A strengthened Human Rights Council

Structural desiderata

Indicated below are a number of desiderata for determining the make-up of a credible HRC.

• The number of members must be large enough to ensure representation by all major state and regional actors, yet small enough to be efficient.
• All major regions of the world must be represented; to the extent feasible, the regions should be similar to those from which SC and ECOSOC/ESEC members are chosen.
• In addition to seats reserved for representatives of specified regions, a substantial number of seats should be filled at large to encourage truly competitive elections of high-quality candidates.
• Council members must be chosen based on their personal integrity, experience and subject expertise, rather than primarily according to their political affiliation, and must be guaranteed legal immunity for any acts taken in the performance of their HRC duties.
• Membership should have a reasonable gender balance.
• The special legal status of indigenous peoples should be recognized by reserving HRC seats for their duly chosen representatives.

Let us examine the basis for each of these recommendations.

The ideal council size is not intuitively obvious. In fact, this question formed one of the few issues on which the reform recommendations of the High-level Panel on Threats, Challenges and Change diverged sharply from those advanced by Secretary-General Annan. The former recommended universal representation, as in the GA; the latter called for a "smaller" body, without specifying what its size might be.[23] In the event, when the CHR was transformed into the HRC only a modest reduction, from 54 members to 47, was achieved. Further reduction would undoubtedly result in greater efficiency. Accordingly, I recommend a council of 36 members, elected to staggered three-year terms, with one-third of the membership chosen in any given year.

As noted for the SC and ECOSOC, the world is presently divided into five regional caucuses for electing HRC members. A division conforming better to current global realities is the 12-region recommendation proposed in Chapter 4.[24] Use of these regions would enable the nomination of HRC candidates in tandem with that of candidates for the SC and ECOSOC/ESEC. The method of nomination is discussed below. The interaction at the regional level required by the selection process will contribute to political integration and facilitate a two-way flow of ideas and resources between UN agencies, the major world regions and the nations and peoples of which those regions are comprised.

While it is politically desirable to have all regions represented to *some* extent in the HRC, there are enormous differences in concern for human rights from one region to another. Table 6.1 indicates the extent of these differences, as of 2010, based on the Freedom House rating system and its threefold classification of nations as "free", "partially free" and "not free" (keeping in mind Freedom House's bias in favour of political and civil rights, rather than those of an economic, social or cultural nature). The range in ratings is exceedingly broad. Two of the three single-nation regions, the United States and India, are rated as free, while China is classified as not free. Among the nine multinational regions, Europe leads with 93 per cent of its nations rated as free, while the Arab League nations, of which 76 per cent are rated as not free, score worst. (Small wonder, then, that the ongoing "Arab Spring" movements swept across much of this region as swiftly as they did.) Thus the probability of finding outstanding candidates for membership in the HRC will be far greater in some regions than in others; hence electing a substantial proportion of all HRC seats from a slate of *at-large* candidates appears warranted. This should lead to genuinely competitive elections and a significant overall increase in the quality of HRC members.

Although the norm in the GA, SC and ECOSOC is for seat holders to faithfully follow instructions from their home governments, human rights

Table 6.1 Freedom House classification of nations within proposed multinational regions, 2010

Region	Free		Partly free		Not free		Total	
	No.	%	No.	%	No.	%	No.	%
Africa South of the Sahara	9	20.9	21	48.8	13	30.2	43	100
Arab League	0	0	5	23.8	16	76.2	21	100
East Asia	3	50.0	2	33.3	1	16.7	6	100
Europe	38	92.7	3	7.3	0	0	41	100
Latin America & Caribbean	23	69.7	9	27.3	1	3.0	33	100
Russia & Neighbours	1	14.3	3	42.9	3	42.9	7	100
Southeast Asia	1	8.3	6	50.0	5	41.7	12	100
West Asia	0	0	4	36.4	7	63.6	11	100
Westminster League	11	73.3	4	26.7	0	0	14	100
Total	88	45.8	57	29.7	47	24.5	189	100

decisions should be based whenever possible on established principles rather than parochial political considerations. The virtually universal tendency for UN delegates to put the interests of their own country ahead of those of peoples whose human rights are being violated is, arguably, the principal reason why much of the work of the CHR/HRC is held in low regard. To correct this deficiency, holders of HRC seats ought to be *individually* vetted prior to election for their expertise in human rights law and experience in dealing with human rights issues.[25] Even now, as previously noted, independent rapporteurs and subject experts, including an 18-member advisory committee, provide the HRC with much of the empirical data and interpretative opinions needed for the execution of its work; but there is no guarantee that their expert advice will be followed. Recommended here is a system more likely to ensure that considerations of law and justice will prevail.[26]

Following their election, HRC members must have the freedom to speak and act in accordance with their understanding of the law. Even though their nominations would come from the countries whose worldview they would presumably represent, once elected they would have to be granted immunity (and, if necessary, sanctuary) for anything they say or do in performing their duties. Without such provisions the integrity and credibility of the HRC will be significantly compromised.

As in most governance organizations worldwide, representation in the United Nations is marked by striking gender imbalances.[27] That this should be the case in respect to the HRC, of all bodies, is particularly ironic and significantly diminishes its legitimacy.[28] Since offences against women are arguably the most pervasive of all human rights abuses, a female perspective seems especially important in dealing with them. Moreover, the perspective of women seems likely to provide a desirable complement to that of many males on many issues that are not gender-related. To ensure fair representation of both sexes in a reformed HRC, I propose that at least one man and one woman be chosen as representatives from each of the 12 regions from which selections would be made; and that neither males nor females shall be more than two-thirds of the total number of representatives from any region.

The status of indigenous peoples in international law has only belatedly been addressed by the United Nations as well as several nations with significant numbers of such persons among their population.[29] Although the sovereignty of indigenous peoples is more circumscribed than that of states which are UN members, their possession of wide-ranging sovereign rights (differing from country to country) is widely recognized. Indigenous peoples often entered into treaties with colonizing nations as if they were their legal equals, only to see their rights steadily and unilaterally eroded with the passage of time and their territories usurped by various means.[30] In recent decades a number of states have restored many rights and control of substantial tracts of land to numerous indigenous groups;[31] and in 1982 ECOSOC, responding to pressure from various NGOs, including the World Council of Indigenous Peoples and the International Indian Treaty Council, established a working group charged with responsibility for writing a universal declaration of the rights of indigenous "populations".[32] A draft declaration was put forward in 1993 and has been under consideration by the CHR and HRC ever since.[33] Article 3 of the draft is especially significant:

> Indigenous peoples have the right to self-determination. By virtue of that right they freely determine their political status and freely pursue their economic, social and cultural development.

Nowhere in the document, however, is there any claim to the right of secession. If there were, there would surely be insurmountable opposition by virtually every state with a significant indigenous population.

Although it would certainly be possible to maintain an HRC without the explicit representation of indigenous peoples, the time has come to rectify – at least in part – the injustice done to such peoples by allocating to them two seats – one for a male and one for a female – out of the total of 36 proposed. This would be, as it happens, in approximate proportion to the total of the world's people (roughly one-eighteenth) made up by indigenous groups.[34] While there is as yet no official definition of "indigenous people" (or, for that matter, of a "people" in general), this does not appear to be an insurmountable problem. The "working" definition proposed in 1986 by the special rapporteur for the Sub-Commission on Indigenous Populations has gained widespread acceptance:

> Indigenous communities, peoples and nations are those which, having a historical continuity with pre-invasion and pre-colonial societies that developed on their territories, consider themselves distinct from other sectors of the societies now prevailing in those territories, or parts of them. They form at present non-dominant sectors of society and are determined to preserve, develop and transmit to future generations their ancestral territories, and their ethnic identity, as the basis of their continued existence as peoples, in accordance with their own cultural patterns, social institutions and legal systems.[35]

Means of implementing structural recommendations

Recapitulating and expanding upon the recommendations made in the preceding discussion, a 36-member HRC would be constituted as follows:

- 24 seats assigned by region: two (one male and one female) for each of 12 regions – six seats for three single-nation regions (China, India and the United States), and 18 seats for nine multinational regions
- two additional seats (one male and one female) for indigenous peoples
- 10 seats elected at large from the 9 multinational regions, following the election of the 26 seats noted above; of these seats, no more than two (one male and one female) could go to a single nation.

Seats would be held for staggered three-year terms, 12 being open for election each year. Incumbents would be eligible for re-election only once.

Nominations from the single-nation regions would be made at the discretion of their respective governments. Nominations from multinational regions would normally be made from their respective caucuses in accordance with the rules established by each caucus, very likely – in some cases – by methods entailing weighted voting (see the discussions of weighted voting in Chapters 4 and 5). In the event that a regional caucus is unable to agree on a slate of candidates, individual countries from within the region would be at liberty to nominate their own candidates.

Nominations for seats for indigenous peoples would be made by the more than 200 representatives of indigenous groups who annually attend sessions of the Working Group on Indigenous Populations, using whatever nomination procedure is deemed appropriate. No two nominees, however, could come from the same world region.

For each open seat there would have to be at least two qualified *individual* candidates. Nominations would be required by mid-June of each year. Nominees would be objectively vetted by the UN High Commissioner for Human Rights, using standardized criteria, and appropriate reviews circulated to the delegations of all UN member nations not later than mid-July. Campaigning, under strict rules for fairness, would be permitted until September, in which month the GA would elect by secret ballot the authorized set of delegates. In cases where the votes cast did not yield the stipulated gender balance, the candidate with the highest number of votes among those of the requisite gender would be chosen.[36]

Were an elected delegate to become unable for any reason to perform his/her duties, he or she would be replaced for the balance of his/her term by the eligible candidate who obtained the next highest number of votes, with due regard to the rules on maximum numbers of delegates by region and gender.

All seat holders would cast equal (unweighted) votes. Decisions on procedural matters would require simple majorities of delegates present and voting. On substantive issues, decisions would require two-thirds majorities of those present and voting, thereby adding to the legitimacy of the relevant HRC resolutions.

Procedures

This chapter has argued that the UN's concern with human rights seems bound to expand in breadth and complexity, and there is a need to elevate the status of the HRC from its present subsidiary position under the purview of the GA to that of a principal organ of the UN system on a par with both the GA and the SC. To enhance its credibility, its delegates would have to be of exceptionally high calibre and free to speak and act without fear of retribution.[37]

Also required is a more prominent role for the OHCHR, and substantially greater funding than at present.[38] In light of the need for regular and close interaction between the OHCHR and the HRC, serious consideration should be given to having the HRC nominate a slate of suitable candidates for that position, leaving the final decision to the GA.

The proposed allocation of decision-making power in the HRC is fundamentally different from the recommendations put forward in earlier chapters for the GA, SC and ECOSOC. On pragmatic grounds, it will be recalled, it was deemed desirable for those bodies to make use of various forms of weighted voting whereby the ability to influence political decisions would have a reasonable relationship to the distribution of political power in the world outside the United Nations. In respect to human rights, however, *principle* should take precedence. Power tends to corrupt and does not provide a valid basis for moral authority. Rather, moral influence should flow from the conformity of one's arguments to the spirit and letter of the law and the appeal of those arguments to our shared humanity. Since this cannot be determined a priori, it follows that each HRC member should have an equal vote. While it would be expecting too much to anticipate debate and voting totally free from national or cultural bias, the suggested method of choosing HRC members and the freedom of those members to speak without fear of reprisal should go far towards promoting principled decisions meriting wide respect.

To ensure adequate time for debate, the term of the HRC should be lengthened. Presently it is much too short to engage effectively with all the issues that the HRC should address. Regular sessions should be expanded to at least four months per year and additional special sessions held as needed. Most of the mechanisms for dealing with human rights issues described earlier in this chapter are theoretically sound and should be retained. The HRC's 18-member advisory committee would become redundant, however, since the proposed new membership of 36 elected delegates would in itself be a merit-based group with substantial expertise.

Throughout the human rights system there is need for greater transparency and accountability and more efficient two-way information flows. This is true not only for agencies within the United Nations *per se*, but also for dealings between the United Nations and its member states. Greater use of the human rights infrastructure already established by regional organizations could facilitate such flows. Although the HRC cannot compel regional organizations to play major coordinative roles in human rights matters, they should be urged to do so. Regional human rights commissions, such as those already existing in Europe and proposed for Africa and Latin America, should be strongly encouraged. Such bodies could work closely with national commissions, related agencies and NGOs, and serve as conduits for human rights initiatives from the global to the local level as well as from the local to the global, thereby reducing the misguided perception that the UN's human rights agenda is, in essence, a means for imposing Western or Northern values on cultures of the global East or South and subverting national sovereignty.

More than in most matters of global concern, human rights issues have given rise to a burgeoning of NGOs, many of which are accredited to ECOSOC and have made useful contributions to UN projects. These contacts should be nurtured, expanded and, in some respects, regularized. The fledgling HRC now offers the most suitable entry point for doing so. To the extent that civil society organizations feel that they have a respected voice in the formulation of UN human rights policy, they will likely lend their much-needed support and expertise to the promotion and use of the UN system as a whole. In return, their being taken seriously by the United Nations will enhance their status in the countries where they operate. How best to strengthen and systematize the relationships of NGOs to the United Nations will be explored in Chapter 10.

The HRC is not intended to become a legislative organ, but it should have a role to play in respect to UN legislation, assuming that such legislation becomes possible. It was argued in Chapters 2 and 3 that the GA should, in fact, be given legislative capability (hopefully in concert with a World Parliamentary Assembly) in dealing with a limited range of matters of truly global concern that cannot be adequately addressed by nations acting on their own. Some such problems will undoubtedly relate to human rights and should be addressed in reports to the GA by the HRC.

Unlike the proposed weighted voting system for the GA and the partially weighted system suggested for ECOSOC/ESEC, all delegates to the HRC would cast a unitary vote, since the independent interpretation of principles rather than the expression of national political power should be decisive in making human rights decisions. One would expect, therefore, that in cases where the GA chose more than one delegate from a given country those delegates might, from time to time, vote on different sides on a particular issue. Such democratic practice is precisely what occurs in democratic national legislatures and would do much to heighten the legitimacy of HRC decisions, even though they would not be legally binding without further UN action.

Conclusion

Since its inception the United Nations has taken enormous strides in advancing the cause of human rights. The UDHR and an ever-expanding body of human rights treaties have set laudable standards for the whole of humanity, notwithstanding the fact that adherence to those standards is typically inadequate. In dealing with egregious breaches of human rights in particular parts of the world, however, UN performance has often been seriously flawed because of the high degree of politicization and frequent arbitrariness of the decision-making process. This has sullied the UN's reputation, cast doubt on its legitimacy, led to diminished national and popular support for the organization and provided a rationale for unilateral great-power initiatives (often contravening international law) in situations where the United Nations was deemed incapable of functioning effectively.

If there is any aspect of the UN system in which bold departures from established political practices are necessary, it is surely in the domain of human rights. This chapter proposes several such departures: electing members of an HRC primarily on the basis of their qualifications (while not totally ignoring their countries or regions of origin); ensuring that the perspectives of all major world regions are represented; mandating a better gender balance in the HRC; providing voices for indigenous peoples; and guaranteeing political immunity to delegates for actions taken in the performance of their duties that are contrary to the expressed interests of the states from which they come.

There is also need to strengthen the UN's human rights machinery, chiefly by establishing the HRC as a major organ on a par with the GA and SC; to allocate greater fiscal and personnel resources to human rights activities; and to intensify relevant monitoring and information flows among various components of the UN system, between the United Nations and its member states, as well as the major world regions, and between the United Nations and civil society.

The more innovative aspects of the proposals put forward in this chapter will surely meet with substantial opposition, not only from nations with a poor human rights record but also (for now) from the United States, which has little faith in the ability of the United Nations to perform as needed. Consequently, the prospects for implementing the recommended changes will remain poor until such time as there is a sea change in public opinion on the need to strengthen the UN system. Nor will such change come about without credible political leadership on UN reform from progressive nations drawn from both global North and South. The United States should form part of such a group. The likelihood that human rights abuses – even to the extent of another genocide – will of themselves become the catalyst for a reform movement with the requisite strength to achieve success is probably low. But, sooner or later, major global threats such as climate change or a serious and prolonged global economic collapse should result in an altered political situation in which improving human rights institutions will form a major part of a more comprehensive and enlightened reform movement. Having workable plans at the ready will hasten the willingness to act.

Pending the anticipated new era, it will still be possible to adapt and adopt specific components of the human rights reform package set forth in this chapter.

Notes

1. Though there were no dissenting votes, the then Soviet-led Eastern bloc of nations, South Africa and Saudi Arabia abstained.
2. In the absence of a clear definition of what constitutes a human rights NGO, it is impossible to provide even an approximate number. Many NGOs concerned with human rights also have other core concerns and their emphases may shift over time.
3. The principal sources consulted for this section were Bertrand G. Ramcharan, "Norms and Machinery", in Thomas G. Weiss and Sam Daws (eds), *The Oxford Handbook on the United Nations*, Oxford and New York: Oxford University Press, 2007, pp. 439–462; Julie A. Mertus, *The United Nations and Human Rights: A Guide for a New Era*, London and New York: Routledge, 2003; Gerd Oberleitner, *Global Human Rights Institutions, Between Remedy and Removal*, Cambridge: Polity, 2007; Joshua Cooper, "Revised Human Rights Structures at UN", *Minerva* 34, May 2009, pp. 35–41.
4. The relevant articles for ECOSOC are 62 and 68. For other UN entities see Articles 1, for the United Nations in general; 13(1), relating to the General Assembly; 55 and 56, applicable to member states; and 76, relating to the Trusteeship Council.
5. For a general statement of the official position see Navanethem Pillay, "Are Human Rights Universal?", *UN Chronicle* 2/3, 2008, pp. 4–8.
6. The phrase is that of Ramcharan, note 3 above, p. 441. The discussion of the differences between the ICCPR and ICESCR is based primarily on this source.
7. A detailed organization chart of the UN human rights system, as of 1994, appears in Erskine Childers and Brian Urquhart, *Renewing the United Nations System*, Uppsala: Dag Hammarskjöld Foundation, 1994. Complex though that chart is, it would have been substantially more so had it related to the situation at the dissolution of the CHR in 2006. Useful thumbnail sketches of some 26 UN bodies with a significant human rights nexus are provided in Mertus, note 3 above, Appendix A, pp. 166–177.
8. Increases were from 18 to 21 members in 1962, 32 in 1967–1968, 43 in 1980 and 63 in 1992.
9. The objectives and key provisions of each of these and other human rights treaties, as well as the dates of their adoption and entry into force and dates of signature and ratification by all acceding countries, are indicated in *Multilateral Treaty Framework: An*

Invitation to Universal Participation, New York: United Nations, 2005. The text of these and other human rights treaties (those adopted up to 1983) as well as of relevant international proclamations and declarations will be found in *Human Rights, A Compilation of International Instruments*, New York: United Nations, 1983.

10. Childers and Urquhart, note 7 above, pp. 109–110.

11. For a comprehensive critique see Andrew Hudson, "Dangerous Potential: Streamlining the United Nations Human Rights Committees", *Australian Journal of Human Rights* 13, 2002, www.austlii.edu.au/journals/AJHR/2002/15.html.

12. Cooper, note 3 above, p. 40.

13. Complete yearly data are provided by UN Human Rights Council, http://www2.ohchr.org/english/bodies/hrcouncil/membership.htm.

14. Failure to contest seats carried over from the CHR to the HRC: in the 2009 elections only 20 countries ran for the 18 open seats; when the United States decided to contest a seat, New Zealand diplomatically withdrew its well-merited candidacy.

15. India and the Soviet Union/Russia served without a break from 1947 to 2006. France served every year but 1977, the United Kingdom every year but 1979 and the United States every year but 2002 and 2006. When the HRC was created in 2006 the United States decided not to run for a seat, but changed its position in 2009 and was duly elected. The People's Republic of China first ran for a seat in 1982, and was then re-elected without a break until 2005.

16. High-level Panel on Threats, Challenges and Change, "A More Secure World: Our Shared Responsibility", UN GA Doc. A/59/565, 2004, para. 283.

17. On 4 May 2004 the United States walked out of the CHR in protest against the uncontested election of Sudan to that body, notwithstanding Sudan's policy of ethnic cleansing, if not – as many would assert – genocide, in Darfur.

18. Oberleitner, note 3 above, pp. 146–149.

19. International Commission on Intervention and State Sovereignty, *The Responsibility to Protect*, Ottawa: International Development Research Centre, 2001.

20. For an exceedingly thorough analysis of the problem see Ambassador Richard W. Williamson, "Sudan and the Implications for Responsibility to Protect", Policy Analysis Brief, October 2009, Stanley Foundation, Muscatine, IA.

21. Termination was recommended by Secretaries-General Boutros Boutros-Ghali and Kofi Annan, in 1994 and 2005 respectively, and endorsed at the GA's 2005 World Summit; but needed follow-up action was not taken. Ralph Wilde, "Trusteeship Council", in Thomas G. Weiss and Sam Daws (eds), *The Oxford Handbook on the United Nations*, Oxford and New York: Oxford University Press, 2007, pp. 149–159.

22. E.g. World Health Organization, 15 September 2005, paras 1.38–1.39; Resolution 1674 (2006), www.who.int/htv/universalaccess2010/worldsummit.pdf.

23. High-level Panel, note 16 above, para. 286; Kofi Annan, "In Larger Freedom: Towards Development, Security and Human Rights for All", UN GA Doc. A/59/2005, 2005, para. 183.

24. The regions need not be fixed, however, and a system allowing UN member nations to belong simultaneously to two regions would be feasible.

25. The High-level Panel on Threats, Challenges and Change, note 16 above, para. 286, recommended that "all members of the Commission on Human Rights designate prominent and experienced human rights figures as the heads of their delegations".

26. Childers and Urquhart, note 7 above, pp. 108–109, argue for a "new kind of forum ... at a level above the [then] Human Rights Commission, a place of intellectual enquiry and discussion, engaging exceptional women and men well-versed in precepts and practices of governance ... [bringing] these together with innovative and highly knowledgeable minds from many disciplines and from non-governmental organizations. ... [and]

broadly representative of the cultures and regions of the membership of the United Nations". This chapter proposes a council that would *replace* the present HRC, rather than being instituted *above* it. The latter option, I believe, would either lead to conflict between the two bodies or, if not, make the HRC redundant.

27. Imbalances within the UN system are documented in Thomas G. Weiss, *What's Wrong with the United Nations and How to Fix It*, Malden, MA: Polity, 2009, pp. 115–119.

28. In June 2011, following the successive elections of five males as president of the HRC, the body finally chose its first woman president. Figures on the gender breakdown among the 47 elected delegates are unavailable, but only four of the 18 members of the HRC's advisory committee were women as of mid-2012. A happy contrast is provided by the OHCHR; of its six high commissioners, three (Mary Robinson, Louise Arbour and Navanethem Pillay) have been women and women have held that post for 12 out of 18 years from its inception in 1994 to 2012.

29. For a succinct discussion of the rights of indigenous peoples see Maivân Clech Lâm, "Minorities and Indigenous Peoples", in Thomas G. Weiss and Sam Daws (eds), *The Oxford Handbook on the United Nations*, Oxford and New York: Oxford University Press, 2007, pp. 532–535. The relationship of indigenous peoples to various components of the UN system is treated in Julian Burger, "Indigenous Peoples and the United Nations", in Cynthia Price Cohen (ed.), *Human Rights of Indigenous Peoples*, Albany, NY: Transnational Publishers, 1998, pp. 3–16; "Indigenous Peoples and the United Nations System, An Overview", author unspecified (probably Working Group on Indigenous Peoples), Leaflet No. 1, circa 2001, available at www.ohchr.org/Documents/Publications/GuideIPleaflet1en.pdf. A more comprehensive presentation is Siegfried Wiessner, "Rights and Status of Indigenous Peoples: A Global Comparative and International Legal Analysis", *Harvard Human Rights Journal* 12, 1999, pp. 57–128.

30. Until 1871, for example, the US Senate ratified treaties with Native American tribes in the same way as it did with sovereign nations in general. Until then, "all of the American Indian treaties appeared to have the nature, as well as the force and effect of international treaty obligations". Wiessner, ibid., p. 97.

31. The most noteworthy example of restoration of territorial control to indigenous peoples is the creation of Nunavut, in northern Canada, in 1999. With a total area of roughly 1.9 million square km (750,000 square miles), Nunavut is the fifth-largest subnational political entity in the world and, if independent, would rank as the world's fifteenth-largest state. Its population, 85 per cent Inuit (Eskimo), is, however, estimated to be a mere 33,000.

32. The use of the word "populations" rather than "peoples" was intentional, in that the UN Charter stipulates that all *peoples* have the right of "self-determination". Even though there is as yet no satisfactory legal definition of "people", the recognition of indigenous populations as "peoples" would imply their right to self-determination and could lead to literally hundreds of unmanageable secessionist demands. Nevertheless, the United Nations did proclaim 1993 as the International Year for the World's Indigenous Peoples (*sic*).

33. The full text of this declaration appears in Cynthia Price Cohen (ed.), *Human Rights of Indigenous Peoples*, Albany, NY: Transnational Publishers, 1998, pp. 377–387.

34. The worldwide total of indigenous peoples was estimated as approximately 300 million in 1993. Extrapolating from that figure, their total population in 2010 would be about 370 million or roughly one-eighteenth of the world total. The country with the largest number of indigenous people is India. "Scheduled tribes", as they are officially designated, account for more than 8 per cent of India's total population and would now be more than 90 million persons, roughly a fourth of the world total.

35. José R. Martínez Cobo, *Study of the Problem of Discrimination against Indigenous Peoples: Conclusions and Recommendations*, Vol. 5, New York: United Nations, 1987,

article 379; cited in Lâm, note 29 above, p. 533. The problem of self-identification introduced by Cobo's definition could create difficulties, especially in Africa, where the question of who is and is not indigenous is not especially salient. On this point see Ayitégan G. Kouevi, "The Right of Self-Determination of Indigenous Peoples: Natural or Granted? An African Perspective", in Pekka Aikio and Martin Scheinin (eds), *Operationalizing the Right of Indigenous Peoples to Self-Determination*, Turku/Abo: Abo Akademi, Institute for Human Rights, 2000, pp. 143–153. For a worldwide conspectus of indigenous groups, with particular regard to their relation to their surrounding societies, see Julian Burger, *The Gaia Atlas of Indigenous Peoples: A Future for the Indigenous World*, New York: Anchor Books, 1988.

36. Given the rule of having a maximum of two-thirds of elected seats for either gender, a region with three seats would have to have a two-to-one gender split; a region with four seats must have an even division; and a region with five seats would have a three-to-two division.

37. This presumes that delegates will be granted diplomatic immunity from prosecution and guaranteed the right of political asylum if and when that becomes necessary.

38. Because it is not possible to disentangle primarily human rights concerns from other issues with a human rights dimension, such as peacekeeping or development, one cannot assign a precise dollar total to UN support for human rights in any recent year. However, by any standard it would be embarrassingly small. The High-level Panel on Threats, Challenges and Change, note 16 above, para. 290, noted that support for the OHCHR came to only 2 per cent of the regular UN budget.

7

A strengthened judicial system

We now have before us the opportunity to forge for ourselves and for future generations a new world order, a world where the rule of law, not the law of the jungle, governs the conduct of nations.
US President George H. W. Bush

Our ideal is a world community of States which are based on the rule of law and which subordinate their foreign policy activities to law.
Soviet General Secretary Mikhail Gorbachev

As an instrumentality for the maintenance of peace and human dignity, the promise of international law exceeds its performance. Law has not yet been able to bring order to the world. All nations pay lip service to prohibiting the use of force, yet very few are prepared unconditionally to abide by their professed restraints.
Benjamin B. Ferencz, Nuremberg war crimes prosecutor

Introduction[1]

Benjamin Ferencz put the matter as clearly and succinctly as anyone could:

[E]very orderly society is based on three foundations:
1. *Laws* to define minimum standards of behavior;
2. *Courts* to serve as a forum for the peaceful settlement of disputes and to determine if the agreed laws have been violated;
3. A system of effective law *enforcement.*[2] (Emphasis in original)

Transforming the United Nations system: Designs for a workable world, Schwartzberg, *United Nations University Press, 2013, ISBN 978-92-808-1230-5*

Chapter 6 considered standards of behaviour in regard to human rights and responsibilities. In Chapter 12 the focus is on persuasion and, in exceptional cases, enforcement where compliance with legal standards is seriously deficient. Here, the principal concern is with courts and analogous legally empowered tribunals. I begin with a brief review of the experience to date of international judicial and quasi-judicial bodies, noting both their successes and their numerous shortcomings. I then put forward recommendations for expanding and strengthening the global judicial infrastructure, both within and alongside the UN system. I acknowledge that the process will long and difficult, but conclude that it will inexorably go forward.

The record to date

Early efforts

It was not until the signing in The Hague, in 1899 and 1907, of the Convention for the Pacific Settlement of International Disputes that acceptance of arbitration or mediation became a widespread – though usually qualified and unreliable – political norm. The institutional fruit of this convention was the establishment of the still-functioning Hague-based Permanent Court of Arbitration. That name, however, is misleading; the so-called "court" is actually little more than a "list of arbitrators who would be available if called upon to settle disputes between states".[3] While it did enjoy modest successes, it was totally incapable of averting serious inter-state conflict, including the cataclysm of the First World War. Something more robust was needed.

Another early, but abortive, initiative was the establishment in 1908 of the Central American Court of Justice in San José, Costa Rica. This court, a true judicial body, considered few cases and was disestablished in 1918.[4]

The shock of the First World War led to a much more ambitious, but ultimately inadequate, attempt to create a judicial body to help maintain international peace. The Permanent Court of International Justice (PCIJ), established in The Hague in 1921 and dissolved in 1945, consisted of eminent jurists representing the major legal traditions of the world. Open to membership from all nations, it was competent to decide "any dispute of an international character which the parties thereto submitted to it".[5] Though the PCIJ did handle some 65 contentious cases and rendered 21 judgments and numerous advisory opinions during its brief existence, it failed to realize the hopes of its founders. The principal reasons – a lack of compulsory jurisdiction and an unwillingness to establish enforcement mechanisms – should have been evident with the benefit of hindsight; yet those same shortcomings now characterize the court's successor agency, the International Court of Justice (ICJ).[6]

The International Court of Justice[7]

Established in 1945, the ICJ replaced the PCIJ and occupies the same stately edifice, the Hague Peace Palace. It seemingly improves on its earlier incarnation in three respects. First, its membership is now virtually universal, extending automatically to all countries belonging to the United Nations.[8] Second, it imposes a legal obligation for parties to a dispute to comply with its rulings. Third, it grants to the UN Security Council the *right to enforce* those rulings in cases where they are flouted. Regrettably, however, the SC has not regarded its enforcement right as an *obligation* and has not once exercised it. In effect, then, the ICJ's authority depends on voluntary compliance. Moreover, the ICJ lacks compulsory jurisdiction, except in respect to some 67 states (as of mid-2012) that have accepted it in advance under the terms of Article 36, paragraph 2 of the ICJ's statute.[9] Absent such prior *ipso facto* general acceptance, both parties to a dispute must agree to have it adjudicated before it can be considered. More than any other deficiency, the absence of *universal compulsory jurisdiction and institutionalized enforcement mechanisms* cries out for correction.

Despite its shortcomings, the ICJ has performed numerous useful services. Its 15 justices, elected from nominees proposed by national groups in the Permanent Court of Arbitration, represent all parts of the world and, allegedly, all major cultures and legal systems. This in itself – along with universal membership – promotes a sense of international community. ICJ verdicts, in respect to both contentious cases and advisory opinions, have established a substantial body of legal precedent; and many ICJ rulings have been cited by national courts as applicable to domestic disputes.[10]

Contentious cases coming before the ICJ involve two state adversaries and result in theoretically binding rulings. As of mid-2011 there was a total of 124 such cases, averaging slightly more than two cases for each of the 66 years of the ICJ's existence. The number 124, however, is deceptively high. In the record year 1999, with 17 cases, no fewer than 10 were brought forward by either Yugoslavia or its successor state, Serbia & Montenegro, questioning the legality of the use of force by individual members of NATO, while Croatia brought another case against Serbia. Additionally, the Democratic Republic of the Congo brought three cases protesting armed activities within its territory by Rwanda, Burundi and Uganda. In no other year were more than six cases added to the ICJ's docket; and in 18 years, including the period 1962–1966, not a single contentious case was introduced. Overall, the ICJ remains greatly underutilized.

Willingness to resort to the ICJ in contentious cases varies markedly by regions and countries. Given their prominence in world affairs and the legal problems ensuing from decolonization, it is hardly surprising that four of the P-5 powers have been involved in numerous judicial disputes.[11] Of the ICJ's 124 contentious cases, the United States was a party, either as "applicant" (plaintiff) or "respondent" (defendant), in 21, France in 13, the United Kingdom in 11 and the USSR/Russia in 5. China, on the other hand, has not been a party in any ICJ dispute. The P-5 numbers might have been even higher were it not for the states' reluctance to submit to litigation when they felt doing so might result in an adverse verdict. Even though they knew in advance that their veto power would make SC enforcement of such a verdict impossible, the negative diplomatic fallout from defying the ICJ would have entailed an unacceptable political cost.

Additional factors have also limited use of the ICJ. Small and poor states often held back, recognizing that they could not match the legal resources of larger and richer nations. Rightly or wrongly, they believed the ICJ was incapable of protecting them from hostile actions by the great powers. And newly independent states, especially in Africa and Asia, often distrusted the ICJ, fearing it would rely on unfamiliar laws developed by their former colonial masters to protect their own national interests.[12] Hence the small number of cases involving countries in Africa and Asia: 22 for the 43 nations of Africa south of the Sahara, 10 for the 22 members of the Arab League and only 9 for the whole of Asia excluding the Arab nations.[13]

Countries of Europe and Latin America, on the other hand, have made relatively abundant use of the ICJ. European countries, exclusive of Russia, have been involved in 65 cases (52 per cent of the total) on widely varying topics; and the nations of Latin America in a total of 25, mainly involving territorial disputes on land, sea or both.

Subjects leading to ICJ litigation have been remarkably varied. Especially common are cases relating to the law of the sea. Less frequent, though well over a dozen cases, are disputes relating to land boundaries (generally involving relatively small areas). Several dozen cases have entailed allegedly improper use of military or paramilitary forces or acts of terrorism. One also encounters cases on seemingly trivial matters – for example a dispute between the Netherlands and Sweden to determine the applicability of a 1902 convention regarding the guardianship of infants.

Individuals, corporations, NGOs and other non-state entities may not bring cases before the court, but may be called on to give testimony. National governments, however, have sometimes acted on behalf of such parties, especially corporations, in pressing essentially economic suits.

Advisory opinions, which are non-binding, provide a court service available solely to UN agencies, ostensibly enabling them to deal better with matters within their purview. An ICJ ruling in regard to the use, or threatened use, of nuclear weapons, for example, was brought to a hearing because of a GA request in 1995. Only 26 advisory opinions have thus far been delivered, and not one request for an opinion was made between 1961 and 1970. As with contentious cases, subjects for advisory opinions are diverse. They have related, *inter alia*, to the conditions for the admission of new UN member states (1947 and 1949); the interpretation of various peace treaties (1949); the legal status and/or claims to self-determination of Southwest Africa/Namibia (1947, 1949, 1955 and 1970), Western Sahara (1974) and Kosovo (2008); reservations to the Convention on Genocide (1950); and maritime safety (1959). But most have concerned the dealings of various UN agencies with particular states or other entities within the UN system.

Even when national governments ignore an advisory opinion, the ICJ's authoritative legal pronouncements may provide ammunition for civil society groups in furthering worthy causes. Thus arguments by opponents of nuclear arms were fortified by the ICJ's 1996 opinion that use of nuclear weapons and even the *threat* to use them would be illegal under international law. Similarly, the 2003 opinion that the wall constructed by Israel in the occupied Palestinian territory of the West Bank was in contravention of international law has been frequently cited by peace activists in Israel and other countries. Civil society is not alone in referencing such opinions; states that would not undertake on their own to bring a case before the ICJ do not hesitate to cite advisory opinions when doing so proves convenient.

Most cases handled by the ICJ have involved the entire court. In 1982, however, in a dispute relating to the maritime boundary between the United States and Canada, a case was referred for the first time to an *ad hoc* chamber. The chamber consisted of only five judges mutually agreeable to the disputants. Since then (to mid-2009), five additional contentious cases have gone to such chambers, each with from three to five judges, thereby making better use of scarce judicial resources.[14]

Should the ICJ's docket expand substantially, the question of relying on chambers will assume greater importance given the time required – often years – to come to a decision in contentious cases. To cite but one example, it took more than 40 months, from 1951 to 1955, to settle a case brought by Liechtenstein against Guatemala establishing a precedent in international law in regard to a country's rights in recognizing foreign citizenship.

Also, the burden on the ICJ could be reduced by establishing additional regional courts or duly authorized circuit courts and specialized courts (e.g. for investment disputes), leaving to the higher court only those cases that cannot be satisfactorily settled at a lower level.[15]

Whatever its shortcomings, the ICJ is generally held in high regard. The probity and expertise of its judges, who are elected to nine-year renewable terms, are widely acknowledged. However, its gender bias is pronounced: of the 108 individuals having thus far served as judges only four have been women.[16]

Less glaring than the gender bias is the regionally disproportionate representation of judges.[17] Assuming the competence of all elected judges, this ought not be a serious problem; but in terms of political legitimacy it could be. One means of gauging representativeness would be to total the length of service by countries in various regions, counting each year served by a judge as a "judicial year". Using data for the 64-year period from 1946 to 2010, I derived an overall total of 955 such years.[18] Of these the totals for the global "North" and global "South" – now representing less than a fifth and more than four-fifths of humanity respectively – come to 518 (54.2 per cent) and 437 (45.8 per cent).[19] Of the judicial years served by nations of the global North, 256 (not quite half) were from the Northern members among the P-5 powers – France, the United Kingdom, the United States and the USSR/Russia – all of which have been continually represented on the ICJ since the court's inception. Five other Northern countries have provided judges accounting for totals of more than 20 judicial years each.

Within the global South one finds striking disparities. Judges from China served from 1946 until 1967 (then representing the Nationalist regime) and from 1985 onward (for the People's Republic), a total of 48 years. (China did not put up a candidate in the interim years.) The Latin American and Caribbean region has also been exceptionally well represented, and the Arab League fared reasonably well. Africa South of the Sahara, however, sent its first judge (from Senegal) to the ICJ only in 1964 and has provided just eight judges, drawn from five nations. Apart from China and Japan, Asia has been especially underrepresented, providing a total of only six judges (three of them from India).

Another indicator of ICJ influence is service as court president. Judges from 16 countries have served in this capacity (as of 2012). Of the total of 22 terms served, four have been from the United Kingdom; two each from France, Poland and the United States; and one from each of 11 other countries. Europe's dominance is clear and the four places for Latin America are noteworthy, but the total absence of the USSR/Russia is even more remarkable.

Evaluating ICJ experience to date, one would have to recognize the court's utility in defusing a number of *incidents* and *difficult situations* that, if unaddressed, could have greatly heightened tensions between states (even involving resort to arms) and would not have lent themselves to other forms of conflict resolution. But many issues brought before the court were of minor importance. Because of the rule that both parties to a dispute must consent to its adjudication, not a single *long-term dispute* involving major, or even middle-level, powers has been brought before, much less settled by, the ICJ. The court has done virtually nothing to address the dispute between India and Pakistan in respect to Kashmir; the Korean War; uprisings in Soviet satellites in Eastern Europe; the Cuban missile crisis; Chinese repression of Tibet; American military interventions in Viet Nam, Afghanistan, Iraq and numerous other countries; wars between Israel and neighbouring Arab states; and so forth. The list is long and – even in retrospect – frightening.

Ad hoc *criminal tribunals and the International Criminal Court*[20]

The Second World War led not only to the creation of the ICJ but also – thanks to the Nuremberg and Tokyo war crimes tribunals – to the establishment of a revolutionary new principle: that members of the international community had a moral and legal obligation to bring to justice *individual perpetrators* of serious criminal offences in violation of customary – even if not yet codified – international law. In the cited tribunals, however, it was only the major victors, rather than the whole of the United Nations or some other institutionalized group of nations, that carried out the legal proceedings. The laws the victors invoked were those of the Hague Conventions of 1899 and 1907, which placed limits on the practice of war, and the Geneva Conventions of 1929, relating to humanitarian behaviour.

Following the war crimes tribunals, the Cold War contributed to a prolonged hiatus in the development of international criminal courts. But the post-Second World War trials did establish the needed precedent for further action against *individual actors* believed to have participated in genocide, ethnic cleansing, crimes against humanity and war crimes, as well as the as-yet-undefined crime of aggression. Accordingly, in 1993 the SC established the International Criminal Tribunal for the Former Yugoslavia (ICTY), and the following year saw the creation of the International Criminal Tribunal for Rwanda (ICTR). As with earlier tribunals, *deterrence*, rather than lust for vengeance, motivated the SC's actions. Arrogant national leaders and their accomplices had to be shown they could face severe legal consequences for egregious criminal actions and that positions of authority did not give them legal immunity.

In addition to the ICTY and ICTR, *ad hoc* "hybrid" tribunals, drawing on both external and domestic staff and resources, were formed over the period 1999–2006 to deal with crimes committed in Bosnia & Herzegovina, Kosovo, Cambodia and Sierra Leone. Rather than adjudicating by permanent established courts comparable to the ICJ, these tribunals were *ad hoc,* dealing only with offences committed over a specific space and time. But such procedures are inefficient and costly.[21] They were also highly politicized and unfair to some of the defendants. This led to recognition that something better was needed.

In 1989 the dormant idea of establishing a *permanent* international criminal court was revived by A. N. R. Robinson, then prime minister of Trinidad & Tobago, speaking at a gathering of Parliamentarians for Global Action; and it gradually acquired momentum among both governments and civil society.[22] Not until July 1998, however, at a GA-convened conference in Rome, was agreement reached on the Statute of the International Criminal Court. Thereafter, in remarkably short time, the statute attained the requisite 60 ratifications to bring it into force in July 2002. This confirmed the principle that *individuals, as well as states, can be objects of international law* and instituted a new global norm that *no person, no matter how high in rank, should be above the law.*[23]

By mid-2012 the number of ratifying nations, known as "states parties", had risen to 116, including virtually all the nations of Europe and South America, well over half the nations of Africa, Japan, the Republic of Korea, Canada, Australia and New Zealand. Conspicuously absent, however, are the United States, Russia, China, India and almost all predominantly Muslim nations. In fact, the administration of President George W. Bush, needlessly fearful that the ICC might provide a means for prosecuting American personnel serving overseas, waged a global campaign to diminish the court's authority.[24]

Based in The Hague, the ICC is governed by the Assembly of States Parties, wherein each member nation casts a single vote. The assembly meets annually and elects the ICC's 18 judges, no two of the same nationality. Judges serve for nine years. The court also includes the Office of the Prosecutor, which is independently responsible for conducting investigations and prosecutions. Its expenses are borne by the states parties, according to a formula based on their economic capacity.

Presently, the ICC's jurisdiction is limited to genocide, war crimes and crimes against humanity, each defined within the 1998 Rome Statute. The crime of aggression will be added to this brief list once its definition is duly ratified. Jurisdiction is limited in several other ways. It is applicable only to crimes committed in the territory of the states parties or by their citizens in other nations or that are referred to the ICC by the SC. Additionally, the statute applies only to crimes committed after its coming into force in 2002. Finally, based on the principle of "complementarity", the ICC can prosecute only when a national court is unable or unwilling to try an indictee on its own. A historically innovative feature of the ICC is its empowerment to order individuals to pay *reparations* to their victims.

As of mid-2012 the ICC had opened investigations in only six situations: first in respect to the Democratic Republic of the Congo, in June 2004; and then with northern Uganda; the Darfur region of Sudan; and Kenya, the Central African Republic and Libya. The indictment in March 2009 of Sudan's president, Omar Hassan Ahmad al-Bashir, for war crimes and crimes against humanity marked the first time that a *sitting head of state* has been indicted by any international tribunal. The second occurred in June 2011, when the ICC ordered the arrest of the since-deceased Libyan president, Muammar Gaddafi. Of the 26 individuals indicted as of June 2012, 11 remain at large. Only four trials have begun and only two have been concluded, one by an acquittal and the other because of the death of the defendant.[25]

Critics of the ICC have voiced concerns about its actual, or possible, unintended consequences. They suggest that fear of being held accountable for their crimes will cause indicted individuals in conflict areas to fight even harder. They note that in retaliation for being indicted, Sudanese President al-Bashir expelled most NGOs working with internally displaced persons in Darfur, thereby causing even greater suffering.[26] They indicate that war crimes trials could run at cross-purposes to the actual or future working of truth and reconciliation commissions of the type instituted in South Africa. They point out that, given the ICC's limited resources and complicated rules of procedure, only a small fraction of alleged criminals can be brought to trial. In this respect, the Rwanda genocide (occurring prior to the ICC's establishment) is instructive. Apart from the small group of major perpetrators indicted (fewer than 70) and tried (fewer than 50) by the ICTR, another 6,500 or so individuals have undergone trials in customary, so-called *gacaca*, courts in Rwanda itself, while another 80,000 are still (as of 2007) in prison and awaiting trial.[27]

While it is still too early to evaluate the utility of the fledgling ICC, its creation does mark a major step forward in global governance. Many observers, however, remain wary of this development. They feel the ICC poses a threat to national sovereignty, notwithstanding the many relevant jurisdictional and procedural safeguards built into the Rome Statute. They presume that it could constrain a state's freedom of action, especially regarding use of force against terrorists and other perceived internal and external enemies. Critics from the global South, especially Africa, allege that the ICC is but another tool of Northern neocolonialism. A final complaint is that the ICC is excessively costly and funds spent for it could better be utilized for other humanitarian purposes. This complaint ignores the fact that conducting fair jury trials in domestic courts is also costly, yet is deemed worth the expense because of the transcendent value of providing justice.

Other global international organization tribunals[28]

Globalization has brought about an ever-expanding and increasingly varied need to regulate economic and other transnational activities and handle related conflicts of interest. It has led to a bewildering array of specialized international organizations (IOs). Including regional bodies, approximately 300 such organizations were in existence as of 2006, nearly 40 of which incorporate judicial or quasi-judicial tribunals and dispute-resolving mechanisms. Even so, the supply of such mechanisms falls far short of the potential demand.[29]

The United Nations and numerous other IOs were recognized by the ICJ in 1949 as "international legal personalities". As such, they and other IOs subsequently created – including some, such as the World Trade Organization (WTO), outside the UN system – can interact autonomously with states in ways that were unthinkable in an earlier, more purely Westphalian era. They may also interact with one another as shapers of customary international law and occasionally as judicial bodies.

The development and codification of international law as it relates to the activities of IOs, as well as of states, are the purview of the 34-member International Law Commission (ILC), established by the GA in 1948. ILC members – no two nationals of the same state – are elected by the GA to five-year terms. They meet annually in Geneva for 10–12 weeks and have been instrumental in drafting a number of important treaties relating to international diplomacy and treaty making.

Although the vast majority of IOs were established after the Second World War, especially following conclusion of the Cold War, some of the most effective and widely respected are considerably older. Of particular note are the International Telecommunications Union (1865), Universal Postal Union (1874) and International Labour Organization (ILO, 1919), all of which have since become "affiliated agencies" of the UN system.[30] While the work of some affiliated agencies is well known – e.g. the World Health Organization (WHO), UNESCO and the Food and Agriculture Organization (FAO) – most (e.g. the International Civil Aviation Organization) perform mundane and obscure regulatory functions. Nations almost universally choose to follow the regulations of the specialized agencies as if they had the force of law, because doing so makes for a more orderly world and is in their economic and social interest. And when differences do arise among member states, the agencies normally manage to devise amicable resolutions through their respective governance mechanisms.

In this regard some of them may be seen as possessing judicial or quasi-judicial competence.[31]

While IO regulations may not be strictly regarded as "law", their long-standing application and – on many issues – virtually universal acceptance gives them the character of "soft law". In that sense the rulings of affiliated agencies and the norms they endorse are often cited in deciding contentious cases coming before various courts and tribunals and in crafting advisory opinions. Additionally, the expertise of IOs has been important in shaping numerous treaties relating to issues within their purview.

Many IOs serve important roles in complementing the work of other insufficiently resourced world and regional courts. By way of illustration, I note below the judicial and quasi-judicial work of three such bodies: the ILO, the WTO and the International Tribunal for the Law of the Sea.[32]

The International Labour Organization

Among IOs, the venerable, Geneva-based ILO is distinctive in its innovative tripartite governance structure. Half of its 56-member governing body is elected from among its member states (182 as of 2009); the other half represents management/employers and labour, with 14 members from each. Core ILO functions are to establish acceptable labour standards, help in framing relevant treaties and monitor observance and protection of labour norms by member states. However, it may also serve as a formal tribunal when a complaint of non-compliance is brought before it or – at its discretion – refer cases to the ICJ or ask the ICJ for an advisory opinion. Complaints may come from member states, workers or employer delegates. The respondents are invariably ILO member states. On receiving a complaint, the ILO governing body submits it to the appropriate member and offers it a chance to respond. Failing such action, the governing body may create a commission of inquiry to look into the case, render a verdict and prescribe corrective action. The offending state usually complies, but may appeal the verdict to the ICJ, which may then uphold, alter or reverse the commission's decision. The ILO accepts ICJ findings as final. As of 2002, 10 commissions of inquiry had been constituted, 2 based on complaints by member states, 6 on complaints by workers and 2 on complaints submitted by the governing body itself.[33]

Additionally, the ILO actively promotes prevention and voluntary settlement of disputes between management and labour through conciliation and mediation, arbitration, adjudication by a tribunal or labour court and, increasingly, types of "alternative dispute resolution", de-emphasizing legalistic methods in favour of unconventional "workplace justice". While many disputes coming before the ILO are not international in nature, the precedents and norms established by that agency have important international implications.

The World Trade Organization

Founded in 1995, the Geneva-based WTO is the successor to the never fully institutionalized General Agreement on Tariffs and Trade (GATT). Its membership as of 2009 included 153 states, which collectively accounted for more than 95 per cent of international trade. Each member officially has one vote, but almost all decisions are made by consensus. Consensus, however, inevitably requires explicit concurrence among the world's major trading powers, typically obtained through informal discussions from which weaker states are excluded.

Most WTO work relates to the progressive liberalization of trade. It monitors compliance with scores of commercial treaties relating to agriculture, trade in services, intellectual property rights, technical barriers to trade, food safety, etc. Without doubt the WTO has had an enormous influence in expanding world trade and lowering transaction costs. Nevertheless, it has come under widespread criticism for systematic bias in favour of multinational corporations – at the expense of labour and the environment – and, allegedly, for widening the income gap between the rich and the poor. A particularly trenchant complaint is that the WTO continues to allow heavy government subsidies to producers of basic commodities (e.g. cotton, maize, soybeans and sugar beets) in the United States and Europe, thereby undermining the economies of developing countries producing those commodities without subsidization.

Inevitably, disputes arise when WTO members complain of rule violations. Evidence is then reviewed in secret by appointed "appellate bodies", whose findings are presented to the WTO General Council (a committee of the whole). Appellate bodies may request *amicus curiae* testimony, but non-state actors generally have no right to provide such testimony unless it is solicited.[34] Following judgments, the council recommends actions to bring the offending state into compliance with relevant treaties. Compliance is almost always obtained, despite the absence of institutionalized enforcement mechanisms.[35]

The International Tribunal for the Law of the Sea

Created in pursuance of the UN Convention on the Law of the Sea, entering into force in 1996, the Hamburg-based maritime tribunal received its first case the following year. Membership includes 157 countries (as of 2009), plus the European Union. (The United States is not a member.) The tribunal's purpose is to provide a comprehensive system for settling disputes arising in respect to the convention's extensive rules regarding territorial jurisdiction over ocean space, exploration for and exploitation of maritime resources, pollution, navigation, research, naval activity and other subjects. But not all such disputes come before the tribunal, since disputing parties may refer cases instead to the ICJ or specially consti-tuted arbitral bodies. Like the ICJ, the tribunal tries "contentious cases" and may also deliver "advisory opinions"; unlike the ICJ, it is open not only to members (i.e. "states parties") but to other actors as well, includ-ing "natural and juridical persons" and "state enterprises".[36]

The states parties elect 21 judges for staggered nine-year terms, with no two judges coming from the same country. The tribunal assigns much of its work to issue-specific and *ad hoc* chambers. Since its first hearings in 1997 it has delivered judgments in only 15 contentious cases (as of 2009). Nine of these involved seizures of ships, cargoes and crews in re-sponse to alleged infractions of the law committed in foreign territorial waters. Most such cases pitted relatively powerful countries against much weaker ones (e.g. France versus the Seychelles); but two involved Japa-nese fishing vessels seized in Russian seas. No case concerned an issue of major international importance, and none has involved significant territo-rial claims.

Regional courts[37]

Important though they are, judicial bodies functioning at the global level are able to deal with only a small proportion of judicable international controversies. Recognizing this deficiency, a number of regional organiza-tions have seen the wisdom of establishing their own courts to deal with international disputes, even including, in certain cases, individual legal complaints with an international dimension. The following discussion re-fers to significant regional initiatives.

As in other international domains, Europe leads the way. Within Europe, non-domestic judicial responsibilities are divided between two main courts. Human rights cases are the responsibility of the European Court of Human Rights, an organ of the Council of Europe, whose jurisdiction extends to all 47 member states. In the less inclusive European Union, now comprising 27 states, the European Court of Justice is responsible for interpreting European law and ensuring its equal application among all members. The two courts cooperate extensively.

Of the two, the Luxembourg-based Court of Justice (officially the Court of Justice of the European Communities) is the older body, having been established in 1952 to meet legal needs of the European Coal and Steel Community. Its jurisdiction expanded in tandem with expansion of the functions and territorial extent of the several communities now incor-porated within the European Union. The court has 27 judges (one for each member country) assisted by eight advocates-general, working mainly in chambers of three or five judges, depending on the nature of the case, or – in especially important cases – as a grand chamber of 13 judges or even in plenary sessions. It deals not only with cases involving two or more member nations but also as an arbiter in disputes relating to the EU's governance and administrative institutions.

The Strasbourg-based European Court of Human Rights was established in 1959. Previously, cases involving serious human rights violations were submitted to the European Commission on Human Rights (created in 1954), whose capacity was rather limited. Even after the court's creation, individuals could not gain access to it without first going through the commission. However, with the adoption in 1998 of a protocol allowing individuals direct access to the court, the commission was abolished. The court was then converted into an institution open to 800 million Europeans (including those in most of Eastern Europe and Russia[38]). There is one judge for each of the 47 contracting parties; but each is expected to act independently rather than as an agent of his/her country of origin.

Applications against contracting parties for human rights violations may now be brought by other states, other parties or individuals. *For the first time in history an individual from one state is given the right to bring a legal suit against another state within a given region.* From 1998 onward the court's caseload expanded dramatically. Previously it had delivered 837 judgments; by the end of 2005 the number of judgments had risen to nearly 6,000, and there has since been a substantial judicial backlog. The range of issues addressed is broad, including such diverse topics as torture, preventive detention, extrajudicial executions (in Chechnya), religiously prescribed and secularly proscribed dress codes, public display of religious symbols and so forth.

In 1979, following Europe's lead, the Organization of American States (OAS) established a regional court, the Inter-American Court of Human Rights, with its seat in San José, Costa Rica. The court functions pursuant to the 1969 American Convention on Human Rights and its jurisdiction extends to all OAS members. It accepts cases only after review by the Commission on Human Rights, established in 1968 with headquarters in Washington, and its caseload is in no way comparable to that of the major European courts.

The Caribbean subregion has also undertaken significant judicial initiatives. The Caribbean Court of Justice was established in 2001. Based in Port of Spain, Trinidad, its jurisdiction extends to 11 anglophone Caribbean nations plus Suriname, and overlaps that of the Eastern Caribbean Supreme Court, established in 1967, which handles cases for six independent states and three British dependencies.

Inspired by the example of Europe, the Organization for African Unity and its successor organization, the African Union (AU), have taken promising steps towards creating courts analogous to those of Europe. The African Commission on Human Rights and Peoples' Rights was established in 1986 as a quasi-judicial body. Its present headquarters is in Banjul, Gambia. The commission has 11 members elected by heads of state and government. Members promote and protect human and peoples' rights and interpret a human rights charter. An African decision taken in 1998 to establish a Court on Human Rights and Peoples' Rights has yet to be implemented. In 2003 an AU protocol authorized establishment of a Court of Justice of the African Union. This court is intended to rule on disputes over interpretation of AU treaties; it could be merged with the not-yet-operational Court on Human Rights and Peoples' Rights and based in Arusha, Tanzania.

Also noteworthy is the Economic Court of the Commonwealth of Independent States, founded in 1992 and headquartered in Minsk, Belarus.[39] This court was intended to deal mainly with issues arising from the break-up of the Soviet Union, but only eight of the 12 Soviet republics that formed the CIS (Commonwealth of Independent States) in 1991 opted to join.[40] Rendering its first decisions in 2004, the court has since reached numerous verdicts in contentious cases as well as issuing advisory opinions. But many of its rulings have not been well received, being based on a confusing mix of post-Soviet republican, old Soviet and international law, and they are generally not regarded as binding.[41] Despite some structural strengthening, the court's future seems problematic.

Finally, we may note some conspicuous absences. Asia in particular is lacking in regional courts. There appears, however, to be some prospect for a future court in the economically well-integrated Southeast Asian (sub)region, in which ASEAN is an increasingly vital actor. East, South and Southwest Asia, on the other hand, do not appear ripe for a court of any kind. In the Arab League, where one might envisage a court based on Sharia law, there is little movement towards creating such a body. Finally, one might think of the Commonwealth of Nations as an international league amenable to a court based on British common law; but I am aware of no serious initiative to establish such an entity.

Recommendations[42]

As the foregoing accounts make clear, there are many possible judicial and quasi-judicial means for resolving – or preventing – international disputes. No single model provides an obvious best fit for all contentious situations. Further, the world's judicial infrastructure, despite recent additions, remains seriously underdeveloped. If, for example, one considers the thousands of cases coming before the European Court of Human Rights since 1998, one can only imagine the enormous backlog the world would confront if all regions were to follow Europe's example in trying to redress legitimate human rights grievances. Paradoxically, however, much of the infrastructure already in place remains underutilized. In particular, much ICJ expertise that could be applied to resolving disputes of global importance has been allocated to settling relatively minor cases that could have been adjudicated by less prestigious jurists, often at the regional level, if the requisite institutions existed. Finally, as demonstrated by the WTO, when tribunals do arrive at resolutions deemed to be *legal*, they will not necessarily be regarded as *just*. The system is capable of substantial improvement. Some recommendations follow.

The ICJ should assert – and be granted – a right to engage in judicial review of the legality of actions of other components of the world's judicial system and agencies within the UN system. When the court is not so engaged, it should focus on *important* cases that pose serious threats to international peace and security. To the extent possible, it should consign applicants in matters of lesser urgency to lower or more specialized courts. All disputes involving maritime law, for example, should be delegated to the International Tribunal for the Law of the Sea. To increase their capability to handle an expanding docket, both tribunals (and others as well) should work increasingly through chambers including only a part of the court's membership.

The jurisdiction of the ICC must be expanded. At a minimum it should include the crime of aggression. Additional domains in which the ICC should be empowered to act – when appropriate action cannot be taken at a national or regional level – should include illicit dealings in the arms trade, piracy and terrorism (by both state and non-state actors). Regional organizations should be encouraged to establish their own equivalents to the ICC wherever possible.

Courts in general should seek to enhance access to adjudication by non-states parties, especially international governmental organizations and international NGOs. In the case of the ICJ this would require amending the court's statute, admittedly a difficult task in that the statute is regarded as part of the UN Charter. Courts in general should also solicit more *amicus curiae* submissions from competent non-state agencies and be more receptive to unsolicited submissions from them.

Following good-faith efforts to resolve an international dispute through bilateral diplomacy, conciliation, mediation and/or arbitration, the SC should be authorized to assign the dispute to whichever court it deems best suited to handle it or, where feasible, mandate *compulsory* mediation or arbitration. The SC should also be more proactive in working with both the ICJ and the ICC. It should establish a post of senior legal adviser; assign more cases to the ICJ than has been its previous practice; recommend indictment by the ICC of egregious criminals, even in cases where states parties to the ICC statute refrain from doing so; authorize – assuming the possibility of success – the apprehension of such criminals by appropriately designated police acting under UN authority; and enforce ICJ decisions whenever possible.

Minimizing SC application of double or multiple standards is particularly important. Presently, it is virtually impossible to call any of the veto-wielding P-5 powers to account for alleged criminal behaviour. And while the SC might, in theory, take action against any other state, its frequent lack of political will and its inadequate enforcement capability – even when the will is present – immunizes many states (not just the P-5) from condemnation and punitive action. Relatively weak nations justifiably complain that they alone are subject to the SC's political decisions. This morally unacceptable situation will not change appreciably until the veto is eliminated (a possibility explored in Chapter 4) and more reliable peacekeeping and peacebuilding regimes are initiated (discussed in Chapter 12).

The GA should, in a phased manner, authorize establishment or expansion of a number of specialized judicial and quasi-judicial tribunals, including the proposed World Court of Human Rights, and budget the requisite financial resources. Budgetary reform (discussed in Chapter 11) will facilitate this process. The foci for new tribunals would likely be quite varied and might include, for example, crimes against the environment, trafficking in human beings and in transplantable human organs, the narcotics trade, sponsorship of terrorism, the arms trade, (mis)use of the internet and international financial fraud.

The GA should also promote establishment of new regional and subregional courts, especially human rights tribunals, and allocate funds to the UN Secretariat to provide relevant technical expertise where needed and requested. Where regional organizations decline to create such bodies or these organizations do not function, the GA should – after a suitable waiting period – establish circuit courts to serve as courts of first instance and thereby lighten the ICJ's excessive caseload. Finally, the GA might authorize monitoring the functioning and alleged malpractices of the WTO, among other agencies, and call for needed corrective measures, even though it might not yet have the power (apart from its moral authority) to ensure their being carried out.

Regional and subregional organizations should, on their own initiative, expand the scope of their judicial and police systems, seek greater coordination with UN and other global agencies (e.g. INTERPOL) in respect to infractions of international law and seek to enforce judicial decisions taken at the global and regional levels.

The annual sessions of the International Law Commission should be substantially extended and its work should be given greater prominence.

States should be required, by treaty, to incorporate within all future treaties provisions indicating the means by which relevant disputes shall be settled.

Finally, there is a need to increase the participation of women in judiciary bodies. Although the general practice of having no more than one justice from a single country in international tribunals may inhibit this trend, the proposal to have ICJ justices – and possibly others as well – nominated by the proposed Human Rights Council, in which women would constitute no less than one-third the total membership, should contribute substantially to achieving better balance.

Conclusion

Over the past century, and especially since the Second World War, the human family has taken appreciable strides in establishing judicial and quasi-judicial institutions with global or regional scope. Nevertheless, these advances represent no more than a beginning, given the magnitude of the task of establishing regimes that will ensure universal access to legal remedies to injustice. Some regions, most notably Europe, are in the vanguard of the march towards that goal. Others are trying, but have a long way to go. Still others seemingly attach little importance to the promotion of human rights. The UN system, in concert with other global agencies, has the potential greatly to enhance the human rights infrastructure. Regional agencies can play a major role. Entrenched interests, which benefit from the existing order, will of course staunchly resist change and rely on the mantle of national sovereignty as a basis for doing so. Thus progress will be fitful and initially slow. But the entrenched interests will ultimately fail. The struggle for just governance is inexorable and will gather momentum in the generations ahead.

Notes

1. The principal sources for this chapter are Benjamin B. Ferencz, *New Legal Foundations for Global Survival: Security through the Security Council*, New York: Oceana Publications, 1994; official website of the International Court of Justice, http://icj-cij.org; James Crawford and Tom Grant, "International Court of Justice", in Thomas G. Weiss and Sam Daws (eds), *The Oxford Handbook on the United Nations*, Oxford and New York: Oxford University Press, 2007, pp. 193–213; Gerd Oberleitner, *Global Human Rights Institutions, Between Remedy and Removal*, Cambridge: Polity, 2007, pp. 152–163.
2. Ferencz, ibid., p. viii.
3. Ibid., p. 41.
4. Ibid., p. 46.
5. Covenant of the League of Nations, Article 14.

6. Ferencz, note 1 above, pp. 46–48.
7. The Statute of the International Court of Justice, annexed to the Charter of the United Nations.
8. Prior to the United Nations becoming a virtually universal organization, non-member states were nevertheless entitled to accede to the ICJ and several did so.
9. A full list of acceding states, along with the dates of their accession, is provided by the ICJ at www.icj-cji.org/jurisdiction/index.phb?p1=5&p2=1&p3=3.
10. Complete lists of contentious cases and advisory proceedings will be found on the ICJ website at www.icj-cij.org/docket/index.phb?p1=3&p2=3 and www.icj-cij.org/docket/index.phb?p1=3&p2=4 respectively. The website provides links to full discussions of each case considered.
11. Of the P-5 powers, only the United Kingdom has accepted (in 2004) compulsory ICJ jurisdiction.
12. Ferencz, note 1 above, pp. 48–52.
13. Statistics in this and the following two paragraphs were compiled by the author from data on the ICJ website, note 1 above.
14. See www.icj-cij.org/court/index.phb?p1=1&p2=4.
15. Robert Sheppard, "Towards a UN World Parliamentary Assembly: UN Reform for the Progressive Evolution of an Effective and Accountable Parliamentary Process in UN Governance in the New Millennium", *Asian-Pacific Law & Policy Journal* 1(4), 2000, pp. 1–20; see especially pp. 15–17.
16. Wikipedia, "Judges of the International Court of Justice", http://en.wikipedia.org/wiki/judges_of_the_International_Court_of_Justice.
17. Totals included in this and the four subsequent paragraphs were compiled by the author from data in ibid.
18. Were it not for occasional vacancies, the total would have been 960 (64 × 15).
19. The "North" is here defined as consisting of Europe (including the whole of the USSR/Russia), the United States, Canada, Australia, New Zealand and Japan; the "South" includes all other countries.
20. This section is based primarily on Richard Goldstone, "International Criminal Court and Ad Hoc Tribunals", in Thomas G. Weiss and Sam Daws (eds), *The Oxford Handbook on the United Nations*, Oxford and New York: Oxford University Press, 2007, pp. 463–478; Ferencz, note 1 above, pp. 67–82; Wikipedia, "International Criminal Court", http://en.wikipedia.org/wiki/International_Criminal_Court.
21. At the height of their work the ICTY and ICTR accounted for more than a tenth of the regular annual UN budget (Goldstone, ibid., p. 467).
22. Ferencz, note 1 above, p. 77.
23. This principle and norm had been accepted in European human rights courts as early as 1954.
24. Goldstone, note 20 above, p. 475.
25. Wikipedia, note 20 above.
26. For commentary on the ways in which al-Bashir flouted and circumvented his indictment by the ICC see Ambassador Richard W. Williamson, "Sudan and the Implications for Responsibility to Protect", Policy Analysis Brief, October 2009, Stanley Foundation, Muscatine, IA.
27. Goldstone, note 20 above, p. 470.
28. This section is largely based on José A. Alvarez, "Legal Perspectives", in Thomas G. Weiss and Sam Daws (eds), *The Oxford Handbook on the United Nations*, Oxford and New York: Oxford University Press, 2007, pp. 58–81; José A. Alvarez, "International Organizations, Then and Now", *American Journal of International Law* 100(2), 2006, pp. 324–347.

29. Discussion of many of these bodies is provided in Laurence Boisson de Chazournes, Cesare P. R. Romano and Ruth Mackenzie (eds), *International Organizations and International Dispute Settlement: Trends and Prospects*, Ardsley, NY: Transnational Publishers, 2002. The chapter in this volume by Cesare P. Romano, "International Organizations and the International Judicial Process: An Overview", pp. 3–36, is especially helpful for non-specialists.

30. Valuable – even if somewhat dated – summaries of the history and functioning of 15 affiliated agencies are provided in *Everyone's United Nations*, 10th edn, New York: United Nations, 1986.

31. Detailed discussions of the legal status, legal competence and manner of operation of scores of international organizations will be found in Philippe Sands, QC and Pierre Klein, *Bowett's Law of International Institutions*, 6th edn, London: Thomson Reuters, 2009; Henry G. Schermers and Nigel M. Blokker, *International Institutional Law: Unity within Diversity*, 4th revised edn, Boston, MA, and Leiden: Martinus Nijhoff, 2003.

32. Details are derived mainly from the official websites of the bodies in question and relevant Wikipedia articles.

33. Anne-Marie La Rosa, "Links between the ILO and the ICJ: A Less than Perfect Match", in Laurence Boisson de Chazournes, Cesare P. R. Romano and Ruth Mackenzie (eds), *International Organizations and International Dispute Settlement: Trends and Prospects*, Ardsley, NY: Transnational Publishers, 2002, pp. 119–132; see also in the same volume Annex C, "International Labour Organization", pp. 258–261.

34. Christine Chinkin and Ruth Mackenzie, "Intergovernmental Organizations as Friends of the Court", in Laurence Boisson de Chazournes, Cesare P. R. Romano and Ruth Mackenzie (eds), *International Organizations and International Dispute Settlement: Trends and Prospects*, Ardsley, NY: Transnational Publishers, 2002, pp. 135–162; see also in the same volume Annex E, "World Trade Organization", pp. 269–272.

35. See Wikipedia, "Dispute Settlement Body", http://wikipedia.org/wiki/Dispute_Settlement_Body.

36. Tullio Treves, "International Organizations as Parties to Contentious Cases: Selected Aspects", in Laurence Boisson de Chazournes, Cesare P. R. Romano and Ruth Mackenzie (eds), *International Organizations and International Dispute Settlement: Trends and Prospects*, Ardsley, NY: Transnational Publishers, 2002, pp. 37–46; see also in the same volume Annex B, "Statute of the International Tribunal for the Law of the Sea", pp. 256–258.

37. Information presented in this section was derived principally from Ferencz, note 1 above, pp. 56–66, and Wikipedia articles on agencies mentioned, generally updated to mid-2009.

38. Only Belarus, whose human rights record is deplorable, is excluded.

39. Account based primarily on Gennady M. Danilenko, "The Economic Court of the Commonwealth of Independent States", *International Law and Politics* 31, 1999, pp. 893–918.

40. Ukraine and Turkmenistan did not sign the formative treaty; Azerbaijan and Georgia signed, but then took no further action. Armenia dropped its membership in 2006.

41. Huliq News, www.huliq.com/2931/armenia-quite-cis-economic-court.

42. A useful complement to this section is provided by Commission on Global Governance, *Our Global Neighbourhood*, New York: Oxford University Press, 1995, pp. 303–334.

8

Coordination of UN specialized agencies and special UN commissions and funds

The development of global governance is part of the evolution of human efforts to organize life on the planet, and that process will always be going on.
Ingvar Carlson and Shridath Ramphal, Commission on Global Governance

Beneath the surface of states and nations, ideas and language, lies the fate of individual human beings in need. Answering their needs will be the mission of the United Nations in the century to come.
Kofi Annan, Nobel Prize acceptance speech

Introduction

Little heralded, yet immensely important in the aggregate, is the wide range of activities performed by a constellation of global and largely autonomous intergovernmental organizations (IGOs), some affiliated to the United Nations and others not; as well as a number of programmes and funds under direct UN management. Some of these affiliated agencies pre-date the United Nations itself, going as far back as 1865 in the case of the International Telecommunications Union (ITU – originally the International Telegraph Union and renamed in 1934); and many, such as the Universal Postal Union (UPU, also pre-dating the United Nations), provide oversight for a variety of mundane but essential activities. Some, such as the International Atomic Energy Agency, owe their existence to the dangers and hopes of the nuclear era. It is not possible within a single chapter to discuss each agency and fund in question. Rather, I first consider in

Transforming the United Nations system: Designs for a workable world, Schwartzberg, United Nations University Press, 2013, ISBN 978-92-808-1230-5

general terms their variety, membership, manner of establishment, staffing, direction, methods of decision-making and systemic cohesion (or lack thereof); then suggest ways by which their work might be more rationally executed and their decision-making systems improved. I conclude with some broad systemic recommendations.

The expansion of global agencies and funds[1]

Study of the proliferation and increasing geographic dispersion of UN-affiliated specialized agencies, important commissions and funds within the United Nations itself and a global network of UN-sponsored training and research institutes indicates that the expansion was *ad hoc*. It followed no preordained plan and was guided by no compelling logical considerations. Nor can one discern any compelling rationale as to why certain activities are carried out under the direct aegis of core organs of the United Nations (e.g. ECOSOC), while others are allocated primarily to essentially autonomous specialized agencies.

Perhaps the most striking conclusion one can draw is that the scope of activities within the UN system has expanded enormously beyond the UN's initial preoccupation with security. Development, human rights, humanitarian concerns and environmental issues now account for much of the system's total staffing and budget. But as new responsibilities were assumed, all too often the United Nations created new organizations or funds to handle them, rather than adding them to the mandates of agencies already in existence. The resultant bureaucratic redundancy has been widely noted and deplored. Yet despite overlap in many areas of concern, there are major organizational lacunae in others. These problems are discussed later in this chapter.

Total full-time employment in the UN system now (2012) approaches the 100,000 mark,[2] and total spending is approximately US$25 billion, a large preponderance of which is accounted for by voluntary donations from UN member states and/or various foundations and other private sources independent of the biennial budgeting mandated by the UN General Assembly (discussed in Chapter 11). In fact, several specialized agencies, most notably the Bretton Woods institutions – the International Monetary Fund (IMF), International Bank for Reconstruction and Development (IBRD or World Bank) and IBRD subsidiary agencies – individually disburse billions of dollars annually. The annual budget of the WHO also runs into the billions. At the opposite extreme is the meagre annual budget of $26 million for the World Tourism Organization, the newest

UN-affiliated specialized agency. Overall, levels of support vary enormously from one agency to another.

Also remarkable is the universality, or near universality, of membership in the specialized agencies, typically running to more than 180 nations. In several cases it reaches a total of 193: all 192 UN member states plus the European Union, which increasingly seeks and is granted membership in leading IGOs. Even the International Atomic Energy Agency has 145 member nations (the lowest total for any of the 14 specialized agencies, exclusive of the Bretton Woods group), despite the fact that far fewer than half that number can realistically hope to make direct use of nuclear energy in the foreseeable future. Similarly, the 168 members of the International Maritime Organization (IMO) include a number of the world's 41 landlocked countries, almost all of which lack a merchant marine; and the 173 members of the UN Industrial Development Organization include many whose industrial potential is, at best, negligible.

Despite the substantial geographical dispersion of headquarters for various UN agencies, the principal affiliated agencies remain almost entirely in New York, Washington and a small group of cities in Western Europe. Geneva is by far the dominant European node; Rome and Vienna also host multiple agencies; and several other cities provide headquarters for a single agency. A slightly more balanced picture emerges in respect to the 13 agencies directly administered by the United Nations. Although 10 of these are in four cities of the global North, Nairobi is the seat of two – the UN Environment Programme (UNEP) and the UN Human Settlement Programme – and Gaza of one, the UN Relief and Works Agency for Palestinian Refugees in the Near East (UNRWA). Greater dispersion is evident in respect to the UN's eight training and research institutions, whose headquarter cities include Tokyo (United Nations University), Santo Domingo (Research and Training Institute for the Advancement of Woman) and San José (University for Peace). And the United Nations University is itself widely dispersed, with some 15 subsidiary, thematically focused campuses: six in Europe, four in Asia, three in North America and one each in Africa and Latin America.[3]

The geographic spread of UN *activities* cannot, of course, be inferred from the locations of headquarters of the responsible agencies. While some operate overwhelmingly from a single location, many others function through networks of regional and/or national offices. These networks are not necessarily all-inclusive, in that certain world areas have little or no need for particular forms of assistance. Moreover, no two networks are exactly alike, which complicates the coordination of development programmes. For example, the FAO maintains five regional offices (Africa, Asia and the Pacific, Europe and Central Asia, Latin America and the

Caribbean, and the Near East and Southeast Asia), while the WHO functions with six (Africa, the Americas, the Eastern Mediterranean, Europe, Southeast Asia and the Western Pacific).

Decision-making within UN-affiliated agencies and commissions directly controlled by the United Nations follows no set pattern. Most in the former group, however, do conform to a more or less standardized model.[4] In general, major decisions are taken at meetings of the agency's plenary body (consisting of the representatives, usually cabinet ministers, of all member states choosing to participate). Plenary bodies are variously designated: general conference, (general) assembly, congress, governing council or, in the case of the IMF and World Bank, governing board. With the exception of the governing boards of the major Bretton Woods institutions, which function throughout the year, these entities meet for relatively brief periods, anywhere from twice yearly to once every four years. Plenary meetings provide venues for making major policy decisions, discussing the organizational budget and electing the members of a relatively small executive body – most commonly designated as executive board, executive council or simply council – to oversee the organization's day-to-day functioning. The size of the executive body – again excluding the Bretton Woods entities – varies from 18 (in the case of the International Fund for Agricultural Development – IFAD) to 58 (UNESCO), with several set at 36; and its composition is usually based on predetermined regional quotas, though the regions vary from one organization to another.[5] In both plenary meetings and those of executive bodies decisions are preferably taken by consensus; but when votes are called for most organizations follow the general UN practice of one nation – one vote. Major exceptions to this rule are the Bretton Woods institutions, in which votes are allocated in rough proportion to the financial subscriptions of the member nations; and the ILO, whose membership was discussed in Chapter 7.

Among UN commissions and funds, the internal organization and decision-making procedures are more varied than those of the specialized agencies. While there is no general template, several bodies do have plenary meetings at intervals of two or more years. The UNCTAD conference, occurring only at four-year intervals, is noteworthy for encouraging participation by other IGOs, as well as numerous NGOs. In contrast to affiliated agencies, decision-making by small elected executive committees is not the rule. However, UNICEF, the World Food Programme (WFP) and the UN Development Programme (UNDP) all have elected, regionally representative 36-member executive boards; and UNEP has a 58-member executive. As with affiliated agencies, UN commissions also follow the one-nation-one-vote rule.

Rationalization and coordination of agencies[6]

Criticism of the UN system includes frequent reference to its extensive redundancy, serious lacunae and/or misplaced emphases in the agendas of its constituent agencies, inadequate coordination of agency activities, inadequate and unpredictable funding, confusing lines of responsibility and reporting, insufficient transparency and accountability, the prevalence of political hypocrisy and double standards, and unrealistic systems of decision-making.[7]

In light of these shortcomings, one may fairly ask whether the so-called "UN *system*" merits being so characterized. On this point Maurice Bertrand, one of the UN's most experienced civil servants,[8] casts an unequivocally negative verdict, branding the organization as a "non-system" and calling for a complete overhaul of the Charter.[9] This "non-system" characterization was echoed by Fomerand and Dijkzeul in their discussion of attempts to coordinate development activities at UN headquarters, between the central offices of various UN agencies and operations in the field, and among UN field agencies themselves.[10] Criticism from within the United Nations itself tends to be more diplomatically muted. Even so, one reads in *Delivering as One*, the report of the Secretary-General's High-level Panel on System-wide Coherence:

> Despite its unique legitimacy, including the universality of its membership, the UN's status as a central actor in the multilateral system is undermined by lack of focus on results, thereby failing, more than anyone else, the poorest and the most vulnerable ... the UN's work on development and environment is often fragmented and weak. Inefficient and ineffective governance and unpredictable funding have contributed to policy incoherence, duplication and operational ineffectiveness across the system. Cooperation between organizations has been hindered by competition for funding, mission creep and by outdated business practices.[11]

Recommendations for improvement have come from many quarters, within and outside the United Nations, and are far too numerous to summarize in this work. I put forward here no more than a few especially important ideas, some of them original, others borrowed from cited sources. Intentionally omitted from consideration are recommendations relative to staff recruitment and budget, dealt with in Chapters 9 and 11 respectively.

With respect to system coherence, one may ask why, for example, there should be three separate agencies in Rome – the FAO, IFAD and WFP – rather than a single entity with an enlarged food and agricultural mandate?

Would not consolidation enable substantial efficiencies in planning, budgeting, staffing, field operations and reporting?

The pros and cons of other possible consolidations should also be explored. Why not incorporate the UN World Tourism Organization within UNESCO, which is already charged with the task of certifying "World Cultural Heritage" and "World Natural Heritage" sites? The functions of the World Intellectual Property Organization (WIPO) might also best be carried out under a broadened UNESCO umbrella. Significant benefits might be realized by merging the ITU and UPU, and by combining the International Civil Aviation Organization (ICAO) and the IMO.[12] Would it not now make sense to put UNRWA under the Office of the High Commissioner for Refugees, or to merge the Human Settlements Programme with the UN Fund for Population Activities (UNFPA)? Finally – in this far-from-complete list – does not economic globalization provide a strong case for combining UNCTAD with the much more powerful WTO and bringing the WTO within the UN system, under the general oversight of a strengthened ECOSOC (or, as suggested in Chapter 5, its proposed successor, an Economic, Social and Environmental Council)?

As previously noted, major international concerns of the contemporary era go well beyond the military security issues that preoccupied the UN's founders. This points to the need for new and/or strengthened agencies to deal with emergent problems. Some suggestions follow.

The word "environment" is nowhere to be found in the UN Charter. Today, however, we recognize that environmental changes present humankind with profound existential threats. Despite this, there is still no UN-affiliated specialized agency dealing primarily with such issues. The Nairobi-based UNEP has an annual budget of only US$142 million (two cents per capita for the earth as a whole).[13] This must be corrected.

Burgeoning populations, especially in the developing world, also pose numerous and serious threats. Struggles over increasingly inadequate supplies of water, land and other vital resources present but one among many likely causes of future conflict. Joblessness among young male population cohorts not only creates conditions conducive to mass civil unrest, but also enhances recruitment opportunities for terrorist networks. The annual budget of roughly $629 million for the UNFPA (nine cents per capita, worldwide) is inadequate. As with UNEP, the status of the fund should be elevated to that of a specialized agency.

Terrorism and other forms of organized international crime – narco-trafficking, trafficking in human beings, illegal financial dealings, smuggling of small arms, etc. – have become globalized and require a more robust and well-coordinated UN response. The logical nexus for such efforts is the politically neutral International Criminal Police Organization, commonly referred to as INTERPOL. Founded in 1923, this Lyons-based agency now has 188 member nations and has done remarkably good work despite its meagre annual budget ($61.4 million in 2007).[14] INTERPOL, too, should become a specialized UN agency and incorporate the Vienna-based UN Office on Drugs and Crime.

Contributing significantly to the inadequate coordination of UN activities is the fact that they are carried out from institutional headquarters scattered throughout the world. Agencies that should be in regular contact with one another may be situated in different continents and separated by thousands of miles. As the following statement by the UN Preparatory Commission makes clear, this was not intended when the organization was founded:

> The principle of centralization should be adopted according to which the permanent seat of the United Nations ... as well as of the specialized agencies should be concentrated in one place, with the exception of the International Court of Justice.[15]

For political reasons this expectation was never realized. The placement of a particular agency in a particular location was seen as a prestigious plum – recognition, as it were, that the site and country selected were politically significant. Efficiency was not the determining factor.

Although increasing internet use will undoubtedly mitigate the problem of geographic separation, setting up teleconferences is time-consuming and cannot adequately substitute for the frequent, unscheduled, open-ended and informal interactions that result from working in close proximity. Childers and Urquhart discuss this problem in their 1994 monograph, *Renewing the United Nations System*.[16] Recognizing the likelihood that the scale of UN activities will increase dramatically in future generations, we should weigh the relative future costs and benefits of geographic consolidation. Admittedly, restructuring would be costly. But deferring needed consolidation to some indefinite future date could prove more expensive in the long run. Additionally, maintaining the present, often dysfunctional, system exacts a heavy price in inadequate delivery of services. Notwithstanding the substantial capital investment in establishing the existing organizational infrastructure of the UN system, Childers and Urquhart's recommendations for a high degree of geographic consolidation appear warranted. Further, beyond the organizational mergers previously suggested, I recommend, in the absence of powerful arguments to the contrary, that UN entities be headquartered in either New York or Geneva. The principal exceptions to this rule would be the long-entrenched, Washington-based Bretton Woods institutions (situated only a few hours away from New York); the World Court and ICC should also remain in their symbolically significant locations in The Hague.

Important as the consolidation of agencies and a more rational distribution of headquarters locations would be, enhanced coherence of activities within the UN system also requires more effective central planning utilizing a cabinet-like system. To be sure, a measure of coordinated planning already exists within the Chief Executives Board for Coordination (CEB).[17] But, judging from the results and continuing engagement with this issue, more is needed. Presently, the CEB has 28 members and meets only twice a year. It brings together the Secretary-General and the heads of the major UN funds, specialized agencies (including the Bretton Woods institutions) and the WTO. Cooperation is promoted through two high-level committees, one on programmes and the other on management, each supervising informal networks of working groups, managers and experts involved in inter-agency work. Neither of these bodies, however, has decision-making authority.[18] The unwillingness of agency heads to bend to the recommendations of an oversight body inevitably contributes to insufficient coordination. Ways must be found to overcome this deficiency. Greater pressure from the Secretary-General, the deputy secretary-general for administration (a post created in 1997), a revitalized ECOSOC (or ESEC, as recommended in Chapter 5) and the GA (possibly empowered with law-making authority) is necessary. Using the power of the budget as a tool to elicit cooperation should be considered.

Whatever the future reform efforts may be, they will not be optimally effective unless decision-making processes are transparent and decision-makers are held accountable for their actions. This objective may be promoted by creating more open channels for communication among agencies within the UN system and the NGOs concerned with their agendas and activities. ECOSOC (or its proposed successor, ESEC) should play a leading role. How this might best be achieved is discussed in Chapter 10.

Apart from coordinating UN agencies operating at the headquarters level, whether in New York or in the many UN regional centres, there is need for better coordination with and among regional and national centres. As with locating the headquarters of UN-affiliated specialized organizations and funds, there is, as Childers and Urquhart demonstrate, little logic to or efficiency in the geographic dispersion of their major field offices.[19] The data in Table 8.1 on Africa illustrate the point. More complete and up-to-date data would reinforce it.

Not only does Table 8.1 show the fragmentation of field operations within the UN system, but in the case of UNESCO even within a single agency, with regional centres in both Dakar and Nairobi. The coexistence of ICAO offices in Cairo and Dakar is easier to justify, in that the area covered by the Arab League is often considered as a region distinct from Africa south of the Sahara. To compound the problem, large parts of Africa are covered by regional offices located in Europe or Southwest

Table 8.1 Location of African regional offices of UN agencies, 1994

City, country	Agencies (and designations of regions represented)
Abidjan, Côte d'Ivoire	IBRD (West Africa), UNICEF (West Africa)
Accra, Ghana	FAO (Africa)
Addis Ababa, Ethiopia	Economic Commission for Africa (Africa), ILO (Africa)
Alexandria, Egypt	WHO (East Mediterranean)
Bujumbura, Burundi	WMO (Africa)
Brazzaville, Republic of Congo	WHO (Africa)
Cairo, Egypt	ICAO (Middle East and North Africa)
Dakar, Senegal	ICAO (Africa), UNESCO (Education, Africa)
Nairobi, Kenya	IBRD (East Africa), UNEP (Africa), UNESCO (Science and Technology, Africa), UNICEF (East Africa)

Source: Erskine Childers and Brian Urquhart, *Renewing the United Nations System*, Uppsala: Dag Hammarskjöld Foundation, 1994, world map on p. 96.

Asia. The UNICEF office in Amman, Jordan, for example, is responsible for activities in North Africa. This spatial disarray cannot be conducive to harmonizing UN field activities. Either a single regional office in Nairobi or, preferably, two offices, one in Nairobi (for Africa south of the Sahara) and the other in Cairo (for the area of the Arab League), would be a superior arrangement. I also recommend 10 additional centres to serve the major world regions proposed for representation in the SC and ECOSOC in Chapters 4 and 5: Geneva for Europe, Moscow for Russia and neighbouring CIS states, Tehran for West Asia (other than nations in the Arab League), New Delhi for India, Beijing for China, Tokyo for East Asia, Bangkok for Southeast Asia and Vancouver for the Westminster League.

Proceeding from the regional to the national level, there is the question of inadequate coordination and competition among UN agencies within individual countries or, in some cases, within small groups of neighbouring countries. This perennial problem has been dealt with extensively in several UN-sponsored reports, as well as by Childers and Urquhart, among others.[20] It has gained increasing salience as large parts of the world fall behind in pursuing their respective Millennium Development Goals. The consensus view is that there should be a single director responsible for all UN-related country programmes, preferably the appointee of UNDP, and operations should be coordinated from a single venue, a "UN house" in which all country programmes would be based. However, despite the fact that UNDP operates in well over 150 countries, there were as of 2007 fewer than 60 UN houses worldwide: 17 in Africa, 16 in Europe and the CIS, 10 in Latin America and the Caribbean, 10 in Asia and the Pacific, and 5 in Arab states.[21]

Finally, we have the often-thorny problem of coordination between UN agencies and various government ministries within the countries where they work. Given the world's diversity, it is inevitable that the agendas of UN agencies may not harmonize with those of their host countries. Attempts to better the lot of women, for example, will often run counter to the local cultural mores of dominantly patriarchal governing elites. More generally, development efforts that threaten existing power hierarchies will meet opposition from those benefiting from the status quo. While some accommodation to local power interests may prove unavoidable, if anything is to be accomplished there must be limits beyond which the resident UN director should not go. Since the United Nations has no legal obligation to provide its services, this gives the director some leverage in dealing with local authorities. No simple approach, however, will fit all situations. Finding an optimal balance will require good intelligence and diplomacy, not only in dealing with host-country ministries but also in persuading UN colleagues in the field, as well as superiors in regional offices and New York, of the correctness of one's position. Effectiveness will ultimately depend on having one capable person in charge in each country hosting UN development programs.

Devising appropriate weighting formulae

As previously noted, decision-making in most UN-affiliated specialized agencies and commissions, when not made by consensus, follows the one-nation-one-vote rule. But the fact that the Bretton Woods institutions are able to function with a system of weighted voting (whether or not one approves of the weighting method) demonstrates that the one-nation-one-vote principle is not sacrosanct. And the governance of the ILO demonstrates that nations need not have a monopoly on decision-making.

In Chapters 2–5 it was argued that appropriately weighted voting – in the GA, proposed WPA, SC and ECOSOC respectively – was preferable to decision-making on a one-nation-one-vote basis. In particular, it was shown that the existing system does not reflect the realities of power in the world outside the United Nations, and that powerful nations would often question the legitimacy of UN decisions with which they disagree and act unilaterally when it suited their perceived national interests. In general, the argument applies also to the agencies discussed in this chapter. The decisions of those agencies would receive greater respect if they were reached by realistically weighted voting formulae.

The following principles should guide the devising of formulae.
- There is need for an optimal (not necessarily equal) balance between the concerns of *stakeholders* – generally speaking, the people – and

those of *shareholders*, the nations that control and/or pay the bills for various activities.

- The balance between the claims of each group should be determined by objective weighted voting formulae.
- Weightings should be appropriate for the functions that the agency in question performs.
- Formulae should yield results that are nuanced and flexible.
- The resultant country weights should be periodically adjusted to reflect changing situations (demographic, economic, etc.) in the world outside the United Nations.

In practice it will not always be possible to apply all these principles, primarily because the requisite data for weighting will not always be available, and when they are available there may be irreconcilable differences of opinion as to their suitability and relative importance. If, for example, we consider the WHO, it is obvious that people, the intended beneficiaries of WHO services, are stakeholders. But who ought to be considered as shareholders? States? Providers of medical services (when not supplied directly by the state)? The health insurance industry (again, in respect to non-state agencies)? All three? And if one does include health service providers, should a paramedic, a village midwife or a tribal shaman count the same as a brain surgeon? Whatever the answers may be, it will be necessary to decide what logical and politically acceptable weight should be given to each recognized group. Finally, who should best provide the requisite data, and what credibility will the provider have?

In light of these problems, a relatively simple default formula, similar or identical to the one proposed for weighted votes in the GA, might be in order. To refresh the reader's memory, the GA formula was:

$$W = (P + C + M)/3$$

in which W is a country's weight, the average of the three terms in the right-hand side of the equation; P its population as a percentage of that of all nations in the United Nations (or all nations that are members of the agency in question); C its contribution to the organization's budget as a percentage of the total; and M its membership as a percentage of the total.

Alternatively, one might wish to assign greater weights to people and contributions than to nations, in which case one might prefer a formula along the following lines:

$$W = (3P + 2C + M)/6$$

The coefficients 3 and 2 in this formula are merely illustrative. Others might find wider acceptance. Those ultimately chosen would be determined by political bargaining in either the specialized agency in question or, in the case of commissions, in the GA.

Space considerations and inadequate knowledge of how specific agencies function preclude my offering suggestions for all UN bodies, but a few suggestions should clarify the general approach. Let us begin with the most important, and most frequently criticized, agencies, the Bretton Woods institutions, which already have a system of weighted voting based almost entirely on the funding contributions of member nations and which allocate virtually no power on the basis of population. If the intention were to assign comparable weights to the interests of shareholders and stakeholders, an acceptable departure from the present system might be the following:

$$W = (5C + 4P + M)/10$$

Here a country's weight, W, would be equal to five times its cash subscriptions, C (as a percentage of the institutional total); plus four times the country's population, P (as a percentage of the total for all member nations); plus M, its membership as a percentage of all members; divided by 10. This maintains the supremacy of the economic term of the equation, but moderates it in such a way as to make the institution appear much more legitimate than it presently does in the global South.

Another example might be the IMO. As in the previously discussed cases, people may be regarded as stakeholders. Nations can be seen as both shareholders and stakeholders. The most relevant shareholder term in the equation, however, might be the registered shipping tonnage of each nation's merchant fleet (often zero), excluding warships and ships sailing under what are termed "flags of convenience".[22] Excluding vessels flying flags of convenience points to a way, incidentally, whereby decision-making formulae could be utilized to reward responsible international behaviour. The following is suggested:

$$W = (5T + 4P + M)/10$$

This formula is similar to those proposed for the Bretton Woods institutions, except that T, standing for tonnage, becomes the chief term in the right-hand side of the equation.[23]

A final, more complex example is a possible formula for the FAO. Here, as with the WHO, people are clearly stakeholders. Everyone must eat. Shareholders would include workers in the agricultural sector.[24] But in terms of contributing to the world's food balance, there are vast differences between capital-intensive farms in the American Midwest and subsistence peasant holdings in Southeast Asia. These must be recognized. Finally, as with the WHO, one should view the state as both a stakeholder and a shareholder. Given these considerations and the fact that relevant data are reasonably abundant and credible, one might put forward the following formula:

$$W = (3P + 2A + 2V + M)/8$$

Here a country's weight, W, would be equal to three times its population, P (as a percentage of the total for all FAO members); plus two times its number of persons in the agricultural sector, A (as a percentage of the total for all members); plus two times the value of the nation's agricultural output, V (as a percentage of the total output of all members); plus the nation's membership, M (as a percentage of the total membership); divided by eight.

It bears repeating that the terms and coefficients in all the foregoing equations are merely suggestive. Political bargaining among concerned parties might yield significantly different choices. The point, however, is to demonstrate that realistic and equitable formulae are possible, and to argue that decisions so made will be regarded as more legitimate and command greater respect than those made under the one-nation-one-vote system.

Conclusion

The reform process in regard to UN-affiliated specialized agencies and commissions operating under the United Nations proper will be long and fraught with political and economic difficulties. Consolidation of agencies and coordination of their activities at various levels – global, regional and national – will encounter substantial resistance. So too will field operations running counter to the perceived interests of local magnates. The chief problems will be resistance from turf-protectors, perceived incompatibility of agendas of the global North and global South, nationalist pride, inadequate funding, lack of requisite political will and, as in all bureaucracies, institutional inertia. Some reforms, however, have already been carried out and others will surely follow as needs become more pressing. Proposing novel – but relevant and feasible – reform paths should speed the process.

Notes

1. The factual accounts in this section are based almost entirely on *The Europa World Year Book, 2009*, New York and London: Routledge, 2009, pp. 48–81 and 93–169.
2. This excludes the Bretton Woods institutions and deployments in UN peacekeeping missions. The number of peacekeepers deployed in any given year fluctuates substantially, but has in several recent years exceeded 100,000, counting both soldiers and police.
3. See "Training Centres and Programmes/United Nations University", www.unu.edu/systems/centres.html.
4. The principal exceptions among UN-affiliated agencies are the ILO, ITU and WIPO.
5. The regional groups are specified largely along continental lines; but in the case of IFAD the threefold division is developed nations, developing oil-producing nations and developing nations that are not oil producers.
6. The discussion in this section is based primarily on Jacques Fomerand and Dennis Dijkzeul, "Coordinating Economic and Social Affairs", in Thomas G. Weiss and Sam Daws (eds), *The Oxford Handbook on the United Nations*, New York and Oxford: Oxford University Press, 2007, pp. 561–581; Erskine Childers and Brian Urquhart, *Renewing the United Nations System*, Uppsala: Dag Hammarskjöld Foundation, 1994, *passim*, especially pp. 67–104; High-level Panel on UN System-wide Coherence in the Areas of Development, Humanitarian Assistance and the Environment, *Delivering as One*, New York: United Nations, 2006. Also quite useful are the trenchant, sweeping and often radical critiques contained in Maurice Bertrand and Daniel Warner (eds), *A New Charter for a Worldwide Organisation?*, Vol. 22, The Hague, London and New York: Kluwer Law International, 1997; Klaus Hüfner (ed.), *Agenda for Change: New Tasks for the United Nations*, Opladen: Leske + Budrich, 1995.
7. Excellent reviews of relatively recent reform proposals (and the shortcomings leading to them) are provided in Jan Woroniecki, "Restructuring the United Nations: A Response to New Tasks, or a Substitute for Action?", in Klaus Hüfner (ed.), *Agenda for Change: New Tasks for the United Nations*, Opladen: Leske + Budrich, 1995, pp. 59–83; Victor-Yves Ghebali, "United Nations Reform Proposals Since the End of the Cold War", in Maurice Bertrand and Daniel Warner (eds), *A New Charter for a Worldwide Organisation?*, Vol. 22, The Hague, London and New York: Kluwer Law International, 1997, pp. 79–111. For the post-1996 period see Fomerand and Dijkzeul, note 6 above.
8. Bertrand was a member of the UN's Joint Inspection Unit (1968–1985) and a high-level panel on restructuring the United Nations (1986); he has written and taught extensively in his native France and in Switzerland on the subject of UN reform.
9. Maurice Bertrand, "The Necessity of Conceiving a New Charter for the Global Institutions", in Maurice Bertrand and Daniel Warner (eds), *A New Charter for a Worldwide Organisation?*, Vol. 22, The Hague, London and New York: Kluwer Law International, 1997, pp. 1–44; the contrasting organizational diagrams on pp. 40–41 are especially relevant.
10. Fomerand and Dijkzeul, note 6 above, p. 561.
11. High-level Panel on UN System-wide Coherence, note 6 above, p. 1.
12. Among newly salient problems that both organizations must confront are terrorism and hijacking or piracy.
13. One might add to this figure a portion of the $68 million budget of the World Meteorological Organization, while recognizing that the principal WMO concern is *weather*, not climate as such.
14. See www.interpol.int/Public/ICPO/default.asp.

15. Executive Committee of the UN Preparatory Commission, UN Doc. PL/EX/113/Rev.1, Part III, Chapter X, sec. 2, para. 10, 12 November 1945, quoted in Childers and Urquhart, note 6 above, p. 45.

16. Childers and Urquhart, ibid., pp. 45–48.

17. Formed in 2000, the CEB replaces the Administrative Committee on Coordination, established in 1946.

18. Fomerand and Dijkzeul, note 6 above, pp. 569–570.

19. Childers and Urquhart, note 6 above, pp. 95–98

20. UN Secretary-General, "Strengthening of the United Nations: An Agenda for Further Change", UN GA Doc. A/57/387, 2002, *passim*, especially pp. 111–121; High-level Panel on UN System-wide Coherence, note 6 above, *passim*, especially pp. 12–15; Childers and Urquhart, note 6 above, pp. 89–95.

21. Fomerand and Dijkzeul, note 6 above, p. 572.

22. "Flags of convenience" are sold by various countries to shipping agencies seeking to avoid compliance with international law (e.g. in respect to environmental regulations) or not wishing to pay their crews union wages. Several such countries are landlocked (e.g. Mongolia's handling of goods bound for or coming from the DPRK). More than half the world's merchant ships now fly such flags and carry on much of the world's smuggling and illegal fishing. Global Policy Forum, "Flags of Convenience", www.globalpolicy.org/nations-a-states/state-sovereignty-and-corruption/flags-of-convnience.html.

23. In the foregoing discussion it was assumed that the recommended merger of the IMO and ICAO will not have taken place; if it had, a different line of reasoning would have been warranted.

24. Statistics for this sector conventionally include cultivators, pastoralists, hunters, gatherers, fishermen and forestry workers, most or all of whom are engaged in food production.

9

Enhancing human resources

The paramount consideration in the employment of the staff and in the determination of the conditions of service shall be the necessity of securing the highest standards of efficiency, competence and integrity. Due regard shall be paid to the importance of recruiting staff on as wide a geographic basis as possible.
UN Charter, Article 101, para. 3

The United Nations shall place no restrictions on the eligibility of men and women to participate in any capacity and under conditions of equality in its principal and subsidiary organs.
UN Charter, Article 8

Introduction[1]

Since its inception the United Nations has experienced serious problems in recruiting, promoting and retaining UN Secretariat and other staff to meet the standards suggested by Charter Articles 8 and 101, cited above. Although lip service has frequently been paid to the ideal of a truly international civil service whose staff do "not seek or receive instructions from any government or other authority external to the Organization", as called for in Article 100, violations of that ideal have been frequent and often egregious.

In the UN's earliest years the nations of the West, led by the United States, were so overwhelmingly in control of the world body that they

Transforming the United Nations system: Designs for a workable world, Schwartzberg,
United Nations University Press, 2013, ISBN 978-92-808-1230-5

frequently turned a blind eye to their own excesses in respect to how business was carried out and saw only the unreasonable demands put on the organization by the Soviet Union and its then satellites. But as the wave of decolonization swept across much of Asia and Africa and UN membership burgeoned, demands for greater equity in recruitment and allocating major positions were increasingly voiced. The "geographic basis" for employment often assumed primacy over "the necessity of securing the highest standards of efficiency, competence and integrity". What was originally polarization along East-West lines morphed into an essentially North-South divide.

Hard on the heels of the rise of the global South, calls for gender equity also became salient. Four major world conferences on women – in Mexico City (1975), Copenhagen (1980), Nairobi (1985) and especially Beijing (1995) – added some sense of urgency to this process, as did the general rise of feminism in and since the 1960s. Feminist leaders came initially mainly from the global North and have only recently been joined by substantial numbers of activists from the South. At the rhetorical level there appears to have been substantial progress; but in terms of concrete action, gains have been inadequate.

Apart from problems relating to geographic origin and gender, the UN Secretariat and affiliated organizations have had to grapple with numerous other issues contributing to low morale and tarnishing the UN's public image. Among these are the often ill-defined and/or overlapping missions of various agencies (discussed in Chapter 8), the difficulty of staffing field missions in undesirable locations, corruption (e.g. the "oil-for-food" scandal), the fallout from sexual misconduct in certain peacekeeping operations, and unrelenting pressures for reform put upon various agencies by those who pay the lion's share of the bills, especially the United States. Many senior-level appointments can credibly be attributed to the political machinations of the P-5 powers, as can failures to reappoint certain individuals deemed unacceptable by one or more of those powers (e.g. the blocking of Boutros Boutros-Ghali for a second term as Secretary-General in 1996 because of the disfavour with which he was viewed by the then administration in the United States).

Despite some reforms in response to past abuses and mounting demands for equity, it is clear the United Nations still has far to go in establishing an optimal, truly international civil service system. Some observers contend that merit-based and geographically based recruitment are fundamentally incompatible. Others, including the present author, disagree. Much of this chapter is devoted to proposing mechanisms by which the two bases for recruitment can be reconciled and greater gender equity achieved. I also suggest means for ensuring that senior-level appointments are made competitively and primarily on the basis of merit.

A review of past practices and reforms

In comparison to the Secretariat of the League of Nations, whose staff peaked at around 900 individuals (not counting roughly 400 in the ILO), the onset of the UN Secretariat was meteoric. An estimated 3,000 persons were hired in the organization's first six months, most of whom, not surprisingly, were nationals of the United States, the United Kingdom and France.[2] Referring to this "swarm" of appointees, the Australian diplomat Sir Walter Crocker observed: "some were friends of delegates, and got through by what is known in international secretariats as political pressures ... Some – and probably the largest number – found their way of ingress through the friendship of a senior officer."[3] Many others were recruited from staff of the League Secretariat or drawn from the ranks of officials in the preparatory commission charged with establishing the United Nations. Merit-based competition for most positions initially played little, if any, role. That legacy continues to hamper reform efforts.

Despite establishment of the International Civil Service Advisory Board in 1948, recruitment procedures were slow to improve and new staff, especially from the Soviet bloc, often found it difficult to pay their primary allegiance to the United Nations rather than their home nations. In 1946 Trygve Lie, the UN's first Secretary-General, acceded to a "gentlemen's agreement" that the major departments within the UN Secretariat were to be controlled by members of the P-5. He also succumbed to pressure from the United States during the "un-American activities" witch hunts of the McCarthy era to allow FBI access to UN facilities and FBI vetting of US staff in the UN Secretariat, 43 of whom were subsequently dismissed.[4]

Lie's successor, Dag Hammarskjöld, laboured mightily to correct already-entrenched shortcomings within the system. He stood up not only to the United States, bringing an end to FBI interventions, but also to the Soviet Union, which sought to impose on the UN Secretariat a so-called "troika" system of leadership by three individuals: one from the United States, one from the USSR and a third from the growing Non-Aligned Movement. In a major speech at Oxford University in 1961, Hammarskjöld responded by asserting staunchly the necessity of a truly independent international civil service. He created the Office of Personnel Services (subsequently renamed the Office of Human Resources Management) to establish uniform recruitment standards, and throughout his administration did much to promote his internationalist vision and raise the morale of UN staff. His preference for staff with permanent commitments to the United Nations was opposed by the Soviet Union, which insisted that its nationals accept only two- or five-year contracts. The inevitable compromise was to opt for a staff in which 75 per cent were on permanent and 25 per cent on fixed-term contracts.[5]

Notwithstanding Hammarskjöld's efforts and numerous additional initiatives, serious personnel problems continued to beset the UN Secretariat, the affiliated organizations and other components of the UN system. Hammarskjöld's successor, U Thant, instituted what proved to be a highly politicized system of under-secretaries-general and assistant secretaries-general that still remains in force. And in the 1960s nationals from developing countries began to be appointed to high-level positions, as well as to an increasing proportion of entry-level posts, often on a permanent basis. Over time, however, the perception grew that permanent appointments were resulting in the UN Secretariat becoming burdened with a substantial load of "dead wood". Concomitant problems were the emergence within the UN Secretariat of various "fiefdoms" and the erosion of common standards for staff recruitment and promotion.[6] In response, during the tenure of Kofi Annan a new staff selection system was instituted and permanent contracts were largely phased out. Since 2004 almost all new contracts are of one of three types: short term (up to six months), to meet specific and pressing needs; fixed term but renewable (up to five years); and continuing, to be granted only to staff having served on fixed-term contracts for at least five years and meeting "the highest standards of efficiency, competence and integrity".[7]

Among organizational reforms was the GA's approval in 1974 of the International Civil Service Commission (ICSC). While this body seeks to establish a common system for the United Nations and affiliated agencies in respect to hiring, salaries and conditions of professional staff employment, not all agencies accept its mandate. The Bretton Woods agencies, in particular, retain their own rules. The fact that their employees enjoy higher salaries and more employment "perks" than do those in other parts of the UN system has contributed to problems in retaining top-level talent and adversely affects the morale of *relatively* disadvantaged UN staff, notwithstanding the fact that most such employees earn(ed) far more within the UN system than they could in their respective home countries.[8]

Complicating ICSC efforts to promote more uniform conditions of service is the fact that the various agencies of the UN system must deal with more than 100 separate employees' unions, grouped within three system-wide associations. Discussion of how these unions interact with the UN bureaucracy, however, is beyond the scope of this book.[9]

A perennial problem has been the underrepresentation of women at all levels of employment. The gender imbalance is especially striking in peacekeeping operations; as of 2008, women constituted a mere 2 per cent of peacekeeping forces worldwide. Among professional staff women fare substantially better, now accounting for 36.9 per cent of all personnel. Only at the lowest levels, however (civil service grades P-1 and P-2), have women achieved gender balance.[10] Among several reasons cited for the inadequacy of female representation are the following:

> First, member states nominate candidates for secretariat posts. Informal networks of support from which women are often excluded operate to nominate men ... Second, the principle of equitable geographical distribution ... sometimes works against women candidates. A highly qualified woman from a member state that is oversubscribed according to the UN's complex calculus for geographical distribution will probably lose out to a male candidate from a member state that is undersubscribed.[11]

Significant progress, however, may be on the way. In 2009 the GA agreed to establish a high-level agency for gender-related activities. This agency consolidated four bodies dealing with gender-related matters into a single entity, UN Women, headed since July 2010 by Under-Secretary General Michelle Bachelet, a former president of Chile and a strong advocate for greater parity in employment and gender-responsive planning and budgeting.[12]

Apart from the gender issue, there is still no approach to consensus on an equitable system of recruitment and placement of professional UN staff to provide an optimal balance between merit-based selection and geographical equity. This is true at all professional levels. Surprisingly, however, a small number of positions are, in principle, to be assigned according to predetermined formulae worked out on an agency-by-agency basis.[13] Excluded from considerations of geographical equity are virtually all "general service" positions (e.g. low-level clerical posts, drivers, custodial staff and the like), who are locally recruited in sites hosting UN agencies. Also excluded are translators, interpreters and persons with highly specialized professional skills (e.g. architects and medical practitioners). Additionally, a number of autonomous bodies (most notably the WFP, UNHCR, UNICEF and UNDP) were totally exempted. This left (as of 1994) a mere 2,550 "professional" positions in the UN Secretariat (51.5 per cent of the total) to be assigned on a geographic basis[14] and another 5,373 in 12 UN-affiliated specialized agencies. In percentage terms, the professional positions to be filled on a geographic basis ranged from a low of 45.3 per cent for the FAO to a high of 93.1 per cent for WIPO.

There is no persuasive rationale for the marked differences between agencies.[15] Nor are there compelling reasons for the formulae employed to fill the rosters of eligible job applicants. Although changed several times, the formula used in the UN Secretariat since 1988 is one that assigns 55 per cent of all geographic positions on the basis of contributions to the regular UN budget, another 40 per cent based on membership (with each UN member, however small, being entitled to an equal number of positions) and a mere 5 per cent on the basis of population. Several specialized agencies use similar formulae, but most appear idiosyncratic and are presumably outcomes of political bargaining. In the UNESCO formula, for example, of the 741 geographically assigned professional posts (74.5 per cent of the total) as of 1996, 76 per cent were allocated by membership, 24 per cent by contributions and none by population.[16] Further, to the extent that regional balance is considered (as in the ITU, UPU, WIPO and WMO), the regions recognized differ markedly from agency to agency.[17]

A GA report summarized the situation as follows:

> Over the years, discussions about equitable geographical distribution have been characterized by two dominant points of view. One group, composed largely of developing countries, wanted more weight to be given to the membership or, alternatively, to the population factor, whereas another group – mostly Member States with high rates of assessment – wanted to keep greater weight on the contributions.[18]

Overall, developed countries fare much better than those less developed. Although accounting for less than a fourth of the world's population, they hold roughly half the professional staff positions, irrespective of the level of such posts.[19]

Of course, the employment debate was never limited solely to geographically assigned posts. As Barbara Crossette observed:

> In reality, many of the 192 member nations of the UN see appointments for their citizens as plums to be picked and not as opportunities to serve. Government leaders try to influence the UN work from within these Secretariat positions. Many people who hold good jobs get quickly addicted to New York life and resist working in the field, especially in dangerous or unsavory places.[20]

Viewed nationally, the employment data reveal many anomalies. As of 2005, 24 of the then 191 member states accounted for more than 72 per cent of all UN Secretariat staff (professional plus general service posts), each providing more than 100 employees. In itself this is not surprising; but the subset of six nations with more than 400 employees each is a curious mix: Ethiopia, France, Kenya, the Philippines, the United Kingdom and the United States.[21] One cannot but wonder how several of those nations managed to fare as well as they did.

Speaking at a retreat for senior UN officials in 2009, Secretary-General Ban Ki-moon rendered the following verdict: "Department heads squabble among themselves over posts and budgets and bureaucratic prerogatives as if they somehow owned them. But our departments, agencies and programs are not personal fiefdoms."[22] There is much room for improvement.

Suggested reforms

A by-no-means-small part of the problem of recruitment relates to the absence of agreement on the meaning of equity.[23] Nor is it clear what is meant by the phrase "on as wide a geographic basis as possible" in Charter Article 101. Given the UN's propensity to assign posts by member *nations*, one might suppose that the differences *between* proximate island nations – say between the tiny Polynesian nations of Samoa and Tonga – were somehow more relevant than the vastly greater cultural, social and economic differences *within* such large and populous states as India, China, Russia, Brazil and the United States. Yet that is neither stated nor implied by the Charter. By adopting formulae favouring such minuscule – albeit sovereign – states as the island nations just noted, one necessarily disadvantages the populations of major states and might preclude representation from ethnic groups numbering in the millions. India, for example, has at least 18 languages spoken by more than a million persons each.[24] It is virtually certain that some of these groups are nowhere represented in the employment rolls of the UN Secretariat or affiliated agencies. Is it just that their chances for employment should be constrained by the politically correct attitude that puts the interests of states, however small, above those of peoples?

The following guidelines are suggested for hiring junior-level administrative staff.[25]

- In the secretariats of the United Nations and affiliated agencies, wherever staffs are enjoined to pay their primary allegiance to *global* institutions the number of positions allocated to *individual* member nations should not, *per se*, be a matter of major concern.
- Nevertheless, it is important for persons with diverse perspectives and cultural orientations to be represented, thereby heightening the sense that *the United Nations belongs to the whole of the human family.*
- The desirable diversity can be adequately obtained through a system based on representation by major world *regions* and *subregions*, rather than primarily by individual nations.

- There is little justification for basing representation quotas on the level of a country's contributions to the budget of the United Nation or its affiliated agencies.
- Merit (judged in respect to inherent intelligence and potential for development) should, within reasonable limits, take precedence over place of origin in assigning civil service positions.
- Although *privilege* is very unevenly distributed worldwide, *human intelligence and the potential for personal development are more or less evenly distributed* among all large population cohorts; thus recruiting worthy entry-level professional staff from all parts of the world is a realizable goal.
- Attaining the aforementioned goal will require establishing a global system of periodic examinations (administered at UN country headquarters) to establish rosters of potential staff from which entry-level professionals will be recruited when and as needed.
- Applicants passing an initial screening examination will be subsidized, if necessary, in getting to a higher-level office for one or more additional rounds of qualifying examinations, including face-to-face interviews with senior UN officials.
- A duly empowered, politically neutral UN Civil Service Commission, functioning under GA auspices, should play a key role in recruitment.
- To overcome existing discrepancies in privilege (based on personal connections, class, national origin, etc.) and inculcate new professional staff with an ethos of global service and a fundamental knowledge of how the United Nations functions, *all* professional recruits will be required to spend an initial year in training under the auspices of a multipurpose UN Administrative Academy (discussed in Chapter 12).
- To weed out individuals who regard UN employment as a potential sinecure, all applicants must be made to understand that approximately four months of the initial training year will be spent at a stressful field location and periodic alternation between headquarters and field posts would be a condition of employment and advancement.

As argued above, geographic diversity can be obtained through a system based on representation by major world regions, rather than individual nations. But to achieve this goal fair and workable allocation formulae are needed. Although there is no obviously optimal formula for allocating positions on UN rosters, some proposals would clearly have much greater, more widespread acceptability than others. The following guides are relevant:
- the regions selected shall be comparable in respect to population, global importance and size (i.e. the differences between the greatest and the least will all be within a single order of magnitude)

- the number of regions within the system shall not be unmanageably large
- the regions selected shall be widely recognized for their economic, cultural and/or political coherence
- *population* should be the most important variable in the allocation formula
- there shall be an *acceptable range* for recruitment above and below the proportional regional or subregional share of the total determined by the formula
- no region or subregion shall have an inordinately large share of the total pool of positions to be filled.

Table 9.1 sets forth a nine-region system consistent with the foregoing desiderata. It – or some reasonably close variant – would presumably be met with considerable approval and be deemed suitable for most future recruitment. The basic formula is simple. Target shares are the means (column *d*) between two percentages: population, expressed as a percentage share of the world total, and a constant, 11.11 per cent or one-ninth of the total. The use of the constant leads to convergence between the means for the most and least populous regions and ensures that no region can be represented to an inordinate degree. Column *f*, indicating a range of acceptable shares in the employment roster, is a set of values 15 per cent above and below the stated means.

If adhered to strictly, the system would yield a possible regional high of 20.64 per cent for South Asia and a possible low of 6.08 for Northern Eurasia, with a ratio of 3.4:1 between those extremes. But projecting population trends into the future – with relatively high rates of increase for South Asia and declining population for Northern Eurasia – the gap could widen substantially. By 2050 South Asia's maximum share may even exceed 25 per cent. Under the circumstances it might be politically prudent to impose an arbitrary regional maximum share of 20 per cent of total civil service employment, which is still substantially better than South Asia's current representation. Additionally, it might be desirable to gradually reduce the accepted range around the targeted mean as the capacity of lagging regions to provide capable personnel expands.

To conform to the stipulated Charter goal of attaining the widest possible geographic representation, it would be appropriate to establish recruitment fields (subregions) within each of the regions of Table 9.1.[26] While some of these might consist of a single country, others would be blocs formed from contiguous groups of related and demographically small states. To ensure that a subregion is sufficiently populous to guarantee the emergence of a pool of highly talented and motivated individuals, some minimum population threshold, say 20 million, should be specified. In all, I suggest the establishment of between 50 and 75 subregions world-

Table 9.1 Suggested regional allocation of UN civil service roster positions

Regions *a*	Population, 2010 Millions *b*	% *c*	Regional Constant (%) *d*	Mean $c + d/2$ *e*	Acceptable range 0.85 *e*–1.15 *e* (%) *f*
Africa South of the Sahara	796	11.63	11.11	11.37	9.10–13.64
East Asia	1,572	22.99	11.11	17.05	13.64–20.46
Europe	543	7.93	11.11	9.52	7.62–11.42
Latin America and Caribbean	577	8.44	11.11	9.78	7.82–11.74
Middle East and North Africa	506	7.40	11.11	9.26	7.41–11.11
North America and Oceania	379	5.55	11.11	8.33	6.66–9.58
Northern Eurasia	279	4.08	11.11	7.60	6.08–8.74
South Asia	1,592	23.28	11.11	17.20	13.76–20.64
Southeast Asia	589	8.62	11.11	9.86	7.89–11.83
Totals	6,840	100.00	100.00	100.00	

Source: Data were derived from *2010 World Population Data Sheet*, Washington, DC: Population Reference Bureau, 2010.
Notes:
Africa South of the Sahara: all African states not members of Arab League; East Asia: China, Japan, DPRK, Republic of Korea and Mongolia; Europe: all European states west of the former USSR, plus the Baltic states, Cyprus and Israel; Latin America and the Caribbean: all American states south of the United States; Middle East and North Africa: all Arab League countries in Africa and Asia, plus Turkey and Iran; North America and Oceania: United States, Canada. Australia, New Zealand and 12 small Pacific island states; Northern Eurasia: Russia and former Soviet republics (other than the Baltic states); South Asia: India and seven additional members of SAARC; Southeast Asia: all members of ASEAN plus Timor-Leste.

wide. Because *intra*-regional differences in culture and other relevant variables will generally be less than *inter*-regional differences, there is no need for more than a single determinant, namely population, in allocating shares of the regional roster totals for each subregion.

By way of example, Table 9.2 indicates how shares might be allocated among seven subregions within the Latin America and Caribbean region. Column *c* indicates a general target share as a proportion of the regional total, while column *d* indicates acceptable deviation below and above that target. In this table the acceptable range around each target is broadened from the 15 per cent employed in Table 9.1 to 25 per cent, in that deviations from statistical norms tend to be greater for small than for large populations. Overall, the proportional differences between the

Table 9.2 Proposed allocation of UN civil service roster positions by recruitment subdivisions of the Latin America and Caribbean region

Subdivision a	Population Millions (2010) b	% of regional total and of roster allotment c	Acceptable range 0.75 c–1.25 c (%) d
Mexico	108.4	18.79	14.09–23.49
Central America	41.9	7.26	5.44–9.08
Caribbean	39.6	6.86	5.14–8.58
Northern Andes	73.3	12.71	9.53–15.89
Central Andes	53.3	9.24	6.93–11.55
Southern Cone	67.2	11.65	8.74–14.56
Brazil	193.3	33.51	24.16–41.92
Totals	576.9	100.00	

Source: Data were derived from *2010 World Population Data Sheet*, Washington, DC: Population Reference Bureau, 2010.
Notes:
Central America excludes Belize; Caribbean includes all islands of the West Indies (including all dependencies), plus Belize, Bermuda and the Guianas; Northern Andes includes Colombia and Venezuela; Central Andes includes Ecuador, Peru and Bolivia; Southern Cone includes Argentina, Chile, Paraguay and Uruguay.

minima and maxima of Table 9.2 (from the Caribbean's 5.1 per cent minimum to Brazil's 41.9 per cent maximum in column *d*) are substantially greater than the corresponding range in Table 9.1, yet still within a single order of magnitude. While the figure of 41.9 per cent as an acceptable maximum for one country may seem unacceptably high, one must recall that that figure is a percentage of the regional total, varying within a range from 7.8 per cent to 11.7 per cent of the world total.

Less complicated than promoting regional equity is the question of gender equity. Although some would-be reformers argue for maximal parity (the reservation, as nearly as possible, of 50 per cent of all posts to women, agency by agency, region by region and at all levels of employment), such a recommendation seems excessively rigid and not conducive to maximizing merit. In some agencies female majorities might prove desirable, and the converse is also true. As with geographic placement, I would advocate establishing acceptable ranges applying equally to both males and females. For the UN civil service as a whole, the acceptable range might be 45–55 per cent. For regions and major agencies, 40–60 per cent might be desirable. And for subregions and minor agencies, ranges as wide as 35–65 per cent might be acceptable. In all cases, female majorities would be regarded no differently than male majorities.

To this point I have considered merit and equity among *junior-level* professional staff. But what of the small pool – presently numbering only in the low hundreds – of agency directors, assistant secretaries-general and under-secretaries-general? To what degree should geographic and gender considerations figure in their selection? This is not an easy question. On the one hand, one can assert that country of origin or gender should never be a bar to selection. At the very least, eliminating such bars would heighten the sense of inclusiveness of the UN system. On the other hand one may argue that if *merit* is to be the principal determinant of acceptability, neither factor should provide the *key* to selection. Political correctness would have to give way to promoting the greater good of the people to be served. Nevertheless, if two candidates for a position were truly of more or less equal merit, it would be appropriate to choose the one from a region of the world that is underrepresented in top-echelon positions or to pass over a candidate from a region that is relatively overrepresented.

Complicating the selection process is the understandable attitude that determining merit among senior staff is not the same as for entry-level professionals. In the latter case, both inherent intelligence and potential for growth should weigh heavily; in the former, the UN system cannot afford the luxury of waiting years for a particular individual to blossom into his/her ultimate capability. Thus, on balance, candidates from developed countries who have been privileged to attend highly prestigious universities, move in circles of politically powerful actors, enjoy careers enabling them to manage substantial budgets and other resources, and participate in influential think-tanks or commissions are more likely to have highly impressive resumes than equally intelligent professionals from countries mired in poverty. Similarly, given prevailing gender attitudes over most of the world, men are more likely to enjoy substantial career advantages over women. These lamentable imbalances, however, should diminish over time as outstanding individuals from an impartially recruited elite civil service staff move up through the ranks within the UN system.

But, say what one will about merit, as the United Nations is presently constituted, quality will often be trumped by political considerations, especially when vetting by the P-5 and election by the GA determine the selection process. As noted by Weiss:

> From the outset of the UN's existence ... the permanent members of the Security Council reserved the right to "nominate" (essentially to select) officials to fill the main posts in the secretary-general's cabinet. This procedure applies virtually everywhere to positions above the director level, and often below as well.[27]

Remedies to the shortcomings noted above have been proposed by a number of leading experts on the United Nations. I would endorse the following recommendations:[28]

- that all vacancies at director level and higher (right up to Secretary-General) be advertised worldwide well in advance of their being filled and specific and rigorous requirements for each such position be made explicit
- that the accuracy of resumes of job applicants be determined by a duly authorized UN body and vetted resumes made available to all members of the GA
- that no post be reserved for a specific country or world region and there be no predetermined order of rotation among regions in filling existing vacancies
- notwithstanding the preceding recommendation, there *could* (but need not) be a requirement that successive holders of specific posts at the level of assistant secretary-general and higher should not come from the same major world region and/or the post should alternate between developed and developing nations
- that GA balloting to select holders of top-level UN posts be secret.

Conclusions

The quality of human resources is a key to the successful functioning of any bureaucracy. Many shortcomings of the UN system can be attributed to deficiencies in the ways by which its personnel have been recruited, placed, utilized and promoted. Despite widespread agreement on what those shortcomings are, the requisite will to take bold corrective measures is still lacking. But, unlike many problems relating to the UN's basic *structure*, which can be corrected only by the lengthy process of Charter reform, civil service reform can be effectively addressed in the relatively short term. How then does one generate the requisite will? Conceivably, disenchantment with the existing system will mount to the level needed to initiate a serious reform process. Alternatively, some major new scandal – even greater than the oil-for-food fiasco – will prove to be a major catalyst for change. Another possibility (already tried with limited success) would be for the chief contributors to the UN budget to withhold payment of their UN assessments until the GA endorses meaningful reform measures. Such an approach, however, would polarize the United Nations to an even greater degree than at present and is not recommended. Mutually beneficial bargains must be crafted.

This chapter has put forward a set of workable ideas that would lead to a truly inclusive, merit-based civil service that would put the welfare of humanity before the interests of individual nations and be seen as equitable in respect to gender balance and the geographic distribution of positions at all employment levels. The existence of such proposals should stimulate the reform process. In no case should the proposed recommendations be regarded as the only ones worthy of discussion. But, assuming they do have merit, they should at a minimum provide a platform for discussing what might work best and why.

Implementing the recommendations in this chapter would, undoubtedly, be costly. But the expense should be looked upon as an investment that will yield long-term organizational benefits. Cheap, as a rule, is cheap. The present cheap system is not sustainable and must be improved.

Notes

1. Balanced overviews for the subjects covered in the first two sections are James O. C. Jonah, "Secretariat: Independence and Reform", in Thomas G. Weiss and Sam Daws (eds), *The Oxford Handbook on the United Nations*, New York and Oxford: Oxford University Press, 2007, pp. 160–174; Charlotte Bunch, "Women and Gender", in Thomas G. Weiss and Sam Daws (eds), *The Oxford Handbook on the United Nations*, New York and Oxford: Oxford University Press, 2007, pp. 496–310; Thomas G. Weiss, *What's Wrong with the United Nations and How to Fix It*, Malden, MA: Polity Press, 2008, pp. 107–124.
2. Marcus Franda, *The United Nations in the Twenty-First Century: Management and Reform Processes in a Troubled Organization*, Lanham, MD: Rowman & Littlefield, 2006, pp. 190–195, provides a trenchant review of recruitment since the UN's inception.
3. Quoted in ibid., pp. 191–192.
4. Jonah, note 1 above, pp. 161–162; Franda, note 2 above, p. 194.
5. Jonah, note 1 above, pp. 162–164; Franda, note 2 above. A fuller account is provided in the biography by Brian Urquhart, *Hammarskjöld*, New York: Alfred A. Knopf, 1972.
6. Jonah, note 1 above, p. 165.
7. Ibid., p. 162.
8. For a revealing set of differences see the comparison of basic UN principles with World Bank and IMF characteristics in Erskine Childers and Brian Urquhart, *Renewing the United Nations System*, Uppsala: Dag Hammarskjöld Foundation, 1994, Table 3, p. 178. Comparable data on average government civil service wages in a sample of 13 countries and academic salaries in six countries are presented in Jean-Marc Coicaud, "International Organizations as a Profession: Professional Mobility and Power Distribution", Research Paper No. 2006/109, United Nations University – World Institute for Development Economics Research, Helsinki, 2006.
9. Key details on this little-studied issue are provided by Franda, note 2 above, pp. 195–199.
10. Weiss, note 1 above, pp. 115–119, provides recent data, with emphasis on staffing peacekeeping operations.
11. Interview with Devaki Jain, 11 October 2005, cited in ibid., p. 119.
12. *Minerva*, "Gender Equality Architecture Reform at the United Nations", *Minerva* 35, November 2009, pp. 60–61; "UN Women", www.unwomen.org/about-us/executive-director/.

13. The data in this paragraph are from Faith Bouayad-Agha and Homero L. Hernández, *Comparison of Methods of Calculating Equitable Geographic Distribution within the United Nations Common System*, Geneva: UN Joint Inspection Unit, 1996, p. viii.
14. Coicaud, note 8 above, p. 6, gives the actual number so employed, as of mid-2005, as 2,581.
15. Ibid., pp. 1–12.
16. Bouayad-Agha and Hernández, note 13 above, pp. viii and 5.
17. Ibid., *passim.*
18. GA Department of Public Information, "Geographic Distribution of UN Staff", UN Doc. GA/AB/3702, 1 November 2005, www.un.org/News/Press/docs/2005/gaab3702.doc. htm, p. 6. Most of the very lengthy title (and the text) concerns matters not relating to UN staff.
19. Abstracted from a much more complete dataset in Coicaud, note 8 above, Table 3, p. 8.
20. Barbara Crossette, "Ban Takes on Turf Wars that Cripple the UN", *UNA-USA E-Newsletter*, 1 October 2009, www.unausa.org/site/pp.asp?c=fvKR18MPjpf&b=4572085.
21. Coicaud, note 8 above, pp. 8–9.
22. Cited in Crossette, note 20 above.
23. Bouayad-Agha and Hernández, note 13 above, p. ix.
24. *Encyclopaedia Britannica 2009 Book of the Year*, Chicago, IL: Encyclopaedia Britannica, 2009, p. 768.
25. Similar, though less ambitious, goals were set forth in Irene Martinetti, "Secretariat and Management Reform", in *Managing Change at the United Nations*, New York: Center for UN Reform Education, 2008, pp. 55–77.
26. As with the regions of Table 9.1, the inclusiveness of subregions would be determined by the UN Civil Service Commission and subject to change over time.
27. Weiss, note 1 above, p. 109; Weiss also discusses several recent questionable appointments, pp. 109–110.
28. Though I have not strictly followed any single author, I have been especially influenced by Brian Urquhart and Erskine Childers, *A World in Need of Leadership: Tomorrow's United Nations—A Fresh Appraisal*, Uppsala: Dag Hammarskjöld Foundation, 1996; Weiss, note 1 above, pp. 191–206.

10

Engaging civil society: NGOs and other non-state actors

A strong civil society promotes responsible citizenship and makes democratic forms of government work. A weak civil society supports authoritarian rule, which keeps society weak.
Kofi Annan, statement to Parlatino, 14 July 1998

Introduction

Inclusiveness. That must become a mantra – arguably the most decisive mantra – for the UN system if that system is to acquire and maintain the legitimacy needed to deal effectively with the manifold challenges of the twenty-first century. When citizens in any society believe their concerns are not taken into account in decisions vitally affecting their well-being, they will question the legitimacy of the body making those decisions and many of their governments will refuse to comply. Hence this work's emphasis on more inclusive decision-making, both within and alongside the UN system.

Despite the UN's design as an organization of *nations*, and the fact that no person is legally an Earth citizen, it has become necessary in many contexts to think of ourselves as such. Mass failure to do so will inevitably exact a price, whether it be a degraded ecosystem, an outbreak of international war, large-scale insurrectionary movements and/or terrorism or greed-induced failures within the global financial system. States have, with rare exceptions, failed to appreciate this. But untold numbers of individuals have reached this conclusion; and many express their position

Transforming the United Nations system: Designs for a workable world, Schwartzberg, United Nations University Press, 2013, ISBN 978-92-808-1230-5

through civil society organizations (commonly designated as NGOs, or non-governmental organizations).

Since the Second World War a remarkable transformation of the still-inchoate architecture of global governance has been the proliferation and increasing influence of NGOs and other non-state actors on the international stage.[1] Among NGOs is a sizeable and diverse *international* sub-group, often dubbed INGOs, whose activities are of particular interest. While most NGOs may be subsumed under the "civil society" rubric, there is no consensus on what the term means.[2] Does it include the corporate sector of the economy? Labour unions? The media? Educational, scientific and professional organizations, possibly including think-tanks? Faith-based organizations, or for that matter religious communities themselves?

I shall not attempt to answer these questions; nor shall I discuss all the types of entities just noted. Rather the focus will be NGOs, especially the subset of INGOs, many of which are recognized by ECOSOC. Since there are tens of thousands of such groups, finding ways of enabling their voices to be heard on an equitable basis poses an enormous challenge; but I propose reforms by which all voices can find expression.

Less fully engaged as yet than NGOs, but wielding vastly greater power, are the world's multinational corporations (MNCs), collectively accounting for much the greater part of the world's total GNI. Since 1999 thousands of these firms have entered into "global compacts" with entities within the UN system. This chapter notes their immense potential benefits and suggests ways of keeping their potential dangers in check.

Non-governmental organizations[3]

The number of NGOs has grown exponentially in recent decades. More than a million are believed to exist. Of these, well above 250,000 working across state borders may be described as INGOs.[4] Although the number affiliated with the UN system is a small fraction of the total, even that select cohort now numbers more than 3,000.

The means by which NGOs enter into consultative status with one or more organs within the UN system is governed by rules established by ECOSOC in accordance with Article 71 of the UN Charter. These rules have been modified in response to reviews in 1950, 1968 and 1996 and the wide-ranging 2004 Cardoso Report (drafted by a commission headed by Fernando Enrique Cardoso, a former president of Brazil), *We the Peoples: Civil Society, the United Nations and Global Governance.*[5] Since 1996 NGOs with consultative status have been grouped within three categories – general, special and roster – determining the extent and manner of their UN relationships. Representatives from all three types may attend conferences and meetings, but only those in the select general category may propose agenda items,[6] while both general and specialized NGOs may make and circulate statements at meetings of ECOSOC and subsidiary bodies.[7] Additionally there is a large but vague fourth category, NGOs accredited to the Commission on Sustainable Development, most of which work with UN agencies in the field.[8] Table 10.1 indicates the increase in the number of each of the main NGO categories and of all three combined.

Obviously, the number of NGOs with which the United Nations seeks to cooperate leads to serious communications problems. How can several thousand NGOs expect to have their individual voices heard, much less their messages studied and acted upon? Only a small proportion – those with a strong membership base, ample funding and sophisticated PR capabilities – presently have a reasonable chance of winning out in the competition for attention. This must be corrected.

Table 10.2 shows changes in the regional distribution of consultative NGOs over the period 1996–2007. These data indicate substantially more rapid increase in the global South (especially Africa and Asia) than in developed countries. Latin America's increase slightly lagged that of the world as a whole. The most striking change occurred in Africa, where the increase was 736 per cent as opposed to 206 per cent for the world as a whole. Nevertheless, the African share remains low. Extrapolating trends into the future, one sees the potential for NGOs in developing countries to play significantly enhanced roles in decision-making and establish a more level global playing field. As they do, the countries where they are based will be more favourably disposed towards development and global governance projects.

Table 10.2 must, of course, be interpreted with caution since membership, funding, expertise and experience vary enormously from one NGO

Table 10.1 Number of NGOs in consultative status with ECOSOC by category for selected years, 1948–2010

Year	General	Special	Roster	Total
1948	13	26	1	40
1968	17	78	85	180
1992	38	297	409	744
1996	76	468	497	1,041
2000	122	1,048	880	2,050
2005	136	1,639	944	2,719
2010	138	2,137	1,070	3,345

Source: Global Policy Forum, www.globalpolicy.org/component/article/176-general/32119-ngos-in-consultative-status-with-ecosoc-by-category.html.

Table 10.2 NGOs in consultative status with ECOSOC by region, 1996 and 2007

Region	1996		2007		Increase, 1996–2007		% of total increase
	No.	%	No.	%	No.	%	
Europe	489	47	1,179	37	690	141	32.2
North America	333	32	924	29	591	177	27.5
Asia	94	9	510	16	416	442	19.4
Africa	42	4	351	11	309	736	14.4
Latin America & Caribbean	73	7	191	6	118	162	5.5
Oceania	10	1	32	1	22	220	1.0
World	1,041	100	3,187	100	2,146	206	100.0

Note: The number of NGOs by region in 1996 and 2007 was calculated by the author from percentages presented as *integer* values, and may therefore differ slightly from the actual figures.
Source: Global Policy Forum, www.globalpolicy.org/tables-and-charts-ql/ngos-tcql/32120.html.

to another. Some NGOs, in fact, have budgets substantially greater than the national budgets of the countries in which they work and also of the UN agencies with which they cooperate.[9] Additionally, there is the question of accessibility: many NGOs operating in countries distant from New York or Geneva simply cannot afford to maintain a presence at or close to those decision-making centres and therefore operate at a considerable disadvantage. As of circa 1999, for example, of the 1,550 NGOs associated with the UN Department of Public Information, only 251 were from the global South, while the proportion in consultative status with ECOSOC was even lower.[10]

Effectiveness depends also on local politics. Some NGOs operate with the active or tacit support of the governments of the countries within which they work. Others act, often at their peril, in defiance of the state, which often regards progressive NGOs as subversive. A strategy commonly followed in the latter case is to seek influential allies among sympathetic governments and NGOs. Those allies then pressure the NGO's home state, sometimes via the United Nations, to institute changes that would not otherwise be possible.[11]

NGOs serve the United Nations in many ways, summarized by Wapner as follows:

> They gather information, offer advice, educate member states, help draft treaties, mobilize governmental and citizen support for UN policies, provide data on the ground conditions relevant to the organization's operations, and gener-

ally supply a specialized knowledge base for UN deliberations and interstate negotiations. They offer these services at a range of United Nations forums, including conferences, ECOSOC and subsidiary body meetings, the Department of Public Information (DPI), and conferences of parties to various international agreements.[12]

NGOs also play roles in broader global arenas. As Forman and Segaar observe:

> Their contribution to global policy increases pluralism, gives voice to the aspirations of politically marginalized groups, and takes up critical issues that might otherwise not surface on the political radar screen. But rather than being simply voices of advocacy and opposition, they are increasingly engaging government and multilateral organizations as partners in global governance initiatives.[13]

The following list of Nobel Peace Prize awards testifies to the impact of INGOs since the UN's founding:[14]
- 1947 – Friends Service Council, American Friends Service Committee
- 1963 – International Committee of the Red Cross, League of Red Cross Societies
- 1977 – Amnesty International
- 1985 – International Physicians for the Prevention of Nuclear War
- 1997 – International Campaign to Ban Landmines
- 1999 – Médecins Sans Frontières.

Additionally, several individual laureates have done much important work through NGOs with which they are identified. The 2002 award, for example, went to Jimmy Carter, who has worked largely through the Atlanta-based Carter Center.

Some of the most notable NGO achievements have resulted from working together in strategic *ad hoc* coalitions to achieve specific goals. The International Campaign to Ban Landmines is one such case. Another example is the Jubilee 2000 campaign, which spread beyond its religiously inspired base and gained partners in some 40 countries in promoting billions of dollars of debt forgiveness for impoverished nations of the global South.[15] Similarly, the London-based International HIV/AIDS Alliance, founded in 1993, soon gained NGO partners throughout the world, resulting in substantial support for combating AIDS in Africa and elsewhere.[16] Finally, we note successes by coalitions of NGOs and other non-state agencies – including the Helsinki Watch Committee within the United States in concert with the Moscow Helsinki Group – in bringing about markedly reduced repression of political dissidents and other improvements in the human rights situation within the Soviet Union.[17]

Of particular importance in respect to global governance is the NGO Coalition on the International Criminal Court.[18] Founded in 1995 by a group of 25 NGOs, among which the World Federalist Movement – Institute for Global Policy (with headquarters in New York and The Hague) was especially prominent, the ICC coalition has since grown to include more than 2,500 organizations throughout the world. Its steering committee of 16 NGOs provides oversight for the coalition's activities, carried out through some 69 national subcoalitions, a clear majority of which are in developing countries. The coalition has received financial support from the European Union, eight individual European governments and such powerful actors as the Ford Foundation and John D. and Catherine T. MacArthur Foundation.[19]

Following completion of the ICC treaty in Rome in July 1998, the coalition focused on promoting ratifications. The requisite sixtieth ratification, sufficient to bring the treaty into force, occurred in July 2002. Additionally, the coalition monitors and supports the work of the court and the associated Assembly of States Parties, and promotes expansion and strengthening of the coalition's worldwide network.[20]

Some NGO coalitions have diffuse agendas, especially regarding the environment and sustainable economic development. For example, the 1992 Rio UN Conference on the Environment and Development, the so-called "Earth Summit", brought together some 2,400 representatives (including the present author) of roughly 1,400 NGOs, along with roughly 15,000 other interested persons (exclusive of the media), to meet in the Global Forum, held in tandem with meetings of the official delegations from 172 participating states. The summit's message, delivered to almost 10,000 on-site journalists, was sweeping and bold, namely that "nothing less than a transformation of our attitudes and behaviour would bring about the necessary changes" needed to save the planet from ecological catastrophe.[21] While the official outcome document, "Agenda 21, The Rio Declaration on Environment and Development", was watered down substantially, due to political pressure from various nations (especially the United States), it was undoubtedly much stronger than it would have been without NGO involvement.

The summit also produced a much stronger *unofficial* document, the Earth Charter, the idea for which originated in 1987. Following the summit, the charter took on a life of its own, with support from not only NGOs but also the government of The Netherlands, UNESCO, Mikhail Gorbachev, numerous municipalities and some 250 universities around the world. Rewritten over the period 1994–2000, the charter advances 16 guiding principles for benign stewardship of Planet Earth. Not surprisingly, it has been strongly opposed by those who see it as a blueprint for world government, a socialist manifesto and/or a subverter of established religion. Whatever the reality, it demonstrates the catalytic power of civil society.[22]

Since Rio, additional UN conferences with enthusiastic NGO participation have included the International Conference on Population and Development in Cairo in 1994; the Beijing Conference on Women in 1995; the World Summit for Social Development in Copenhagen, also in 1995; deliberations producing the Kyoto Protocol in 1998; the UN Millennium Summit in 2000 (contributing to adoption of the Millennium Development Goals); the UNCED + 10 Earth Summit in Johannesburg in 2002; the Copenhagen and Cancún Conferences on Climate Change in 2009 and 2010 respectively; and the Rio + 20 Conference in 2012.

NGO-led initiatives related to these conferences and others organized outside the UN ambit have produced numerous controversies, sometimes resulting in a powerful conservative backlash. Citing the need for *"fair trade*, rather than *free* trade", NGO opposition to the WTO brought an estimated 50,000 protesters to the WTO gathering in Seattle in 1999, shut down the WTO meeting in Cancún four years later and made its influence felt in the WTO's so-called Doha Development Round in Doha, Hong Kong, Geneva, Paris and Potsdam over the period 2001–2008.[23]

Finally, we must consider the World Social Forum, held annually since 2001 in response to the perceived excesses of economic globalization.[24] Though first convened by the municipal government of Porto Alegre, Brazil, the participants were from the outset largely representatives of NGOs. Attracting some 12,000 in its initial meeting, the gathering grew to 60,000 in its second year and more than 150,000 by 2005, with participants from across the world sometimes representing more than 1,000 organizations. In some years the forum was held in one city, in others – beginning in 2006–2007 – at multiple sites (35 in 2010). Representation from the global North has always been substantial, and resentful allegations, especially at the 2007 Nairobi forum, that Northern NGOs presumed to have authority to speak on behalf of peoples of the South became a source of tension. Although the forums produce no binding outcomes and initiate no concrete development projects, they are major shapers of economic and social opinions and cannot be cavalierly ignored by either UN or national decision-makers.

NGO challenges to policies of UN agencies and existing governments and their questioning of the privileges of ruling elites inevitably engender political opposition. Commenting on this, Edwards observes:

It is increasingly common to hear senior agency staff, academics, and journalists echo the complaints of some governments (especially in the Southern hemisphere) that NGOs are self-selected, unaccountable, and poorly rooted in society, thereby questioning their legitimacy as participants in global debates. It is not that ... civic engagement is being questioned: more that the practice of civic engagement may be distorted in favour of organizations with greater resources and more access to decision-makers in capital cities, perhaps marginalizing grass-roots constituencies in the process.[25]

This critique has undeniable validity. The North-South NGO divide surfacing in Nairobi and elsewhere (just as it does in many UN organs and deliberations), as well as the rich-poor divide in both the North and the South, must be addressed if NGOs are to function to their fullest potential. Moreover, in all parts of the world there are NGOs whose *bona fides* are suspect. Some are led by unreasonable zealots, narcissists or corrupt charlatans. Others were created as vehicles for providing employment and funding for staff with little aptitude for and/or dedication to their organization's ostensible purpose.[26] Some were created in response to changes in accreditation rules in 1996, when, in an effort to give developing countries a greater voice, it was decided to allow NGOs operating in *only one* country to enjoy consultative status. The unintended result was the establishment of numerous spurious "GONGOs" (government-organized non-governmental organizations).[27] The independence and integrity of NGOs may also be compromised by their acceptance of contributions from corporations whose economic interests might be adversely affected by the adoption of specific policies that the NGO may, absent such funding, choose to promote.[28]

Moreover, while NGOs are often touted for their alleged ability to bring expert scientific and technical knowledge to bear on major issues, the fact that individual NGOs often work at cross-purposes indicates that at least some of those positions must be ill advised. One need only consider the polarization of groups arguing "pro-life" and "pro-choice" positions in regard to abortion, especially in the United States, for proof of this observation.

Fortunately, the general thrust of the criticisms noted, especially those relating to the North-South divide and the resultant differential access to UN agencies, is acknowledged by many large and well-led agencies, as well as the United Nations itself. Among NGOs headquartered in the North, many would, presumably, be amenable to an increasingly sensitive UN consultative regime.

Criticisms notwithstanding, there can little doubt that the role of NGOs is, on balance, strongly positive and will increase substantially with the passage of time. In a BBC interview Kofi Annan put the matter this way:

You have no idea of how we work with civil society and the NGOs. They can lead and say things that I cannot say. There are times we don't like what they say or do, and times when they don't like what we say or do and there are moments when they are ahead of us. They can lead and say things I cannot say. We cannot operate in the field without our essential partners, the NGOs.[29]

With respect to legitimacy and function, the aforementioned Cardoso Report observed:

> The legitimacy of civil society organizations derives from what they do and not from whom they represent or from any kind of external mandate. In the final analysis they are what they do. The power of civil society is a soft one. It is their capacity to argue, to propose, to experiment, to denounce, to be exemplary. It is not the power to decide.[30]

Voices for all

Presently, the various organs of the UN system cannot consider more than a small proportion of the tens of thousands of NGO voices. This problem can be substantially mitigated. One key to doing so would be the establishment of a group of elective and representative thematically focused *civil society coordinating councils* (CSCCs). Five such councils are envisaged, one each to deal with human rights, environment, development, peace and security, and democratic governance. Participation would be open to all NGOs willing to abide by their rules and pay a modest membership fee. The work of the councils would be marked by transparency, fairness, accountability and statutory legitimacy.

Establishing viable CSCCs would be a complicated and time-consuming undertaking and I shall not here go into the many needed details.[31] In brief, the process would begin with establishment by the GA of an expert commission for each of the five thematic foci. The mandate of each commission would be to create, within a period of five years, a structure and set of rules for nominating and electing CSCC members, as well as operating instructions once a CSCC is established. Membership should be balanced in regard to both regional and gender composition. Commissions would be authorized to consult as needed with appropriate agencies within the UN system and civil society agencies.[32]

CSCCs would, in principle, be open to participation by any NGO. In practice, however, a workable system would require specific eligibility conditions. Each would-be participant would have to file a membership application and, once admitted, would have to submit an annual report in one of the six working languages of the United Nations. They would also have to pledge to abide by codes of ethical conduct, promising not to indulge in or support violence, to be civil in their discourse and publications and, in the case of religiously based NGOs, to refrain from proselytizing in UN-related projects.[33] Further, all organizations would be required to pay some modest fee, pro rata in accordance with their financial resources, to defray the administrative costs of the CSCC. While most participating NGOs would probably elect to be affiliated with only one CSCC, there would be no bar to multiple memberships provided that an NGO fulfilled the requirements of each. Failure to meet CSCC obligations or the filing of falsified reports would result in forfeiture of participation rights. Given the stated requirements, many NGOs, especially those that are mismanaged or involved in questionable activities, would probably choose not to participate in the system. Many others, probably a substantial majority, will stay out because they operate only within a single nation.

In view of the tremendous economic gulf between the world's wealthiest and poorest countries, an additional requirement for NGOs headquartered in countries with a per capita GNI above the global average (roughly $8,875 in 2010) would be the payment of some subsidization fee, on a progressive sliding income scale, to facilitate the participation of CSCC members from countries with a below-average GNI. Additional matching funds for meeting this end might be budgeted by the GA.[34]

As with any deliberative body, the size of each CSCC would ideally be small enough to be efficient, yet large enough to carry out its mission effectively. Depending on the thematic focus, bodies ranging in size from 50 to 125 elected councillors would likely prove suitable. Membership would be balanced in terms of gender (not less than one-third female or male) and geography. The geographic problem, as will be demonstrated, is more complex.

Devising a viable and fair system of *weighted voting* to elect CSCC members would be a thorny undertaking. On the one hand it would have to consider populations to be served within some acceptable regional framework. On the other hand it would have to reflect the great variations in the capability of existing NGOs. In respect to the latter, cumulative weights could be assigned via a system of *points* for relevant variables, as follows.

- *Budget.* Using a geometric scale, points would be assigned in a stepwise manner in accordance with regularly increasing multiples of some base figure. Doubling is suggested. If, say, the base figure were $100,000, all agencies with annual budgets up to that amount would receive one point. Those with an annual budget between $100,000 and $200,000 would get two points, those in the $200,000–400,000 range three points, and so forth. Using this geometric progression, an NGO would reach 12 points with a budget of $102.4 million dollars. Few agencies would exceed this figure, and it is doubtful that any would exceed 15 points.
- *Geographical range of activities.* One additional point would be assigned for every country in addition to that of the headquarters in

which a given NGO had paid staff working on organization projects. Most NGOs would receive no points in this respect, while a few would receive several dozen or even more. An arbitrary maximum, say 40 or 50 points, might be established.

- *UN consultative status.* Six points might be assigned to NGOs with "general" status, four to those with "special" status and two to those with "roster" status (cf. Table 10.1). The vast majority of NGOs would receive no points on this variable.

The number of points per NGO, given the above determinants, would probably range from one to more than 100.[35] (One could, however, set an arbitrary maximum of say 100.) Scores for all NGOs would be recalibrated at regular intervals.[36] The total number for all participating NGOs within the purview of the CSCCs cannot be confidently predicted. This is so not only because we cannot possibly know, at this juncture, how many NGOs will opt to participate, but also because of the absence of empirical research (so far as I am aware) to determine point totals for NGOs likely to participate. Nevertheless, I imagine that within a few years the totals in all cases would number no fewer than several thousand. Within each group it seems likely – using the data in Table 10.2 as a partial guide – that NGOs from the global North would presently account for at least 80 per cent of the total and very likely more than 90 per cent.[37] Thus it follows, in the absence of countervailing measures, that in any at-large CSCC election the combined voting power of Northern NGOs would likely lead to a council marked by serious and unacceptable geographic inequities. Although that problem would diminish over time, it must be addressed in the planning stage if a viable system is to be established.

A compromise solution might entail a weighting formula balancing the interests and relative strengths of intended service *receivers* (i.e. the people of the world) and service *providers* (i.e. NGOs). The following formula might achieve this end:

$$C = (P + N)/2$$

where C represents the percentage of the total number of councillors to which a given major world region would be entitled; P indicates the region's population as a percentage of the world total; and N indicates the total number of points of all participating NGOs in the region as a percentage of the world total. C, then, will be the average of P and N. Table 10.3 illustrates how the system might work. It presents a set of estimates as of the year 2025 – there being virtually no likelihood of the system's coming into effect before that date.

Should the estimates be close to the mark, the average distribution of seats in the five proposed NGO coordinating councils in 2025 would be

Table 10.3 Hypothetical regional allocation of seats in 100-member Civil Society Coordination Council, as of 2025

Regions a	Population % b	NGO points % c	Mean weight $(b + c)/2$ d	Councillors e
Africa South of Sahara	13.5	4.5	9.00	9
East Asia	21.0	7.5	14.25	14
Europe	7.0	35.0	21.00	21
Latin America & Caribbean	8.5	6.5	7.50	7 or 8
Middle East & North Africa	7.0	5.5	6.75	7
North America	5.0	32.0	17.50	17 or 18
Northern Eurasia	3.5	1.5	2.50	2 or 3
South Asia	25.5	3.5	14.50	14 or 15
Southeast Asia & Pacific	9.5	4.5	7.00	7
Total	100.0	100.0	100.00	100

Notes:
Percentages in columns *b* and *c* are rounded to nearest 0.5 per cent.
Population figures for 2025 are based on projections of Population Reference Bureau, *2009 World Population Data Sheet.*
NGO points are the author's rough estimates based in part on extrapolations from the data of Table 10.2 and on subjective estimates of average regional point weights.

such as to give a slight majority to NGOs based in the global South and would show modest improvement (from a Southern perspective) over the present situation wherein NGOs from the global North enjoy an advantage. Moreover, the South's edge would likely increase with the passage of time. But one should keep in mind the important asymmetries between Northern and Southern NGOs. Among those asymmetries is the fact that many Northern-based NGOs (e.g. Oxfam, Amnesty International and the relatively new and meteorically rising Avaaz) draw a significant part of their membership and staff from the global South, whereas the converse is almost never the case.

The period during which councillors would meet face to face would not be fixed; but a predetermined starting time and minimum duration for plenary meetings of the council, perhaps as little as one month, would be established. Annual meetings could alternate between New York and Geneva. When not in face-to-face session, the council's work could be carried out by an executive committee elected by the councillors from their own ranks, assisted by a secretariat of modest size. Much of the work would rely on the internet. On specific issues, at any time of the year, member organizations could be polled to ascertain their views on controversial matters. Their votes would then be counted with reference to their respective point weights.

Figure 10.1 illustrates how the work of a council – in this case the CSCC for Human Rights – would relate the work and concerns of member NGOs to the functioning of the UN system. It shows a number of vertical and horizontal linkages – all involving two-way information flows – among organizations operating on various planes, from that of the grassroots NGOs themselves upward to the UN's existing and proposed major organs (exclusive of the ICJ). Some linkages would take the form of required annual reports; others would be *ad hoc*.

The most important CSCC functions would be to receive, discuss, harmonize and prioritize recommendations from NGOs, acting in *coalitions* focused on promoting shared goals within the CSCC's purview, and then to pass on those recommendations annually in a consolidated report to the UN agency or agencies most concerned (in this case the Human Rights Council). To the extent feasible, the CSCC would make the progress of its deliberations available via the internet to the participating coalitions as well as NGOs, and receive feedback from them which it would then use in shaping the final draft of its reports. Minority reports could also be transmitted. In either case an accounting would be provided of NGOs willing to go on record in support of, or opposition to, the report. Additionally, the CSCC would study and comment upon relevant debates and resolutions within the UN system and pass its own views down to participating coalitions. Coalition staff would then discuss the UN and CSCC reports and transmit them – possibly with additional commentary – to individual member NGOs. They would also transmit feedback to the CSCC.

At the UN level, the relevant UN organ – here the HRC – would be obliged to *discuss and comment upon* CSCC reports and transmit its findings to the UN Secretariat and other major UN organs. The UN Secretariat would translate the CSCC and HRC reports into the UN's official languages, append to them relevant resolutions by various UN agencies and make the reports available to the public through the Department of Public Information. While the HRC would not be obliged to take *substantive action* on those reports, it would undoubtedly take them into account. Other major UN organs would also likely consider CSCC and HRC reports.

Apart from required annual reports, the CSCC would respond to unscheduled *ad hoc* requests for its views from concerned UN agencies. It would, however, be understood that in the interests of expeditiously obtaining needed information or advice (especially in emergency situations),

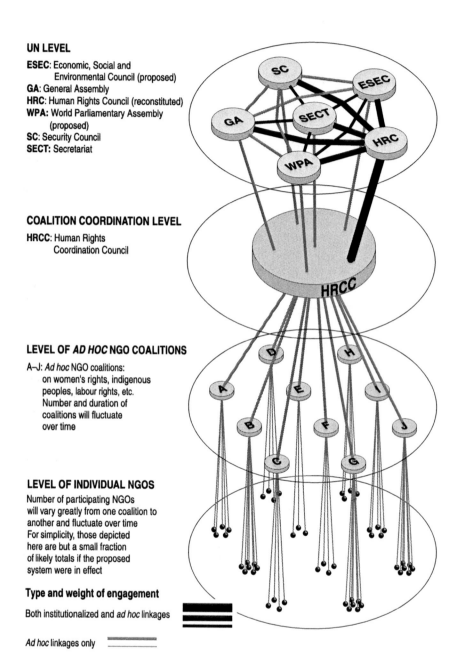

UN LEVEL

ESEC: Economic, Social and
Environmental Council (proposed)
GA: General Assembly
HRC: Human Rights Council (reconstituted)
WPA: World Parliamentary Assembly
(proposed)
SC: Security Council
SECT: Secretariat

COALITION COORDINATION LEVEL

HRCC: Human Rights
Coordination Council

LEVEL OF *AD HOC* NGO COALITIONS

A–J: *Ad hoc* NGO coalitions:
on women's rights, indigenous
peoples, labour rights, etc.
Number and duration of
coalitions will fluctuate
over time

LEVEL OF INDIVIDUAL NGOS

Number of participating NGOs
will vary greatly from one coalition to
another and fluctuate over time
For simplicity, those depicted
here are but a small fraction
of likely totals if the proposed
system were in effect

Type and weight of engagement

Both institutionalized and *ad hoc* linkages

Ad hoc linkages only

Figure 10.1 Proposed system of engagement of human rights NGOs with major
UN organs and human rights engagements among these organs

those agencies could go directly to the coordinators of specific coalitions or even to individual NGOs. By the same token, there would be no bar preventing individual NGOs or coalitions from bypassing the CSCC and seeking to reach influential allies – whether countries or other agencies – which might agree to further some urgently pressing initiative.

In essence, Figure 10.1 seeks to indicate an orderly way of bringing greater fairness, legitimacy, transparency and accountability to UN-NGO relationships. While the proposed architecture may appear complicated, the present jerry-rigged system is actually more complex. Nevertheless, Figure 10.1 presents an oversimplified picture, excluding many types of linkages that would continue under *any* future NGO dispensation. Such linkages connect NGOs with affiliated IGOs (e.g. the World Bank, WHO, UNESCO, etc.), regional agencies (e.g. the European Union), governments at national and lower levels, foundations and other donor agencies, think-tanks, unaffiliated political activists, corporations and so forth.[38]

Moreover, Figure 10.1 simplifies the dynamic process of coalition building. Coalitions are often formed at multiple levels, depending on the political context and the actors with which they seek to work. With respect to human rights, for example, separate coalitions might be formed in regard to eliminating violence against women, gaining equality for women in the economic domain, promoting reproductive rights and better family planning, and other vital issues. For certain purposes, however, all these would merge within a larger, all-encompassing women's coalition. Similarly, indigenous peoples might form separate coalitions in the Americas, Southeast Asia, Oceania and elsewhere, but unite in a super-coalition when dealing with the CSCC.

In summary, the main thrusts in creating CSCCs would be to provide a means whereby all legitimate voices can be heard and counted, and maximize and systematize the flow of information and informed understanding between NGOs at or near the grassroots level of the global governance system and various UN agencies at its apex. The system proposed represents a *pragmatic compromise*. It is neither perfectly democratic nor based solely on the realpolitik of economic power or on presumed technical and scientific expertise. Rather, it combines diverse desiderata in a way that is at once maximally inclusive and reasonably equitable. Finally, it is amenable to change as the world evolves.[39]

The private commercial sector

Unlike NGOs, which have interacted with various parts of the United Nations virtually since the organization's founding, significant officially sanctioned cooperation between the private commercial sector and the

United Nations is a recent phenomenon. To be sure, there were modest inputs from individuals prominently associated with the business world – largely in the form of economic advice to UNDP and predecessor programmes in the 1950s and 1960s – but few funding or contractual ties.[40] In that governments wedded to a capitalistic economic model controlled the United Nations, GATT, the Bretton Woods institutions and other key agencies, they were able to shape policies and organizational structures to their liking; and there was, consequently, little incentive for *corporations per se* to become directly involved.

With the wave of decolonization cresting in the 1960s, the global economic climate changed substantially. A "new international economic order" was called for. In 1975, at the urging of ECOSOC, the Commission and Centre on Transnational Corporations were founded. For most of the next two decades these bodies sought ways of enhancing the capacity of newly independent nations to deal with transnational corporate interests and establish new codes of ethical corporate conduct. Western/Northern responses to this perceived Southern agenda were to transfer much of the commission's oversight to UNCTAD, increase the OECD's role in developing codes of corporate behaviour and obtain compatible declarations from the ILO.[41]

In 1986 changed leadership in UNDP ushered in a more cooperative period. Previously:

> UNDP's corporate self-image was long that of the servant of each developing country in which it was resident, but ... [it was] decided to change that by adding a "second track" of work: advocating (but not requiring) a set of policies that the program was convinced would contribute to development. These included the protection of the environment and the promotion of women, NGOs, and the private sector.[42]

Soon afterwards, following the collapse of the Soviet-led bloc, UNDP began openly to promote development through the private sector in all parts of the world and to help establish direct linkages with major corporate actors.

The pro-business climate grew even warmer with Kofi Annan's accession in 1997 to the post of Secretary-General. The following year the US business magnate Ted Turner provided an unprecedented billion-dollar gift to support UN causes and activities. This was followed by munificent bequests from other US corporate leaders, including Bill Gates. But whereas Turner's gift was not earmarked for any specific programme, that of Gates was tied to the WHO's fight against HIV/AIDS. Though few observers would question the altruistic nature of this and other recent large grants, one should consider the problematic precedent that they set, namely that wealthy, unaccountable corporate actors can leverage their financial power to bend programmes and priorities of particular agencies within the UN system to their own advantage.

The year 2000 marked the most innovative and, arguably, the most controversial economic undertaking of the Annan era, the formal launching of the UN Global Compact (GC). The GC has been described as:

> the largest voluntary corporate citizenship initiative in the world, whose mission is to ensure that business – in partnership with other social actors, including Governments, organized labour, non-governmental organizations (NGOs) and academia – plays an essential role in achieving the United Nations vision of a more sustainable and equitable global economy. Its participants voluntarily commit to advance ... universal principles on human rights, labour standards, environmental protection, and anti-corruption ... derived from core UN treaties.[43]

Participating firms are expected – even if not legally required – to incorporate these principles in their normal operations, undertake projects advancing broad social goals and render an annual accounting: a "communication on progress" on those projects for posting on the GC website.

Hailed for its enlightened approach and, *inter alia*, its potential to promote realization of the Millennium Development Goals, the GC took off quickly. By 2007 the number of participating businesses was roughly 3,000, including 108 of those on that year's "Global 500" list of the *Financial Times*. These 108 firms collectively employed almost 10 million workers, had approximately $5 trillion in assets and garnered annual revenues of $3.5 trillion. Most participating firms, however, were of relatively small or medium size. Slightly more than half were based in developing countries, while only 4 per cent had headquarters in North America.[44] By 2010 the programme had attracted participation from more than 6,000 businesses in 135 countries.[45]

In 2005–2006 a new, more elaborate governance framework was established for the GC. It entailed greater involvement from representatives of governments, donor agencies, corporations, labour organizations, eminent unpaid volunteers and other civil society stakeholders, and more comprehensive reporting and networking at local, national and UN levels.[46]

Projects undertaken under the GC umbrella are quite diverse, including, for example, assistance with various levels of education, social networking, improvements in telecommunications infrastructure, pipeline construction, small business training, strengthening judicial institutions and human rights training.[47] The geographic scope of projects is also impressive. Thus GC initiatives call into question the widely held assumption that corporations exist *solely* to maximize shareholder profits, and lead one to wonder how much further the GC approach can and should go. With respect to motives, the Secretary-General observed:

> For-profit enterprises are usually not in the business of philanthropy. They need a clear sense as to why partnerships in support of United Nations goals make good business sense. They could have many motives for engagement, which could include image-building, safeguarding long-term investments, building future markets, improving the quality of suppliers and contributing to more stable and predictable business environments.[48]

In a speech on "creative capitalism" delivered at the World Economic Summit meeting in Davos, Switzerland, in 2008, Bill Gates put the matter more simply, stating: "We have to find a way to make the aspects of capitalism that serve wealthy people serve poorer people as well."[49]

Not surprisingly, despite statements and actions such as this and Warren Buffett's 2006 pledge to donate $31 billion to the UN-friendly Gates Foundation,[50] verdicts on the GC vary. Many critics look with disdain on the whole enterprise, regarding it essentially as a UN sell-out to the business world, notwithstanding its demonstrable benefits to millions of people throughout the world: "some civil society groups and academics see it as a way for businesses to cloak themselves in UN legitimacy while continuing unsavory practices". On the other hand, "old suspicions linger ... [and] some in the business community worry that the initiative is an attempt at global regulation".[51]

To date, so far as I am aware, there have been no accusations of egregious improprieties in respect to carrying out GC obligations; but the Global Compact Board is empowered to investigate serious violations should any occur. Lax observance is another matter; in 2006 some 335 companies that had missed filing two consecutive annual reports of progress were "delisted" from the GC roster.[52] But despite the generally good record to date, as the programme expands oversight problems will inevitably multiply, as will the likelihood that corporate PR professionals and participating governments will "spin" unpleasant facts in unwarranted ways. As occurs frequently in the United States, corporate lobbyists and campaign contributions amounting to *de facto* bribery can subvert supposedly democratic processes; and there is danger of similar improprieties emerging in a UN system with a substantially increased global economic role.

While it is probably not necessary to make major changes in an already elaborate governance system, prudence suggests a need for enhanced oversight capability. One way of enabling this would be to expand the mandate and resources of the UN Secretariat Ethics Office established in 2006.[53] Additionally, one might require formal ECOSOC/ESEC approval for projects exceeding specified budgetary levels and/or those affecting more than a stipulated number of people.

Conclusions

Recent decades have witnessed a tremendous increase in the number of NGOs and other civil society actors, a phenomenal worldwide explosion in the use of electronic media, dramatic reductions in the cost and difficulty of international travel, and the resultant establishment of numerous issue-specific globally engaged civil society coalitions. Although existing methods of accrediting NGOs to work with agencies within the UN system are commendable, as far as they go, they are still incapable of giving a meaningful voice to most such organizations. Relatively weak and poor agencies of the global South generally operate at a substantial disadvantage in comparison to a select, mainly Northern set of privileged actors. This chapter has proposed institutional mechanisms by which these deficiencies in the state-centric global governance system can be fairly and rationally mitigated. Essential to the proposed system are the establishment of regular lines of two-way communication and institutionalizing issue-specific NGO coordinating councils, within each of which the views of member organizations can be considered, reconciled and transmitted to appropriate UN organs.

I have also noted the recent dramatic increase in the involvement of MNCs in projects involving local development programmes along with UN agencies. This development, under the aegis of the UN-sanctioned Global Compact programme, offers both great future hope and great future risk.

Notes

1. For an excellent discussion of the ways by which networks of non-state actors have learned to work cooperatively see Margaret E. Keck and Kathryn Sikkink, *Activist beyond Borders: Advocacy Networks in International Politics*, Ithaca, NY: Yale University Press, 1998. Regrettably the United Nations does not figure prominently in their analyses.
2. Among discussions of this question, I especially commend that of John E. Trent, *Modernizing the United Nations System: Civil Society's Role in Moving from International Relations to Global Governance*, Opladen: Barbara Budrich Publishers, 2007, pp. 9–10, 30–42 and *passim*.
3. In addition to ibid., good discussions of NGOs in relation to the UN system are provided in Paul Wapner, "Civil Society", in Thomas G. Weiss and Sam Daws (eds), *The Oxford Handbook on the United Nations*, Oxford and New York: Oxford University Press, 2007, pp. 254–263; Michael Edwards, "Civil Society and Global Governance", in

Ramesh Thakur and Edward Newman (eds), *New Millennium, New Perspectives: The United Nations, Security and Governance*, Tokyo, New York and Paris: United Nations University Press, 2000, pp. 205–220.

4. Wapner, ibid., p. 257.
5. Panel of Eminent Persons on United Nations-Civil Society Relations, "We the Peoples: Civil Society, the United Nations and Global Governance", UN Doc. A/58.817, 7 June 2004.
6. Within the general category, the Inter-Parliamentary Union enjoys a particularly favoured status.
7. Wapner, note 3 above, p. 258.
8. Wikipedia, "Consultative Status", http://en.wikipedia.org/wiki/Consultative_Status, plus list at http://habitat.igc.org/ngo-rev/csd-list.html.
9. Trent, note 2 above, p. 31.
10. Edwards, note 3 above, p. 213.
11. Keck and Sikkink, note 1 above, *passim*.
12. Wapner, note 3 above, p. 258.
13. Shepherd Forman and Derk Segaar, "New Coalitions for Global Governance: The Changing Dynamics of Multilateralism", *Global Governance* 12(2), 2006, pp. 205–225, at p. 216.
14. See http://nobelprize.org/nobel_prizes/peace/laureates.
15. Wikipedia, "Jubilee 2000", http://en.wikipedia.org/wiki/jubilee.2000.
16. See www.hivpolicy.org/blogs/HPEO216b.htm.
17. Keck and Sikkink, note 1 above, p. 24.
18. Trent (note 2 above, *passim*, but especially pp. 109–160) argues persuasively that, for the foreseeable future, major reform of the global governance system can come about only through initiatives emanating from NGOs and other components of the UN system, in that the present holders of power are either unable or unwilling to reform themselves and surrender a modicum of the power they currently possess.
19. Coalition for the International Criminal Court, www.iccnow.org//?mod=coalition; Wikipedia, "Coalition for the International Criminal Court", http://en.wikipedia.org/wiki/Coalition_for_the_International_Criminal_Court.
20. Wikipedia, ibid.
21. UN Conference on the Environment and Development (1992), www.un.org/geninfo/bp/enviro.html.
22. Wikipedia, "Earth Charter", http://en.wikipedia.org/wiki/Earth_Charter.
23. Wikipedia, "Doha Development Round", http://en.wikipedia.org/wiki/Doha_Development_Round.
24. Wikipedia, "World Social Forum", http://en.wikipedia.org/wiki/World_Social_Forum.
25. Edwards, note 3 above, p. 209.
26. These observations are based in part on the author's first-hand experiences in a number of countries. They are also supported by the comments of Cyril Ritchie in his printed overview of the Conference of Non-Governmental Organizations in Consultative Relationship with the United Nations (CONGO), Civil Society Development Forum, Geneva, 28–30 June 2007. CONGO Secretary Ritchie was at pains, however, to note that the cited defects were probably no different, proportionally, from those among "bankers, bishops or footballers".
27. Peter Willetts, "The Cardoso Report on the UN and Civil Society: Functionalism, Global Corporatism, or Global Democracy?", *Global Governance* 12(3), 2006, pp. 305–324, at pp. 318–319.
28. See, for example, Johann Hari, "The Wrong Kind of Green: How Conservation Groups Are Bargaining Away Our Future", *The Nation*, 22 March 2010, pp. 10–19.

29. Kofi Annan, BBC interview, 15 September 2005, quoted in Trent, note 2 above, p. 242.
30. Panel of Eminent Persons, note 5 above, p. 3.
31. A full exposition will be found in Joseph E. Schwartzberg, "Institutionalizing a Role for NGOs in the Work of the UN", in Paolo Bargiacchi (ed.), *Liber Amicorum*, Milan: Giuffré Editore, 2013.
32. Among active civil society agencies from which likely candidates might be drawn are the CONGO; CIVICUS, the World Alliance for Citizen Participation; Earth Charter International; the International Civil Society Forum for Democracy; the Union of International Organizations; the Global Partnership for the Prevention of Armed Conflict; and the World Federation of United Nations Associations. There would, however, be no bar to appointing individuals with no current institutional affiliation.
33. UN Fund for Population Activities, "Culturally Sensitive Approaches: Building Bridges among Faith-Based Organizations and Secular Development Practitioners", www.unfpa. org/culture/fbo.html. Faith-based organizations meet with suspicion in many quarters. They are thought, sometimes rightly, to be equally or more interested in proselytizing than in providing other needed human services; and many of them are perceived as agents of Western/Northern neoimperialism. Thus, in certain culturally sensitive domains, interaction between UN agencies and faith-based organizations has resulted in the development of codes of conduct to guide what sorts of activities may or may not be countenanced. Especially noteworthy in this regard is the code developed by the UNFPA in respect to family planning and dealing with the HIV/AIDS epidemic.
34. Travel support for representatives of NGOs in the global South was recommended by the Cardoso Report; but, as Peter Willetts pointed out (note 27 above, p. 317), the United Nations had by then already taken such an initiative, establishing and funding the Non-Governmental Liaison Service.
35. For example, the 2006 budget of Catholic Relief Services came to $560 million, enough for 14 points on this geometric scale; it would have more than 100 additional points for its services in an equivalent number of countries (where it reaches more than 100 million people); and another six points for its "general" ECOSOC accreditation. Its total point score would probably be approximately 125, possibly more than that of any other agency. Catholic Relief Services, http://crs.org; Caritas.org, www.caritas.org.
36. I have intentionally avoided assigning points on the basis of organizational membership for several reasons: first, many influential NGOs are not membership organizations; and second, membership criteria differ enormously from one organization to another, with some requiring no more than a personal indication of interest in the NGO's work while others have a dues requirement, in some cases substantial.
37. Adding the 2007 percentages for Europe, North America and Oceania, plus an estimate for the wealthier nations of East Asia, yields a Northern total of roughly 67 per cent. But given the financial resources and geographical reach of Northern NGOs, the estimates suggested seem reasonable.
38. Keck and Sikkink (note 1 above, *passim*) prefer to discuss "networks" rather than "coalitions" or "alliances".
39. In this sense, the proposal responds to Willett's (note 27 above) criticism of the lack of coherence in recommendations of the Cardoso Report, which allegedly attempted to be all things to all people, satisfying very few.
40. A succinct account of attempts by business interests to play a role in global governance from the first Hague Peace Conference onwards is provided in Craig N. Murphy, "Private Sector", in Thomas G. Weiss and Sam Daws (eds), *The Oxford Handbook on the United Nations*, Oxford and New York: Oxford University Press, 2007, pp. 264–274.
41. Ibid., pp. 267–269.
42. Ibid., p. 269.

43. Georg Kell, Anne-Marie Slaughter and Thomas Hale, "Silent Reform through the Global Compact", *UN Chronicle* 1, 2007, pp. 26–29, at p. 26. A list of 10 "universal principles", grouped under the treaties to which they relate, is provided.
44. Ibid., p. 26.
45. "Corporate Progress on Environmental and Social Issues Is Tangible, But Far from Sufficient, Global Survey Shows", www.unglobalcompact.org/news/127-06-07-2011.
46. "Global Compact Governance", www.unglobalcompact.org/aboutthegc/stages_of_development.html; "The UN Global Compact Board", www.unglobalcompact.org/the_global_compact_board.html.
47. The examples given are abstracted from a longer list cited in a report by the Secretary-General, "Enhanced Cooperation between the United Nations and All Relevant Partners, in Particular the Private Sector", UN GA Doc. A/58/227, 18 August 2003, pp. 11–14.
48. Ibid., p. 15.
49. Reported in "Bill Gates Issues Call for Kinder Capitalism", *Wall Street Journal*, 24 January 2008, http://online.wsj.com/article/SB120113473219511791.html.
50. Robert Smith, "Buffett Gift Sends $31 Billion to Gates Foundation", www.npr.org/templates/story/story.php?storyId+5512893.
51. Both quotations are from Kell, Slaughter and Hale, note 43 above, p. 29. For additional, mainly positive, evaluations see John Gerard Ruggie, "global_governance.net: The Global Compact as Learning Network", *Global Governance* 7(4), 2001, pp. 371–378.
52. Kell, Slaughter and Hale, note 43 above, pp. 29–30.
53. United Nations, "Reform at the United Nations, Ethics Office Establishment and Terms of Reference", www.un.org/reform/ethics/index.shtml.

11

The problem of funding

He who pays the piper calls the tune.
Old English proverb

No taxation without representation.
Pre-US Revolutionary War slogan

In this world nothing can be said to be certain, except death and taxes.
Benjamin Franklin

Introduction

How best to finance the manifold tasks entrusted to the UN system has been a major concern since the UN's founding. It raises highly contentious questions. What are the correct operative principles? How might the burden be most fairly and effectively shared? Should funding come from parties other than the member states. If so, to what extent? Should there be a single consolidated budget, or separate budgets for different agencies? Who should be responsible for establishing the budget(s)? How large should the budget(s) be? How should the United Nations deal with countries that are delinquent in meeting their payment obligations? The answers are not self-evident and responses have changed over time. In particular, the proportions of total funding provided by the regular budget, by the peacekeeping budget and by voluntary funding have fluctuated markedly.

Transforming the United Nations system: Designs for a workable world, Schwartzberg, United Nations University Press, 2013, ISBN 978-92-808-1230-5

This chapter discusses each of these issues. But the concern is less with past practice than to suggest reforms needed to meet the fiscal demands of the future, which will likely be at least an order of magnitude – perhaps two orders – greater than they are at present. These demands will call for establishing new sources of revenue and, in turn, institutionalizing new agencies for collecting and processing that revenue.

I begin with an overview of the current budgetary apparatus. I then present data on funding to date for the regular budget and national assessments, and note how different groups of nations regard those obligations. I next consider budgeting and sources of revenue for peacekeeping and other activities not covered by the regular budget. Noting that expenditures outside the regular budget constitute an increasingly large share of total UN expenditures, I explore possible sources of future funding. Finally, I propose a coherent set of reform recommendations.

Budgetary practices

Financial mechanisms[1]

According to Article 17 of the UN Charter, the GA shall "consider and approve the budget of the Organization", apportion expenses among UN members and "consider and approve any financial and budgetary arrangements with [UN] specialized agencies". This is, arguably, the most important among the few functions for which the GA exercises *binding* authority. Since the budget is deemed to be an "important" substantive issue, the requisite majority vote for approval is, in principle, two-thirds. In practice the budget has, with but one exception, been approved by consensus since 1986.

Since 1973 budgets have been prepared on a two-year cycle, and planning for each biennial budget begins two years before it goes into effect.[2] The Secretary-General and UN Secretariat are charged with the planning responsibility, which they carry out in accordance with rules established by the GA; and the GA has the duty of discussing, recommending changes in and approving the budget. Work is allocated as follows.

- The Fifth Committee discusses the budget, topic by topic, and issues relevant reports to the GA plenary.
- The elected Advisory Committee on Administrative and Budgetary Questions discusses budgetary topics of its own choosing and reports on them to the GA.
- The Committee for Programmes and Coordination, a subsidiary of both the GA and ECOSOC, considers the budget within its so-called "stra-

tegic framework" and prepares whatever recommendations it deems necessary.

- The Board of Auditors carries out an external audit of UN accounts, funds and programmes, and reports on them.
- The Committee on Contributions recommends the scale of assessments for UN member states.

There is unquestionably redundancy within this system. That may presently be seen as a justifiable safeguard against sloppy, less-than-candid or clearly dishonest reporting. However, a simpler, more effective system is possible.

The regular budget

Although critics often complain about the UN's burgeoning cost, the regular budget has always been remarkably – one might even say incredibly – low.[3] In its first budgeted year, the approved regular budget came to a mere $18.9 million. In *percentage* terms, growth in the budget was moderately high during the UN's early years; but, considering the very low starting point, *absolute* increases were modest. The $100 million mark was crossed only in 1965, $500 million in 1978 and the billion dollar mark in 1990. The 2010 budget came to just over $2.5 billion, or $0.37 for each person on this planet! (*Can the world really justify such extravagance?*) But the figures cited are in *current* dollars, as of the dates indicated. Adjusted for inflation, based on the US consumer price index, growth over the past four decades has been quite modest. Using 1971 as a reference year, when the budget came to $194 million, the Global Policy Forum found that the nominal budget of $2,073 million for 2007 (the last year for which calculations were made) translated to only $404 million in *constant* 1971 dollars. In short, in real terms the *regular* budget slightly more than doubled over a period of 36 years. This works out to an annual growth rate of approximately 2 per cent. The picture is significantly different, however, in respect to the peacekeeping budget and programmes funded by voluntary contributions (discussed later).

Throughout the UN's history arrearages in payments have been commonplace. A state in arrears to the extent of two years of its assessed obligations shall, in accordance with Article 19 of the Charter, have its vote forfeited, unless it is ruled – as has frequently happened – that the causes were beyond the state's control.[4] To avoid forfeiture, many states – at times including the United States – have paid just enough of their back dues to avoid losing their GA voting rights. In practice, states whose votes have been forfeited have either had pariah governments (e.g. Saddam Hussein's Iraq) or been under some sort of UN sanction (e.g. South Africa under the apartheid regime).

The scale of UN assessments has periodically been re-examined and adjusted in accordance with mathematical formulae for determining the percentages of the regular budget to be assessed for each member nation. The formulae in question were fairly complicated, never uniformly applied and frequently modified (usually at three-year intervals); but they were always keyed largely to per capita GDP (or later GNI) and presumed capacity to pay.[5] In effect, this resulted in "offsets" for a majority of countries (those with below-average per capita incomes) and compensatory increases for most wealthy states. Additionally, there were adjustments for countries with heavy debt burdens and politically negotiated assessment floors and ceilings. Initially the minimum member payment was set at 0.04 per cent of the total budget, but this figure was successively reduced to 0.02 per cent in 1974, 0.01 per cent in 1978 and its present level of 0.001 per cent in 2001. The United States has always paid the largest share, beginning at 39.89 per cent in 1946, with staged reductions to 33.3 per cent in 1954, 25 per cent in 1974 and then, following great pressure from the US Senate, 22 per cent in 2005 (well below the US share of world GDP, then roughly 29 per cent).[6] In consequence, Japan, wealthier members of the European Union and Canada, Australia and New Zealand had to make up the resultant funding shortfall. In the 2010–2011 biennium the top five contributors were assessed 55.3 per cent of the total regular budget, the top 15 81.5 per cent and the remaining 177 only 18.5 per cent. (Data are provided in Appendix 1.)

Table 11.1 highlights the enormous disparities in budgetary assessments over the period since the UN's founding. Yet despite these differences, the United Nations clings to the legal fiction of the sovereign equality of nations and accords all members equal votes in the GA and most other UN agencies. As previously noted, the gaping disconnect between the diplomatic pretence of equality, on the one hand, and the behind-the-scenes political recognition of inequality on the other contributes to perennial tension between the strong and the weak, the large and the small, the rich and the poor. The weak zealously defend their ability to command two-thirds majorities in votes on almost all substantive matters. Since 1987, however – at the insistence of the US delegation – the one substantive matter on which *consensus* decisions have been required is the adoption of the budget.[7]

The budgetary role of the United States is highlighted in Table 11.1 because so much of the UN's success – or lack thereof – depends on the level of its support from the United States. Apart from the pronounced US lead, when compared to the second-ranking power (except for 2005) the US share of contributions has doubled relative to the average for all states (line *f*). More dramatically, its assessment as a multiple of that of

Table 11.1 Highest, average and lowest assessments for regular UN budget for selected dates, 1946–2010

	1946	1955	1965	1975	1985	1995	2005	2010
a US assessment (%)	39.89	33.33	31.91	25.00	25.00	25.00	22.00	22.00
b Second-ranking member	UK	USSR*	USSR*	USSR*	USSR*	Japan	Japan	Japan
and its assessment (%)	11.98	15.08	14.92	11.60	10.54	13.95	19.47	12.53
c Average assessment (%)	1.887	1.315	0.862	0.694	0.629	0.524	0.521	0.521
d Minimum assessment (%)	0.04	0.04	0.04	0.02	0.01	0.01	0.001	0.001
e Line a as multiple of line b	3.33	2.21	2.14	2.16	2.37	1.79	1.13	1.76
f Line a as multiple of line c	21.1	25.3	37.0	36.0	39.7	47.7	42.2	42.2
g Line a as multiple of line d	997	893	798	1,250	2,500	2,500	22,000	22,000
h Number of UN members	53	76	116	144	159	191	192	192
i Members paying minimum	8	9	58	80	78	96	45	38
j Line i as % of line h	15.09	15.00	50.00	55.56	49.06	50.26	23.43	19.79

Notes:

*USSR percentages do not include separate assessments for Ukraine and Byelorussia.

Figures in lines c and e–j were calculated by the author.

Sources: Assessment percentages for 1946–1985 are derived from a table providing complete data up to the year 1991, sent to author in 1993 by Marc E. M. Gilpin and Mya M. Than of the then UN Contribution Service. Assessments for 1995 are from Europa World Year Book, 1996, Rochester: Europa Publications, 1996; and for 2005 from Europa World Year Book, 2006, London and New York: Routledge, 2006. Assessments for 2010 are from UN Secretariat, "Assessments of Member States' Advances to the Working Capital Fund for the Biennium 2010–2011 and Contributions to the United Nations Regular Budget for 2010", ST/Adm/Ser. B/789.

countries with minimum assessments (line *g*) rose from 997 to 22,000 over the period 1946–2005.

Study of the complete year-by-year array of assessment data for the period 1946–2010 reveals many additional remarkable facts. I cite but a few.[8]

- The P-5 nations accounted for more than half the total budget in every year up to 1980, when their combined assessments slipped to 47.9 per cent.
- The P-5 share of the total budget decreased steadily from its 1946 high of 71.1 per cent to 34.3 per cent in 2005.[9]
- The P-5 nations were the five top contributors every year until the UN's admission in 1971 of the German Federal Republic, which then assumed third place; ever since 1974 Japan and Germany have ranked second and third respectively.
- The most dramatic decline occurred in the USSR/Russia, which went from a high of 15.1 per cent in 1955 to 10.0 per cent at the time of the USSR's implosion, and then, as the Russian Federation, to a low of 1.1 per cent in 2000.
- Since its entry into the United Nations in 2002 Switzerland's assessment has exceeded the total for all 53 nations of Africa combined; in 2010 the respective figures were 1.130 per cent and 1.103 per cent.
- As of 1946 it was theoretically possible for an aggregation of economically weak nations accounting for just 10.2 per cent of the total budget to command the two-thirds voting majority needed to pass a substantive resolution in the GA. By 1975 this proportion fell to 2.4 per cent, and then to a mere 1.7 per cent in 2010.

Observers have drawn radically different conclusions from reviewing the UN's fiscal history. The continuing retention of power – one might even say the continuing stranglehold – within the United Nations of the P-5, despite their relative decline in funding, is regarded with disfavour in many quarters: by the former Axis powers, most notably Japan and Germany, whose economies now substantially outstrip those of France and the United Kingdom and vastly exceed that of Russia; by such newly emerging powers as India, Brazil and South Africa, which also feel entitled to SC seats; and, more generally, by the vast majority of the G-77. On the other hand, given the low assessment rates of the G-77, most developed nations are leery of their demands to have a greater say in the decision-making processes of the United Nations and its affiliated agencies.

The funding picture could not but rankle fiscally conservative – and often xenophobic – American legislators. Beginning in the 1980s, the US relationship to the United Nations, especially on budgetary matters, became especially stressful. Withheld and/or late payment of US assessments, for both the regular and peacekeeping budgets, pushed the United

Nations to the brink of insolvency. This economic power game gained for the United States a number of concessions that have compromised the UN's effectiveness ever since. Apart from the aforementioned requirement for budgetary consensus, the most important concession, arguably, was the agreement in 1991 to hold the United Nations to a nominal zero-growth budget.[10] With no allowances for inflation, this meant a significant diminution in budget in real terms in subsequent years. (Not until 2003 was this unsustainable condition reversed.) Additionally, the United States sought and obtained dozens of additional concessions, including a substantial reduction in UN staffing and promises that the United Nations would not create a standing UN army and would prohibit discussion of international "taxes".[11] The United States was not alone, however, in its desire to limit UN spending. In particular, the economically troubled Soviet Union/Russia supported it on some issues. But the onus for the damage done was borne mainly by the United States, the world's undisputed economic superpower.

In fact, it was the USSR that initiated the practice of withholding payments in respect to UN actions with which it disagreed. The action triggering this move was the UN's alleged lack of neutrality in handling the Congo peacekeeping mission of 1960–1964. In the Soviet view this provided sufficient grounds for non-payment, not only by the USSR but also its satellites, other allies and even France. Facing the loss of its GA vote for having accumulated a debt to the United Nations greater than two years of its assessments, the Soviet Union threatened to pull out of the United Nations altogether if that sanction were to be imposed. To avert so drastic an outcome the United States, which had previously urged application of Article 19, backed down and agreed that peacekeeping expenses would form part of a special account separate from the "regular budget".[12]

The peacekeeping budget

In contrast to the highly regulated – even if often contentious – process by which the UN's regular budget is established, funding for peacekeeping missions since the Suez crisis of 1956 has been carried out on an *ad hoc* basis, given that the need for such missions cannot be reliably forecast and that the United Nations never has a substantial cash reserve to draw upon when serious emergencies arise. The first signs of significant stress were brought about by the costs of peacekeeping during the previously noted Congo operation in the early 1960s. Although costs for that mission appear modest in contrast to recent operations, a number of poor, newly independent countries, mainly in Africa, withheld their assessed payments. The GA responded by establishing a system of discounts based on the poverty levels of different sets of countries, hoping that wealthier nations would make up the shortfall. Although that desired outcome was not realized, a precedent was established. In subsequent decades numerous assessment formulae were devised, with even less predictability or regularity than for the regular budget.[13] The general rule, however, was to reduce assessments of the poor even more than for the regular budget (with deductions, in 10 per cent increments, from 10 per cent to 90 per cent of the regular budget assessment). Conversely, wealthier nations – especially the P-5 – were assessed at higher rates. But, as with the regular budget, the United States insisted on an arbitrary ceiling: originally 33.3 per cent and subsequently 27 per cent, though many American legislators regard 25 per cent as appropriate.[14]

Over the years – and especially since the end of the Cold War as missions increased dramatically – expansion in the peacekeeping budget greatly outpaced growth in the regular budget. However, the level of actual *spending* fluctuated markedly. Because arrearages in regard to peacekeeping have been greater than in the regular budget and contributions may be in kind as well as in cash, comparable year-to-year data are hard to come by; but a reasonably good time series from 1946 to 2005 was constructed by the Global Policy Forum.[15] The data show marked year-to-year fluctuations, with dramatic annual drops and increases. In the peak year, 2005, expenditures exceeded $4.7 billion. While this sum may appear large, it represented a mere 0.42 per cent of that year's global total of $1.118 trillion ($178 per capita) for military expenditures.[16]

The 11 leading nations in respect to peacekeeping *assessments* (but not necessarily in *payments*) as of the 2010 budget are, in descending order: United States, 27.17 per cent; Japan, 12.53 per cent; United Kingdom, 8.16 per cent; Germany, 8.02 per cent; France, 7.56 per cent; Italy, 5.00 per cent; China, 3.94 per cent; Canada, 3.21 per cent; Spain, 3.18 per cent; Republic of Korea, 2.25 per cent; and Russia, 1.98 per cent. Their collective share came to 83.01 per cent of the total; that of the top five was 63.44 per cent.[17]

Individual missions vary enormously in cost. In the most recent years for which statistics are available (2007–2010), the annual range was from $16 million for the UN Military Observer Group in India and Pakistan to $1.57 billion for the African Union/UN Hybrid Operation in Darfur. One additional mission, MONUC in the Democratic Republic of the Congo, also cost more than $1 billion per year; and at least six others more than $100 million each.[18]

The unpredictability of not only financial *demand* but also *supply* (of peacekeepers, logistical support and funding) creates severe political stress and unconscionable suffering among endangered populations for whose needs peacekeeping operations are organized. Failures to respond adequately – in Rwanda, Darfur, Somalia, Cambodia, Yugoslavia and elsewhere – are major blots on the UN's record or, more properly, on those of its recalcitrant members. Preventing future failures calls, *inter alia*, for major funding reforms.[19]

Voluntary contributions

Finally, we come to voluntary contributions, not mentioned in the UN Charter. As with peacekeeping, the volume and sources of such funding are highly unpredictable. Determining which agency gets what, from whom and when is based on mixed altruistic, political and economic motives. The purposes of funding are largely established by leading donor nations. The GA, which controls other aspects of funding, plays a relatively minor role. It can elect officers for the programmes and specialized agencies which voluntary funding supports; but if the individuals elected pursue agendas at variance with those of the donor(s), it is likely that the funding spigot will soon be turned off. Funding cut-offs may also result from economic stress in donor countries.

A blatant example of political pressure affecting voluntary funding was the decision of the US administration of George H. W. Bush to terminate support for the UN Fund for Population Activities because of its perceived anti-natal policies. That decision, however, was countered by increased UNFPA funding from countries in Europe and reversed during the Clinton administration.[20]

Also affecting willingness to contribute are the location of an agency's headquarters and the nationality of the director. Italy, for example, has always been *a*, if not *the*, leading contributor to the FAO, headquartered in Rome. Similarly, Japan was a leading contributor to the UN High Commissioner for Refugees (UNHCR) as long as it was headed by Sadako Ogata.[21]

Political expediency plays an important role. UNRWA has been the principal UN-related entity providing economic support for Palestinian refugees (numbering 4.7 million as of 2010). It could not function directly under the GA or have that body determine its budget because of the adverse political reactions that would ensue; rather, it has functioned ever since 1950 exclusively through voluntary funding, largely from America.[22]

I am not aware of any published tabulation of voluntary funding covering the entire period of the UN's existence, but the Global Policy Forum has prepared a table indicating expenditures for eight major programmes and funds for the period 1971–2007.[23] That period was one of great and relatively steady growth, from a total of $584 million in 1971 to $12.29 billion in 2007. The $1 billion mark was passed in 1975, $2 billion in 1979, $4 billion in 1991 and $8 billion in 2003. In circa 1994 the total of *voluntary* contributions, then somewhat over $5 billion, passed that of *assessed* contributions – for both regular and peacekeeping budgets – for the first time. Table 11.2 provides additional data on the meteoric expansion of voluntary funding.

Voluntary contributions come overwhelmingly from wealthy nations. Three nations accounted for more than half the 2002–2003 total: the United States, with 36 per cent, followed by the United Kingdom and Japan with 9 per cent and 8 per cent respectively. Collectively the European Union accounted for 35 per cent of the total, while Norway, a non-EU nation, alone provided 6 per cent. Among non-OECD countries China was in the lead, but its contributions came to not quite 1 per cent. The rest of the world contributed approximately 15 per cent.[24] In relation to population, remarkable disparities appear among the wealthy contributors. For example, Norwegian per capita contributions were almost 11 times higher than those of the United States. Even within the European Union there were striking differences: the 6 per cent contribution of the Netherlands was, per capita, more than 16 times that of France, whose contributions came to only 1 per cent of the world total.[25]

While one can easily appreciate the desire of donor nations to maintain control over the programmes they voluntarily support and see the benefits such funding makes possible, the dramatic increase in resort to voluntary funding finds many informed critics. In a trenchant critique published in the *UN Chronicle*, Iqbal Haji, an officer in the UN Department of Economic and Social Affairs, observes:

> The situation is tantamount to "UN a la carte." It strikes at the root of the Charter provisions for financing UN activities in that it enables a group of countries, no matter how small, to finance activities under the UN label, that are in accord with their national priorities.

This has serious implications for the governance of the United Nations. Consider the following:

- The largest part of voluntary funding has centered upon issues that do not reflect the priorities of the vast majority of the Member States. They also happen to be a sensitive issue for bilateral aid (for example, it is difficult to press developing countries bilaterally on family planning). There is much analysis also to show that the $1 billion worth of food aid that is channeled through the World Food Programme is in reality worth much less, for it is a mechanism to get rid of surplus food that emerges from the anachronistic and heavily subsidized agriculture in the United States and the European Union. (These subsidies greatly harm the agricultural export prospects of many developing countries.)
- These voluntary-funded activities are in reality controlled largely by the western donor agencies. This is so, notwithstanding the executive boards and governing councils that "supervise" their activities. Anyone who has attended

Table 11.2 Expenditures of selected UN programmes and funds, 1971, 1991 and 2007

Year	UNDP	UNEP	UNFPA	UNHCR	UNICEF	UNIDO	UNRWA	WFP	Total
1971	290	*	17	9	57	33	49	130	584
1991	1,248	94	229	863	752	**	315	1,338	4,839
2007	3,861	279	629	1,346	2,767	**	654	2,753	12,283

Notes:
Figures are in millions of US dollars.
In addition to expenditures indicated here, there were voluntary contributions to UN specialized agencies amounting to $182 million in 1971 and $3,281 million in 2007.
* UNEP was first funded in 1973, when its expenditures were $13 million.
** In 1986 UNIDO became a specialized agency; its funding in 1985 was $138 million.

Abbreviations:
UNDP – UN Development Programme
UNEP – UN Environment Programme
UNFPA – UN Fund for Population Activities
UNHCR – UN High Commissioner for Refugees
UNICEF – UN Children's Fund
UNIDO – UN Industrial Development Organization
UNRWA – UN Relief and Works Agency for Palestinian Refugees in the Near East
WFP – World Food Programme

these meetings knows that their role is heavily circumscribed by the donor countries. A false image of democratic control is conveyed. The secretariats of these activities are also donor-determined, notwithstanding the presence of many developing country nationals.[26]

Iqbal calls for a study on the "compatibility between the spirit and the letter of the Charter" with respect to the new funding situation and urges donor countries to examine the possibilities of reorganizing many of their activities involving overseas development assistance. Although his criticisms may be too sweeping, his recommendations are fundamentally valid. Ways of eliminating the problems to which Iqbal refers are examined later in this chapter.

A temporal budget-specific overview

Figure 11.1 provides an overview of the growth of the various UN budgets between 1971 and 2007, as well as the increasing arrearages accumulated by member nations.[27] Data for 1991 are also included because that was a pivotal year in which the Cold War came to an end, bringing about a substantial surge in peacekeeping operations. The budgetary and arrearage figures provided are in both *current* and *2007 constant* dollars, adjusted for inflation over the period since 1971.[28] Thus the increases depicted are those of the budget and arrearages in *real* terms.

Significant facts derivable from Figure 11.1 include the following.

- The annual rates of *nominal dollar* growth in overall funding appear quite high: 10.8 per cent in the period 1971–1991 and 6.4 per cent in the period 1991–2007. However, in terms of *constant dollars*, adjusted for inflation, annual growth rates in the two periods were moderate: 4.3 per cent and 3.8 per cent respectively.
- The share of the *regular* budget in the overall total spending has markedly decreased in the period covered, going from 13.5 per cent in 1971 to 10.2 per cent in 1991 and 8.2 per cent in 2007.
- The share of the *peacekeeping* budget has risen strikingly, from 2.1 per cent in 1971 to 5.4 per cent in 1991 and 20.6 per cent in 2007.[29]
- The proportion of total spending accounted for by *specialized agencies* (FAO, UNESCO, WHO, etc.), counting assessed and voluntary contributions, declined substantially, from 34.1 per cent in 1971 to 30.7 per cent in 1991 and 21.9 per cent in 2007.
- Within the combined funding for specialized agencies, the proportion coming from *voluntary donations* has steadily risen, from roughly 47 per cent in 1971 to 50 per cent in 1991 and 60 per cent in 2007.
- In all three referenced years, *voluntary* funding has been close to or slightly more than double *assessed* funding.

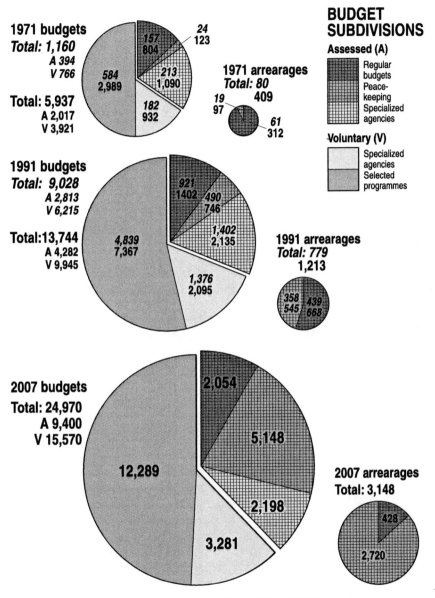

Figure 11.1 UN budgets and arrearages, 1971, 1991 and 2007
Note: All figures are in US$ millions. For 1971 and 1991 figures in italics are in US$ millions as of these years; non-italic figures are in millions of constant dollars as of 2007, adjusted for inflation.

213

- The proportion of spending going to *special UN programmes and funds* has stayed close to half in all three referenced years.
- The annual rate of growth in *arrearages* significantly exceeded that of funding as a whole, being 12.1 per cent in the period 1971–1991 and 9.0 per cent in 1991–2007.
- The amount of arrearages in proportion to the budget has risen steadily: 5.3 per cent in 1971, 8.8 per cent in 1991 and 12.6 per cent in 2007.
- The proportion of all *arrearages for peacekeeping* has shown a phenomenal increase: 24 per cent in 1971, 45 per cent in 1991 and 86 per cent in 2007.

These findings suggest some hypotheses warranting further reflection.
- Global forces are at work that drive *steady growth in the UN system* despite its many imperfections.
- Growth will demand *substantial increases in levels of UN funding*, necessitating new funding formulae and innovative funding mechanisms.
- *Enhanced funding for peacekeeping* will be especially needed in the near future.
- When wealthy nations do engage with the needs of the rest of the world they will not follow the agenda of the G-77 nations that control the GA.
- Increasing arrearages, especially for peacekeeping, suggest that a growing proportion of UN members have doubts about the legitimacy and/or wisdom of many SC resolutions.

Alternative sources of funding

Ways by which the United Nations might enhance its financial support system have engaged the imagination of statesmen, scholars and political activists since the organization's founding.[30] And the many proposals advanced have met with staunch resistance throughout that period, especially from observers who envisage and fear an excessively powerful global government that might, through taxation and other means, infringe upon the sovereign prerogatives of their respective states. Nevertheless, the system has already witnessed substantial expansion and has become increasingly complex. These trends are likely to continue in the century ahead, given the growing need for global action in numerous domains.

Probably no proposal has been more widely and seriously discussed and promoted than the so-called Tobin tax, named for the Nobel laureate economist James Tobin, who proposed it in 1971 (though with no particular reference to the United Nations).[31] The tax envisaged would be a very small levy on currency transactions. Such mainly speculative, non-productive transactions now amount to well above a trillion US dollars per day. Thus with a tax rate as low as 0.001 per cent, or possibly even less – which, Tobin tax advocates argue, would not harmfully restrict currency trading – one should be able to collect more than $1 billion per trading day, or at least $200 billion a year, even after deducting collection costs and allowing for a modicum of tax evasion.[32] Yet despite the apparent simplicity and attractiveness of Tobin's proposal, the idea has been roundly criticized by economists and others. It would allegedly inhibit the liquidity of capital, dampen financial initiatives and be widely avoided by shifting transactions from such traditional financial centres as London, New York, Frankfurt and Tokyo to offshore tax havens such as the Cayman Islands.

While I support the Tobin tax in principle, I do not believe it will be needed in the foreseeable future for two fundamental reasons. First, the United Nations presently lacks – and will for decades to come continue to lack – the infrastructure required to collect the tax and allocate efficiently the vast increase in funding that it promises to provide. Second, the funding the United Nations will require for the next several decades can be raised through much simpler means. Collecting a Tobin tax would require the creation of a new worldwide UN-controlled fiscal agency, and would contribute unnecessarily to strongly negative and counterproductive perceptions of the United Nations in wealthy countries.[33]

The following two quotations – by Fidel Castro and a US congressman – epitomize the gulf between commentators at the extremes of the spectrum in regard to support for a Tobin tax:

> May the tax suggested by Nobel Prize Laureate James Tobin be imposed in a reasonable and effective way on the current speculative operations accounting for trillions of US dollars every 24 hours, then the United Nations, which cannot go on depending on meager, inadequate, and belated donations and charities, will have one trillion dollars annually to save and develop the world. Given the seriousness and urgency of the existing problems, which have become a real hazard for the very survival of our species on the planet, that is what would actually be needed before it is too late.[34]

> The United Nations remains determined to rob from wealthy countries and, after taking a big cut for itself, send what's left to the poor countries. Of course, most of this money will go to the very dictators whose reckless policies have impoverished their citizens. The UN global tax plan ... resurrects the long-held dream of the "Tobin Tax." A dangerous precedent would be set, however; the idea that the UN possesses legitimate taxing authority to fund its operations.[35]

To varying degrees, the opposing views held about the Tobin tax would be mirrored in respect to many other possible taxes that would likely inhibit socially undesirable behaviour (making them analogous to "sin taxes", widely imposed on alcohol and tobacco) while simultaneously raising vast sums of needed revenue. Among these would be a carbon tax levied in proportion to the total industrial generation of CO_2, or perhaps of CO_2 in excess of some permissible threshold; a tax on emission of pollutants into the air, ground and surface water and the oceans; and a tax on international trade in armaments.[36]

Taxes on benign international transactions – such as international air or ocean travel, international postal service, use of the electromagnetic spectrum, the internet and e-mail, and even international trade in tangible goods – have also been suggested. So too have taxes on the extraction of natural resources, which may or may not be benign depending on local circumstances.[37] Attempts to institute these taxes, as with those noted previously, while intrinsically logical, would inevitably run into strong nationalistic opposition. They are likely, however, to find renewed support in future decades as funding needs expand.

During negotiations on the Law of the Sea Treaty, an idea attracting strong support in some quarters was to tax the extraction of petroleum and natural gas from rigs on the continental shelf beyond the territorial waters of any state (most of which at the time were legally defined as extending specified distances – from three up to 12 nautical miles – from a nation's shores), or the exploitation of the vast resources of manganese nodules and other metals and mineral compounds available in deep seabed locations. The idea was then advanced that the high seas, the underlying ocean bed, Antarctica, polar ice floes and even the moon, other heavenly bodies and outer space were parts of our "common heritage", belonging to all humankind, and could be subject to taxation for the common good. However, the invention of the concept of the 200-nautical-mile "exclusive economic zone", within which coastal states could operate exclusively or, if they chose, lease exploitation rights to others, foreclosed the near-term likelihood of deriving much revenue from the global maritime commons.[38] Whether revivifying the common heritage principle will gain traction remains to be seen.

A proposed new system

With a view to establishing a simple, effective and politically acceptable UN budgetary system, the following propositions are put forward.
1. The present complicated and contentious system used to establish UN member state assessments for both regular and peacekeeping budgets should be replaced by one wherein all states are assessed at a very small, *affordable* and *equal* percentage (say 0.1 per cent, initially) of their respective gross national incomes.[39]

2. The revenue thus raised should more than suffice to cover all the costs for functions presently carried out by the UN system, not only via funds raised in the regular and peacekeeping budgets, but also for the specialized agencies and activities made possible by voluntary contributions.
3. Funds remaining after meeting these obligations should be put into an *escrow account* to enable the United Nations to respond expeditiously to unanticipated peacekeeping emergencies and major natural disasters.
4. Voluntary contributions should be accepted only if they are provided on the understanding that the donor will not be able to determine or unduly influence the leadership or agenda of the agencies or programmes being funded.
5. To increase the probability that nations actually pay their respective assessments, those payments shall be *factored into formulae for weighted voting* in the GA, SC, ECOSOC/ESEC and other UN agencies.
6. Failure to make payments on time and/or in full will result in proportional reductions of a nation's weighted vote; and protracted failure may result in total forfeiture of voting rights until such time as the problem is corrected.
7. Interest will be charged on late budgetary payments at clearly specified rates.

The arithmetic indicating the revenue potential of the proposed scheme is simple. If the system were in place in 2010, given the total GNI of $58.65 trillion for all 192 UN members in 2009 (the latest year on which assessments for 2010 could be calculated) a uniform assessment rate of 0.1 per cent of GNI would yield a return of $58.65 billion, more than twice the total current spending for the entire UN system. Of that total, the US share, 24.73 per cent, would come to $14.50 billion, while that of Tuvalu, with the smallest economy of any UN member state, would come to only $30,000.

This total revenue projection would not only suffice to meet all current commitments within the UN system, but also allow substantial expansion of those activities to meet high-priority development goals, pay off debts to various nations for peacekeeping services and still leave a substantial remainder to go into the proposed escrow account for peacekeeping and other emergency needs.

The demonstrable efficacy of the proposed system in promoting global economic and social justice and in responding to peacekeeping needs would greatly revive popular and diplomatic support for the UN system. It would also facilitate orderly expansion in the staffing and capability of key UN agencies. That expansion would, in turn, set the stage for a gradual upward adjustment of the uniform rate of assessment, say from 0.1 per cent to 0.125 per cent or whatever other figure the GA might approve.

Whatever the adjusted rates might be, it would probably take decades before any nation would experience genuine hardship in meeting its UN financial commitments.

Nevertheless, as with any proposal for radical reformulation of long-standing practices, one would anticipate serious initial doubts about and opposition to the above recommendations. Let us consider what those concerns might be and why they should be dispelled.

With respect to the proposed uniform assessment rate (proposition 1), many observers would take issue with what appears to be an abandonment of the progressive principle built into the tax systems of most liberal democracies, as well as all existing UN assessment formulae of which I am aware, i.e. the idea that it is fair to tax the rich at higher rates than those for the poor. But in national tax systems the *per capita* taxes are vastly greater than in respect to the United Nations. Although a uniform, non-progressive tax rate at the *national* level might inflict substantial economic hardship on much of the population, that is hardly the case regarding the United Nations.

For example, the present regular UN budget assessments for Bangladesh, Ethiopia, Nigeria and Viet Nam come to *less than three cents per capita per year!*[40] (The US figure would be less than two dollars per year.) Poor though these countries are, increasing that assessment tenfold would not make an appreciable difference. In this context it is worth noting that the countries named – like the world's major powers – all manage to allocate revenues for their respective military establishments at financial levels vastly greater than those required of them as members of the United Nations. And what can they show for it?[41] Very little.

There is, of course, a proper place for progressivity in economic decision-making in the UN system. But, for the foreseeable future, that place ought to be in *the way in which revenues are spent*: in improving the lot of the impoverished, investing in human capital through better health and education programmes, thereby enhancing the productive capacity of society, and so forth. Rather than comparing differential assessment rates, one should advocate an improved system in which *all* nations benefit. Such a world would be less prone to terrorism and other forms of violence, allowing substantial reductions in military spending.

Viewed from the perspective of contemporary politics, however, one must recognize that the existing assessment and budgetary system leads to UN-bashing by ardent nationalists who mistrust international initiatives, which they perceive as harbingers of a dreaded "socialistic world government". In the United States criticism of the United Nations has long been in vogue and indulged in by many politicians from both major parties. Since few Americans are aware of how trivial US financial contributions to the United Nations actually are in comparison to military spending and other federal expenditures, it has been easy for demagogues, and even moderate legislators, to frame the argument by emphasizing that the United States provides 22 per cent of the regular budget, pays at an even higher rate (25 per cent) for peacekeeping and carries the lion's share in respect to voluntary funds, yet gets only one vote out of 193. The facts that the US share of the world's GNI was about 29 per cent when it bullied the United Nations to have its regular budget assessment reduced to its present level and that it pays less in comparison to its wealth than any other developed nation would, of course, not be noted. Nor would critics question the US veto power in the powerful SC.

Now suppose that the United States were to pay at the same uniform rate, 0.1 per cent of its GNI, as even the poorest country in the world. In that circumstance, it would become very difficult to make a credible argument that the United States was being unfairly exploited. Whereas the current assessment rate, *22 per cent of the total regular budget*, would strike most ordinary American citizens as inordinately high, the proposed uniform rate of assessment, *a mere 0.1 per cent of the total US GNI*, would – paradoxically – strike them as an easily bearable obligation, notwithstanding the fact that the latter rate would impose on the United States a financial load 25 times as great as the former.[42] Further, if timely payments to the United Nations were to be reflected in enhanced voting power, the United States would have a powerful incentive to favour the proposed fiscal reforms. The key to understanding this paradox is that the *percentages*, 22 per cent and 0.1 per cent, would loom larger in the minds of most individuals than the unknown *total sums* to which those percentages refer, namely the UN budget and the US GNI. Various polls indicate that most Americans believe their government already allocates a vastly larger share of its budget to foreign aid of all sorts, including contributions to the UN system, than is actually the case. For example, according to the 2010 round of the annual poll of the Program on International Policy Attitudes: "Asked how much of the federal budget goes to foreign aid the median estimate is 25 percent. Asked how much ... would be *an 'appropriate' percentage* the median response is 10%" (emphasis added). The actual amount is roughly 1 per cent; but over the years since the poll's inception in 1995 "the most common median estimate was ... 20 percent".

Presently, even with a president as UN-friendly as Barack Obama, the problematic nature of UN budgeting procedures, the low overall level of funding and the inability of the United States to prevail in many budgetary debates have led to increased US reliance on alternative agencies for promoting basic economic goals. In addition to working through the Bretton Woods institutions, the WTO, the OECD and the G-7 or G-8, the United States and other key economic players now appear increasingly to be bypassing the United Nations and formulating international economic policies through the newly emerging G-20.[43] Bound by no restricting set of rules – such as those of the UN Charter and more than six decades of GA resolutions – the informal G-20 consortium will, some observers believe, be able to achieve what the United Nations cannot. The rest of the world will remain voiceless and have to adapt to new realities as best it can. Thus, absent significant reform, the unwieldy GA, along with an often-dysfunctional ECOSOC, may in fact become the largely irrelevant entities that their critics already accuse them of being.[44]

With respect to voluntary contributions (proposition 4), some critics would question the wisdom of moving the UN system away from its heavy dependence on such largesse. One should ask, however, why voluntary funding was deemed necessary in the first place. While a certain amount was required – as noted, for example, in respect to UNRWA – voluntary funding was necessitated mainly because of excessive GA parsimony in framing the regular budget. And that parsimony was, in turn, due to the refusal of the United States and other wealthy nations to meet the budgetary expectations of the world's less developed states, an overwhelming GA majority. By allowing nations to provide voluntary funds with the expectation that they should – and in fact could – control how those funds were to be used, the United Nations fosters an unhealthy climate of distrust. Moreover, the fact that voluntary funds can be terminated whenever the donor wishes makes long-term planning risky and difficult. The solution, then, is to rely less on voluntary funding, and to establish rules precluding unwarranted control by the donors where such funding is authorized. Funds such as UNICEF, which rely mainly on small contributions from thousands of private donors, would be obvious exceptions to this rule.

The case for proposition 5, namely to make assessed payments one of several terms in weighted voting formulae, has been set forth in preceding chapters. Here it need only be underlined that the willingness of wealthy nations to approve greatly enhanced levels of funding will largely be linked to the expectation that they will receive a reasonable and proportional enhancement of their decision-making power. Such a bargain offers a mutually beneficial trade-off between the rich and poor nations of the world.

Enhanced voting power, however, should be based not on the level of *assessments*, but rather on the level of timely *payments* over a specified period (say three or five years) preceding the establishment of a given budget cycle. Failure to pay would, according to proposition 6, automatically result in a diminution of a nation's weighted vote. Further, to ensure greater fiscal discipline, the GA should stipulate that failure to pay assessments for the equivalent of, say, five times the current rate would cause a nation to forfeit its *full* weighted vote and its voting privileges would be restored only when its debt, including interest payments, was fully paid. Thus instead of the United States threatening to withhold dues payment so as to influence UN decisions or force specific reforms, it would have a powerful incentive to pay what it owes in full and on time.

Finally, it should be noted that while the seven propositions put forward in this section are intended to form a coherent and politically optimal whole, it would be possible – though not optimal – to adopt one or several of them without accepting the entire package. One could, for example, change to a system of weighted voting without accepting the idea of a uniform rate of assessment, or vice versa. Nor would creating an escrow account be an *essential* feature of the proposed new system.

Summary and conclusions

Funding the UN system is complicated, undependable and contentious, consuming more time and energy than it should. Moreover, despite substantial increases in agency budgets, funding levels remain far from adequate for the effective performance of many UN functions. Further, the ratio of arrearages to the regular and total budgets has increased substantially in recent decades. Accordingly, the system has found it expedient to rely increasingly on voluntary contributions, potentially creating political problems where donor and UN agendas diverge.

Additionally, differences in national assessment levels vary substantially in both relative and absolute terms and also from one budget to another. For individual nations they have also varied dramatically over time. Determining and justifying these differences have tended to polarize the United Nations along political lines (initially East-West and later North-South) and created an atmosphere of pervasive distrust. The United States has been especially strident in criticizing the system, and has employed various tactics to bully the GA into accepting changes in funding and budgeting procedures.

Calls for new revenue-raising mechanisms have assumed many forms. The most notable is the proposed Tobin tax. But this and all other new forms of taxation meet with staunch nationalistic opposition. While not ruling out eventual adoption of any suggested reform, this chapter proposes simpler, more coherent means of meeting the UN's funding needs. In brief, it advocates doing away with the multiple budgets that the GA must now establish and substituting a single consolidated budget; assessing all nations, however rich or poor they may be, at a uniform low and affordable rate based on their respective GNIs, which should at least double present funding levels; establishing an escrow account from resultant surplus funding to enable the United Nations to cope with unforeseeable future emergencies; including payments to the United Nations as one among several elements in weighted voting formulae; and responding to national failure to meet funding obligations with automatic proportional reduction of the nation's weighted vote. Although these proposed changes would work best as an integrated package, it would be possible to adopt one or more of them separately from the others.

Notes

1. For a succinct account of the evolution of UN financing mechanisms up to the year 2007 see Jeffrey Laurenti, "Financing", in Thomas G. Weiss and Sam Daws (eds), *The Oxford Handbook on the United Nations*, New York and Oxford: Oxford University Press, 2007, pp. 675–700. Unless otherwise stated, the facts presented in this section are taken from this source.
2. The following description is based on UN Dag Hammarskjöld Library Research Guide, "UN Regular Budget", www.un.org/depts/dhl/resguide/specrb.html#acabq.
3. The budgetary data in this paragraph are derived from Laurenti, note 1 above, pp. 690–694; Global Policy Forum, www.globalpolicy.org/un-finance/tables-and-charts-on-un-finance/the-un-regular-budget/27466.html.
4. The Secretary-General certifies each January which states are in arrears.
5. At least 30 different proposals by single countries or country blocs (the European Union, the G-77 and Canada/Australia/New Zealand) were put forward during the debates within the Fifth Committee of the GA over the 2010–2012 period. These are systematically analysed in respect to income measures (gross national income versus purchasing power parity), base periods, currency conversion rates, debt burden and other adjustments, and floor and ceiling assessments in a study by Emanuel Evans, "Scale of Assessments – An Overview of Methodology Proposals by Member States", Center for UN Reform Education, 18 November 2008, www.centerforunreform.org/node/374/print.
6. For sources of data in this paragraph, see notes at the bottom of Table 11.1.
7. Laurenti, note 1 above, p. 688–689.
8. The sources used to derive each of the bulleted facts that follow are those listed at the bottom of Table 11.1.
9. Since 2005, however, owing largely to the rise of China and the partial economic recovery of Russia, the P-5 share has increased to 39.5 per cent.
10. The original US demand also included a call for weighted voting; but it could not muster the requisite support and had to settle for decision-making by consensus, as was the practice in the League of Nations.
11. Laurenti, note 1 above, pp. 689–690.
12. Ibid.
13. Ibid., pp. 687–690.
14. Henry L. Stimson Center, "US 'Cap' on UN Peacekeeping Funding", www.stimson.org/fopo/?SN=FP200607251040.
15. Global Policy Forum, "Peacekeeping Operations Expenditures, 1947–2005", www.globalpolicy.org/tables-and-charts-ql/un-finance-tcql/the-un-peacekeeping-operations-budget.html.
16. Stockholm International Peace Research Institute, *SIPRI Yearbook 2006, Armaments, Disarmament and International Security*, Oxford: Oxford University Press, 2006, p. 15.

17. UN Department of Peacekeeping Operations, DPI/2429/Rev 7, March 2010.
18. *Europa World Year Book, 2009*, London: Routledge, 2010, pp. 81–93; *Europa World Year Book, 2010*, London: Routledge, 2011, pp. 82–95.
19. Additional discussion of peacekeeping costs is provided in Chapter 12.
20. Laurenti, note 1 above, pp. 694, 696.
21. Ibid.
22. Ibid., p. 694; UNRWA, www.unrwa.org.
23. Global Policy Forum, "Expenditures of Selected UN Programmes", www.globalpolicy. org/un-finances/tables-and-charts-on-un-financing-of-the-un-programmes-funds-and-specialized-agencies/27483.html.
24. Laurenti, note 1 above, Figure 39.2, p. 695.
25. International per capita comparisons were calculated by the author.
26. Iqbal Haji, "The 'Problem' of Voluntary Funding", *UN Chronicle*, Winter 1997, http:// findarticles.com/p/articles/mi_m1309/is_n4_v34/ai_20518066.
27. Global Policy Forum, "Total UN System Contributions", data compiled by Klaus Hüfner (Global Policy Forum) and Michael Renner (Worldwatch Institute), www.globalpolicy. org/un-finance/tables-and-charts-on-un-finance/un-system-budget/27505.html. Data on regular budget and assessed portion of budgets for specialized agencies represent approved budgets rather than actual expenditures.
28. 2007 is an appropriate terminal year for this analysis, in that it pre-dates the financial turmoil of the global economic system since 2008.
29. Budgeting for peacekeeping, however, has fluctuated dramatically over the period analysed.
30. Widely ranging recommendations are presented in Harlan Cleveland, Hazel Henderson and Inge Kaul (eds), *The United Nations: Policy and Financing Alternatives, Innovative Proposals by Visionary Leaders*, Washington, DC: Global Commission to Fund the United Nations, 1995. While those recommendations reflect virtually all the funding ideas touched upon in this chapter, none is comparable to the principal proposal of the present author, presented in Chapter 14.
31. The following discussion is based on a lengthy Wikipedia article presenting the pros and cons of the Tobin tax, as evaluated by numerous economists and statesmen: Wikipedia, "Tobin Tax", http://en.wikipedia.org/wiki/Tobin_tax.
32. Originally Tobin proposed, for the sake of discussion, a levy of 0.5 per cent. Subsequent proponents have progressively lowered that figure. Currently the rate of 0.001 per cent seems to be most preferred, though lower percentages have also been suggested.
33. The negative views put forward in the US Congress are summarized by Laurenti, note 1 above, pp. 696–697.
34. Fidel Castro in an address delivered on 1 September 2001 at the World Conference against Racism, Racial Discrimination, Xenophobia and Related Intolerance, quoted in Wikipeda, note 31 above, p. 16.
35. Statement on "International Taxes" made by US Congressman Ron Paul on 6 March 2006 for the Ron Paul Library, quoted in Wikipedia, note 31 above, pp. 16–17.
36. Discussed in Chadwick F. Alger, "Widening Participation", in Thomas G. Weiss and Sam Daws (eds), *The Oxford Handbook on the United Nations*, New York and Oxford: Oxford University Press, 2007, pp. 712–713.
37. Ibid.
38. For many relevant articles see *The Ocean Yearbook*, Chicago, IL: University of Chicago Press, 1979–2005.
39. If adopted, this proposition would eliminate the need for the GA's Committee on Contributions and greatly simplify the work of the plenary Fifth Committee.

40. Calculations by the author using World Bank data.

41. In the countries named the ratios of military spending to what they would pay to the United Nations if assessed at a uniform rate of 0.1 per cent of their GNI were roughly Bangladesh, 11:1; Ethiopia 15:1; Nigeria, 8:1; and Viet Nam, 20:1. Ratios based on present assessment rates would be several times higher. For relevant country-wise data see Stockholm International Peace Research Institute, note 16 above, Table 51.3, "Military expenditure by country", in constant US dollars for 1998–2007 and current US dollars for 2008. The author's rough calculations were based on the figures for 2008 in current dollars.

42. See   www.worldpublicopinion.org/pipa/articles/brunitedstatescanadara/670.php.   Thus one may safely infer that few Americans would object to the United States being assessed a mere 0.1 per cent of its GDP as its share of the total expenses of the UN system.

43. "About G-20", www.g20.org/about_what_is_g20.aspx.

44. It is too early to form judgements on this matter. For an optimistic perspective see Bruce Jones, "Making Multilateralism Work: How the G-20 Can Help the United Nations", Policy Analysis Brief, Stanley Foundation, Muscatine, IA, April 2010.

12

Peacekeeping, peacebuilding and disarmament

An ounce of prevention is worth a pound of cure.
Benjamin Franklin

I know not with what weapons World War III will be fought, but World War IV will be fought with sticks and stones.
Albert Einstein

Mankind must put an end to war, or war will put an end to mankind.
John F. Kennedy

The threat to use force is neither credible nor effective if there is no ability or preparedness to use it.
Commission on Global Governance, 1993

Introduction

Maintenance of peace and security was the paramount goal of those who drafted the UN Charter in 1945. It would very likely remain the paramount goal if the Charter were being rewritten today. Yet the deaths of more than 50 million persons – overwhelmingly civilians – in, or as a direct result of, interstate and civil wars since the conclusion of the Second World War indicate that success in meeting that goal has been far from satisfactory.[1] Among the many reasons are structural shortcomings of the UN Charter, with one set of rules for the P-5 and another for all other

Transforming the United Nations system: Designs for a workable world, Schwartzberg, *United Nations University Press, 2013, ISBN 978-92-808-1230-5*

nations, and the concomitant unrealistic decision-making systems.[2] More critical analysis is needed.

In what follows I first consider UN mechanisms for dealing non-violently with threats to peace and security, and suggest how they might be made more effective. Second, I review peacekeeping missions involving uniformed personnel and related peacebuilding initiatives. I then examine UN steps to address the problem of peacekeeping, especially in post-conflict situations. This chapter proposes a number of correctives, including creation of new institutions: a UN Peace Corps (UNPC) that will enable more robust and effective responses to existing and potential threats, a UN Administrative Reserve Corps (UNARC) to provide highly trained personnel to restore viable post-conflict polities and establish a climate for peacebuilding, and a UN Administrative Academy (UNAA) for training UNARC personnel. Peacekeeping, however, must be pursued not only at the *local* level, but also on the *global* stage. Accordingly, I also consider the challenges of arms control and disarmament, especially in regard to weapons of mass destruction. Finally, we need a revisionist perspective on the threat of international terrorism.

The pacific settlement of disputes

Chapter VI of the UN Charter relates to "The Pacific Settlement of Disputes". Article 33 stipulates that parties to disputes "likely to endanger the maintenance of international peace and security" shall seek solutions "by negotiation, enquiry, mediation, conciliation, arbitration, judicial settlement, resort to regional agencies or arrangements, or other peaceful means of their own choice". This admonition – despite its broad menu of options – has frequently been ignored. The onus of compliance is put on states and local opposition groups. But since in most disputes one party sees itself as substantially more powerful than the other, that party has little incentive to place trust in potentially unsympathetic external actors. It will favour either negotiation on its own terms or no action at all. Thus more proactive policies by legitimately interested outside agencies are necessary.

Ideally, many disputes should initially be handled by regional bodies, such as the European Union, OAS or Organization of African Unity, not only because those bodies presumably possess the knowledge to deal efficiently with the problem, but also because they have the greatest stake in promoting a peaceful regional climate. Additionally, when regions deal with their own problems, the disputants and neighbouring states are less likely to sense unwarranted neocolonial meddling in their affairs. Competent courts already exist in several regions, but more are needed. Though judicial settlements are an obvious expedient, others noted in the preceding paragraph would also be worth pursuing if the conflicting parties agree. In certain circumstances highly respected INGOs (e.g. Human Rights Watch or the International Crisis Committee) might also play supportive roles, either in coaxing disputants to the bargaining table or in providing expert testimony.

When agencies outside the UN system fail to initiate meaningful negotiation and the problem is deemed sufficiently serious, UN action will be necessary. Normally the Security Council, on the request of one party to the dispute, would (in accordance with Article 34) be the initiating agency. But when the SC chooses not to become involved, the General Assembly (under Article 35) could do so. Either the SC or the GA could call for involvement by the Secretary-General. Conversely, the SG could direct the attention of either or both bodies "to any matter which in his opinion may threaten the maintenance of international peace and security" (Article 99).

One tool at the SG's disposal is the appointment of special representatives to the Secretary-General and other roughly equivalent personal representatives to investigate threats to the peace and – more often – conflicts already under way, and report their findings to him and other concerned UN agencies.[3] As of mid-2010 there were 60 such authorized posts: 32 for countries in Africa, 6 for the Americas, 7 for Asia and the Pacific, 4 for Europe and 9 for the Middle East. Appointees have come from all major world regions, but decisions as to the home region of the appointee have varied widely. Thus 18 of Africa's posts were staffed by Africans, while not one of the 9 Middle Eastern posts was held by a citizen of any country within that region. While most representatives were little-known diplomats, the "special envoy for Haiti" appointed in 2009 was former US president Bill Clinton.[4] Assuming availability of highly skilled, well-informed and impartial individuals, greater use should be made of this potentially pre-emptive mediatory tactic.

Presently, the number of significant conflicts in the world far exceeds the capacity of regional and UN mechanisms to deal with them. Some *system for prioritizing* UN involvement is needed. I recommend the following.

- First, that the SC and GA shall determine the severity of problems brought to their attention.
- Second, that in situations presenting particularly serious threats, a time frame should be established within which the disputants would be expected to show progress towards a peaceful resolution.
- Third, absent satisfactory progress, a course of remedial action shall be prescribed by the SC, beginning – wherever feasible – with intervention by the appropriate regional agency/agencies.
- Fourth, when timely regional intervention proves ineffectual, one or more of the following measures shall be *mandated*: that an advisory opinion be sought from the International Court of Justice; that the case

be referred to expert impartial mediators; and/or that, in the event of unsuccessful mediation, the case shall be referred to either a specially appointed board of arbitrators or the ICJ or some other appropriate international judicial body for a *binding decision.*

• Finally, that decisions reached by whatever means shall be reinforced by *binding* SC resolutions, and such resolutions shall specify sanctions or other enforcement mechanisms in the event of non-compliance.

These recommended courses of action are all consistent with Article 1 of the UN Charter and require no structural changes in the organization. Prioritizing and handling the methods selected would largely depend on available UN personnel and funding. Currently both are severely limited, but measures for their substantial expansion are proposed elsewhere in this work. Effective action will also depend on improved decision-making systems in the SC and GA, hopefully utilizing weighted voting and elimination (or non-use) of the veto. Though the types of action proposed are largely unprecedented, they should prove highly cost-effective. Pre-emptive diplomatic and judicial intervention will inevitably be much more economical and humane than the present propensity to allow treatable problems to fester and degenerate into violence and state failure.

Sanctions call for special comment. They have assumed numerous forms: general trade embargoes, selective trade embargoes (e.g. on imports or exports of petroleum), arms embargoes, travel restrictions, aviation sanctions (e.g. no-fly zones), freezing of assets in foreign banks, cut-offs of economic assistance, severance or limitation of diplomatic relations and so forth.[5] Though not violent, they are decidedly coercive. Many have greatly harmed innocent civilian populations, while having little impact on ruling elites.[6] While sanctions were little used prior to the end of the Cold War, Iraq's invasion of Kuwait in 1990 ushered in a more active period. But because of poor monitoring, inadequate enforcement, illicit smuggling and overt defiance by sanctioned governments – and others sympathetic to them – most sanctions regimes have met with little success and been characterized as "blunt instruments" of diplomacy.[7] Widespread revulsion against civilian suffering brought about by sanctions has resulted in greater moderation since 1995 and led to numerous conferences and studies of ways of establishing "smart" sanctions regimes.[8] Nevertheless, the record leaves much room for improvement.

Peacekeeping and peacebuilding: The record to date

Recognizing that the measures for maintaining peace stipulated in Chapter VI of the UN Charter would not always prove effective, the drafters of that document also included Chapter VII, "Action with Respect to

Threats to the Peace, Breaches of the Peace and Acts of Aggression".[9] However, the system devised has repeatedly failed to work as intended. Article 43 calls for all UN member nations to make available to the SC, on call, "armed forces, assistance and facilities, including rights of passage" to help maintain peace and security; and Article 47 calls for a Military Staff Committee "to advise and assist the Security Council". In practice, the needed forces were as a rule reluctantly provided and in insufficient numbers for their assigned missions. Although the Military Staff Committee, consisting of "the Chiefs of Staff of the permanent members of the Security Council or their representatives", was created, it was from its inception an ineffectual reflection of the political polarization of the Cold War. Rather than the *peace-enforcement* measures originally envisaged, SC resolutions to deal with breaches of the peace typically established *peacekeeping* missions; and these were often mounted only *after* the signing of truces and cease-fires, thereby establishing conditions with at least a modicum of peace for UN forces to maintain. Such unanticipated exercises were often informally referred to as "Chapter Six-and-a-half" missions.

Although the SC is unquestionably the principal UN organ concerned with matters of war and peace, the Charter also allows the GA to play a significant role. Chapter IV, Article 11 states that the GA:

> may consider the general principles of co-operation in the maintenance of international peace and security ... may discuss any questions relating to the maintenance of peace and security brought before it by any Member of the United Nations, or by the Security Council, [or] may call the attention of the Security Council to situations which are likely to endanger peace and security.

However, according to Article 12, "While the Security Council is exercising in respect to any dispute or situation the functions assigned to it, the General Assembly shall not make any recommendation with regard to that dispute or situation unless the Security Council so requests."

The first decade of the UN's existence witnessed the authorization of only a few SC-sanctioned UN peacekeeping missions. These were all modest undertakings, mainly to provide observers of truces, such as that between the newly founded state of Israel (established in 1948) and its Arab neighbours, and in the following year the mission to oversee the cease-fire agreed by India and Pakistan in the disputed state of Kashmir.[10]

But the Korean War, initiated in 1950, put the system established by the Charter to a particularly difficult test. In the face of the DPRK's invasion of the Republic of Korea, meaningful SC action was precluded by the Russian veto. Under the circumstances the United States, already engaged in the conflict, succeeded in its call for an emergency GA session, which adopted Resolution 377 (V), the so-called Uniting for Peace resolution, declaring:

> If the Security Council, because of lack of unanimity of the permanent members, fails to exercise its primary responsibility for the maintenance of international peace and security in any case where there appears to be a threat to the peace, breach of the peace, or act of aggression, the General Assembly shall consider the matter immediately with a view to making appropriate recommendations to members for collective measures, including in the case of a breach of the peace or act of aggression the use of armed force when necessary, to maintain or restore international peace and security.[11]

The resolution provided *post hoc* legitimization of the American intervention and a basis for introducing forces from numerous allied nations in support of the US-led effort.

In 1956, only a few years after the truce ending the Korean War, the United Nations again found it necessary to resort to the Uniting for Peace resolution, in response to the joint Anglo-French-Israeli takeover from Egypt of the recently nationalized Suez Canal and the adjoining Sinai Peninsula. In this instance the United States and Soviet Union were united in opposing the action. The result was not only a pullout of the British and French, but also establishment of the UN Emergency Force (UNEF) to provide a buffer between the remaining Israeli and Egyptian forces.[12] UNEF was a more robust undertaking than previous missions. With roughly 6,000 uniformed personnel, it was the first mission that could actually play an *active peacekeeping* role, rather than that of a truce *monitor*. That role, however, was short-lived. In 1967 Egypt ordered withdrawal of all UNEF forces and, when Secretary-General U Thant acceded, renewed war between Israel and Egypt (as well as Syria) quickly ensued.

Since its initial use, the Uniting for Peace resolution has been employed 10 times.[13] While the end of the Cold War suggested to some that further resort to this expedient has become unnecessary, it could prove applicable in Syria and future crises elsewhere.

Until 1960 the number and scale of UN peacekeeping operations put no unmanageable burden on the organization. But the scope, severity and duration of the Congo mission begun in that year resulted in unprecedented expenses that strained the financial capability of many new, recently decolonized members. Additionally, objections to what some nations perceived as improperly non-neutral actions by the UN mission led to refusals by the Soviet bloc and France to pay their shares of mission costs. Ultimately, this led to establishing separate budgets for peacekeeping and rearrangements in assessment, as indicated in Chapter 11.[14]

Only two more large-scale missions were launched up to the end of the Cold War: UNEF II, from 1973 to 1979, renewed the mission separating Israeli and Egyptian forces in the wake of the so-called Yom Kippur War; and the UN Interim Force in Lebanon, started in 1978 and still in the field, supervised withdrawal of Israeli forces from southern Lebanon and assisted in restoring Lebanese government in that region.

Following the Soviet Union's implosion, however, matters changed dramatically:

> Between 1987 and 1994, the Security Council tripled the number of resolutions it issued, tripled the peacekeeping operations it authorized, and multiplied by seven the number of economic sanctions it imposed per year. Military forces deployed in peacekeeping operations increased from fewer than 10,000 to more than 70,000. The annual peacekeeping budget skyrocketed correspondingly from $230 million to $3.6 billion in the same period, thus reaching to about three times the UN's regular operating budget of $1.2 billion.[15]

As with earlier missions, UN peacekeeping operations in the post-Cold War period varied greatly in size, duration and expense. Several were staffed by fewer than 100 uniformed personnel, whereas others had forces in excess of 25,000 soldiers and police, to which were added substantial numbers of civilians – largely locally recruited – performing tasks beyond the capability of the uniformed contingents.

Space limitations preclude detailed discussion of mission successes and failures. Especially noteworthy among the former was shepherding Namibia to independence and political stability (1989–1990). Other successes entailed the negotiation of cease-fires, disarmament of hostile forces, human rights reforms, repatriation of refugees, implementation of peace agreements, withdrawal of foreign troops, creation of local police forces and restoration of viable civil administrations.[16]

Failures, however, were also numerous.[17] Among them was the ultimate fiasco of three overlapping missions in Somalia from 1991 to 1995, most notably the United Task Force, authorized by the United Nations but led by the United States with minimal UN control. These missions were tasked with facilitating provision of humanitarian relief to the famine-stricken Somali population and stabilizing a country wracked by civil war. The missions were manned by contingents from dozens of nations, and coordinating their efforts was difficult.[18] Additionally, the missions witnessed considerable fighting between UN forces and local warlords – "mission overreach" – resulting in hundreds of civilian deaths and scores of UN troop fatalities.[19] The Somali experience marked the end of US commitment of ground forces to UN-controlled peacekeeping missions and fostered an aversion to active engagement by other wealthy countries. It also contributed to the UN's shameful refusal to strengthen the small UN mission in Rwanda, thereby enabling the 1994 genocide in which up to 800,000 Rwandans were murdered.[20] Yet despite frequent cries of "Never again!", it appears that reluctance to confront genocidal actions is being repeated in several parts of Africa.

Another striking failure to protect innocent civilians occurred in connection with the 1992–1995 UNPROFOR mission in the former Yugoslavia. The lack of a mandate to engage hostile forces, except in self-defence, encouraged Serbian forces in Bosnia to defy UN directives, eventually permitting the slaughter of roughly 9,000 Muslim men and boys in the UN-defined "safe area" of Srebrenica.[21]

Inadequate rules of engagement have led to additional embarrassments. In Sierra Leone, for example, 500 UN peacekeepers were taken as hostages by rebel forces in 2000. Rather than launching a UN rescue mission, that task was carried out by an independent British force.[22]

We must also note widespread scandalous activities – rape, prostitution, paedophilia and other criminal behaviour (corruption, arms trafficking and extortion) – that have tarnished UN missions on four continents since the early 1990s. Lapses in MONUC (UN Organization Mission in the Democratic Republic of the Congo) have been especially egregious. Attempts to address these problems have had limited success.[23]

The UN's frequent inability or unwillingness to respond satisfactorily to threats to peace has, since 1990, led to authorization of scores of multinational operations that were/are not under UN control. Most were under the terms of Charter Articles 52 and 53 of Chapter VIII, dealing with "Regional Arrangements". But the Charter is silent as to how regions shall be defined and recognized. Is the Economic Community of West African States (ECOWAS), for example, to be regarded as a region in its own right or as part of the region of Africa? May regions overlap, thereby allowing countries to be simultaneously parts of more than one? Of particular note is the fact that NATO, with well over half the world's military strength, is regarded by the United Nations as a *regional* entity.[24]

Many Chapters VII and VIII missions have already been concluded.[25] Of these, the first and by far the largest was the 1990 US-led Gulf War coalition, with participation by 580,000 troops. Others with forces exceeding 10,000 included the aforementioned US-led mission to Somalia (1992–1995), several NATO operations in Bosnia & Herzegovina (1995–2005) and an Australian-led force in East Timor (1999–2000).[26] Though most Chapter VIII undertakings were more successful in carrying out their mandates than were UN-directed missions, they were often criticized for being highly politicized operations and more disposed to the use of lethal force.

Among the largest Chapter VIII missions (with over 50,000 troops at peak strength) was ISAF (International Security Assistance Force), the

NATO contingent supporting the US-led mission to Afghanistan. In second place was KFOR, the NATO force in Kosovo (with 43,000 troops at maximum strength). All others had fewer than 3,500 troops – usually much less – and 12 (nine mounted by the Organization for Security and Co-operation in Europe – OSCE) consisted exclusively of civilian staff. NATO forces accounted for the vast majority of troops deployed. By contrast, the three missions of the Russian-dominated CIS, operating in Trans-Caucasia and Moldova, totalled only 5,339 troops. Another noteworthy difference between NATO missions and those of the CIS (and of African organizations) is that the former functioned mainly *outside* the area of its member states, whereas the latter were confined to countries within their respective regions.

Apart from UN-sanctioned missions, individual nations and regional organizations also undertook missions, ostensibly for peacekeeping, without bothering to obtain SC approval or despite having tried unsuccessfully to do so.[27] These included several US interventions in the Caribbean region over the period 1954–1965 that were allegedly consistent with provisions in the OAS Charter. Similarly – arguably following the US precedent – brutal Soviet crackdowns on political rebels in Hungary and Czechoslovakia, in 1956 and 1968 respectively, were said by Moscow to be justified under the Warsaw Pact. It was thus no great political stretch for ECOWAS to employ military actions to restore stability to the conflict-torn states of Liberia, Sierra Leone and Guinea-Bissau in 1990 and subsequent years. Numerous other interventions (e.g. by India in what was to become Bangladesh in 1971, and by Viet Nam in Pol Pot's Cambodia in 1978) were launched with varying degrees of justification.

Given UN inaction (or inept action) following the Cold War, the United States, the one remaining superpower, increasingly arrogated unto itself the role of world policeman, expending staggering sums in developing hundreds of overseas bases and embarking on numerous military forays into countries presumed to pose threats to either America or its allies. US interventions were not only frequent but often characterized by questionable tactics. Consider, for example, the 79 days of NATO (overwhelmingly US) aerial bombardment of Yugoslavia, allegedly to save Kosovo from ethnic cleansing and/or genocide. Because of its casualty-averse military doctrine, the United States refused to commit ground troops to the effort, though doing so might have accomplished American goals in no more than a week or two of fighting. Thus NATO forces suffered not one fatality, while the death toll among Kosovars – whom they were supposedly seeking to assist – plus innocent civilians throughout Yugoslavia was well into the thousands.[28]

Later US actions in the protracted conflicts in Afghanistan and Iraq were of a different order of magnitude. In its proclaimed "global war on terror", a response to the murder of some 3,000 persons at New York's

World Trade Center and other sites on 9/11 2001, the United States became the principal agent in devastating two countries and the deaths of hundreds of thousands of innocent civilians, either through direct military action or the indirect effects stemming from the destruction of national infrastructure and other causes. Additionally, the US anti-terrorism campaign has frequently resorted to use of unmanned drone aircraft, targeting suspected terrorists in Pakistan, Yemen, Somalia and other countries. Undoubtedly some terrorists have thereby been eliminated, but so too have hundreds of innocent civilians, victims of so-called "collateral damage". Yet horrible though many post-9/11 responses may now appear, relatively few observers in a world inured to systemic violence questioned their legitimacy when they began in 2001.

To summarize, UN efforts to deal with threats to peace and security have proved seriously inadequate. They have failed to avert or halt (as in Syria) many international and civil wars. Many missions launched were ill coordinated, underfunded and understaffed, falling far short of achieving their mandated goals. Moreover, missions have been largely confined to small and/or weak nations, whereas powerful states, especially those wielding veto power in the SC, have waged war with impunity.

Dual or multiple standards also were applied in funding and staffing peacekeeping missions.[29] Consider, for example, the contrast between the average of $3.5 billon spent annually by NATO and the United Nations combined in Bosnia & Herzegovina between 1995 and 2003, and the expenditure in 2004 of only $2.38 billion for *all seven* UN missions in Africa.[30] With respect to troop contributions, there has been ever-increasing reliance on forces from developing nations, many of which arrive at their missions poorly equipped and/or inadequately trained. In recent years a substantial majority of all forces have come from South Asia and Africa.[31] Several explanatory factors may be advanced. First, it has become politically unpopular in many wealthy nations, especially the United States, to have their troops serve – and sometimes die – under foreign command, even under the UN banner.[32] Conversely, for many developing countries service in UN missions is a matter of prestige and honour. Additionally, being a leading troop contributor strengthens the claim of some states (e.g. India and Nigeria) to be entitled to a seat on the SC.

However, troop "contributions" are not really *contributions* (a matter seldom candidly discussed), but rather a form of mercenary engagement. The "contributing" countries receive from the United Nations a set payment in dollars per soldier per month ($1,028 since 2002), a small fraction of which normally goes towards troop salaries. By the standards of most recipient countries this is generous compensation. Additionally, the United Nations reimburses member states for equipment, civilian personnel and support services.[33] Thus soldiers are supplied at the UN's expense and receive on-the-job training and experience that will heighten their value to their home country following UN service. In effect, then, for not a few countries peacekeeping has become a lucrative undertaking.[34]

Attempts at reforming the existing system

Although robust missions mounted by major powers were generally able to achieve their military goals within relatively short time frames, they fared less well in establishing stable regimes in strife-torn countries. Although a *pax Americana* may have appeared attainable as recently as the year 2000, US forces have since become severely overextended; and the idea of the United States – or even a US-led NATO – playing the (uninvited) role of world policeman would now find few adherents. Outside the United States, distrust of the motives and capabilities of the world's one remaining superpower – and of the West in general – is widespread and deep.

Thus an *appropriately reformed United Nations* must reassert itself as the principal global source of legitimate peacekeeping authority and develop the ability to mount more robust, speedier, more reliable and more principled responses to serious security threats. There will still be considerable latitude for the operation of *regional agencies*; but they should, wherever possible, act in accordance with UN-approved principles and with specific UN authorization resolutions.

Numerous official and unofficial reports – most notably by Secretary-General Boutros Boutros-Ghali (in 1992 and 1995),[35] the Commission on Global Governance (1995)[36] and the Panel on United Nations Peace Operations (2000, the so-called Brahimi Report)[37] – have sought to address the problems of peacekeeping and peace enforcement and recommended corrective measures. Although they did result in numerous improvements, most recommendations were ignored or watered down and none has eliminated the serious systemic shortcomings discussed above. But an important structural change, the establishment of the Department of Peacekeeping Operations (DPKO), separate from the Department of Political Affairs, was instituted in 1992.

Among the recommendations of both the Commission on Global Governance and the Brahimi Report was the creation of a *standing UN rapid deployment force* capable of intervening speedily to prevent mass atrocities such as the Rwandan genocide.[38] But despite the Charter's call for member nations to place military forces and facilities at the disposal of the SC, the idea of a standing UN force remains highly contentious.[39]

In 1997, in response to a Danish-led initiative – with major contributions also from Canada and the Netherlands – an international force was established. The Standby High Readiness Brigade for UN Operations (SHIRBRIG) never exceeded 5,000 troops (drawn from 16 countries), however, and did not become operational until the year 2000. SHIRBRIG undertook only five missions, all in Africa: one for peacekeeping along the Ethiopian-Eritrean border, and the others, much smaller in scale, for "capacity building" and training local forces. No mission lasted longer than seven months and the experiment was terminated in 2009.[40] SHIRBRIG did, however, help pave the way for larger UN, AU and/or ECOWAS deployments in Liberia, Côte d'Ivoire and Sudan.[41]

SHIRBRIG's shortcomings, largely predictable in retrospect, led to its own voluntary demise. First, each participating country retained the right to abstain or withdraw from any mission, and that privilege was often invoked. Second, some countries reneged on promised contributions, thereby hindering "force generation". Third, most of the world's major liberal democracies failed to participate.[42] Fourth, chains of command were unclear, leading to frequent decision-making problems both within SHIRBRIG and between SHIRBRIG and the DPKO and host-country functionaries, resulting in inadequate operational coherence. Finally, there were inevitable diseconomies of scale in an operation as small as SHIRBRIG.

Leery though they were of joining SHIRBRIG, the major European powers recognized a need for an EU multilateral rapid-deployment force that might work, when necessary, with NATO and/or the United Nations without being bound to either. In 2001 the European Union adopted the European Capabilities Action Plan.[43] This led to plans for meeting a wide range of needs in regard to the interoperability, deployability and sustainability of land, sea and air forces of the EU's member states (then 19, now 27) by 2010.[44]

The EU plan called for small, highly mobile "battle groups" as an efficacious vehicle for crisis management. Such battalion-sized units, generally numbering around 1,500 troops, commonly included elements from several adjacent nations, one of which was designated as the "lead nation".[45] This model was established after a chain of events in Ituri province of the Democratic Republic of the Congo in 2003, when the local security situation deteriorated rapidly and MONUC, the UN mission deployed there, could not adequately protect the province's native and refugee populations. Needing swift action, the SC authorized France to lead a multinational 1,800-troop force to the region. That deployment, the first EU military engagement outside Europe itself, restored order within a few months, following which MONUC assumed control.[46]

Spurred on by France, the United Kingdom and Germany, countries across the European Union, along with Norway and Turkey (members of NATO but not of the European Union), began to organize battle groups, each of which would be on call in rotation for a six-month period, beginning in 2007.[47] Units were to be made available within 15 days of a deployment resolution and sustainable in the field for up to 120 days, after which they would presumably be replaced by a larger force authorized by NATO, the United Nations or some other capable agency.

While impressive on paper, many of these planned goals remain unachieved. The efficacy of battle groups has not yet been demonstrated. The system suffers from deficiencies similar to those plaguing SHIRBRIG.[48]

Presently the world cannot rely on peacekeeping by regional organizations. Inevitably, then, we must reconsider the United Nations. In this regard the recommendations of the aforementioned Brahimi Report are especially pertinent. This detailed and far-reaching document emphasized the need for "robust" (a diplomatic term for forceful) responses, where needed, to protect civilian populations and, arguably, counter egregious defiance of existing accords. Unlike previous UN practice, it observed that "neutrality" in the face of criminal behaviour is tantamount to "complicity with evil", and that: "No failure did more to damage the standing and credibility of United Nations peacekeeping in the 1990s than its reluctance to distinguish victim from aggressor."[49] The conclusion reached is that UN peacekeeping missions must have "bigger forces, better equipped and more costly, but able to be a credible deterrent" to unacceptable behaviour.[50]

Additionally, the report emphasized the need for "rapid and effective deployment capability".[51] Pending its achievement, however, the report called for a UN "stand-by arrangements system", with brigade-sized units available for deployment on short notice and establishing rosters of highly trained military, police and civilian personnel willing to assume key posts. But it does not challenge reliance on the willingness of member nations to provide troops and other forms of support whenever needed, or the fact that troops can be withdrawn at the pleasure of the contributing nations. Further, while arguing for coordination, it fails to address adequately the insuperable difficulties of trying to cobble together efficient forces composed – as has been the norm – of troops and other personnel from literally dozens of nations, with widely varying training (often irrelevant), experience and operational doctrines. More importantly, the report does not effectively challenge frequent misuse of sovereignty as a cover for state-sponsored criminal behaviour. Nor does it question the prerequisite of government consent for launching a peacekeeping operation, no matter how viciously a regime may behave in dealing with its own citizens. In short, the report would continue to allow sovereignty to trump humanity.[52]

Shortly after submission of the Brahimi Report, at the instigation of Lloyd Axworthy, Canada's then foreign minister, another history-making panel was convened: the International Commission on Intervention and State Sovereignty (ICISS), whose report, *The Responsibility to Protect*, was issued in 2001.[53] Composed of 12 members from 11 countries (including five from the global South), ICISS took as its charge "the 'right of humanitarian intervention,' the question of when, if ever, it is appropriate for states to take coercive – and in particular military – action against another state for the purpose of protecting people at risk in that other state".[54] The basic principles ultimately put forward were as follows:

A. State sovereignty implies responsibility and the primary responsibility for the protection of its people lies with the state itself.

B. Where a population is suffering serious harm, as a result of internal war, insurgency, repression or state failure, and the state in question is unwilling or unable to halt or avert it, the principle of non-intervention yields to the international responsibility to protect.[55]

These proposed principles fundamentally challenged the traditional notion of sovereignty whereby a state enjoyed the *right* to do whatever it wished within its own borders free from interference by outside powers. *Responsibility* became the other side of the sovereignty coin.

It would not follow, however, that *any* outside state or other political actor could take it upon itself to judge that a given state had failed to live up to its sovereign responsibilities to its own citizens and take military action to correct the wrong. Rather, such action would have to be authorized by the SC (in which the P-5 would be enjoined not to exercise their power of the veto); or, absent SC action, by the GA under the Uniting for Peace procedure; or by an appropriate regional organization in accordance with Chapter VIII of the Charter (subject to later SC approval).[56] Thus unilateral initiatives like that of the United States in deposing Saddam Hussein's odious regime in Iraq could not be excused under the R2P doctrine.

Although duly sanctioned military intervention would become possible under an R2P regime, it was to be regarded as applicable only when some threshold had been passed in respect to large-scale loss of life or large-scale ethnic cleansing; and, even then, only as a "last resort" after all other options had failed. Additional "precautionary principles" included "right intention" (i.e. the need to avert human suffering, rather than to achieve some other political goal); "proportional means" (i.e. ensuring that the scale, duration and intensity of the intervention would be limited to what was necessary to achieve the desired human objective); and the existence of "reasonable prospects" for success, with the consequences of action not being worse than those of inaction.[57]

Reactions to the radical ICISS report were diverse.[58] Many nations, especially in the global South, initially viewed R2P as a means by which to justify neocolonial adventurism and hegemonic policies. The fact that the United States used the pretext of "humanitarian intervention" among its justifications for invading Iraq could not but fuel scepticism.[59] Were it not for the warm support that the report received from Secretary-General Kofi Annan and the endorsement provided in the report of the High-level Panel on Threats, Challenges and Change, the R2P principle might not have been accepted.[60] The major sticking point was the reformulation of the meaning of sovereignty. Even before the ICISS report was published, Kofi Annan put the matter this way:

state sovereignty, in its most basic sense, is being redefined ... States are now widely understood to be instruments in the service of their peoples, and not vice-versa. At the same time individual sovereignty – by which I mean the fundamental freedom of each individual, enshrined in the Charter of the UN and subsequent international treaties – has been enhanced by a renewed and spreading consciousness of individual rights. When we read the Charter today, we are more than ever conscious that it aims to protect individual human beings, not to protect those who abuse them.[61]

The most controversial portions of the ICISS report related to military action. There were reasonable concerns about how to decide when the threshold of unacceptable violence had been passed; how to judge that all options other than the last resort, force, have been exhausted; and how to ascertain in advance that that the consequences of military intervention, once authorized, would not be worse than the consequences of inaction.[62] (The last of these three questions loomed particularly large in considering armed intervention in the Sudanese region of Darfur.) The US position was that while R2P was acceptable in principle, it ought not *obligate* any country to intervene; nor should it *preclude* intervention in the absence of UN authorization.[63] But such a position, if adopted, would have made the United Nations virtually irrelevant. The African Union took a different stance. In a document known as "The Ezulwini Consensus" it expressed general agreement with the R2P principle, but argued that regional organizations should be empowered to act on their own when necessary, though SC approval would be sought "after the fact".[64]

Prevention of violence and *rebuilding* in the wake of violence were also major thrusts of the proposal, and arguably the most important parts.[65] Among the provisions was the need for improved measures of early warning and analysis, implying improved UN capability for gathering and processing intelligence, which – if perceived as espionage – provided a justifiable source of concern. More favourably regarded were the post-intervention rebuilding provisions, including commitments to security, justice and reconciliation, development and a viable administrative system.

Given the concerns of many nations in respect to R2P, it was adopted only in a diluted and truncated form – a mere three paragraphs – at the 2005 UN summit. "It was clear from the outset," one analyst observed, "that creative ambiguity would be the order of the day with respect to authority."[66] The principal operative section read as follows:

> The international community, through the United Nations ... has the responsibility to use appropriate diplomatic, humanitarian and other peaceful means, in accordance with Chapters VI and VIII of the Charter, to help to protect populations from genocide, war crimes, ethnic cleansing and crimes against humanity. In this context, we are prepared to take collective action, in a timely and decisive manner, through the Security Council, in accordance with the Charter, including Chapter VII, on a case-by-case basis and in cooperation with relevant regional organizations as appropriate should peaceful means be inadequate and national authorities are manifestly failing to protect their populations ...[67]

Despite the unanimity achieved at the 2005 summit, the R2P principle was not explicitly invoked by the SC until its adoption of Resolution 1973 in March 2011 to establish a no-fly zone in Libya, in hopes thereby of protecting the civilian population of the rebel-held city of Benghazi from threatened massive retribution by the regime of Muammar al-Qaddafi. But subsequent NATO-sanctioned actions went well beyond what the no-fly resolution authorized. Moreover, SC failure to adopt resolutions in respect to the violent suppression of dissent in Yemen, Syria and Bahrain (a key US ally) properly raised questions about applying double standards in the use (or non-use) of the R2P principle.[68]

In Sudan, where the government-supported campaign of genocide and ethnic cleansing in Darfur would appear to have provided even greater justification for R2P intervention than in Libya, the UN response was ill funded and carried out mainly by forces provided by the African Union, with minimal UN support. While some measure of stability (stabilized misery) was achieved, little has been done to address the basic causes and possible remedies for the abuses committed.

Peacebuilding – in addition to peacekeeping – was a concern of both the Brahimi Report and the ICISS, and also addressed in the report of the High-level Panel on Threats, Challenges and Change, "A More Secure World: Our Shared Responsibility".[69] The first of these documents declared that peacebuilding:

> defines activities undertaken on the far side of conflict to reassemble the foundations of peace and provide the tools for building on those foundations some-

thing that is more than just the absence of war. Thus, peace-building includes but is not limited to reintegrating former combatants into civilian society, strengthening the rule of law ... improving respect for human rights through the monitoring, education and investigation of past and existing abuses; providing technical assistance for democratic development ... and promoting conflict resolution and reconciliation techniques.[70]

The specified goals are all worthy and practical; but I would add to the thought that peace is not just *the absence of war* the conviction that peace – in the words of many peace activists (echoing Martin Luther King, Jr) – should be viewed as *the presence of justice*. Thus peacebuilding should promote political, social and economic justice, together with the rule of law.

Following the recommendations of the high-level panel, the 2005 summit outcome document put forward a proposal for "achieving sustainable peace, recognizing the need for a dedicated institutional mechanism to address the special needs of countries emerging from conflict".[71] In particular, it advocated a new international advisory body, the Peacebuilding Commission (PBC), whose main purpose would be:

> to bring together all relevant actors to marshal resources and to advise on and propose integrated strategies for post-conflict peacebuilding and recovery ... [to assist in laying] the foundations for sustainable development ... [and to] provide recommendations and information to improve the coordination of all relevant actors within and outside the United Nations.[72]

The new PBC was established through parallel resolutions by the GA and SC. It works through a standing organizational committee with 31 members drawn from members of the SC (all the P-5 and two others), ECOSOC (selected by regions) and top providers of military and police personnel for peacekeeping missions. No country has more than a single member. Deliberations are open to representatives from the World Bank, IMF and other major donor agencies. The ancillary Peacebuilding Fund was established to ensure speedy release of resources needed in launching PBC activities.[73] Much of the work, however, would be done through country-specific meetings with differing configurations of participants, including representatives from the nation under consideration, other countries in the region, relevant regional and subregional organizations and concerned committee members.[74] Finally, we must note the GA's establishment in 2006 of the small Peacebuilding Support Office within the UN Secretariat, charged with responsibility to gather and assess information on financial resources to assist the work of the PBC. This entity became necessary because of the GA decision (responding to US pressure) to fund the PBC entirely through *voluntary* contributions.[75]

Conceptually, the PBC appears to be a major advance.

> What distinguishes peacebuilding from more conventional peacekeeping and
> humanitarian assistance is its focus on causes of conflict and the use of a wide
> range of multifunctional instruments to consolidate and entrench peace pro-
> cesses. Peacebuilding therefore tries to transform the social and political con-
> text of conflict so that human beings can live in a stable and secure social,
> political and economic environment. It recognizes that unless the peace process
> addresses the underlying causes of violence, human security will be threatened
> – a direct expression of the link between human rights and peace and security,
> as implied by the Charter.[76]

Operationally, however, the distinction between peacekeeping and
peacebuilding is often unclear. While some peacebuilding efforts within
missions launched prior to the establishment of the PBC did meet with
considerable success, others became enmeshed in problems of coordination and coherence similar to those that have bedevilled so many activities
under the broad umbrella of the UN system.[77] Whether PBC initiatives
will avoid such pitfalls remains to be seen.

In the first five years of the PBC's existence, five relatively small countries
– Burundi, Sierra Leone, Guinea-Bissau, the Central African Republic
and Liberia, in that order – successfully requested placement on its
agenda and have received post-conflict assistance (e.g. with disarmament
efforts, reintegration of combatants into society, combating drug trafficking, electoral assistance, etc.).[78] Additionally, they and several others – also
African – received very modest financial support from the Peacebuilding
Fund and a peacebuilding and recovery facility. While it is too early to
attempt a cost-benefit analysis, the following evaluation does not augur
well for the future:

> [There has been] ... a series of weak and under-resourced initiatives which are
> unlikely to fulfill their promise any time soon. This tepid support for institu-
> tional capacity building has political consequences as it tells the world's skep-
> tics that the advocates of R2P are less than ready to put their money, their
> peacekeepers, and their expertise where their mouths are.[79]

In addition to the PBC, the year 2005 also saw the creation within the
UN Secretariat of the UN Democracy Fund (UNDEF), under the authority of the Secretary-General.[80] UNDEF's purpose is to work with
civil society – with approval from the relevant governments – to promote
democratic institutions. It is, in fact, the only UN organ primarily concerned with civil society organizations. To its credit, UNDEF does not
promote any particular variety of democracy, but judges each request for
assistance in terms of the local political and social context. Its governance

structure, through an appointed advisory board, is innovative. The board consists of one representative from each of the seven largest donor nations, six chosen regionally, two members from civil society entities and four individuals serving in a personal capacity.

Like the PBC, UNDEF is funded from voluntary contributions. In its first five years it received contributions from 38 states totalling $110 million, a paltry sum. The principal contributors have been the United States and India. Project support is competitively determined. Of the 7,278 applications up to 2009, only 335 were funded, mainly for community development projects. Others related to women's empowerment, youth leadership, human rights, the rule of law, strengthening the media and an omnibus category designated as "tools of democratization".

Little known, but much older than UNDEF, is the UN Volunteers (UNV) programme.[81] Established by the GA in 1970, UNV is headquartered in Bonn, Germany, and maintains liaison offices in Tokyo and New York. Its work is coordinated with UNDP. Since its founding, UNV has placed more than 50,000 volunteers to perform a broad range of on-site functions in over 130 countries. Additionally, it maintains a roster of over 70,000 professionals who are *seeking* assignments. More than 75 per cent of assigned volunteers come from developing counties and over 30 per cent serve within their own countries. Recent recruitment rates have increased to more than 7,500 annually, and volunteers now constitute a third of all international civilian staff working in UN peacekeeping operations. The minimum age for service is 25 years. Recruitment and assignment involve more than 2,000 NGOs. Volunteers work with UN agencies, as well as non-profit and private organizations, on tasks including many relating to organizing and running elections and service to peacekeeping and humanitarian projects. Volunteers have annually renewable contracts and receive a modest living allowance, generally paid by the host agency but sometimes by donors to the UN's Special Voluntary Fund. The German Development Service (Deutscher Entwicklungsdienst) is the major contributor.

A standing UN Peace Corps[82]

Commendable though they were, past attempts to reform UN peacekeeping and peacebuilding have been far from adequate. Eventually the United Nations will have to create more robust, capable, efficient and cost-effective agencies to perform a growing array of relevant tasks. This and the following two sections present recommendations for establishing three needed institutions: a UN Peace Corps, a UN Administrative Reserve Corps and a UN Administrative Academy.

The envisaged UN Peace Corps would be a *strong, standing, multi-purpose military body made up of globally recruited, elite, highly trained volunteers under direct UN command.*[83] It would not depend upon the unreliable support of individual member nations or blocs of nations. Its establishment will be both difficult and costly, with annual expenditures substantially greater than those allocated for all current peacekeeping missions. But the ultimate benefits would enormously outweigh the investment, not merely with respect to conflicts and destruction averted, but also in the vast reductions in national military expenditures that the force would make possible.

Functions of the UNPC

The more numerous and worthwhile the tasks that the UNPC can perform, the greater its appeal should be. Thus rather than thinking solely of being able to respond rapidly to pressing military emergencies, one should also consider additional functions for the UNPC, many of which could keep units productively occupied during periods when they are not required to play an active, specifically military role.

In the relatively narrow *military mode* would be all functions already assigned to UN-authorized peacekeeping missions: patrolling cease-fire lines and monitoring violations, protecting civilian populations in conflict zones, overseeing the evacuation of refugees, guarding emergency relief supplies to war-affected areas, clearing minefields, disposing of ordnance, dismantling selected military installations and/or weapons-making plants, putting interpositionary forces in place to prevent the spread of conflict to areas under threat of invasion and – when the SC deems necessary – engaging in Chapter VII peace-enforcement operations.

Additional *peacebuilding* functions would be to restore – in concert with civilian specialists from UN agencies, other IGOs and NGOs – some semblance of order in failed states or situations where sovereignty is being transferred from one state to another. Many developmental and humanitarian undertakings would be feasible: constructing roads, airports and other components of the economic infrastructure of host countries; upgrading local drinking-water supplies, sanitation and other aspects of public health; training activities to improve the skills of the local citizenry; and logistic support to other agencies in times of famine and natural catastrophe. Another potential task would be election monitoring, an activity in which the United Nations has become increasingly adept. Cost-sharing arrangements for such activities would necessitate contracts with host governments, various agencies within the UN system and others.

The UNPC would enhance the value of human capital through training internationally recruited male and female volunteers, especially from developing countries. Apart from technical skills that volunteers would acquire, one must consider habits of discipline, devotion to duty and the *esprit de corps* that a well-run military unit would impart. Such intangible benefits have enormous potential to contribute to nation building and social development once volunteers complete their service and return to their home countries. Service would provide veterans with a badge of honour and respect, and enhance their ability to function as development agents.

Moreover, UNPC service would bring elite young adults from different countries into close working contact with one another and help eliminate negative cultural and gender stereotypes and establish enduring bonds of amity. It would also enhance the ability of volunteers to communicate in newly acquired languages. The economic and social benefits should be obvious. Additional benefits would be derived from recreational pastimes, such as organized sporting events (including matches between UNPC and host-country teams), cultural activities within host countries and foreign travel during periods of paid leave. Finally, establishing a corps of volunteers inspired by an ethos of global service and common allegiance to humanity, rather than to specific countries, would promote a salutary planetary consciousness.

Recruitment and training

Service in the UNPC would be open equally to qualified men and women throughout the world. This presupposes establishing offices for screening, testing and selecting would-be volunteers. Most such offices could be permanently annexed to those of the existing network of UN country coordinators; others would operate perhaps for only one or two months per year, at localities making enlistment a practicable option in areas where travel costs are high in relation to average income levels. The physical, mental and moral requirements for eligibility should be sufficiently high to ensure formation of an elite body. Establishing the requisite standards and the means of overseeing adherence to them would be assigned to an appointed subcommission entrusted with drawing up arrangements leading up to the UNPC's formation.

Recruits would undergo an initial period of rigorous basic training, the length of which would vary depending on whether preliminary language instruction was necessary. Recruits failing to meet stipulated achievement criteria during the training period would be honourably discharged. Terms of service, following basic training, would be four additional years for all non-commissioned ranks and could normally be renewed only once, though exceptions might be made for needed specialists. This stricture would preclude creating a large body of career soldiers. (Regularly making vacancies for new recruits would also greatly expand the number of beneficiaries of UNPC service.) To ensure continuity of command, training and operational functions, however, the length of permissible service for officers and a small cadre of key non-commissioned officers should be longer than for lower ranks.

On pragmatic grounds, the number of operating languages within the corps would have to be limited. Initially, English, French and Spanish would best serve, given their widespread distribution and status as either official or auxiliary languages in most countries. While not all recruits would initially be proficient in any of these three, those whose native tongue was closely related to one of the UNPC languages should be able to learn the new language well enough to use it effectively within six months or so following recruitment. (Portuguese-speaking recruits, for example, would be expected to learn sufficient Spanish during their training to fit easily into a Spanish-speaking command.) Within each command a single language would be used for training and most operational purposes. This would require development of comparable training and operations manuals in all three working languages. Many, however, could be translated and/or adapted from existing military manuals. Others could be developed from materials prepared by the International Peace Academy.[84]

As in any substantial military force, specialized units would be necessary in the UNPC and would require appropriate training. Apart from basic weapons and tactical training for all volunteers, specialized training in engineering, mechanics, communications, intelligence, medical, military administration, police and other duties would be imparted. All volunteers would also be given training to enhance their negotiating skills and cultural sensitivity.

Emoluments would be generous. In addition to uniforms, food, billeting and other necessities, as well as paid leave, all personnel would receive a salary appropriate for the area in which they served. Supplementary payments sufficient to make up differences between high- and low-paying field salaries would be deposited in home-country accounts and become available to volunteers on honourable conclusion of their service. Post-service educational benefits (comparable to the remarkably successful GI Bill of Rights for US veterans) should also be instituted. Service would be therefore regarded not merely as a job, but as a hard-won privilege.

Command and control

Largely following recommendations of the Norwegian Commission of Experts,[85] the UNPC chain of command would run from the SC through the SG and an International Military Staff Committee within the UN Secretariat to a UN *headquarters command* and thence to *three regional commands*. However, given the occasional need for swift and robust action – say in times of impending genocide or major natural catastrophes – departures from standard operating procedures should be permissible. Specifically, following a formal emergency appeal from a simple majority of SC members, whether or not that majority included members of the P-5, the Secretary-General should be authorized to initiate rapid deployment of a limited force – say up to 10,000 troops – for a period not to exceed six months. The SC would then have time to debate the wisdom of the initial deployment and either terminate or continue it, possibly at a larger or smaller scale. This departure from past practice could avert immense suffering and enormous post-emergency expenditures.

The recommended emergency provisions would enable the United Nations to give long-overdue credence to the R2P principle. But they should not be employed lightly. In particular, it would be necessary to uphold established criteria of legitimacy: "seriousness of purpose, proper purpose, last resort, proportional means and balance of consequences".[86]

Taking into consideration numerous geographical, logistical and political factors, the following division of responsibilities is suggested: a Western Command for the Americas, with Spanish as the chief operating language; a dual Central Command for Europe, Africa and the Middle East, one component of which would use French and the other English; and an Eastern Command for the balance of Asia and Oceania, with English as its operating language. There could be units within each command, however, using languages other than the official command language. For example, English-speaking brigades trained under the Central Command might be transferred to the Western Command for service in English-speaking areas of the Caribbean.

Some may regard the subordination of English within the Western Command structure and the lack of Russian- and Chinese-speaking commands as significant shortcomings. But one must recognize pragmatically that, for the foreseeable future, the UNPC is unlikely to be called upon to intervene in crises originating in or involving the United States, Russia, China or, for that matter, any other veto-wielding SC member. Nor, in all likelihood, would the UNPC be asked to intervene in the areas of many other stable and peaceful states (e.g. Canada or the Scandinavian countries). But should any *major* power be guilty, in the near future, of armed aggression posing a threat to peace too great for the UNPC to handle, other *ad hoc* mechanisms for dealing with the issue would have to be devised. Ultimately, however, elimination of the SC veto would go far towards remedying this unavoidable limitation of the present proposal (as well as all others calling for standing UN peacekeeping forces).

Generally, troops from only one regional command would be used in a specific military mission, and the size of the force would normally suffice to carry out its mandate. Nevertheless, there may be times when obdurate military resistance to a given UNPC intervention would be sufficiently great to require transferring forces from other commands. Thus each command would provide, in effect, a strategic reserve for the others. Also conceivable are occasions when available units from the combined UNPC commands would be insufficient for a specific assignment. In such cases, the UNPC would still form the nucleus and spearhead of the SC-authorized force needed to meet the threat, with additional units provided by individual member states (as originally envisaged in Chapter VII of the UN Charter). Mustering the necessary will would provide the key to success. Failure to do so would simply invite future defiance of UN authority by nations bent on aggression, genocide or other unconscionable behaviour.

The headquarters of each regional command, along with a substantial part of the staff, should be placed on bases leased from politically stable countries with relatively democratic regimes within regions where they will likely be needed. The countries selected should offer facilities for logistical support by sea and air from powers capable of providing it. If the system were currently in place, suitable candidates might be Costa Rica or Uruguay for the Western Command; Senegal or Tunisia for the French-speaking component of the Central Command and Jordan, Ghana or South Africa for the English-speaking component; and Malaysia or the Philippines for the Eastern Command. A limited number of additional bases, including supply depots, could be established at strategically situated leased sites in each command. Preference would be given to democratic nations.

Initially, the UNPC would have to rely on major powers for naval and air support, using leased vessels and aircraft in much the same way that the DPKO does at present. In principle, however, there is no reason why the UNPC should not eventually acquire its own logistic capability.

A final, but crucial, requirement with respect to command and control is that the criteria for intervention and the rules of engagement once intervention is sanctioned must be clearly specified.[87]

Costs and benefits

The costs of establishing and maintaining the proposed UNPC would substantially exceed those of all current UN peacekeeping operations. Costs under the present DPKO system passed the $5 billion mark in 2007, when the United Nations had a monthly average of roughly 83,000 soldiers and police in the field.[88] Total annual costs then worked out to not quite $60,000 per uniformed person.[89] As of 2010, the annual cost per man/woman in uniform in the world's major armed forces (including land, sea and air forces) varied over a remarkably wide range. Sample figures, calculated to the nearest $1,000, were India $32,000, Turkey $34,000, China $52,000, Russia $56,000 (a drastic decline from the Cold War period), South Africa $73,000, Brazil $105,000, Japan $220,000, France $249,000 and the United States $446,000.[90] For countries towards the upper end of this spectrum, much of the expense indicated derives from expenditures for sophisticated equipment, especially offensive weapons systems for the air force and navy (often including costs for research and development). However, high-tech lethal ordnance would be inappropriate for the UNPC. Thus it seems reasonable to suggest a cost per soldier of approximately $85,000 per year (in 2010 dollars).

If we assume a total force of 300,000 for all three commands once the UNPC attains full strength, and average annual maintenance costs of $85,000 per soldier to cover food, uniforms, billeting, weapons, ammunition, basic equipment, supplies, salaries, prescribed savings, other overhead expenses and optional post-service educational benefits, that would yield a total of roughly $25 billion when the UNPC is functioning in a non-military mode. Employment of civilian specialists and local support personnel (largely for base maintenance) would raise that figure by several billion dollars. Actual military operations would add significantly to this sum, especially for leasing needed ships and aircraft for logistical support. In the initial years of the UNPC, costs would obviously differ from what they would be once the commands were brought to full strength. On the one hand, there would be substantial start-up costs for recruiting and for building and supplying military bases (though significant savings could be realized by utilizing UNPC cadres for much of the work). On the other hand, the initial force would be substantially smaller than the full complement, and expenses for post-service benefits would be negligible.

While the anticipated expenses of the UNPC may at first appear prohibitive, they pale in comparison to the world's national military outlays, which in 2010 totalled $1.63 *trillion*, or to the $698 billion budgeted that year by the United States alone (not counting enormous additional costs for prosecuting the wars/ocupations in Iraq and Afghanistan).[91] One should also compare the likely UNPC costs to the vastly greater expenses for wars it could avert, not merely in military operations but also the incalculable cost of lives lost, destroyed infrastructure and massive environmental degradation, as well as their multiplier effects, for "victors" (if one can use that term) and vanquished alike.

To put the matter in perspective, consider the cost of involvement in UNAMIR (the UN Assistance Mission in Rwanda) after genocide claimed roughly 800,000 lives in roughly 100 days, and the related costs for relief efforts in Goma in the adjacent Congolese Kivu province, where many additional thousands of refugees fell victim to disease and the ravages of armed militias.

> During the slow process of creating UNAMIR, the Security Council made it clear that it wanted the operation conducted at minimal expense. Only a fraction of the US $200 million estimated cost of the operation was ever received by the UN. Only a portion of the troops required to implement UNAMIR's mandate ever arrived in the theatre. The lack of funding and material support for UNAMIR stands in sharp contrast to the money spent by the international community in aid and human resource support once the crisis attracted the attention of the international media.[92]

The United States alone provided US$350 million in aid in the first *six weeks* of the Goma tragedy. How many more Rwandas and Gomas will it take for the global community to liberate itself from its penny-wise, pound-foolish mode of response to looming threats of genocide, aggression and other catastrophes?

Although nobody can foretell the future, some economic speculation is warranted. Let us suppose that, in some future year, the costs of the UNPC, including those of actual military operations, total $50 billion (roughly 10 times the 2007 UN peak). Suppose further that the sense of heightened security generated by the UNPC's capacity to contain conflicts before they get out of control (contrary to what happened, for example, in the former Yugoslavia) would induce the world's nations to reduce annual military budgets (exclusive of combat costs) by roughly a fourth, say by $400 billion (in 2010 dollars). If these hypothetical figures are accepted (though savings in national military expenditures could be vastly greater), they alone would yield a cost-benefit ratio of 8:1, making the UNPC a phenomenally good investment. Consider also the enormous additional savings accruing from the many likely instances in which the very existence of the UNPC would avert destructive wars – or the imputed value of preventing even one campaign of genocide.

Finally, consider the benefits that would flow from the UNPC's *non-*military functions. Though largely unquantifiable, those benefits might more than outweigh the UNPC's cost. Thus unless my assumptions are substantially wide of the mark, by any reasonable calculus the UNPC would clearly warrant implementation.

Since anticipated UNPC costs will exceed the present costs of the entire UN system, one must consider how such an undertaking could best be financed. The simplest method (discussed in Chapter 11) would be to assess all UN member nations a uniform, but very low, percentage of their respective GNIs (say 0.1 per cent), which in itself would yield revenues of roughly $62 billion (as of 2010). But many other creative proposals for enhancing UN revenues have also been advanced. Of these, the most appropriate in respect to the UNPC would be proportional and progressive levies on defence expenditures and/or international arms sales. Apart from their inherent logic, such levies would provide an inducement for arms control and disarmament. However, given the power of the military-industrial complex, none of the workable ideas is matched by the requisite will to effect the needed change. Governments must overcome their myopia and recognize the phenomenal benefits that would accrue from prudent investment in bold peacekeeping initiatives.

Transitional arrangements

The above is a set of general recommendations, not a detailed plan capable of being effected in the short term. To get from our present system to the proposed UNPC, the United Nations should first enhance its capability for timely reaction to crises. This will require establishing a rapid deployment force of relatively modest size under *direct UN command*, backed up by standby national contingents capable of responding swiftly and robustly to future security threats up to a level significantly greater than in the former Yugoslavia and other recent operations. Even that limited goal, however, will not be reached without international determination – especially among leading powers – to act decisively to prevent future conflicts.

As future successes are achieved, and as recognition spreads that there are indeed reliable UN mechanisms for preventing violence, the justification for large national military establishments will diminish. Then, given mounting popular demand for reduced tax burdens, nations should be increasingly willing to divert portions of their bloated military budgets towards supporting the UNPC. This will be more likely if military authorities have done the necessary planning.

In several countries, most notably the Nordic states, Canada and the Netherlands, which have had extensive and exemplary experience in both UN and non-UN military operations as well as in the International Peace Academy, much thought has been given to issues touched on in this chapter. It seems appropriate, then, to suggest that a group of highly trusted states and NGOs – but *not* any major power – be delegated now by the SC to draw up a blueprint and timetable for phased implementation of the UNPC. Precedents exist. In the Korean and Gulf Wars groups of countries, led by the United States, were empowered to act on behalf of the United Nations. Why then should there be any serious objection to assigning responsibility to a select group in an undertaking where the prospects for major enduring benefits are enormously greater? Devising command structures, operational procedures and recruiting mechanisms to launch the UNPC should now be entrusted to a small group of capable peaceloving states.

A UN Administrative Reserve Corps

However capable the staff of a UN peacekeeping mission may be, one can expect only so much from an essentially military body in bringing about a political climate conducive to sustainable peace. Assistance from civilian specialists will be needed. But, thus far, obtaining effective assistance has proved to be highly problematic. The situation is candidly set forth in the Brahimi Report as follows:

> To date, the Secretariat has been unable to identify, recruit and deploy suitably qualified civilian personnel in substantive and support functions either at the right time or in the numbers required. Currently, about 50 per cent of field positions in substantive areas and up to 40 per cent of the positions in administrative and logistics areas are vacant, in missions that were established six months to one year ago and remain in desperate need of the requisite specialists. Some of those who have been deployed have found themselves in positions that do not match their previous experience ... Furthermore, the rate of recruitment is nearly matched by the rate of departure by mission personnel fed up with the working conditions that they face, including the short-staffing itself. High vacancy and turnover rates foreshadow a disturbing scenario for the start-up and maintenance of the next complex peacekeeping operation, and hamper the full deployment of current missions.[93]

Given the problems described, I propose establishing a new institution, the UN Administrative Reserve Corps. The corps envisaged would consist of well-trained civilians capable of responding, on short notice, to the wide range of administrative needs related to ongoing and concluded UN peacekeeping and peacebuilding missions and to creating or restoring a viable society. At full strength, UNARC would be made up of at least 10,000 (preferably 15,000) elite graduates of a three- or four-year training programme at the UN Administrative Academy, described below. All UNARC personnel would receive specialized training in the main languages, cultures and history of a particular world region, and would also obtain some specialized expertise such as finance, personnel management, law, police administration, sanitation and public health, communications technology and so forth.

Upon completing their UNAA studies, graduates would enter into a 10-year contractual obligation to UNARC and be subject to calls to duty as, when and where their services might be required. Thus UNARC would resemble the ready military reserves now maintained by many countries. Trainees would be recruited mainly from the administrative services of national governments and selected primarily from the global South. To ensure their availability when needed, the United Nations would negotiate memoranda of understanding with the countries from which the volunteers came whereby the governments would agree to the temporary release of trainees and reservists called up for service and promise to restore them to their former positions, should the volunteer so desire, with no loss of seniority once their UN training and service were completed. Some trainees would, on graduation, be assigned immediately to UN peacekeeping or peacebuilding missions with pressing civilian staff needs. The remainder would return to their home countries. While the minimum reserve obligation would be for 10 years, it would be possible for those wishing to do so to extend their reserve status beyond that period. The United Nations would exercise final discretion in this matter.

Most UNAA graduates on UN duty would initially serve in junior positions under more experienced personnel from the DPKO appointed as chiefs or deputy chiefs of mission or to other senior posts. However, reservists of proven ability would likely be marked for positions of increasing responsibility in subsequent assignments. Some might even obtain permanent posts within the UN system. Salaries would be modest in comparison to those paid to civilians working on contract in peacekeeping missions or to professional UN staff. But, given the high value of their UNARC education, the discrepancy would be justifiable. Moreover, even the modest salaries envisaged would be significantly better than those most corps personnel would earn in their home countries.

Apart from active duty, reservists would have opportunities to participate in periodic camps within major world regions to enable them to refresh existing skills, acquire new skills and be briefed in lessons learned from completed or ongoing UN missions. Participation would be appropriately remunerated.

UNARC's size would vary over time. The corps would, of course, not even come into existence until graduating the first cohort of trainees three years after the academy's inauguration. Thereafter, UNARC would grow at the rate of 1,000 or more persons per year, depending on the need for additional personnel and the UNAA's ability to expand. Much would also depend on the willingness of reserve personnel to extend their commitments beyond the 10-year minimum. Maintaining a corps in the order of 15,000 individuals seems a reasonable and attainable goal.

Conceivably, many UNAA graduates will never be called upon for active duty. Given the uncertainties of politics, one cannot confidently predict future personnel needs. But even if an individual were never called to service that does not mean that the money spent on her/his training would have been wasted. On the contrary, developing human capital, which would be one of UNARC's missions, should reap numerous dividends. As with the UNPC, service by well-trained personnel in the administration of their respective homelands could contribute greatly to their economic, social and political development. Many graduates, with or without foreign experience, would likely acquire skills enabling them to rise quickly in the ranks of their home country's bureaucracy.

The costs of creating and maintaining UNARC, like those for UN peacekeeping and peacebuilding, would be modest in comparison to the benefits. In this context one might again reflect upon the immense costs of military intervention in Afghanistan and Iraq and subsequent – often amateurish – US-led attempts at state building.

Apart from the potential contributions already indicated, the political stability that use of UNARC personnel would promote would reduce the likelihood of reversion to armed conflict and inhibit the spread of terrorist networks. If even a single major act of terrorism were thereby to be averted, the benefits could be incalculable.

A UN Administrative Academy[94]

The UN Administrative Academy envisaged for training UNARC personnel would initially provide instruction in English, Spanish and French and have three campuses situated in stable, democratic host countries, such as Canada, Costa Rica and Switzerland. In Canada it might be based at the Lester B. Pearson Canadian International Peacekeeping Training Center in Cornwallis, Nova Scotia; in Costa Rica at the UN University for Peace in San José; and in Switzerland at the UN complex in Geneva. In time a fourth campus, offering instruction in Arabic, might also become feasible.

Faculty and administrators would be drawn largely from the pool of persons with UN peacekeeping experience, supplemented by others with specialized expertise. Support staff would be locally recruited.

Trainees would be selected competitively, based on tough annual qualifying examinations. While an attempt would be made to attract qualified individuals from all major world regions, special efforts would be directed at recruiting from developing countries. Eligibility requirements would include possession of a baccalaureate degree or equivalent experience, falling in the age range 21–35, being in good health and having a moral record free from serious blemish. Applications and testing would be managed through national offices of UNDP. Where needed, travel support to reach testing places would be provided.

In addition to students recruited for UNARC, the academy could be used for training incoming junior professional staff of the UN Secretariat, who, as suggested in Chapter 9, would undergo a one-year orientation programme (including a four-month stint in a stressful field location) prior to assuming posts within the UN system.

Making competitive examinations the chief determinant of eligibility entails costs not present in the current system for recruiting civilian staff for UN peacekeeping missions, in which, arguably, class privilege, personal connections and country of origin play too large a role. Top posts in such missions tend to be staffed disproportionately by personnel from relatively affluent countries or elite social strata from a relatively small number of developing countries. The sensitivity of such individuals to the cultures and economic situations of locales where they will likely serve can often be questionable. While there can be no guarantee that those with less privileged backgrounds would be better equipped to perform their jobs, it does seem likely that properly trained UNAA graduates would demonstrate the requisite empathy and understanding.

UNARC-bound students would receive modest monthly stipends in addition to food and lodging. Where appropriate, stipends would be supplemented by allowances for dependants. Books, supplies and related expenses would be borne by the academy. Paid leave and travel allowances would enable students to make periodic home visits. The period of instruction would normally be three years, though certain specializations might require a fourth year. The third year of training would include a four- to six-month field internship, within an existing peacekeeping mission where possible, or otherwise in some other troubled nation. Internships with government agencies, UN field operations (e.g. UNDP, UNICEF or the WFP) or NGOs would be negotiated.

Subjects of instruction and curricular emphases would evolve based on experience. But experience already accumulated by administrative training programmes presently maintained by certain states (e.g. training for the Indian Administrative Service) would be tapped in devising curricula.[95]

The UNAA would establish a core curriculum that all students would have to master. It would include instruction on the history, structure and functioning of the UN system, especially in respect to peacekeeping and peacebuilding, since civilian and military staff will have to be able to work together effectively in the field. Other core activities would include study of management techniques, workshops in effective written communication, honing critical skills in reading history and political propaganda, and training in cultural sensitivity and conflict resolution. Since most

UNARC staff would eventually train local personnel to take over their functions, instruction in pedagogy would also prove useful.

Specialized courses would include human rights law, police supervision, fiscal management, community development, basic education and educational reform, public health and sanitation, and disaster relief. Intensive multidisciplinary study of at least one major world region would be compulsory, and specialized language training – especially in such linguas franca as Arabic, Persian, Swahili, Hausa, Hindi/Urdu and Malay/Bahasa Indonesia – would be encouraged. Diverse means of testing would be utilized. Students failing to maintain high achievement standards would be dismissed from the programme.

Apart from academic offerings, the UNAA would seek to instil in students a global ethos stressing loyalty to humanity as a whole (complementing allegiance to one's own nation) and a sense of planetary stewardship. Thereby, as with the UNPC, it would significantly promote planetary citizenship and inculcate in its students an *esprit de corps* that would substantially enhance their effectiveness.

The costs of creating the academy, like those of UN peacekeeping and peacebuilding in general, would be modest in comparison to the benefits.[96]

Arms control and disarmament

Serious though they are, the threats to peace thus far considered in this chapter pale in comparison to those presented by weapons of mass destruction (WMD). Despite substantial cuts under the terms of a renewed Strategic Arms Reduction Treaty (START), an estimated 9,300 and 13,000 nuclear devices remain in the hands of the United States and Russia respectively.[97] A small fraction of either of those two arsenals could bring an end to all forms of higher life on this planet. Even the much smaller stockpiles of the seven other nuclear-armed nations could wreak unprecedented levels of destruction. Moreover, in addition to nuclear weapons, chemical and biological weapons are capable of exacting death tolls on a scale vastly greater than those experienced from all causes in the First and Second World Wars.[98] Finally, the destructive capabilities of what are misleadingly called "conventional" weapons are also staggering.

Oddly, despite the magnitude of the threat of WMD, most otherwise politically engaged citizens have became, over a period of decades, remarkably inured to their existence. That complacency was shaken, however, by the 2001 terrorist attacks on the World Trade Center and the Pentagon, in which hijacked aircraft were made to function as WMD. This dramatically successful assault on the world's only remaining superpower – along with subsequent acts of terrorism in London, Madrid, Bali and elsewhere – provided a needed wake-up call, reminding people that not only states but also non-state actors can become highly effective deliverers of destruction. The spectre of a lone, perhaps deranged, individual detonating a suitcase-sized nuclear device in the heart of one of the world's major metropolises is no longer a science-fiction fantasy. Yet the global response to old and new threats has been ill coordinated and far from adequate. The United Nations has been significantly involved, but not nearly to the degree needed.[99] Rather, most of the international effort to deal with WMD and non-state terrorism, whatever its form, has taken place through diplomatic channels outside the UN arena.

I highlight below only a few key events relating to nuclear and other forms of WMD, and briefly evaluate the adequacy of relevant policies and institutions. I then offer recommendations for dealing with the problems of arms control and disarmament.

Since the first use of nuclear weapons in 1945 the world has witnessed repeated oscillations between periods of mounting nuclear provocation and interludes of relative sanity, when realization of the looming peril of nuclear war, whether by accident or design, resulted in diplomatically negotiated steps back from the brink of catastrophe.

Among positive diplomatic milestones are two that are noteworthy even though the proposals to which they relate never came fully into effect. The first of these was the so-called Baruch Plan of 1946, presented to the newly created UN Atomic Energy Commission. This bold proposal would have given control of all nuclear technology to an International Atomic Development Authority, which would then control or manage all nuclear-related activities – including mining, research, transportation and nuclear energy production and use – and carry out unfettered inspections of nuclear facilities. It also called for sanctions for non-compliance. Not surprisingly the Soviet Union, then intent on developing its own nuclear capability, opposed the plan, arguing that it put "control" ahead of "disarmament" and would thereby ensure continuation of the US nuclear monopoly.[100]

The second proposal was the Joint Statement of Agreed Principles of General and Complete Disarmament, negotiated in Belgrade in September 1961 by John J. McCloy and Valerian Zorin, on behalf of the United States and USSR respectively. That plan, unanimously endorsed by the GA, called, *inter alia*, for general and complete disarmament; peaceful settlement of disputes in accordance with the UN Charter; limitation of armed forces to what was needed to maintain internal order; provision by states of manpower for a UN peace force; elimination of nuclear stockpiles and delivery systems; balanced implementation by stages until completed, with appropriate international oversight of each stage; unrestricted access to all places necessary for effective verification; and strengthening of institutions for maintaining peace.

The timing of the foregoing accords is remarkable in that they were forged during a period of maximal Cold War bellicosity, between the construction of the Berlin Wall in the summer of 1961 and the Cuban missile crisis in October 1962. This raises the question of whether the entire diplomatic effort might not have been little more than a devious PR charade. I think not. Rather, I subscribe to the theory that the negotiations were attributable to dovish factions in the governing hierarchy of the two concerned states. However, given the then prevailing levels of mutual distrust, the accords were given little public exposure and their sensible and far-reaching provisions – which I would wholeheartedly resurrect and make applicable to all nuclear powers – were soon countermanded by US and Soviet hawks.[101]

Although one may dismiss the accords as too good to be credible and though they never reached the stage of being drafted as a formal treaty, they did have enduring consequences and established a normative framework for subsequent negotiations. Perhaps the most important outcome was negotiation of the 1970 Nuclear Non-Proliferation Treaty (NPT). The NPT, however, was a partial success at best, in that Israel, India and Pakistan – all now nuclear powers – were not among the 187 ratifying nations. The DPRK, a fledgling nuclear power, did ratify the treaty, but later withdrew after giving the requisite six-month notice. Additionally Iran, despite being a signatory, has now allegedly embarked on a nuclear weapons programme.[102] Finally, though seldom noted in the Western press, the P-5 powers have not lived up to their obligation, under Article 6 of the treaty, to work towards the *total* elimination of all their nuclear weapons.[103]

Also flowing from the McCloy-Zorin accords was the recreation in 1978 of the Disarmament Commission, which was in turn succeeded in 1981 by the Conference on Disarmament. Membership in the conference expanded in several stages, and by 2005 reached an unwieldy total of 65 nations. Since conference decisions are made by consensus, each member nation has a veto. Predictably, its accomplishments have been few and hard won.[104]

Worldwide, popular and governmental support for nuclear disarmament is abundant. In the United States recent converts to the idea of complete disarmament include numerous prominent statespersons, both Democrats and Republicans, some previously regarded as Cold War nuclear hawks. Disarmament advocates now include President Obama, two-thirds of all former secretaries of state and many other important political figures.[105]

NGO networks have also been active. Especially noteworthy have been the combined efforts of the International Association of Lawyers

Against Nuclear Arms, the International Network of Engineers and Scientists Against Proliferation and International Physicians for the Prevention of Nuclear War (the last being awarded a Nobel Peace Prize in 1985). In 2007 this consortium published the remarkably thorough "Model Convention on the Prohibition of the Development, Testing, Production, Stockpiling, Transfer, Use and Threat of Use of Nuclear Weapons and on Their Elimination".[106] This report provides a workable text for a treaty fully consistent with the terms set forth in the McCloy-Zorin accords.[107]

Although the Conference on Disarmament has achieved little in respect to limiting *nuclear* weapons, its record and that of the preceding Disarmament Commission in regard to *chemical* and *biological* weapons are significantly better. In 1993, after years of discussion, it proposed the Convention on the Prohibition of the Development, Production, Stockpiling and Use of Chemical Weapons; and by 1997 that treaty garnered enough ratifications to go into effect. A major feature of this treaty is that:

> it includes robust and intrusive verification and compliance monitoring mechanisms ... [including] inspections of factories and production facilities ... and "challenge inspections" that give "each State Party ... the right to request an on-site challenge inspection of any facility or location in the territory or in any other place under the jurisdiction or control of any other State Party for the sole purpose of clarifying and resolving any questions concerning possible non-compliance with the provisions of this Convention."[108]

Foreshadowed by provisions of the McCloy-Zorin accords, this was a precedent-setting breakthrough in surmounting the sovereignty barrier to effective disarmament proposals.[109]

Less impressive is the Biological and Toxin Weapons Convention of 1975 banning use of biological weapons and the development, stockpiling, acquisition, production or transfer of biological agents and toxins not needed for legitimate medical and research purposes. Though ratified by 150 states, that group does not include certain states of "proliferation concern". Moreover, the treaty does not provide for a verification regime.[110]

Even more disappointing has been the UN's disarmament efforts in regard to the complex array of so-called "conventional" weapons, many of which are exceedingly sophisticated and lethal. Although the Register of Conventional Arms has been established, it is a non-binding mechanism for reporting on exports and imports of major weapons systems (aircraft, tanks, military vehicles, etc.), and fails to cover small arms or light weapons.[111]

The only significant treaty in the latter respect provides for a ban on anti-personnel landmines. This landmark achievement, embodied in the

Ottawa Convention of 1997 and now ratified by more than 150 states parties, went into effect in 1999. Among non-signatories, however, are such major states as the United States, Russia, China and India. A noteworthy aspect of the treaty is that it came about because of intense pressure from civil society organizations working under the umbrella of the International Campaign to Ban Landmines. The Canadian campaign organizer, Jody Williams, was awarded a Nobel Peace Prize for her work.[112]

Terrorism

Terrorism, until fairly recently, was regarded by most states as a manageable irritant, a "weapon of the weak". Dealing with the problem was typically entrusted to small groups of national intelligence specialists and law enforcement personnel, with little coordination of effort from one nation to another. Since the traumatic events of 9/11 2001, however, terrorism has emerged as a major global issue. While it continues to be addressed mainly at the national level, it has also become a significant concern to various parts of the UN system, most notably the SC, the GA, the SG, the Commission on Crime Prevention and Criminal Justice, and the Department of Disarmament Affairs.[113]

Largely because of Cold War considerations and the lack of consensus in defining terrorism, pre-2001 SC responses to terrorist acts were relatively few and far between. Among them were several resolutions condemning politically motivated assassinations; a 1970 resolution calling for states to take measures to safeguard air traffic, following a spate of hijackings in the late 1960s; condemnations of several other hijackings and acts of aerial sabotage (most notably over Lockerbie, Scotland, in 1988); and denunciation in 1999 of the bombing by Al Qaeda of US embassies in Kenya and Tanzania.[114]

In general SC resolutions tended to be reactive, in the wake of specific egregious terrorist events. By contrast, the GA was more concerned with norms and principles. It negotiated 13 international legal conventions relating, *inter alia*, to hijacking, crimes against internationally protected persons, hostage taking, terrorist bombings and acts of nuclear terrorism. The division of labour changed in 1999, however, when, recognizing the growing international role of Al Qaeda, the SC passed Resolution 1269, creating a special committee to deal with terrorism and stating that it "unequivocally condemns all acts, methods, and practices of terrorism as criminal and unjustifiable, regardless of their motivation, in all their forms and manifestations, wherever and by whomever committed".[115] And in the immediate aftermath of 9/11 the SC unanimously adopted a binding resolution requiring all states to take measures to prevent and suppress financing of terrorist acts, prevent their territory from being used by terrorists or their supporters and exchange information and cooperate with one another to counter terrorism. Shortly thereafter the existing committee on terrorism, previously known as the "1269 Committee", was strengthened and reconstituted as the Counter Terrorism Committee.[116] State responses to the new directives have generally been good.

Nevertheless, attempts to deal comprehensively with terrorism are bedevilled by the absence of a universally acceptable definition. In particular, many argue that violent acts committed to advance "legitimate" national liberation movements (e.g. the struggles of the African National Congress against South Africa's former apartheid regime) should not be classified as terrorism. Additionally, it is widely asserted that the crime of terrorism should not be made applicable solely to non-state actors, and officially sponsored "state terrorism" should also be criminalized. In this regard the High-level Panel on Threats, Challenges and Change recommended that terrorism should include:

> any action, in addition to actions already specified by the existing conventions ... that is intended to cause death or serious bodily harm to civilians or noncombatants, when the purpose of such an act ... is to intimidate a population, or to compel a Government or an international organization to do or abstain from doing any act.[117]

Though many diplomats (and the present author) find this definition satisfactory, it has failed to cut the Gordian knot. The previously cited concerns, largely held by recently decolonized states, persist.

Prior to 9/11 the United States and several other nations occasionally responded forcefully and unilaterally to terrorist acts on their own soil, which was well within the ambit of international law. Forceful unilateral responses to acts against their citizens in *other* countries were more problematic. US retaliatory air strikes against presumed agents of terrorism in Sudan and Afghanistan following the bombings of US embassies in East Africa are cases in point.[118]

Responses to the horrendous events of 9/11 were decidedly different. Although the United Nations did not sanction the ensuing US invasion of Afghanistan, it did strongly condemn the Afghan regime for its complicity in the Al Qaeda attacks. Moreover, it gave implicit support to the takeover of the country by US and British forces, by sponsoring a conference in Bonn, Germany, which led to the SC's creation in December 2001 of the Afghan Interim Authority, as well as the International Security Assistance Force to work with it. By 2009 ISAF included roughly 65,000 troops from some 42 countries, mainly members of NATO, to which command was transferred in 2003.[119] This UN-ISAF nexus went well beyond any previous UN initiative relating to international terrorism, though the crux of the effort was promoting good governance rather than combating terrorism as such.

Apart from the United Nations, international efforts to counter terrorism have increasingly turned to the International Criminal Police Organization, commonly referred to as INTERPOL.[120] Founded in 1923 and based in Lyons since 1989, INTERPOL now has 188 member nations, maintains seven regional offices around the world and uses four official languages: English, French, Spanish and Arabic. Its main purpose is "to facilitate international police cooperation even when diplomatic relations do not exist between particular countries". Its extensive files include information about suspected actors and activities associated with terrorism. When requested, it coordinates the circulation of alerts and warnings on terrorists in member countries. INTERPOL also provides guidelines to help member countries report on terrorist activity and encourages the reporting of crimes potentially linked to terrorism, such as suspicious financial transactions, weapons trafficking, money laundering, falsification of documents and seizures of nuclear, chemical and biological materials. Greater use of INTERPOL would probably yield high dividends.

While vigilance in dealing with terrorism is essential, it is in order to question, in closing, whether responses to that threat are efficient and whether some of them might actually be counterproductive. Many American responses have been highly problematic. By "declaring war on terrorism" and invading and occupying countries where terrorists were known or *believed* to be based, the United States treats terrorist organizations, in effect, as if they had the same legal status as a nation (though, paradoxically, captive terrorist suspects are systematically denied the legal protection a nation's soldiers would enjoy under the Geneva Conventions). Would it not be more prudent to treat terrorists as *criminals* and deal with them not by military campaigns but rather through patient, unrelenting, multilateral *police*-type operations? Invasions and, in recent years, increasing use of unmanned drone bombing aircraft inevitably bring about substantial "collateral damage" among innocent civilian populations. Can the tens of thousands of civilian casualties inflicted in Iraq, Afghanistan, Yemen, Somalia and Pakistan possibly be regarded as justifiable retribution for the 3,000 or so innocents who died on 9/11? Do two wrongs ever make a right?

Apart from the moral questionability of US policy, one must examine its practical efficacy. For every innocent person slain or maimed, there is a likelihood of creating new recruits to terrorism among grieving and often destitute survivors. Thus it is virtually certain that there are many more terrorists in the world today than was the case when the global "war on terror" was declared.

Additionally, one must consider the corrosive effects of the surveillance system in respect to civil liberties, especially the right to privacy. Further, the costs are staggering. In a remarkably detailed exposé of the burgeoning American intelligence system, the *Washington Post* observed:

> The government has built a national security and intelligence system so big, so complex and so hard to manage, no one really knows if it is fulfilling its most important purpose: keeping its citizens safe ... No one knows how much money it costs, how many people it employs, how many programs exist within it or how many agencies do the same work.[121]

The estimates provided are mind-boggling: 1,271 government agencies, 1,931 private companies and 854,000 individuals holding "top secret" security clearances. Clearly, the fear industry is a big and – for some – highly profitable business. Are the gains commensurate with the shredding of trust and the diminution of personal freedom, not to mention the allocation of tens of billions of dollars that might better have been spent on education, health and other social services?[122]

What, then, are the alternatives? First, in place of knee-jerk, violent and costly responses to acts of terror, we need carefully thought out, appropriately calibrated strategies in which each action taken is dispassionately weighed against its likely beneficial and potentially injurious effects. We must not seek quick-fix military solutions. War is not the answer, though internationally sanctioned, well-disciplined, minimal-force police actions would certainly be warranted. Nor can the United Nations or individual nations expect much benefit from externally imposed regime changes that attempt to reshape states into some preconceived, idealized democratic image. Ultimately, the community of nations can most effectively *combat terrorism by removing its causes*: injustice, social marginalization, economic exploitation, racism and ignorance.

Conclusions

This chapter has demonstrated that the United Nations has played a prominent and multifaceted role in seeking to maintain international peace and security since its creation in 1945. At times it has met with marked success, at others no success at all. Most often results have been mixed. The spotty record is attributable to numerous factors: organizational inertia, problematic coordination of authority, questionable legitimacy in decision-making, institutional lacunae, inadequate financial and human resources, North-South tensions, realpolitik and so forth. In a vicious cycle, distrust keeps the United Nations weak, and the UN's weakness in turn perpetuates distrust. Reforms are sorely needed.

Reforms called for in this chapter include the following.

- Increased resort to proactive diplomacy in addressing international disputes.
- Greater reliance on regional bodies as peace-promoting intermediaries.
- Judiciously targeted *sanctions* when UN and regional efforts at conflict resolution are persistently rebuffed.
- Speedy implementation of the peacekeeping recommendations of the Brahimi Report, especially in respect to creating a rapid-response capability.
- Over a longer term, establishing a standing globally recruited, all-volunteer, elite, highly trained, multipurpose UN Peace Corps, directed by a revitalized Military Staff Committee, organized in three regional commands and ready to respond on short notice to serious threats to the peace anywhere in the world.
- Use of the UNPC brigades for constructive projects when they are not actively engaged in peacekeeping missions.
- Institutionalizing an elite UN Administrative Reserve Corps to facilitate, in concert with the UNPC and other UN agencies, the establishment of stable societies in post-conflict situations.
- Creating an elite UN Administrative Academy to train members of UNARC.
- Total abolition – based largely on the McCloy-Zorin accords of 1961, as well as more recent proposals – of weapons of mass destruction (nuclear, biological and chemical) and establishment of effective inspection regimes.
- Adoption of a more deliberative approach in confronting terrorism, with greater international and interregional cooperation and greater use of INTERPOL.
- Greatly increased efforts to address the root conditions of injustice that create and sustain terrorist networks.

Notes

1. A total of not quite 41 million conflict-related deaths over the period 1945–2000, broken down by conflict and year, is detailed by Milton Leitenberg, *Deaths in Wars and Conflicts in the 20th Century*, Occasional Paper 29, 3rd edn, Ithaca, NY: Cornell University Peace Studies Program, 2006, pp. 73–83. Leitenberg also provides data for numerous serious conflicts for the period 2001–2006. Extrapolations from Leitenberg's figures for ongoing conflicts, plus estimates for new conflicts, yield a total of over 50 million.

2. Thorough analyses are provided by Michael Andregg, *On the Causes of War*, Minneapolis, MN: Ground Zero Minnesota, 1999; Ronald J. Glossop, *Confronting War*, 4th edn, Jefferson, NC: McFarland, 2001, pp. 57–105. That there is but a *single overarching*

cause is argued in Mortimer J. Adler, *How to Think About War and Peace*, New York: Fordham University Press, [1944] 1995.

3. *Global Governance* 16(2), 2010, devotes a "special focus" section to "Postwar Mediation in UN Peace Operations: The Role of Special Representatives of the Secretary-General". It contains the following: Timothy D. Sisk, "Introduction: The Role of SRSGs and the Management of Civil Wars", pp. 237–242; Katia Papagianni, "Mediation, Political Engagement and Peacebuilding", pp. 243–264; Marie-Joëlle Zohar, "SSRG Mediation in Civil Wars: Revisiting the 'Spoiler' Debate", pp. 265–280; Cedric de Coning, "Mediation and Peacebuilding", pp. 281–299.

4. United Nations, "Special and Personal Representatives and Envoys of the Secretary-General", www.un.org/en/peacekeeping/sites/srsg/tables.htm.

5. A complete list of UN resolutions establishing, altering and terminating sanctions of various sorts, country by country and chronologically up to 2003, is provided in David W. Malone (ed.), *The UN Security Council: From the Cold War to the 21st Century*, Boulder, CO, and London: Lynne Rienner, 2004, Appendix 3.

6. Anup Shah, "Iraq – Post 1991 Persian Gulf War/Sanctions", *Global Issues*, www.globalissues.org/article/707/Iraq-post-1991-persian-gulf-warsanctions, updated 2 October 2005. This article cites the interview in which then Secretary of State Madeline Albright was asked on US television if she "thought that the death of half a million children [from sanctions in the 1990s] was worth the price" and replied: "This is a very hard choice, but we think the price is worth it."

7. For an excellent account see David Cortright, George A. Lopez and Linda Gerber Stellingwerf, "Sanctions", in Thomas G. Weiss and Sam Daws (eds), *The Oxford Handbook on the United Nations*, Oxford and New York: Oxford University Press, 2007, pp. 349–369.

8. Discussed by David Cortright and George A. Lopez, "Reforming Sanctions", in David W. Malone (ed.), *The UN Security Council: From the Cold War to the 21st Century*, Boulder, CO, and London: Lynne Rienner, 2004, pp. 167–189.

9. Curiously, however, a definition of the crime of "aggression" has yet to be officially adopted.

10. These two missions, the UN Truce Supervision Organization and the UN Military Observer Group in India and Pakistan, remain in operation.

11. Rama Mani, "Peaceful Settlement of Disputes and Conflict Resolution", in Thomas G. Weiss and Sam Daws (eds), *The Oxford Handbook on the United Nations*, Oxford and New York: Oxford University Press, 2007, pp. 300–322.

12. Bruce D. Jones, "The Middle East Peace Process", in David W. Malone (ed.), *The UN Security Council: From the Cold War to the 21st Century*, Boulder, CO, and London: Lynne Rienner, 2004, pp. 392–393; Michael W. Doyle and Nicholas Sambanis, "Peacekeeping Operations", in Thomas G. Weiss and Sam Daws (eds), *The Oxford Handbook on the United Nations*, Oxford and New York: Oxford University Press, 2007, pp. 323–348, at p. 325.

13. Mani, note 11 above, p. 309.

14. Jeffrey Laurenti, "Financing", in Thomas G. Weiss and Sam Daws (eds), *The Oxford Handbook on the United Nations*, Oxford and New York: Oxford University Press, 2007, pp. 675–700, at pp. 687–668.

15. Doyle and Sambanis, note 12 above, p. 333.

16. Ibid., p. 327; Malone, note 5 above, Appendix 1.

17. Several key failures are discussed by Michael Pugh, "Peace Enforcement", in Thomas G. Weiss and Sam Daws (eds), *The Oxford Handbook on the United Nations*, Oxford and New York: Oxford University Press, 2007, pp. 370–386, especially pp. 374–377.

18. Missions with troops from dozens of countries are common. The hybrid AU/UN mission in Darfur has troops from 58 nations.

19 Malone, note 5 above, Appendix 1.

20. BBC News, http://news.bbc.co.uk/2/hi/africa/3573229.stm.

21. Pugh, note 17 above, pp. 374–375.

22. Ibid., p. 376.

23. Stockholm International Peace Research Institute, *SIPRI Yearbook*, Oxford: Oxford University Press, 2009, pp. 105–115; *Washington Post*, "U.N. Faces More Accusations of Sexual Misconduct", www.washingtonpost.com/wp-dyn/articles/A30286-2005Mar12.html.

24. The methodological and political implications of questions raised in this paragraph are discussed in Kennedy Graham, "Towards a Coherent Regional Institutional Landscape in the United Nations: Implications for Europe", Bruges Regional Integration & Global Governance Papers No. 1, United Nations University and College of Europe, Bruges, 2008. A more extensive discussion appears in Kennedy Graham and Tania Felicio, *Regional Security and Global Governance: A Study of Interaction between Regional Agencies and the UN Security Council, with a Proposal for a Regional Global Security Mechanism*, Brussels: VUB Press, 2006.

25. A tabulation of the concluded missions in Malone, note 5 above, Appendix 2, includes the mission name and acronym, inclusive dates, mandate and staffing statistics.

26. The mission titles, acronyms, list of contributing countries, staffing, number of casualties and costs (for 2010) are all provided in Stockholm International Peace Research Institute, *SIPRI Yearbook*, Oxford: Oxford University Press, 2011, Table 3A.2, pp. 123–153.

27. A useful discussion is provided by Waheguru Pal Singh Sidhu, "Regional Groups and Alliances", in Thomas G. Weiss and Sam Daws (eds), *The Oxford Handbook on the United Nations*, Oxford and New York: Oxford University Press, 2007, pp. 217–232.

28. The figure of 10,000 deaths is given by Leitenberg, note 1 above, p. 79, though some in that total undoubtedly preceded and followed the bombing campaign.

29. An excellent critique, focusing largely on North–South disparities, is provided by Fred Tanner, "Addressing the Perils of Peace Operations: Towards a Global Peacekeeping System", *Global Governance* 16(2), pp. 209–217. Tanner advocates much greater use of regional organizations.

30. Sidhu, note 27 above, p. 228.

31. As of May 2010 uniformed personnel in the field (troops and police) numbered 101,867, coming from 115 countries. Leading contributors (and their contributions to the nearest 1,000) were Pakistan, 11; Bangladesh, 10; India, 9; Nigeria, 6; Egypt, 6; Nepal, 5; Ghana, 4; and Jordan, 4. These nations were all formerly within the British Empire and thus share, to some extent, a common military culture and are better able to function under the command of English-speaking officers than are troops from other nations. The chief contributor from the global North was Italy, with roughly 2,100 troops. Collectively the P-5 accounted for only 4,775 uniformed personnel. France and China each contributed roughly 2,000. The United States, with 83, ranked last among the P-5. For month-by-month statistics by contributing countries see UN DPKO, www.un.org/en/peacekeeping/contributions.

32. Fatalities among UN peacekeepers as of mid-2010 numbered not quite 2,000.

33. United Nations, "United Nations Peacekeeping: Financing Peacekeeping", www.un.org/en/peacekeeping/operations/financing.shtml, p. 3.

34. In some cases (e.g. Nepal and Fiji) payments for UN peacekeepers form a substantial part of total GNI.

35. Boutros Boutros-Ghali, "An Agenda for Peace – Preventive Diplomacy, Peacemaking and Peacekeeping", report of the Secretary-General pursuant to statement adopted by

summit meeting of the Security Council, 21 January 1992, UN Doc. A/47/277-S/2411, 17 June 1992; Boutros Boutros-Ghali, "Supplement to An Agenda for Peace: Position Paper of the Secretary-General on the Occasion of the Fiftieth Anniversary of the United Nations", UN Doc. A/50/60-S/1995/1, 3 January 1995.

36. Commission on Global Governance, *Our Global Neighbourhood*, Oxford and New York: Oxford University Press, 1995.

37. UN General Assembly, "Report of the Panel on United Nations Peace Operations" (Brahimi Report), UN Doc. A/55/305-S/2000/809, 17 August 2000.

38. Apart from governmental initiatives, many essays have advocated a standing emergency response force. Most influential, perhaps, was that of Brian Urquhart, "For a UN Volunteer Military Force", *New York Review of Books* 40(11), 10 June 1993, pp. 58–60. A more detailed exposition is put forth in H. Peter Langille, *Bridging the Commitment-Capacity Gap: A Review of Existing Arrangements and Options for Enhancing UN Rapid Deployment*, Wayne, NJ: Center for UN Reform Education, 2002. An excellent collection, with contributions from five continents, is Robert C. Johansen (ed.), *A United Nations Emergency Peace Service: To Prevent Genocide and Crimes Against Humanity*, New York: World Federalist Movement – Institute for Global Policy, 2006.

39. An elaboration of the SHIRBRIG concept is found, *inter alia*, in H. Peter Langille, "SHIRBRIG: A Promising Step Towards a United Nations That Can Prevent Deadly Conflict", www.globalpolicy.org/component/content/article/199/40961.html. A chronology of relevant events is provided in Joachim Koops and Johannes Varwick, *Ten Years of SHIRBRIG: Lessons Learned, Development Prospects and Strategic Opportunities for Germany*, Berlin: Global Public Policy Institute, 2008, pp. 7–11.

40. An exceptionally instructive report is provided in SHIRBRIG, "SHIRBRIG Lessons Learned Report", 1 June 2009, Standby High Readiness Brigade for UN Operations, Hevelte.

41. Operational limitations and shortcomings are discussed throughout ibid., and also in the critical study by Koops and Varwick, note 39 above.

42. Italy was the most populous participating country.

43. Wikipedia, "Helsinki Headline Goal", http://en.wikipedia.org/wiki/Helsinki_Headline-Goal.

44. European Union, "Headline Goal 2010", General Affairs and External Relations Council of the European Union, Brussels, 2004.

45. EU Directorate-General for Exernal Policies, "The EU Battlegroups", DGExPo/Pol-Dep/Note 2006_145, 12 September 2006; Wikipedia, "Battlegroup of the European Union", http://en.wikipedia.org/wiki/Battlegroup_of_the_European_Union.

46. Wikipedia, "Operation Artemis", http://en.wikipedia.org/wiki/Operation_Artemis.

47. Wikipedia, note 45 above, pp. 4–5.

48. Polish Institute of International Affairs, *Bulletin* 3(79), 11 January 2010.

49. Brahimi Report, note 37 above, unnumbered third page of "Executive Summary".

50. Ibid.

51. Ibid., unnumbered fifth page.

52. A critical analysis of all aspects of the report and an accounting of official actions to which they gave rise (up to 2003) were prepared by staff of the Henry L. Stimson Center, a Washington-based think-tank that was deeply engaged in all phases of the Brahimi project. See William J. Durch, Victoria K. Holt, Caroline R. Earle and Moira K. Shanahan, *The Brahimi Report and the Future of UN Peace Operations*, Washington, DC: Henry L. Stimson Center, 2003.

53. ICISS, *The Responsibility to Protect*, Ottawa: International Development Research Centre, 2001. In addition to the Canadian government, several leading foundations helped finance the commission's work.

54. Ibid., p. vii.
55. Ibid., p. xi.
56. Ibid., pp. xii–xiii.
57. Ibid., pp. xii.
58. Alex J. Bellamy, *Responsibility to Protect: The Global Effort to End Mass Atrocities*, Cambridge: Polity Press, 2009, provides an exceptionally thorough critical analysis of ICISS negotiations, the responses to its report in both the United Nations and the wider diplomatic community, and relevant subsequent action.
59. Ibid., pp. 68–69.
60. High-level Panel on Threats, Challenges and Change, "A More Secure World: Our Shared Responsibility", UN GA Doc. A/59/565, 29 November 2004. Section II, "The Case for Collective Security", para. 29, argues that the "privileges of sovereignty" entail "the obligation of a State to protect the welfare of its own peoples". Section IX deals with rules and guidelines for the use of force, Section X with peace enforcement and peacekeeping, and Section XI with post-conflict peacebuilding. The panel's recommendations were generally endorsed by UN Secretary-General Kofi Annan, "In Larger Freedom: Towards Development, Security and Human Rights for All", UN GA Doc. A/59/2005, 21 March 2005, paras 122–126.
61. Kofi Annan, "Two Concepts of Sovereignty", *The Economist*, 18–24 September 1999, pp. 19–20.
62. Bellamy, note 58 above, pp. 150–153.
63. Ibid., pp. 85–86.
64. Executive Council, African Union, *The Common African Position on the Proposed Reform of the United Nations*, Addis Ababa, Ext/EX.CL/2 (VII), 7–8 March 2005, pp. 8–9.
65. ICISS, note 53 above, pp. 19–27 and 39–45.
66. Bellamy, note 58 above, p. 85.
67. UN General Assembly, "Resolution Adopted by the General Assembly, 2005 World Summit Outcome", UN Doc. A/RES/60/1, 24 October 2005, para. 139.
68. Ian Williams, "Libya, the UN and the R2P Debate", 24 March 2011, www.guardian. co.uk; Jayshree Bajoria, "Libya and the Responsibility to Protect", Council on Foreign Relations, www.cfr.org/libya/libya-responsiilty-to-protect/p24480.
69. High-level Panel, note 60 above.
70. Brahimi Report, note 37 above, para. 13.
71. Ibid., para. 97. The section on "Peacebuilding" comprises paras 97–105. The recommendations were consistent with those of High-level Panel, note 60 above, Section IV, and Annan, note 60 above, para. 114.
72. UN General Assembly, note 67 above, para. 98.
73. Ibid., paras 101–102.
74. Ibid., para. 100.
75. Bellamy, note 58 above, pp. 186–187.
76. Fen O. Hampson and Christopher K. Penny, "Human Security", in Thomas G. Weiss and Sam Daws (eds), *The Oxford Handbook on the United Nations*, Oxford and New York: Oxford University Press, 2007, p. 549.
77. An excellent analysis of the problem is in Roland Paris, "Post-conflict Peacebuilding", in Thomas G. Weiss and Sam Daws (eds), *The Oxford Handbook on the United Nations*, Oxford and New York: Oxford University Press, 2007, pp. 404–426. Diverse approaches are discussed in Bellamy, note 58 above, pp. 167–194.
78. UN Peacebuilding Commission, "Peacebuilding Commission Agenda", www.un.org/peacebuilding/pbcagenda.shtml.
79. Bellamy, note 58 above, p. 199.

80. For a review of UNDEF's first five years see Roland Rich, "Situating the UN Democracy Fund", *Global Governance* 16(4), 2010, pp. 423–434. This account is based entirely on that source.

81. "UN Volunteers", www.unv.org, with links to "About Us", "What We Do" and "Partnerships Overview"; Wikipedia, "United Nations Volunteers", http://en.wikipedia.org/wiki/United_Nations_Volunteers.

82. This section is a distillation and slight modification of arguments put forward in Joseph E. Schwartzberg, "A New Perspective on Peacekeeping: Lessons from Bosnia and Elsewhere", *Global Governance* 3(1), 1997, pp. 1–15.

83. For purposes of this discussion, the word "military" also subsumes police functions.

84. International Peace Academy, *Peacekeeper's Handbook*, New York: Pergamon Press, 1984, has already been used widely in training contingents of national armies for potential peacekeeping operations. SHIRBRIG assistance in developing materials for use in Africa is also relevant. Noteworthy, too, is UN DPKO, *Handbook of United Nations Multidimensional Peacekeeping Operations*, New York: UN DPKO, 2003.

85. Norwegian Commission of Experts, *A Proposal for United Nations Security Forces (UNSF)*, Leliagracht: World Association for World Federation, 1989.

86. High-level Panel, note 60 above, pp. 50–51.

87. Brahimi Report, note 37 above, *passim*, provides excellent analyses of command and control issues. Also valuable is Brian E. Urquhart, "Peacekeeping: A View from the Operational Center", in Henry Wiseman (ed.), *Peacekeeping: Appraisals and Proposals*, New York: Pergamon Press for International Peace Academy, 1983, pp. 161–172.

88. See www.un.org/en/peacekeeping/contributors/2007.

89. If, however, one includes roughly 7,000 internationally recruited civilian personnel and a substantially larger number of locally recruited personnel, costs per person employed would be significantly lower.

90. Figures were calculated by the author using 2010 data from *SIPRI Yearbook*, note 26 above, Table 4.A.4, "Military expenditures by country, in constant US dollars", pp. 205–211; and data on armed forces (excluding paramilitary, gendarmerie, border patrols and reserves) from *Encyclopaedia Britannica Book of the Year, 2012*, Chicago, IL: Encyclopaedia Britannica, 2012, pp. 822–827.

91. *SIPRI Yearbook*, note 26 above, p. 194.

92. Government of Canada, *Towards a Rapid Reaction Capability for the United Nations*, Ottawa: Government of Canada, 1995, p. 6.

93. Brahimi Report, note 37 above, para. 127.

94. The content of this section appears in somewhat different form in Joseph E. Schwartzberg, "Needed: A United Nations Administrative Academy", *UN Chronicle* 43(1), special number on "The Challenge of Building Peace", 2006, pp. 14–16.

95. A precedent for the present Indian programme is that of the British East India Company at Haileybury College in England over the period 1806–1857. Despite its obvious – and in some respects distasteful – colonial associations, the Haileybury programme produced many outstanding administrators and scholars. It provided a corps of dedicated and efficient company servants who were able to communicate effectively with one another and deeply understood what their jobs demanded. The best relevant work is Frederick Charles Danvers, Harriet Martineau, Monier Monier-Williams and Stuart Colvin Bailey, *Memorials of Old Haileybury College*, Westminster: Archibald Constable & Co., 1894.

96. In 2002 I made detailed estimates of what a UNAA might cost *per annum*. I determined that a fully running institution with three campuses, each with an academic staff of about 150, several hundred support personnel (for technical, secretarial and maintenance services) and roughly 1,000 stipend-receiving trainees, would require an annual

budget of not much more than $100 million (at 2002 prices), roughly equivalent to the then cost of the University of Minnesota's College of Liberal Arts (with approximately 15,000 students).

97. A thorough analysis of the many forms of nuclear threat is found in a powerful work by Tad Daley, *Apocalypse Never*, New Brunswick, NJ: Rutgers University Press, 2010. Daley argues that in the absence of total nuclear disarmament, some form of nuclear cataclysm, by accident or design, is virtually inevitable in the foreseeable future.

98. Ibid., pp. 345–412, contains abundant data on nuclear forces and development programmes; chemical and biological weapons are discussed on pp. 413–433.

99. A succinct account of one domain of relevant UN action is provided by Keith Krause, "Disarmament", in Thomas G. Weiss and Sam Daws (eds), *The Oxford Handbook on the United Nations*, Oxford and New York: Oxford University Press, 2007, pp. 287–299.

100. Ibid., p. 289.

101. The US Department of State did make public in September 1961 a 10-page document entitled "Freedom From War: The United States Program for General and Complete Disarmament in a Peaceful World", Department of State Publication 7277. The specific date is not noted, but it was probably prior to the signing of the McCloy-Zorin accords on 21 September. The document put forward the essential elements of those accords and actually expanded on them. The final sentence, relating to Stage III of a three-stage disarmament process, reads: "The peace-keeping capabilities of the United Nations would be sufficiently strong and the obligations of all states under such arrangements sufficiently far-ranging as to assure peace and the just settlement of disputes in a disarmed world." See http:dosfan.lib.uic.edu/ERC/arms/freedom_war.html.

102. Krause, note 99 above, pp. 292–293.

103. Daley, note 97 above, p. 115 and *passim*.

104. Krause, note 99 above, p. 289.

105. Discussed by Ivo Daalder and Jan Lodal, "The Logic of Zero: Towards a World Without Nuclear Weapons", *Foreign Affairs* 87(6), 2008, pp. 80–95.

106. International Association of Lawyers Against Nuclear Arms, International Network of Engineers and Scientists Against Proliferation and International Physicians for the Prevention of Nuclear War, *Securing Our Survival (SOS): The Case for a Nuclear Weapons Convention*, Cambridge, MA: IPPNW, 2007. This updates and expands a 1999 monograph by the same three organizations plus Lawyers Committee on Nuclear Policy, *Security and Survival: The Case for a Nuclear Weapons Convention*. The 2007 work includes detailed comments responding to questions about the feasibility or wisdom of various provisions of the draft convention.

107. Daley, note 97 above, pp. 162–163, succinctly summarizes the major recommendations of the proposal.

108. Ibid., pp. 293–294.

109. Although provisions for effective inspection were built into the McCloy-Zorin accords, they did not come about without a struggle. In a dispatch to McCloy shortly before completion of the negotiations, Zorin wrote that intrusive inspections would represent "an international system of legalized espionage". Reported by Marcus Raskin, "The McCloy-Zorin Correspondence", *Bulletin of the Atomic Scientists*, February 1983, pp. 34–36.

110. Krause, note 99 above, p. 294.

111. Ibid., pp. 295–296.

112. Ibid., p. 296; Wikipedia, "Ottawa Treaty", http://en.wikipedia.org/wiki/Ottawa_Treaty.

113. The role of these agencies is discussed by Jane Boulden, "Terrorism", in Thomas G. Weiss and Sam Daws (eds), *The Oxford Handbook on the United Nations*, Oxford and New York: Oxford University Press, 2007, pp. 427–436.

114. Ibid., pp. 428–431.
115. Quoted in ibid., p. 430.
116. Ibid.
117. High-level Panel, note 60 above, para. 162, cited in ibid., p. 432.
118. The Sudan strike mistakenly targeted a pharmaceutical plant that was not engaged, as alleged, in manufacturing chemical weapons.
119. Wikipedia, "War in Afghanistan (2001–Present)", http://en.wikipedia.org/wiki/War_in_ Afghanistan_(2001-present), *passim*.
120. Information in this paragraph is from the INTERPOL website, www.interpol.int/ public/icpo/default.asp.
121. Dana Priest and William Arkin, "Top Secret America", three-part analysis, *Washington Post*, 19 July 2010, pp. A1, A8–9; 20 July 2010, pp. A1, A8–11; 21 July 2010, pp. A1, A10–11. Quoted passage is from 19 July, p. A1. Research for this project was carried out over a period of two years.
122. Ibid.

13

Towards a sustainable planet and an expanded common heritage

Infinite growth of material consumption within a finite world is an impossibility.
Ernst F. Schumacher

The earth is our mother; whatever befalls the earth befalls the sons and daughters of the earth. All things are connected like the blood that connects one family.
Chief Seattle, native American

Introduction: Contending paradigms

This chapter discusses a number of global issues with particular reference to two related and increasingly important paradigms. The first is the paradigm of *sustainability*, as opposed to a commitment to continuous economic growth. The second is that certain spaces or things should be regarded as parts of the *common heritage of humankind*, as opposed to the belief that all spaces shall be subject to the control of individual states and all things are commodities subject to private ownership.

Since well before the founding of the United Nations, *growth* has been the dominant paradigm guiding the economic policies of virtually all UN member states. Thus it is hardly surprising that growth promotion should have so long underlain policies not only of the United Nations itself but also of affiliated agencies, including the autonomous Bretton Woods institutions. At the national level it mattered little whether the government of a given country pursued neoliberal, democratic socialist, communist or other agendas; all were committed to steady expansion of gross national

Transforming the United Nations system: Designs for a workable world, Schwartzberg, United Nations University Press, 2013, ISBN 978-92-808-1230-5

product. A truth as simple as that of E. F. Schumacher, cited above, relative to the impossibility of infinite growth within a finite world was, all too often, either irresponsibly denied or swept beneath the policy carpet. Following the preferences of politically powerful actors, the virtually universal economic pursuit was to produce more.

But a cascade of independent thinking outside government has challenged conventional wisdom. As early as 1796, Robert Malthus's carefully reasoned *Essay on the Principle of Population* questioned the long-term ability of any society to provide sustenance for its growing population, noting the tendency of population to increase in a geometric progression, while the output of food tends to increase in a much slower arithmetic progression.[1] In the aftermath of the Second World War a steadily expanding body of neo-Malthusian writers resurrected the twin spectres of widespread famine and resource scarcity.[2] Numerous civil society organizations heightened public consciousness of environmental issues, demonstrating the need for conservation and the necessity of cultivating sustainable lifestyles. Outside the West, Mahatma Gandhi, among others, promoted voluntary simplicity, noting that the "Earth provides enough for everybody's need, but not enough for everybody's greed."[3]

Faced with mounting concern about population expansion, resource depletion, environmental degradation, climate change and widening economic inequities, agencies within the UN system accorded those issues ever-greater salience. Many came to espouse a new paradigm, *sustainable development*, defined as "development that meets the needs of the present without compromising the ability of future generations to meet their own needs".[4]

A corollary to the belief in unbridled economic growth is the conviction – among individuals and corporations – that growth is best promoted through the private ownership and management of various forms of property: land and natural resources, capital and even intangibles, such as intellectual property. The analogue at the national level is sovereignty, implying *exclusive* state possession and control of a given portion of terrestrial space on land and sea and in the air.

I shall not here propound the relative merits of capitalist versus communally managed economic systems. Each is desirable in particular situations. The pendulum has swung back and forth between high degrees of regulation and policies of *laissez faire*. The United Nations and each member state must determine its own optimal balance. While there can be no denying that the capitalistic system has led to formerly unimaginable levels of affluence for substantial portions of humankind, the unbridled pursuit of profit characterizing that system has also led to numerous ills. It seems appropriate, then, in many contexts to promote and where possible institutionalize systems – known as "commons regimes" – based on shared ownership of resources and cooperation among stakeholders to establish a sustainable balance between use and conservation. In such systems *stewardship* replaces exploitation as the dominant method of resource management.[5]

Within the UN system, the concept of the commons has been promoted in several agencies. In particular, the United Nations has already endorsed the idea that spaces outside those over which individual nations exercise some form of jurisdiction – portions of the high seas, the underlying seabed, the Antarctic, outer space, the moon and other heavenly bodies – shall be treated as the "common heritage" of humankind. Designated world natural and cultural heritage sites may also be so considered, as may the genetic codes of all plant and animal species, including humans. Finally, intellectual and artistic creations are deemed to fall within the public domain once an appropriate period of patent or copyright protection for their creators has elapsed.

Belief in sustainability implies a commitment to intergenerational equity. That question was addressed by UNESCO in its 1997 Declaration on the Responsibilities of the Present Generations Towards Future Generations. Article 4 reads as follows:

> The present generations [*sic*] have the responsibility to bequeath to future generations an Earth which will not one day be irreversibly damaged by human activity. Each generation inheriting the Earth temporarily should take care to use natural resources reasonably and ensure that life is not prejudiced by harmful modifications of the ecosystems and that scientific and technological progress in all fields does not harm life on Earth.[6]

My own recommendations relative to sustainable development and global commons regimes are set forth later in this chapter. They include calls for greater transparency and better surveillance of actions injurious to the environment; and for establishing binding mechanisms to promote environmental accountability, adjudicate serious offences and sanction responsible parties. To provide oversight of portions of the global commons, I recommend creation of a Common Heritage Council.

Economic and environmental sustainability: The record to date[7]

Management of natural resources was an occasional, but not prominent, matter for UN consideration in its early years. *Sustainable* management, however, was not the issue; rather, the dominant context was that of clashing North-South perspectives. In the global South, many – often newly independent – nations were justifiably concerned about assuring sovereign control over their own resources. They were opposed by countries of the North, whose investors and governments were fearful of nationalization of those resources under unacceptable terms. In particular, the possibility of losing access to petroleum and other strategic resources was a preoccupation of *developed* nations during the Cold War era. The interests of *developing* nations, however, were upheld by the GA in its 1962 UN Declaration of Permanent Sovereignty over Natural Resources.[8]

A new course was set in 1972, with the convening in Stockholm of the UN Conference on the Human Environment. This landmark event highlighted the nexus between environmental protection and economic development. It led to the establishment of the UN Environment Programme and stoked the demand for a "new international economic order", which the GA proclaimed in 1974. It also provided a conceptual platform for subsequent studies and conferences. Later initiatives included creation in 1980 of the Independent Commission on International Development, chaired by a former West German chancellor, Willy Brandt; and in 1987 of the World Commission on Environment and Development, chaired by Gro Harlem Brundtland, a former prime minister of Norway. The latter body oversaw publication of the far-sighted report *Our Common Future*, and reinforced the concept of "sustainable development".[9]

Dwarfing all previous environment-related events was the UN Conference on Environment and Development (UNCED), often known as the Earth Summit, held in Rio de Janeiro in 1992. UNCED and several follow-up conferences and their largely disappointing aftermath are discussed in Chapter 10.

An important outcome of the Rio conference was the adoption of the UN Framework Convention on Climate Change (UNFCCC). That led, in turn, to the drafting of the 1997 Kyoto Protocol. This landmark treaty sought, for the first time, to commit certain nations (37 industrialized, relatively wealthy "Annex I" countries) to setting legally binding quantitative goals for the amounts by which they would reduce emissions of greenhouse gases (GHGs) below 1990 levels by a deadline date of 2012. In general, the more industrially advanced a nation was, the greater its targeted reduction. The global average was set at 5.2 per cent. This goal, however, was to be but a beginning; the ultimate object being to avert catastrophic anthropogenic changes in the earth's climate system, mainly in the form of global warming.[10]

Open for acceptance in 2002, the protocol received the requisite number of ratifications – by at least 55 nations collectively producing not less than 55 per cent of the world's total CO_2 emissions as of 1990 – by 2004 and entered into force the following year. Ratifications reached 191 by December 2010. But, as with so many other treaties, the United States

– which accounted for 36 per cent of all GHGs in 1990 – was conspicuously absent from the roster of signatories. Other major emitters, including China, India and Brazil, were not among the Annex I nations on whom the burden of reduction fell; they merely had to declare their *intentions* to limit GHG-producing activities. In fact, they are among a group of rapidly developing countries whose emissions are rising quickly, rather than declining. The perceived double standard is a major bone of contention from the perspective of the United States and some other wealthy nations.

The protocol provides for various "flexibility mechanisms" to enable Annex I countries to meet their targets, and presumes that those countries will somehow persuade major GHG producers (mainly large corporations) within their borders to help meet national commitments. It also calls on industrialized countries to help finance GHG mitigation efforts in non-Annex I nations and share relevant technology with them. But without meaningful sanctions for non-compliance, many nations failed to achieve their individual goals; and the overall global goal was also unmet.

The Kyoto Protocol and related behaviour by major international actors have been the object of much criticism and heated debate. Relevant diplomatic and scientific negotiations among the "conferences of parties" (i.e. UNFCCC ratifiers) have been held almost continuously since the turn of the century. They included a large, but essentially abortive, international gathering in Copenhagen in 2009 and a more promising conference in Cancún, Mexico, in 2010. The Cancún meeting resulted in establishing more precise emission reduction targets, refinement of recommended mitigation mechanisms, greater expectations for accountability, pledges by industrialized nations to provide $30 billion in "fast-start finance" to support climate action in the developing world and agreement to establish a Green Climate Fund as well as the Cancún Adaptation Framework for better environmental planning.[11] What will be translated into meaningful action remains to be seen.

Space limitations preclude discussion of numerous additional UN meetings on environmental issues: biodiversity, forest protection, fisheries, whaling, protection of coral reefs, etc. Suffice it to say that, while these have helped raise global environmental consciousness and promoted steps towards mandatory changes in national policy and behaviour, the customary mismatch between needs and committed resources persists among relevant agencies within the UN system. The international community has yet to come to grips with looming existential challenges. Major changes in global rule-making mechanisms are essential.

Apart from establishing new norms, the United Nations seeks to promote more viable environments through field programmes under the auspices of UNDP and projects relating to food, public health, the welfare of children and women, and other matters. The dawning in 2000 of a new millennium was accompanied by much soul-searching. Providing grist for the mills of that year's official Millennium Summit meeting of the GA were the recommendations of the Millennium Development Forum, a gathering in New York of representatives from more than 1,000 civil society organizations from over 100 countries. The forum's most significant outcome was the adoption of the Millennium Development Goals (MDGs), to be reached by the year 2015.[12]

1. Eradication of extreme poverty and hunger.
2. Achievement of universal primary education.
3. Promotion of gender equality and empowerment of women.
4. Reduction of child mortality.
5. Improvement of maternal health.
6. Combating HIV/AIDS, malaria and other diseases.
7. Ensuring environmental sustainability.
8. Developing a global partnership for development.

These basic goals were, in turn, divided into 21 subgoals, most of which set numerical targets by which to measure success on a country-by-country basis. While sustainability was not prominently advocated, three subheads were exceptions: Target 7.A called for integrating sustainable development into country policies and programmes, and reversing the loss of environmental resources; 7.B called for reducing loss of biodiversity; and 7.C called for halving the proportion of the population without sustainable access to safe drinking water and basic sanitation.

Target 8 subgoals, while not focused on sustainability *per se*, are noteworthy in calling for greater fairness in trading regimes and financial transactions, dealing comprehensively with the debt problems of developing countries, improved poor-country access to essential drugs, better dissemination of new technology (especially for information and communications) and attention to the needs of the world's least developed countries as well as landlocked and small island states.

Many countries, alas, have failed to adopt or adhere to policies that would enable them to achieve their MDG targets. The UN system seems also to be failing in many respects. Promises came cheaply; the financial wherewithal to translate them into reality has been inadequate. As with the 1970s' call for a new international economic order, only a handful of wealthy countries came close to fulfilling the recommendation that they allocate 0.7 per cent of their GNI towards meeting the MDGs (the Nordic bloc and the Netherlands were exemplary exceptions). Nevertheless, the G-8 finance ministers did agree in 2005 to provide the Bretton Woods institutions and the African Development Bank with sufficient funds to cancel roughly $50 billion of debts incurred by a group of "heavily indebted poor countries".[13] At the regional level there are bright spots, especially in East Asia and, to a lesser degree, South Asia. On the other hand in large areas, most notably in Africa south of the Sahara, progress has been scant or marked by pockets of regression.[14] In retrospect, one may question the wisdom of setting sweeping planetary goals rather than devising policies on a country-by-country basis, taking into account the unique resources and deficiencies of each.

The global commons

Discussions of sustainability must be understood in connection with concerns about national sovereignty and the question of whether states should continue to enjoy an unfettered right to do whatever they wish within their own borders, irrespective of the effects on neighbouring peoples and lands or even the planet as a whole. But are there, or should there be, shared transnational spaces or natural features – the atmosphere, the seas, surface and ground water, or the biosphere – over which the actions of one state may be legitimately and legally constrained by others adversely affected by those actions? My answer is "yes". Certain spaces and things should be legally regarded as "global commons". This issue is considered below.

Antarctica[15]

Although the words "common heritage" appear nowhere in the 1959 Antarctic Treaty, the spirit of the document conforms with that principle. The treaty, which governs the whole of terrestrial space – land, ice, sea and air – south of 60° S latitude, calls in numerous places for sharing scientific and other (e.g. logistic) information, personnel and facilities throughout the Antarctic region. Additionally, it declares that the use of Antarctica shall be for peaceful purposes only and in accordance with the principles of the UN Charter, and that any dispute arising in respect to Antarctica shall be peacefully resolved.

The treaty had 12 original signatories. Seven of these – Argentina, Australia, Chile, France, New Zealand, Norway and the United Kingdom – had already staked claims to portions of the continent and nearby islands; the other five were Belgium, Japan, the Soviet Union, South Africa and the United States. While the treaty did not nullify existing territorial claims, it put them all in abeyance and precluded additional claims by any nation.[16] All UN member states were free to ratify the treaty and by 2010 the number of acceding nations had risen to 48, collectively accounting for more than two-thirds of the earth's total population. Noteworthy accessions include Germany (1974), China and India (both 1983).[17] Signatories that have actually conducted scientific research projects in Antarctica – now numbering 27 – are accorded the status of "consultative parties" and entitled to participate in meetings held approximately every other year to deliberate on matters of shared concern (protection of seals and whales, preventing pollution, etc.). Other signatories may attend as observers.[18]

Throughout its history – even during the Cold War – the Antarctic Treaty has been scrupulously followed. All nations conducting missions in the Antarctic have done so with unfettered freedom of access to any territory claimed and any facility established by other treaty states. Apart from regulated tourism, Antarctica has been spared from commercial exploitation, and its pristine physical state has been well preserved. In short, management of Antarctica offers proof that a common heritage regime covering extensive territories not subject to individual state sovereignty can work when the parties to that regime so decide.

Outer space

Oddly, the first UN treaty embodying the principle of the commons as applicable to the *whole of humanity* related not to any portion of *earth* space, but rather to *outer* space. The act in question, the Treaty on Principles Governing the Activities of States in the Exploration and Use of Outer Space, Including the Moon and Other Celestial Bodies, generally referred to as the Outer Space Treaty, was opened for signature by the United States, the Soviet Union and the United Kingdom in January 1967, not quite a decade after the Soviet launching of Sputnik in 1957. It entered into force in October 1967, and by 2011 had been ratified by 100 nations.[19] Its opening articles were precedent setting:

Article I. The exploration and use of outer space, including the moon and other celestial bodies, shall be carried out for the benefit and in the interests of all countries, irrespective of their degree of economic or scientific development, and shall be *the province of all mankind* [emphasis added]. Outer space, including the moon and other celestial bodies, shall be free for exploration and use by all States without discrimination of any kind, on a basis of equality and in accordance with international law, and there shall be free access to all areas of celestial bodies. There shall be freedom of scientific investigation in outer space, including the moon and other celestial bodies, and States shall facilitate and encourage international co-operation in such investigation.

Article II. Outer space, including the moon and other celestial bodies, is *not subject to national appropriation* [emphasis added] by claim of sovereignty, by means of use or occupation, or by any other means.

The treaty also addresses other matters: prohibiting the placement of WMD in space (including earth orbits); declaring that space, the moon and other celestial bodies shall be used for peaceful purposes only; establishing rules of international responsibility for damages attributable to space activities; and so forth.[20] Some of these (e.g. precluding the militarization of space) have been dealt with more fully in subsequent treaties, but in no case have the commons provisions been challenged. What the treaty fails to establish is the altitude above the earth's surface at which outer space begins. This could lead to future legal controversies.

Of course, it was one thing to talk about sharing space *prior to* the landing of a US spacecraft on the moon in 1969 and quite another *after* that successful venture. In 1979 the so-called Moon Treaty – officially the Agreement Governing the Activities of States on the Moon and Other Celestial Bodies – was finalized. While it declared that "The Moon and its natural resources are the common heritage of mankind", it has not obtained many ratifications, and not even one from a nation with space exploration capability.[21]

Treaties aside, future space exploration is likely to be determined more by economics than by politics. Few nations possess the financial and technical resources to be significant players. Though they may question making their endeavours part of a global enterprise, they do recognize the benefits of international cooperation among capable parties. A US-Russian agreement on cooperation in outer space was reached in 1992;[22] and in 1995 American cosmonauts, transported by the US space shuttle *Atlantis*, joined the Russian crew aboard the space station Mir (launched in 1986).[23] In 1998 Russia launched the first module of the even more ambitious International Space Station, to which numerous additional modules, mainly provided by the United States, have since been added. Additional cooperating parties are Canada, Japan and the European Union, all of which have contributed funds, technical expertise and crew members. This cooperation is certainly laudable, but it is hardly a *global* undertaking.[24]

The oceans

In November 1967, a mere 10 months after promulgation of the Outer Space Treaty, in an electrifying speech before the GA, Arvid Pardo, the then Maltese permanent representative to the United Nations, called on that body to consider the oceans and seabed beyond the national jurisdiction of coastal nations as the "common heritage of mankind". That was the first official use of that phrase before the United Nations.[25] At the time the prevailing view, derived from the writing of the Dutch jurist Hugo Grotius (early seventeenth century), was that coastal nations could control a narrow maritime fringe – most commonly from three to 12 nautical miles wide – which came to be known as the "territorial sea", beyond which lay the "high seas", regarded as *mare liberum*, i.e. open to the free use of all nations.[26] However, modern technological developments – in relation to navigation, fishing, mining (both offshore and deep sea), ecosystem protection, sea-based weapons, defence, scientific research, etc. – necessitated rethinking a wide range of issues relating to sovereignty in and control over ocean space. As envisaged by Pardo, application of the common heritage principle would enable the United Nations to tap into the vast wealth of the oceans in terms of both biotic and mineral resources, and thereby create a fund that would facilitate narrowing the gap between the rich and poor nations of the world.[27]

After much negotiation in various venues – in both global North and global South – over the period 1973–1982, a new consensus on governance of the oceans was embodied in the UN Comprehensive Law of the Sea Treaty (also referred to as UNCLOS III).[28] In 1994, one year after the sixtieth ratification, the treaty entered into force, thereby becoming part of the body of international law regulating the rights and responsibilities of nations in a broad range of ocean-related matters.[29] Since 1994 ratifications have increased to 160 (as of 2010). The United States, which does abide by almost all terms of the convention, is among 19 nations having signed but not yet ratified the document, and is the only major power withholding approval.[30]

Many issues dealt with by UNCLOS III relate to the extent and management of specific territorial zones, defined largely in relation to their proximity to so-called "baselines" (combinations of low-tide coastlines and straight lines connecting certain promontories and offshore islands). Among those zones – some of which were new legal concepts – were "internal waters" on the landward side of baselines; a "territorial sea" with a standardized width of 12 nautical miles immediately outward from the baselines, within which nations enjoy virtually full sovereignty (limited only by the right of "innocent passage"); "contiguous zones", also 12 nautical miles wide and adjacent to the territorial sea, wherein nations have jurisdiction in respect to pollution, smuggling and other legitimate concerns; and "exclusive economic zones" (EEZs), extending 200 nautical miles outward from a nation's baselines and creating areas within which coastal nations enjoy exclusive rights to marine and submarine resources. In the hundreds of cases in which the specified zones of neighbouring nations overlap, the allocation of maritime space was to be diplomatically negotiated, most commonly on the basis of "median lines" equidistant from the coasts of each.

Additional rules established "archipelagic waters" and "archipelagic states" (e.g. Indonesia, Fiji and the Bahamas), a *legal* (as opposed to *geological*) continental shelf, territorial regulations in respect to islands (as opposed to uninhabitable rocks and reefs), rights of landlocked states, guaranteeing them free access to ports, etc.

There were also decisions relating to "the Area", defined as the ocean space beyond the EEZs, within which a newly established International Seabed Authority (a small body headquartered in Jamaica) would have the right to extract oceanic subsoil minerals and lease mining rights to nations and corporations capable of carrying out such operations. Only in the Area would the common heritage principle be applied. In fact, the words "common heritage" do not appear in the treaty until Article 136, which introduces the mechanisms and rules for governing the Area. Whether such rules will eventually prove workable is moot, in that the economic costs of deep-sea ocean mining are such that no extractive operations have yet been attempted or appear likely in the near term.

Finally, one must note the treaty's establishment of the still underutilized International Tribunal for the Law of the Sea. This court (discussed in Chapter 7), located in Hamburg, provides but one among several means of resolving maritime disputes.

Given the complex configuration of the world's oceans and their irregular punctuation by individual islands and archipelagos, EEZs occupy an enormous share – approximately 39 per cent – of oceanic space, roughly 54 million square miles (140 million km^2).[31] To this one must add several million square miles of "continental shelf" subject to some degree of control by individual states. The allocation of EEZ space produces some rather remarkable results because of the possession by certain countries of far-flung island outposts. The United States ranks first, with 12.2 million km^2. France is in second place with 11.0 million km^2, thanks to its control of the widely dispersed islands of French Polynesia (4.8 million km^2). In rank order thereafter are Australia, Russia, New Zealand, Indonesia, Canada, the United Kingdom, Japan, Chile and Brazil. Ranking twelfth is the island nation of Kiribati, whose EEZ of 3.4 million km^2 is roughly 4,200 times as great as its land area of 810 km^2. That is a lot of space entrusted to a nation with only 93,000 inhabitants! Additional island states with small land areas and populations but vast EEZs include Micronesia, the Marshall Islands, the Solomon Islands, Seychelles, Mauritius and Fiji, all with EEZs exceeding a million square miles. The microstate with the highest ratio of sea to land area (roughly 29,000:1) is Tuvalu.

That problematic state of affairs is, arguably, a factor underlying the reluctance of the United States to ratify UNCLOS III and would help explain its protracted attempts to negotiate changes in Part XI of the treaty relating to the extraction of minerals outside any state's territorial waters. (The minerals in question include petroleum and natural gas, "polymetallic nodules" – mainly manganese – and a variety of deep-ocean brines.[32]) Nevertheless, despite the drafting in 1994 of a supplementary agreement that addresses most American concerns, UNCLOS III, even as modified, has yet to come to a vote in the US Senate.

Rather than creating ocean spaces that would build upon the common heritage principle, UNCLOS III appears to have resulted in a stunning capitulation to the territorial demands of coastal states, large as well as small, rich as well as poor. While much ocean space does remain outside the EEZs, the mineral wealth found on scattered portions of the Area's seabed has thus far produced no revenue for either poor nations or rich corporations. Were Pardo alive today, he would lament this outcome. Even in his lifetime he expressed disappointment with the establishment of vast EEZs, noting that mankind's once promising common heritage had been reduced to "a few fish and a little seaweed".[33] Yet there are compensating benefits to creating what is, in effect, a Constitution for the Oceans, a set of rules governing manifold uses of the oceans and seabed. But while having a set of rules is generally good, there is – as with so many other issues of UN concern – a dearth of enforcement capability. This matter is considered later.

Additional commons?

To this point, discussion of the commons has related primarily to relatively remote domains: the Antarctic, the "Area" within the high seas, and outer space. However, exciting though penetration of *outer* space may be, our use of *inner* space will have a much greater impact on our collective well-being for generations to come. Previously, it was assumed that the space over which a nation enjoyed exclusive sovereignty included not only its surface but also the air above it, without limit, and the ground below down to the centre of the earth; but that assumption had little practical meaning prior to the advent of air travel. In an age of both air and outer space travel, as well as of large-scale climate change and atmospheric pollution, management of inner space must be reconsidered. Accordingly, one can now make a strong case for converting the atmosphere – which no country had a role in creating – into a global commons.

To the best of my knowledge, the words "common heritage" do not appear in any treaty relating to the atmosphere. Nevertheless, the fact that nations have seen fit to enact such treaties points to their realization that what happens in and to the atmosphere is a vital common *concern*. I have already discussed the 1992 UNFCCC, the Kyoto Protocol annexed to it in 1997 and the Cancún accords of 2010 modifying the CO_2 emission goals set in Kyoto. But there were other treaties and conventions as well. One – to which civil society pressure made a major contribution and which proved to be remarkably successful – was the 1987 Montreal Convention for the Protection of the Ozone Layer, the erosion of which – due mainly to chemical reactions with chlorofluorocarbons (CFCs) in the form of anthropogenic aerosols – significantly heightened the risk of cancer.[34]

The atmosphere is of concern not only because of what humans put into it – GHGs, CFCs, soot and other particulates (many of them carcinogenic), etc. – but also because of its role as the medium through which telecommunication signals travel. These signals, on various wavelengths of the electromagnetic spectrum, recognize no national borders. As early as the first International Radiotelegraph Conference in 1906, the need for regulating sea-to-shore radio transmissions was accepted by the 29 participating maritime states. Since then, regulation and monitoring have steadily expanded under a succession of agencies. By 1932 a system for assigning radio frequencies within the electromagnetic spectrum in such a way as to avoid interference between stations was firmly in place. Regulation and monitoring functions were assumed in 1947 by the newly founded International Telecommunications Union, functioning as a specialized agency within the UN system. The ITU's purview has since expanded to the regulation of wireless cellular phones – of which billions are already in use – and communications satellites.[35]

Although one might suppose that the logic of ITU regulation of various forms of radio communication would be applicable also to the internet, that position is staunchly resisted by the US government. The reasons are easily understood, in that the internet's development was initially underwritten by the US Department of Defense, beginning as early as 1969. Oversight has since shifted several times: to the US Defense Communications Agency in 1973, the Internet Configuration Control Board in 1979 and the Internet Corporation for Assigned Names and Numbers (ICANN) in 1998. ICANN operates under the aegis of the US Department of Commerce. Its principal functions are to coordinate the assignment of unique internet domain names, establish operational protocols and maintain the interoperability of various systems.[36] Its global success in these areas is beyond dispute. Nevertheless, many voices call for greater participation by stakeholders outside the United States. Following the UN-sponsored 2003 World Summit on the Information Society, the 40-member Working Group on Internet Governance (WGIG) was established by Secretary-General Kofi Annan. This body included government servants, representatives from the private sector and members of civil society, drawn from all major regions of the world.[37] In 2005, at a summit meeting in Tunis, it was agreed to establish the Internet Governance Forum to discuss various governance models proposed by the WGIG.[38]

Nevertheless, it appears that no major change in the internet regime will occur in the near future. Some observers believe that calls by many countries for a greater voice mask their governments' desire to be able to monitor and censor messaging to and from their citizens.[39] The prominent role of internet users in respect to political uprisings in North Africa, the Middle East and elsewhere provides ample reason to give credence to this motive.

Apart from the atmosphere, inner space includes our physical and biotic environment, in respect to which scores of international treaties have been adopted. Among topics addressed are the exclusion of various types of WMD (nuclear, chemical and biological) from the seabed; transnational movement of hazardous materials; protection of specific types of environment (wetlands, tropical forests, etc.); protection of endangered species (migratory birds, whales, etc.); management of transboundary watercourses and international lakes; access to environmental information; and liability in the event of environmental damage.[40] Many of these treaties are worldwide in scope; others relate only to limited areas such as the Alps, the Mediterranean region, West and Central Africa, and the South Pacific.[41] If the treaties have any common denominator it is that they embody a sense of *stewardship* among the contracting parties, a sense that may in time evolve into a normative belief in our common heritage.

A little-noticed development in respect to the common heritage concept is the proliferation of "world heritage sites" deemed by UNESCO to be properties with "outstanding universal value". The official list of such sites as of June 2010 had 911 entries, of which 704 were designated as cultural sites (e.g. China's Great Wall, India's Taj Mahal and Italy's Venice), 180 as natural sites (e.g. Australia's Great Barrier Reef and Yellowstone Park in the United States) and 27 as "mixed". These sites were distributed among 154 countries out of the 187 states parties to the World Heritage Convention of 1972.[42]

While the idea of creating such sites pre-dates the Second World War, the movement gained little traction until 1959 in the face of threatened destruction of Egypt's Abu Simbel temples by the proposed construction of the Aswan High Dam. While the temples were unequivocally a part of the cultural heritage of Egypt, UNESCO managed to coordinate the collection of US$80 million from individuals and governments worldwide who regarded the temples as part of the *world's* cultural heritage as well as that of Egypt. Miraculously, by 1968 both temples were relocated to high ground and preserved for posterity.[43]

For natural heritage sites, the story is markedly different. While the United States, for example, deserves much credit for initiating the worldwide national park movement by establishing Yellowstone Park in 1872, the wonders protected within that area were put there by *nature*, not by the US government or even by Native Americans. Thus the case for making the park a *world* heritage site is even stronger than for any cultural creation.

Following the Abu Simbel operation, UNESCO summoned the assistance of the International Council on Monuments and Sites as well as the International Union for Conservation of Nature in drafting what ultimately became the 1972 convention noted above. This convention prescribes criteria for qualifying for recognition as a world heritage site, procedures for applying and for vetting applications, and the responsibilities that states parties assume for site management and maintenance.[44]

States parties reap substantial benefits from becoming trustees of world heritage sites. Such sites form prized elements of the national patrimony, and are sources of national pride and major promoters of tourism. Tourists benefit in that placement of sites on the UNESCO register typically generates better information on them, improved transportation infrastructure and better facilities at the site itself. Further, UNESCO's rules preserve the essential character of heritage sites and protect them against tawdry commercialization. Finally, the world benefits from the enhanced international understanding that flows from familiarity with locales sufficiently distinctive to merit inclusion in the UNESCO roster.[45]

Apart from its concern with world heritage sites, UNESCO's purview extends to culture in general. Articles 7 and 8 of its 1997 Declaration on the Responsibilities of the Present Generations Towards Future Generations read:[46]

Article 7 – Cultural diversity and cultural heritage
With due respect for human rights and fundamental freedoms, the present generations should take care to preserve the cultural diversity of humankind. The present generations have the responsibility to identify, protect and safeguard the tangible and intangible cultural heritage and to transmit this common heritage to future generations.

Article 8 – Common heritage of humankind
The present generations may use the common heritage of humankind, as defined in international law, provided that this does not entail compromising it irreversibly.

Article 8 is noteworthy in linking the sustainability and common heritage paradigms.

In Article 1 of the 1997 Universal Declaration on the Human Genome and Human Rights, UNESCO further proclaimed: "The human genome underlies the fundamental unity of all members of the human family, as well as the recognition of their inherent dignity and diversity. It is the heritage of humanity." In light of this perception, Article 4 asserts: "The human genome in its natural state shall not give rise to financial gains."[47]

Article 4 has major implications for the pharmaceutical industry, which has isolated and patented numerous human genes for use in diagnostic testing and other purposes. In the United States alone, as of 2010 approximately 40,000 patents had been granted on roughly 2,000 human genes (about a tenth of the human genome). While many of these have been transformed from their "natural state", many others have not and may thus be said *not* to constitute "inventions" and therefore *not* to be subject to private appropriation.[48] A particularly egregious practice engaged in by some pharmaceutical firms is gathering and patenting genes from rural populations in Asia and Africa with a view to their commercial use and with little or no compensation to the donors.[49]

Further, although the UNESCO declaration refers only to the *human* genome, one may argue that genes derived from the genetic codes of all plants and animals – extensively used in the pharmaceutical, biotechnology and other industries – are equally non-human creations, a part of our common heritage, and not subject to appropriation for private gain. Numerous lawsuits seem likely based on such reasoning.[50]

Finally, I call attention – if only in passing – to the view that *all* intellectual, technical and artistic creations should, after appropriate periods of exclusive ownership conveyed by patents and copyrights, become part of the public domain and made available to *all* would-be users. The principal agency (among several) charged with promoting this norm is the Geneva-based World Intellectual Property Organization, established as a specialized agency of the United Nations in 1974. But, as with so many other UN agencies, WIPO is beset by major conflicts of interest between developed and developing countries, the former seeking maximum protection for the intellectual property of their citizens and corporations and the latter seeking transfer, especially of technology, on the most liberal of terms.[51]

Recommendations

Throughout this work, I have noted the UN's propensity to deal with serious problems by the piecemeal establishment of new agencies. Regrettably, however, these agencies were seldom provided with sufficient staff and fiscal resources to carry out their mandates effectively. Moreover, they tended to deal primarily with *symptoms* of a given problem (e.g. hunger), often failing to address the root *causes*. While some new agencies may still be needed, it is more important that the United Nations uses existing agencies to maximum advantage. This presupposes greater mission coherence, better oversight, more reliable funding and wiser use of human capital. Additionally, there is need for greater mission transparency, more accountability and enforceable sanctions when nations wilfully fail to conform to established norms.

A good starting point would be an overhaul of ECOSOC, ideally recast as ESEC (Economic, Social and Environmental Council) to enable it better to coordinate and report on UN activities within its purview.[52] This was discussed at length in Chapter 5 and the case need not be repeated here. Nor need I review recommendations in Chapters 3 and 8 regarding the roles of the GA and the UN's affiliated agencies and special commissions and funds.

Whatever structural reforms are made, policy formulation will have to reconcile the demands of stakeholders with markedly differing perspectives: those preferring market-based decisions and those inclined towards government planning;[53] industrialized and relatively unindustrialized states; rich and poor; states under severe environmental stress or threat and states relatively free from such concerns. To the extent practicable, the common heritage principle should be honoured. Policies will inevitably evolve by trial and error in the crucible of experience. But, given the dangers ahead, one would hope that progress along the learning curve – especially by powerful actors – will be accelerated by willingness to compromise, to recognize that all stakeholders deserve a meaningful voice in decision-making, to accept the policy implications of scientific evidence (especially relating to climate change) and to embrace an ethos that puts global welfare and intergenerational equity ahead of the near-term interests of particular nations and corporate giants.

Adherence to some common heritage norms should be legally binding, especially for norms relating to environmental goals where performance failure by a given state has significant adverse effects on the well-being of citizens of other states. However, legally binding rules mean little unless there are penalties for those who flout them. Hence, unpalatable as the prospect may seem, there is a need to develop credible systems for penalizing egregious transgressors and to muster the political resolve and mechanisms to apply them.

Admittedly, it is hard to imagine what sort of system could be established to enable the imposition of penalties on a major power such as the United States or China, or even on a defiant middle-level power. On reflection, however, several plausible measures emerge. The simplest would depend on a "naming and shaming" procedure. Even great powers have become sensitive to their standing before the "court of public opinion" and to the possibility that their being officially condemned might influence ordinary citizens around the world as they make decisions on whose goods they buy, where they travel and whom they support politically. Some enlightened leaders already recognize that all nations, like all citizens, must be equal before the law. Conceivably, it might take no more than a single acceptance by a major power of an adverse verdict against it to transform the global political climate in respect to environmental responsibility.

Additionally, it should be feasible for egregious flouters of established norms to be singled out for sanctions in the form of reduction or forfeiture of their voting power in various organs of the UN system. Wilful offenders might lose their votes entirely until such time as they modified their behaviour in a way prescribed by some duly constituted legal authority. Denying nations the right to participate in debates might also be effective. Another possible penalty might be payment of a prescribed fine in order to be allowed to have forfeited rights restored. Other sanctions provisions are already specified in Chapter VII of the UN Charter. Those imposed by the SC would carry special weight.

Sanctions, however, should normally be a last resort. Their consideration and imposition should be entrusted to duly authorized courts, commissions or panels. Wherever possible, contentious cases should be referred to regional organizations. Only when they cannot be dealt with effectively at a regional level should they be considered by a global agency.

Wise management of the global commons should become a major goal of the UN system. Although a new agency for this purpose does not appear to be a high priority in the near future, growing populations, higher living standards and diminishing resources will surely increase demands to privatize and exploit spaces and resources forming parts of our common heritage. It is therefore necessary to think about institutional mechanisms needed to protect the commons. A new agency – perhaps even a *core* agency – will be needed, specifically a *UN Common Heritage Council* (UNCHC).

Given the rapidity of technological change and of anthropogenic changes in the terrestrial ecosystem, one cannot confidently stipulate what the purview and composition of the UNCHC should be. Nevertheless, I suggest a council comprising 60 *experts* serving in their *individual* capacities rather than as political representatives of specific *states*, most of which remain wedded to the principle of exclusive sovereignty, an idea antithetical to that of a global commons. More specifically, I propose the following.

- Five groups of 12 experts each, representing biological sciences (including medicine and public health), physical sciences, social sciences, humanities (including law and religion) and the private sector.

- Rules establishing minimum and maximum representation of all the major regions of the world, defined more or less along the regional lines set forth for the SC (in Chapter 4) and ECOSOC (Chapter 5), as per Table 13.1.
- Gender balance such that neither males nor females shall have less than one-third or more than two-thirds of the total UNCHC membership; and, to the extent possible, neither males nor females shall have less than one-third or more than two-thirds of the total membership from a given region.
- A minimum of two members from indigenous communities, a minimum of two members from landlocked states (whose perspectives on UNCLOS will differ from those of maritime states) and at least one member from a UN roster of "small island states" (many of which are particularly susceptible to environmental threats).
- All UNCHC representatives, no matter how chosen, would cast *equal votes*.

The maximum and minimum regional representation in the UNCHC would be determined with reference to the proportions of the weighted votes of each region in ECOSOC. The proportion elected from a given region would be not less than half or more than one-and-a-half times the region's proportional weighted vote in ECOSOC, rounded to the nearest integer. For example, if Region X had a total weighted vote of 20 per cent in ECOSOC (one-fifth of the total), then its share of the UNCHC membership would have to fall in the range of 10–30 per cent of the UNCHC total of 60 seats, i.e. a minimum of six and a maximum of 18

Table 13.1 Ranges of regional membership in hypothetical UN Common Heritage Council

Region	Total weight in ECOSOC (%)	Maximum UNCHC membership	Minimum UNCHC membership
Africa South of the Sahara	11.25	10	3
Arab League	5.97	5	2
China	8.46	8	3
East Asia and Pacific	9.74	9	3
Europe	20.79	19	6
India	6.34	6	2
Japan	5.42	5	2
Latin America and Caribbean	10.74	10	3
Russia and Neighbours	2.66	6	2
United States	11.72	11	4
Western Asia	5.35	5	2
Westminster League	1.24	2	1

seats. Table 13.1 indicates regional ranges of UNCHC membership if the proposed system were in place today.

Additional suggested rules are as follows. Members would serve staggered six-year terms, one-third of the total being elected every two years. No member would serve more than two consecutive terms. Nominations would be made by ECOSOC/ESEC, with due regard to the specified membership criteria and with at least two candidates for every vacant position. Civil society organizations would be encouraged to suggest worthy candidates to ECOSOC/ESEC. Elections would be conducted by the GA, jointly with the World Parliamentary Assembly should the latter body be established.

The council would meet for at least six weeks every spring and report to ECOSOC/ESEC, which would in turn discuss UNCHC reports and pass on its recommendations to the GA and – hopefully – the WPA for further action. When not in session, UNCHC members would remain in regular contact with one another via the internet and other media. The council would establish its own agenda, but be responsive to relevant requests from other UN agencies. Members would be guaranteed political immunity for anything they may say or write in pursuance of their duty.

In the remainder of this section, I consider several commons-related issues that the GA, ECOSOC and – should it come into existence – the UNCHC ought to address.

In discussing UNCLOS, I noted the creation of EEZs accounting for nearly two-fifths of ocean space. That decision was, in my judgement, a feckless act of political expediency, resulting in a tremendous reduction of what should have remained the common heritage of humankind. Although it is easier for one political actor – in this case the GA – to give something of value to others than to take back all or portions of the gifts bestowed, I would argue that the United Nations should establish an *eminent domain principle* enabling it to reclaim the greater part of the world's EEZs. Exempted areas would be the territorial seas of maritime states and their contiguous zones, jointly extending 24 nautical miles from their respective baselines. This recommendation is, admittedly, fraught with legal and political difficulties, and its execution might necessitate compensation for adversely affected poor states. Such compensation could come from a financial pool derived from leasing and licensing fees for approved, sustainable commercial uses (fishing, mining, tourism, etc.) of ocean space.

The eminent domain principle should, in time, also be extended to the atmosphere. This portion of our common heritage could become a major source of UN revenue through a variety of mechanisms: fees paid to obtain radio frequencies, pro rata assessments on telecommunications messaging, small surcharges on air travel and so forth. While these charges would not be politically popular and would fall disproportionately on wealthy nations, they would reduce alternative funding of UN programmes and benefit poorer states.

If fees are to be assessed on uses of the atmosphere, it will be necessary to define where the atmosphere ends and *outer* space begins. Although no official definition presently exists, a simple border would be a spherical surface 350 km (210 miles) above mean sea level. This altitude is roughly the upper limit of the ionosphere, the outermost of four conventionally recognized atmospheric layers. (The others, from low to high, are the troposphere, within which our weather is generated, the stratosphere and the mesosphere.) The ionosphere is especially important in that ionized particles therein reflect radio waves, making wireless telecommunications possible. Additionally, it is the layer that must be reached if artificial earth satellites are to achieve orbit.

Conclusions

Our world is on a self-destructive, non-sustainable course because of its commitment to unlimited economic growth and the concomitant depletion of resources and degradation of the environment, including spaces deemed to be part of the common heritage of humankind. Major conferences, including many sponsored by the United Nations, have highlighted the problems and put forward achievable goals and action strategies. Other worthy recommendations have come from organs of the United Nations itself. Yet while many observers recognize what needs to be done to save the people of the earth from short-sighted, self-serving governmental and corporate actors, actions taken by the United Nations – including the creation of new agencies – are typically tepid, ill funded and inadequately staffed. Repeated failure to obtain desired results has led to widespread scepticism about the UN's capabilities and the charge that it is a hopelessly bloated, ineffectual bureaucracy.

Sooner or later, however, the human family – acting through the United Nations, regional organizations, national and local governments and civil society – will have to muster the requisite determination to confront its existential perils with seriousness of purpose and a sufficiency of needed resources, A reformed ECOSOC – hopefully recast as ESEC – can play a major role in coordinating that effort. So too could the proposed UNCHC with respect to the vast terrestrial and extraterrestrial spaces regarded as our common heritage. But it is doubtful that the proposed reform of ECOSOC/ESEC or the establishment of the UNCHC can be realized without strong backing from other key components of the UN system. Both recommendations would necessitate backing from the

GA, ideally endowed with the ability to make *binding decisions*, the proposed WPA and the Secretary-General. Early support from progressive and highly respected UN member nations and regional organizations will also be needed. And well-orchestrated campaigns by civil society organizations would speed the reform process. But whoever the change agents may be and whatever strategy they may employ, it will be important that they prominently include representatives of both global North and global South.

Notes

1. Robert Malthus, *An Essay on the Principle of Population, as It Affects the Future Improvement of Society*, 1st edn published anonymously, London: J. Johnson, 1796; editions 2 (much revised) to 6 published under Malthus's name between 1803 and 1826.
2. Works that have especially influenced the author include William Vogt, *Road to Survival*, New York: Sloane Associates, 1948 and Whitefish, MT: Kessinger Publishing, 2009; Paul R. Ehrlich, *The Population Bomb*, Cuthogue, NY: Bucaneer, 1971; Donella H. Meadows, Dennis L. Meadows, Jergen Randers and William W. Behrens III, *The Limits to Growth: A Report for the Club of Rome's Project on the Predicament of Mankind*, New York: New American Library, 1977.
3. The original source of this much-cited observation is uncertain and the wording varies from one source to another.
4. World Commission on Environment and Development, *Our Common Future*, Annex to Doc. A/42/427, New York: United Nations, 1987, Ch. 2, p. 1.
5. Among modern scholars writing on common property regimes, none has contributed more than the late Elinor Ostrom, whose analyses of what she calls "common pool resources" over a period of decades earned her the Nobel Prize in Economics in 2009.
6. UNESCO Culture of Peace Programme, "Declaration on the Responsibility of the Present Generations Towards Future Generations", adopted on 12 November 1997 by General Conference of UNESCO, 29th session, Paris: UNESCO, 1997.
7. A summary of the UN's role is found in Richard Jolly, Louis Emmerij and Thomas G. Weiss, *UN Ideas That Changed the World*, Bloomington and Indianapolis, IN: Indiana University Press, 2009, pp. 149–162. See also Fen O. Hampson and Christopher K. Penny, "Human Security", in Thomas G. Weiss and Sam Daws (eds), *The Oxford Handbook on the United Nations*, New York and Oxford: Oxford University Press, 2007, pp. 539–557; Nico Schrijver, "Natural Resource Management and Sustainable Development", in Thomas G. Weiss and Sam Daws (eds), *The Oxford Handbook on the United Nations*, New York and London: Oxford University Press, 2007, pp. 592–601. The account in this chapter relies primarily on these sources.
8. World Commission on Environment and Development, note 4 above.
9. Discussed in Jolly, Emmerij and Weiss, note 7 above, pp. 149–155.
10. Wikipedia, "Kyoto Protocol", http://en.wikipedia.org/wiki/Kyoto_Protocol; see also Jolly, Emmerij and Weiss, note 7 above, pp. 157–160.
11. UNFCC Secretariat, "UN Climate Change Conference in Cancún Delivers Balanced Package of Decisions, Restores Faith in Multilateral Process", press release, 11 December 2010.

12. For background information see www.un.org/millenniumgoals/bkgd.shtml. A summary and critical analysis are provided in Wikipedia, "Millennium Development Goals", http://en.wikipedia.org/wiki/Millennium_Development_Goals.

13. Wikipedia, ibid., p. 6.

14. For goal-by-goal and country-by-country progress see "Millennium Project", www.unmillenniumproject.org/goals/index.htm.

15. The following text is based largely on Antarctic Connections, a website maintained by the US National Science Foundation, www.antarcticconnection.com/antarctic/treaty/treaty-text.shtml.

16. This leaves a substantial area of Antarctica, the so-called "Pacific Sector", a wedge of territory from 90° to 150° W longitude with no claimant, as the only significant unclaimed land territory on the planet. On the other hand a large area, including the Palmer/Antarctic Peninsula, has three overlapping claims, namely those of Argentina, Chile and the United Kingdom.

17. Scientific Committee on Antarctic Research, "Signatories to the Antarctic Treaty", www.scar.org/treaty/signatories.html.

18. Antarctic Connections, www.antarcticconnection.com/antarctic/treaty/index.shtml.

19. Wikipedia, "Outer Space Treaty", http://en.wikipedia.org/wiki/Outer_Space_Treaty, p. 1, last modified 25 July 2012.

20. "International Space Treaties", www.islandone.org/treaties/.

21. Wikipedia, "Moon Treaty", http://en.wikipedi.org/wiki/Moon_Treaty.

22. Wikipedia, "International Space Station", http://en.wikipedia.org/wiki/international_space_station, p. 6.

23. Wikipedia, "Mir", http://en.wikipedia.org/wiki/Mir.

24. Wikipedia, note 22 above, p. 2 and *passim*.

25. Wikipedia, "Common Heritage of Mankind", http://wikipedia.org/wiki?Common_heritage_of_mankind, p. 1, last modified 16 February 2011.

26. Schrijver, note 7 above, pp. 598–599.

27. Wikipedia, "Arvid Pardo", http://en.wikipedia.org/wiki/Arvid_Pardo.

28. Prior attempts to deal with maritime territorial issues included the UNCLOS I conference of 1956–1958, resulting in four now-superseded treaties, and the abortive UNCLOS II negotiations of 1960.

29. UNCLOS III is the longest and most detailed treaty ever prepared under UN auspices.

30. Wikipedia, "United Nations Convention on the Law of the Sea", http://en.wiki/United_Nations_Convention_on_the_Law_of_the_Sea.

31. Area figures in this and subsequent paragraphs are from Wikipedia, "Exclusive Economic Zones", http://en.wikipedia.org/wiki/Exclusive_Economic_Zones#rankings_by_area.

32. Ibid.; also Schrijver, note 7 above, pp. 599–600.

33. Quoted in Wikipedia, note 27 above, p. 2.

34. Paul Wapner, "Civil Society", in Thomas G. Weiss and Sam Daws (eds), *The Oxford Handbook on the United Nations*, New York and Oxford: Oxford University Press, 2007, pp. 254–263, at p. 258.

35. Valery Timofeev, "How ITU Processes and Regulations Have Helped Shape the Modern World of Radio Communications", International Telecommunications Union, Geneva, 2011, www.itu.int/itunews/manager/display.asp?lang=en&year=2006&isssue+03&ipage=radiotelegraphy&ext=html.

36. Wikipedia, "Internet Governance", http://en.wikipedia.org/wiki/internet_governance.

37. United Nations, "United Nations Establishes Working Group on Internet Governance", UN Press Release PI/1620, 11 November 2004, www.un.org/News?Press/docs/2004/pl1620.doc.htm.

38. Wikipedia, "Working Group on Internet Governance", http://en.wikipedia.org/wiki/Working_Group_on_Internet_Governance.
39. Ibid.
40. Wikipedia, "List of International Environmental Agreements", http://en.wikipedia.org/wiki/List_of_international_environmental_agreements.
41. Ibid.
42. UNESCO, "World Heritage List", http://whc.unesco.org/en/list.
43. UNESCO, "World Heritage Convention", http://whc.unesco.org/en/convention.
44. Ibid.
45. Observations based on author's visits to scores of world heritage sites on every inhabited continent.
46. UNESCO Culture of Peace Programme, note 6 above.
47. UNESCO, "Universal Declaration on the Human Genome and Human Rights", UNESCO, Paris, 1997.
48. Wikipedia, "Gene Patent", http://en.wikipedia.org/wiki/Gene_Patent.
49. UNESCO, "The Patentability of Living Organisms Debated at UNESCO Symposium", UNESCO, Paris, 2001.
50. Ibid.
51. Wikipedia, "World Intellectual Property Organization", http://en.wikipedia.org/wiki/World_Intellectual_Property_Organization.
52. An excellent discussion of coordination measures is found in Jacques Fomerand and Dennis Dijkzeul, "Coordinating Economic and Social Affairs", in Thomas G. Weiss and Sam Daws (eds), *The Oxford Handbook on the United Nations*, New York and Oxford: Oxford University Press, 2007, pp. 561–581.
53. The tension between planning and market-based approaches and the periodic shifts in their relative favour are analysed in Jolly, Emmerij and Weiss, note 7 above, pp. 118–129.

14

A new global governance architecture

I am not an advocate for frequent changes in laws and constitutions, but laws and institutions must go hand in hand with the progress of the human mind. As that becomes more developed, more enlightened, as new discoveries are made ... institutions must advance also to keep pace with the times. We might as well require a man to wear still the coat which fitted him when a boy as civilized society to remain ever under the regimen of their barbarous ancestors.
Thomas Jefferson

Man's capacity for justice makes democracy possible; but man's inclination to injustice makes democracy necessary.
Reinhold Niebuhr

World government is necessary; therefore it is possible.
Giuseppe A. Borgese

Introduction

Our future is not pre-ordained. At the global, regional, national and local levels decision-makers have innumerable options for influencing what is yet to come. Each choice comes with its own set of benefits and drawbacks, its own risks and uncertainties, its own time and space horizons, its own likely casts of relative winners and losers. Further, apart from their own choices, societies must also reckon with and respond to the often-unforeseeable choices of other human actors (e.g. rogue states, terrorists).

Transforming the United Nations system: Designs for a workable world, Schwartzberg, *United Nations University Press, 2013, ISBN 978-92-808-1230-5*

Finally, there is the powerful agency of nature, whether it be processes that humans help set in motion or amplify (e.g. global warming, loss of biodiversity) or the shock of cataclysmic events (e.g. earthquakes, tsunamis, violent storms, floods, droughts). Obviously, any attempt at predicting the future will be fraught with uncertainty. Yet plan we must, because maintenance of the status quo is demonstrably untenable.

This work puts forward proposals for reforming the decision-making processes of all major components of the UN system; for creating new organs where necessary; and for ways to connect civil society organizations more effectively to the UN system. I do not suggest that my proposals are necessarily the best that can be devised. They are merely the best I can presently think of in light of my limited and imperfect understanding of how various agencies have worked to date and appear likely to function in the future. Nor would I state that there is any obviously best sequencing of the proposed reforms (though suggestions are offered in Chapter 15). Nor, finally, do I suppose that every selected target for reform needs to be addressed in the foreseeable future. My aim is to promote *a world that is workable*, not a future utopia.

In broad terms, my strong preference is for *a constitutional system of democratic, federal world government*, characterized by a division of powers among executive, legislative and judicial branches and with clearly specified checks and balances to ensure none of the three branches gains ascendancy over the others. Along with Albert Einstein and many others, I am convinced that such a democratic world government would offer the greatest scope for maximizing and sustaining human well-being, promoting justice and ensuring political stability.[1] Yet I recognize that most readers will take issue with my conclusion and be inclined to settle for some less radical alternative. Those readers, however, are presumably from a privileged – but diminishing – segment of world society, that of the politically, economically and socially advantaged global North. It is only natural they should wish to preserve a system that perpetuates their privileges, even while offering occasional expedient concessions to the relatively disadvantaged global South. In that the North is still politically, economically and militarily dominant, it can, if it so chooses, delay the reform process or, perhaps, stop it dead in its tracks. But to do so will become increasingly risky in a rapidly changing and electronically networked world, a world in which new powers are emerging and the knowledge of blatant injustice anywhere swiftly becomes internet news virtually everywhere else. In short, an unjust world cannot long remain a peaceful world.

I would like to believe, along with the highly regarded international relations scholar Alexander Wendt – among others – that a single world state is the inevitable end-stage of our planet's political development.[2]

But I cannot. Wendt's avowedly teleological and highly theoretical argument posits progression through five stages: "a system of states, a society of states, world society, collective security, and the world state", essentially a transition from global anarchy to a stable global order.[3] My doubts hinge on the abundant historical evidence of human greed and stupidity, and the possibility that miscalculation can lead to a global conflagration that will bring civilization to an end. Also, I find it strange that Wendt barely acknowledges – in only one footnote! – the existential dangers posed by "exogenous shocks that could prevent world state formation – an asteroid impact, plague, ecological collapse, and so on".[4] That he should specifically mention the low-probability threat of asteroid impact while failing to discuss the far greater near-term threat posed by global warming seems peculiar. Moreover, I question Wendt's time perspective. He guesses "that a world state will emerge within 100–200 (?) years".[5] Although many other students of international relations would likely go along with such a judgement or suggest an even lengthier time horizon, given the inertia within and acceleration of the global warming process, a more realistic and prudent view is that we may have no more than a generation in which to get our planetary house in order – assuming that we have not already passed a point of no return; perhaps not to the extent of creating a full-fledged world state, but, at a minimum, a system sufficiently reformed to stave off ecological catastrophe.[6]

In what follows I put forward my preferred vision for a new global governance architecture, acknowledging the low probability that it will be created in quite the form I propose. I do so, however, in the hope and expectation that the model envisaged will generate creative discussion and lead to refinements on at least a few of my proposals.

A new architecture for global governance

The design presented is that of a system of democratic federal world government. By definition, a federal system must function at two or more levels. In this section and the next I focus on the global level, as illustrated in Figure 14.1. In the last section I consider the regional, national and lower levels.[7]

General remarks

Only the more important proposed UN agencies are indicated in Figure 14.1. Even so, it may strike readers as an excessively complex bureaucracy. The system portrayed, however, is far less complicated than that of the United States or, I would judge, the bureaucracies of most of the

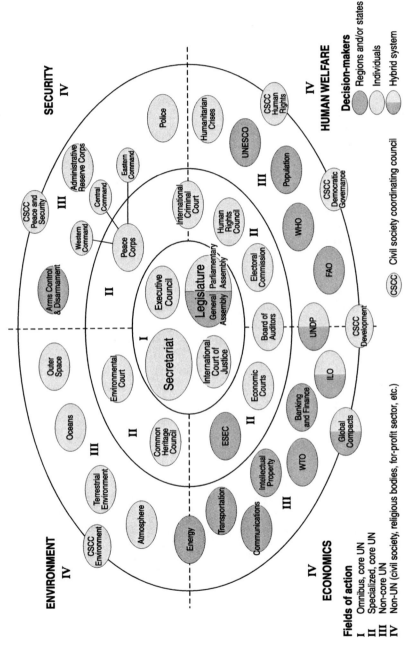

Figure 14.1 Hypothetical infrastructure at global level of a future system of global governance

ENVIRONMENT
IV

SECURITY
IV

HUMAN WELFARE
IV

ECONOMICS
IV

Decision-makers
- Regions and/or states
- Individuals
- Hybrid system

CSCC   Civil society coordinating council

Fields of action
I   Omnibus, core UN
II Specialized, core UN
III Non-core UN
IV Non-UN (civil society, religious bodies, for-profit sector, etc.)

Labels within figure:

Police
Humanitarian Crises
CSCC Human Rights
UNESCO
Administrative Reserve Corps
Eastern Command
Central Command
Population
CSCC Peace and Security
III
Western Command
Peace Corps
International Criminal Court
Human Rights Council
II
CSCC Democratic Governance
WHO
Arms Control & Disarmament
II
Executive Council
Parliamentary Assembly
Legislature
General Assembly
Electoral Commission
FAO
Outer Space
Environmental Court
I
Secretariat
International Court of Justice
Board of Auditors
UNDP
CSCC Development
Oceans
III
II
Common Heritage Council
Economic Courts
ILO
Banking and Finance
Terrestrial Environment
ESEC
WTO
Global Compacts
Atmosphere
Intellectual Property
CSCC Environment
IV
Energy
Transportation
Communications
III

world's larger states. In considering the agency descriptions below, the reader would benefit from reviewing related antecedent reforms proposed earlier in this work.

Each shaded oval on the graph represents a particular agency, the principal concern of which is specified. (Acronyms are used for well-known agencies – UNESCO, WHO, etc. – that would be retained in the future system.) Agencies are situated in accordance with the centrality of their position within the UN system as well as in respect to their focal concerns. *Core agencies*, those that would presumably be specifically called for in the anticipated constitution, are situated in fields I and II. Field I includes agencies with *omnibus mandates*, while *specialized core agencies* are plotted in the concentric field II. *Non-core UN agencies* are shown on the UN periphery, in field III. Beyond them in field IV (though not shown) are thousands of civil society agencies (mainly INGOs) that are *legally outside the United Nations*, but whose activities increasingly influence UN decision-making. Such agencies may be considered as components of the system of global *governance*, but not of the *government per se.*

With the exception of the omnibus core agencies, ovals are situated according to four *functional domains*: security (upper right), human welfare (lower right), economics (lower left) and environment (upper left). This essentially heuristic classification is not intended to suggest that the domains are mutually exclusive. In fact most agencies have multiple concerns, often in two or more domains, but they are arranged within each domain sequentially and – somewhat subjectively – with regard to both their *most important* and their *subsidiary* concerns (e.g. "Police" is placed within the security domain, but closest to human welfare). Several agencies (e.g. UNDP) are placed on the dividing line between their two most important domains.

Five ovals marked "CSCC" on the boundary separating the UN system from the non-UN field represent civil society coordinating councils (Chapter 10). Similarly situated is the oval relating to the global compacts. The rationale for these decisions is explained below.

Finally, each agency is shaded to indicate whether the proposed decision-makers therein are to be *regions* and/or *states* (dark grey), as opposed to *individuals* (light grey) or, for several agencies (e.g. the ILO), hybrid entities comprising both state and non-state actors. In general, agency members representing regions or states would be nominated by national governments, with no fewer than two candidates for each vacant post, and elected concurrently by both legislative chambers. Agency members serving in their individual capacity (excluding those in the Executive Council) would be nominated by the Executive Council, subject to approval by both legislative chambers. In all cases there would be provisions to assure reasonable regional and gender balance.

UN core agencies with omnibus concerns (field I)

Agencies within the innermost field of Figure 14.1 are those whose purview would extend to *all* the major domains of UN concern. Three of them correspond to the branches of government – executive, legislative and judicial – presently found in virtually all national democratic governments. The fourth, the Secretariat, would make up much of the UN civil service.

The envisaged *Executive Council* would be made up of a specified number of elected *individuals* – I suggest 12 – rather than representatives of member *states*, as is now the case for the SC. The manner of their selection is discussed later. The principal functions of the Executive Council would be:

- periodically to review and report on the state of the world
- to present to the Legislature a programme calling for binding and non-binding resolutions
- to suggest a biennial budget
- to nominate individuals to serve on federal courts and direct other major UN agencies
- to act expeditiously in case of breaches of the peace or major humanitarian crises (subject to subsequent legislative approval).

Super-majorities within the council (say eight councillors) would also be empowered to veto legislative decisions.

The envisaged *Legislature* would be *bicameral*. One house, the *General Assembly*, would represent *states* (including future regional federations), while the other, the *World Parliamentary Assembly*, would represent *people*. WPA representatives would be popularly elected from multi-member constituencies using a system of proportional representation. Unlike the present GA, the future Legislature would be empowered to enact *binding* legislation. Such legislation would require the concurrence of varying super-majorities – depending on the issue – in both houses. Procedural votes and recommendatory resolutions would be by simple majorities. Voting to override an Executive Council veto would require substantial majorities, say 75 per cent, in both chambers. Binding legislation would be limited to a restricted – but constitutionally expansible – range of subjects *of truly global concern*. Operating on the EU principle of subsidiarity, legislation on all *non-global* matters would be the province of regional organizations, nations or subnational entities. (This is analogous to the provision of the Tenth Amendment of the US Constitution – the so-called "reserved powers clause" – and similar provisions of other federal constitutions.) Additionally, the Legislature would function as an *electoral college*, electing not only the Executive Council but also the Secretary-General and his/her principal assistants. It would vote to approve or disapprove Executive Council nominees for numerous key positions, including judges in the courts indicated in Figure 14.1 and the directors of major agencies. Finally, the Legislature would debate the budget submitted by the Executive Council and modify it as it saw fit.

The supreme judicial body, the *International Court of Justice*, would be composed of jurists nominated by the Executive Council and approved by the Legislature. It would try only cases deemed to be of *major importance*. Litigants would be restricted to states (including regional federations), rather than individuals or corporations. Cases could be referred to the ICJ by either or both houses of the Legislature, by one of the other courts indicated in Figure 14.1 or by regional or national courts. The ICJ would have the right to *rule on the constitutionality* of laws passed by the global Legislature or lower-level legislatures in situations where legislation or practices allegedly conflicted with the global constitution. While ICJ verdicts would normally be binding, the court would also have the right – as at present – to render *advisory opinions* on the legality of actions and policies contemplated by UN agencies or member nations.

UN administration would largely be carried out by the *Secretariat*, whose future staff will probably number in the hundreds of thousands (not including Secretariat staff assigned to the agencies indicated in fields II and III of Figure 14.1). The Secretariat would be headed by an elected Secretary-General, aided by a number of elected under- and assistant secretaries-general. Given the wide-ranging roles envisaged for the Executive Council, the powers of the future Secretary-General would be less than at present and limited mainly to administrative and ceremonial duties. The Secretariat would seek to facilitate execution of the decisions and programmes of other UN agencies. It would also be responsible for translating the texts of UN documents into all the official UN working languages, and facilitating liaison among UN agencies and between UN and non-UN agencies at the global and lower levels.

UN core agencies with specialized concerns (field II)

As with the agencies discussed above, those indicated in field II would all be constitutionally prescribed, given the importance of their respective mandates. They are discussed below in clockwise order.

The *UN Peace Corps* would deal with serious threats to the peace in situations in which diplomacy and other peaceful methods of conflict resolution proved inadequate. In that most of its standing force would be deployed in locations away from the United Nations itself, only the headquarters staff (the successor, in principle, to the Military Staff Committee called for in Article 47 of the present Charter) is included in field II.

Jurisdiction of the *International Criminal Court* would extend, as at present, to individuals indicted for serious crimes under international law, not only those currently specified – genocide, ethnic cleansing, war crimes and crimes against humanity – but also aggression, illicit arms trading, human trafficking, narco-trafficking and other egregious offences. It would select a manageable number of cases referred to it by other UN agencies, member nations, victimized groups or the civil courts of regional bodies (e.g. those of the African Union or European Union) unable to make a final determination on a particular case. It would also relegate cases to lower courts or *ad hoc* tribunals as needed. Though the ICC would report to the ICJ, its decisions would normally be final and binding.

The proposed *Human Rights Council* would – unlike the present council, functioning under the aegis of the GA – be reconstituted as a major organ of the United Nations in its own right. Its members would be elected by the Legislature on the basis of merit, rather than being appointed by member nations. Selection would pay due regard to regional balance and gender equity. Additionally, seats would be reserved for representatives of indigenous peoples. The HRC's mandate would be broader than that of the present body, reflecting the widening ambit of human rights concerns. It would pay particular heed to marginalized populations, especially ethnic or religious minorities, and to the rights of women, children and other vulnerable groups. As needed, the HRC would refer egregious human rights violators to the ICJ, ICC and/or the Executive Council and Legislature, and recommend ways of dealing with the problem.

If the future United Nations is to enjoy the trust and win the allegiance of the world's peoples and other political actors, transparency and accountability must be built into all parts of the governance system. Two agencies are envisaged to deal with these needs: an *Electoral Commission* and a *Board of Auditors*. The former would recommend rules to ensure the fairness of elections to the WPA and, where needed, assist in delimiting electoral constituencies. Additionally, on request by the Executive Council, it would monitor national elections conducted in situations likely to result in serious violence or fraud. It should become a rule that *no* national election would be regarded as legal unless it is so certified by the Electoral Commission.

The Board of Auditors would regularly examine the financial accounts of all entities within the UN system and bring to the attention of the Executive Council and Legislature serious cases of financial waste, mismanagement, corruption, bribery, extortion or fraud. It would also examine financial interactions between entities within the UN system, as well as those with outside governments and private contractors, and bring shortcomings to light.

Where necessary, individuals or corporate bodies indicted for offences noted in the previous paragraph could, on the recommendation of either the Executive Council or Legislature, be brought to trial before the *Economic Court*, which could impose fines or other appropriate penalties, including removal from office, prison terms, fines and/or confiscation of ill-gained funds or property.

The *Economic, Social and Environmental Council* would carry out functions similar to those of today's ECOSOC. It would coordinate the activities of UN-affiliated field III agencies in all domains other than security.[8] Some such agencies, most notably the Bretton Woods institutions, are presently virtually autonomous entities that – not infrequently – function at cross-purposes to UN-sponsored programmes. Others, most notably the WTO, are now completely independent of the UN system. But all should be brought under the UN umbrella. ESEC would also have oversight over numerous special funds and programmes that are insufficiently coordinated (e.g. the WFP, UNICEF, UNDP, etc.). These measures should enable greater programmatic coherence than presently exists.

The *UN Common Heritage Council* (UNCHC) would be created to oversee management of humankind's "common heritage", namely spaces – Antarctic, oceanic, atmospheric and extraterrestrial – and elements of the biosphere over which no country should enjoy the right of exclusive ownership or jurisdiction. Councillors, elected on the basis of merit, would be individuals representing diverse non-state constituencies. UNCHC functions would include determination and collection of appropriate fees – subject to legislative approval – for the use of commonly held spaces or resources (e.g. the electromagnetic spectrum), establishing standards for protecting physical and biotic environments, and maintaining oversight of world natural and cultural heritage sites.

Finally, the *Environmental Court* would try serious cases of violation of environmental norms not amenable to resolution by lower-level bodies. It could try cases involving IGOs, nations, NGOs, corporations or individuals, and impose the same types of penalties as those noted for the Economic Court.

Non-core UN agencies (field III)

In discussing agencies within field III of Figure 14.1 I again proceed in a clockwise direction.

The security domain

An *Arms Control and Disarmament Agency* would have an unlimited right to carry out, on short notice, intrusive inspections anywhere in the world to ensure that illegal arms build-ups of atomic, biological, chemical and/or so-called "conventional" weapons had not occurred. Additionally, the agency would be authorized to dismantle or otherwise dispose of all weapons in excess of those needed to maintain domestic law and order.

The largest security agency would be an all-volunteer, internationally recruited, elite *UN Peace Corps*. Though indicated here with three separate regional commands, the UNPC would have the capacity for globally coordinated action. In that most UN member nations in this hypothetical future world would have submitted to disarmament regimes and have little cause to resort to armed conflict, most UNPC deployments would presumably be to help ensure or restore peace in situations of *intra*-state – mainly ethnic – conflict, which seems unlikely to abate substantially until well after the establishment of a functional world government. When not actively deployed in a military mode, the UNPC would devote much of its effort to training the militias of UN member states. It could also undertake constructive projects, such as strengthening the material infrastructure of host states, improving public health facilities and so forth.

Working closely with the UNPC would be the *UN Administrative Reserve Corps*, drawn from pools of reserve administrative specialists who would have previously graduated from a UN Administrative Academy (not indicated in Figure 14.1). UNARC's main function would be to help prevent the breakdown of civil administration in areas of severe political strife and restore normality in areas where civil administration had already collapsed.

Many threats to society not requiring a military response would more appropriately be addressed by a *police agency*. Such an agency would deal with a wide range of international malefactors: cells of terrorists, mafia-type organizations, pirates, smugglers and other criminal elements operating across state borders. The envisaged agency, which would take over and expand upon the functions now carried out by INTERPOL, would have the right to operate throughout the world – if so directed by the Executive Council – and apprehend and bring to justice indicted individuals and groups accused of committing serious international crimes. Implicit in the agency's creation would be substantial expansion of the UN's *intelligence* capability.

The human welfare domain

Several major agencies operating within this domain would be strengthened continuations of existing UN-affiliated organizations, specifically UNESCO, the WHO and the FAO. Others would incorporate functions now performed by specially funded programmes such as UNICEF, the UNHCR, etc.

Let us begin with an agency designed to respond to *humanitarian crises*. Whether dealing with refugees fleeing from civil strife or populations devastated by natural catastrophes, there is little difference in the services needed to alleviate suffering, provide food and shelter, stave off disease and deal with psychological trauma. The requirements – human skills, food, medicine and other supplies, field equipment, shelter and needed logistic support – will be similar in either case. Thus the proposed agency would take over the largely redundant roles now performed, *inter alia*, by the UNHCR and UNICEF.

UNESCO's functions are manifold. As at present, its principal future roles would be in promoting education, science and culture. Improving basic education would remain a top priority. But all functions would evolve in light of changing technology (especially in respect to the internet, bio-engineering and nanotechnology). Other areas of concern would include ecotourism and, in conjunction with the Common Heritage Council, oversight of world heritage sites.

A reformed *population* agency would take over functions now carried out mainly by the UNFPA. Its purview would extend to family planning (including reproductive health services), eliminating gender gaps in education, promoting maternal and infant health, reducing infant mortality, increasing life expectancy and combating sexually transmitted diseases.

The functions of the *World Health Organization* would partially overlap those of the population agency (e.g. in respect to sexually transmitted diseases), but would relate to all communicable diseases. They would include developing protocols for dealing with pandemics, such as severe acute respiratory syndrome (SARS) and other diseases not yet on the medical horizon. Ways of dealing with illnesses caused by industrial carcinogens, radioactivity, nutritional deficiencies and unsafe drinking water would also be on the WHO's agenda. Sanitation and basic health education would be particularly important.

The *Food and Agriculture Organization* would work mainly with farmers and consumers in poor countries. In addition to seeking to increase production, the FAO would promote better ways of storing, transporting, processing and marketing agricultural commodities and educate consumers in regard to human nutrition. Finally, it would try also to influence policy in agriculturally advanced countries, in that the quantity and prices of food, seeds, fertilizers and pesticides they export greatly influence production costs and commodity prices – even the very viability of agriculture – in the rest of the world.

Working closely with the population agency, the WHO and the FAO – among other agencies – would be the *UN Development Programme*, shown in Figure 14.1 as straddling the border between the human welfare and economics domains. As at present, UNDP will interact with national development-related ministries throughout the developing world. In most host countries it would be the lead UN agency and seek to incorporate

UN-funded initiatives smoothly into their respective development plans and help formulate coherent, well-integrated, efficient and cost-effective programmes.

The economic domain

As in the human welfare domain, agencies within the economic domain would function under the oversight of ESEC.

Since its founding in 1919, the *International Labour Organization* has been a singularly effective agency. Its role should be maintained and expanded. Included within that role are the development of labour codes and standards regarding freedom of association, forming labour unions, collective bargaining, work conditions, just compensation, child labour, forced labour, discriminatory hiring, etc. The ILO also monitors adherence to codes and standards and would recommend sanctions for egregious violators, including both states and individual corporations. A likely major future concern will be migrant workers, whose numbers will probably increase dramatically in coming decades.

I have previously noted the sometimes conflicting agendas of the Bretton Woods agencies and other components of the UN system, and the need to bring the former more fully within the UN ambit. Figure 14.1 indicates a single *banking and finance* agency in place of the presently fragmented Bretton Woods system. Deciding on the functions and strength of the future bank will inevitably be highly contentious, given the financial power of its most important members and their vested interest in the status quo. Presently, decision-making power is roughly proportional to funds subscribed, which is mainly a function of GNI (basically one dollar – one vote). A more equitable formula is essential. Also needed are greater transparency, an end to insistence on "conditionality" (having to agree to economic liberalization and privatization as preconditions for receiving loans), lower interest rates and greater leniency in respect to loan repayments when the economies of debtor nations are adversely affected by conditions beyond their control (e.g. skyrocketing increases in prices for food and petroleum). The IBRD must also be weaned away from ecologically harmful mega-projects that advance the careers of bankers, government officials, engineers and contractors while providing few benefits for most inhabitants of the project areas.

Present IMF oversight of the global financial system (exchange rates, balance of payments issues, financial reporting, etc.) also needs reform, mainly via tighter regulation. Assuming that the world does eventually adopt an overarching government, one would expect it to empower the World Bank to create money and establish a common world currency. Although most economists would not now warm to this recommendation, the case has been persuasively argued by others.[9]

The *World Trade Organization*, presently an autonomous body with the power to make binding decisions, must be incorporated into the future UN system. There it would continue its present functions of negotiating reduced barriers to international trade, preventing dumping of commodities in foreign markets, developing codes for product safety, promoting transparency in respect to conditions under which exported goods and services are produced (e.g. by using child or prison labour), providing a forum for negotiations and settlement of trade disputes, conducting research and analysis, and assisting developing countries to adjust to WTO rules. While the WTO does provide many benefits, its presently opaque system of dispute resolution, favouring wealthy countries with unlimited access to legal expertise, will in the future require greater openness and equitability.

The *World Intellectual Property Organization* would continue its present mission of promoting creative intellectual endeavour, protecting intellectual property and facilitating the transfer of technology to developing countries. The last of these goals, however, may at times conflict with the former two. Proper balance must be established based on principles of equity for all concerned parties.

The global explosion in *communications* technology, especially via the internet, is profoundly reshaping interactions among individual citizens, NGOs and national and international governmental organizations. Attempts to control and censor information flows call for appropriate monitoring, regulation and exposure. Additionally, the virtual monopoly now enjoyed by ICANN over internet regulation should eventually give way to a more democratically governed system. That system would not only regulate emerging communications technologies, but also assume the more traditional functions of the present UPU and ITU.

The world's *transportation* systems are undergoing rapid change, often leading to seriously harmful environmental consequences. Automobiles are major generators of greenhouse gases, and the spreading adoption of an automobile-oriented culture contributes to unsustainable economies consuming inordinately large shares of our planet's material resources. The envisaged transportation agency would promote new, more economically and ecologically benign forms of transport technology, both private and public. It would also assume the functions of the present International Civil Aviation Organization and International Maritime Organization.

Closely related to the issue of transportation is that of *energy* in general. The proposed agency most concerned with this issue straddles the Figure 14.1 boundary between the economic and environmental domains. Devising efficient, cheap, safe and sustainable ways of providing energy to domestic, industrial and agricultural consumers presents enormous challenges. Future use of nuclear energy is especially problematic. Without substantially increased regulation, the pace of change will be much too slow to arrest seriously harmful ecological effects. Careful monitoring and, when needed, imposing sanctions for non-adherence to established guidelines are necessary. These tasks should be assumed by an energy agency that would, among other functions, incorporate the present roles of UNEP and the International Atomic Energy Agency.

The environmental domain

Apart from the energy agency, four agencies are indicated in this domain. All would report to both the proposed UNCHC and ESEC. Although views vary on the extent to which the land portion of the terrestrial environment (including Antarctica), the oceans and the atmosphere should be regarded as parts of the common heritage of humankind, it is clear that management of those spaces cannot be divorced from the management of those that are nationally and privately controlled. And exploration and eventual use of *outer* space will also entail shared costs and benefits.

The envisaged agency for the *atmosphere* would take over functions now performed by the World Meteorological Organization. These relate not only to the scientific study of global warming but also to forecasting and recording of weather and standardized record keeping. Monitoring GHG emissions and the generation of polluting aerosols would be an agency responsibility. Finally, the agency would be actively involved in research and advocacy relating to the mitigation of ecologically harmful processes.

The agency dealing with the *terrestrial environment* (including Antarctica) would be concerned with soil pollution, loss of agricultural land due to salinization and urban sprawl, toxic chemicals in consumer goods, hydrological issues (especially diminishing supplies of fresh surface and ground water), glacial melting, flooding and drought, hazard mitigation, protection of endangered species, despoliation of natural landscapes and numerous other issues.

The *oceans* agency would deal with issues covered by the Law of the Sea Treaty: territorial claims to portions of ocean space, means of dispute resolution, access rights for landlocked states, navigation rights, fisheries (including whaling), protection of coral reefs and endangered species, deep-sea and offshore mining, pollution, research, preventing militarization of the seabed and so forth.

The *outer space* agency would oversee exploration and use of outer space, including the moon and other heavenly bodies. It would assign band widths on the electromagnetic spectrum, license access to satellite positions in geo-stationary space orbits, control space traffic and deal with claims for damages due to collisions of satellites with space debris or from debris falling to earth. Other functions will undoubtedly emerge as technology advances.

Non-UN agencies and their UN interface

Governance, as I have noted, is not synonymous with government. Civil society actors, especially NGOs, are increasingly mobilizing ordinary citizens to influence legislation and government policies, often meeting with notable success. Such organizations are growing rapidly in both number and size. Since political legitimacy depends largely on the sense that governmental bodies listen to the voice of the people and take their concerns seriously, it is essential that any future system of democratic government incorporates mechanisms whereby popular concerns can gain a hearing. The proposal put forward in Chapter 10 for achieving this goal is to establish five *civil society coordination councils*, each of which would examine, weigh and consolidate the salient concerns of groups of NGOs working on related clusters of issues: *peace and security, human rights, democratic governance, development* and the *environment*. These CSCCs are indicated by ovals on the border between fields III and IV of Figure 14.1.

Also shown on this interface between the United Nations and outside agencies is an oval relating to a proposed agency to help negotiate and monitor *global compacts* (Chapter 10). Such compacts provide arrangements whereby non-governmental entities – mainly corporations – may cooperate with UN agencies and agencies within specific countries to promote development goals (e.g. organizing small businesses, community development, eradicating infectious diseases). Thousands of such compacts already exist, and it is to be hoped that an increasingly enlightened economic ethos will lead to substantial expansion of this type of initiative.

Apart from the agencies just noted, field IV would contain countless altruistic individuals and philanthropic *corporate actors* whose opinions, hopes and fears merit attention. To the extent that they can make their voices heard, they will form meaningful parts of the governance system at every level from the global to the local.

A plural executive

Perhaps the most pervasive fear among those opposed to the idea of world government is that it might/would somehow come under the control of an evil autocrat, a future Hitler or Stalin. Alternatively, many believe that a world government would become an imperial state controlled by a single hegemonic power or a small cabal of relatively rich and/or militarily powerful states.[10] There is, however, no reason why either of those possibilities should come to pass, assuming the constitutional establishment of a democratic world federation with the previously presented division of powers, system of checks and balances, comprehensive bill of rights – or perhaps two such bills, one for people, the other for member states – and adherence to the doctrine of susbsidiarity in respect to legislation and administration.

There is one additional key measure that should preclude the dreaded scenarios noted above, namely the institution of a plural executive. In such a system, rather than having a single person serve as president or prime minister, there would be a democratically elected *Executive Council*. The largely honorific role of "president" would be held on a rotating basis, say for two months at a time. Though the details obviously differ, this essentially has been the system successfully employed in Switzerland under several constitutions, beginning in 1848 when, shortly after its last war (a brief civil conflict), that country converted from a confederal to a federal form of government.[11] It is a system admirably suited to a polity with entrenched social divisions based on language, religion and local historical experience. In the Swiss case it has helped prevent the ascendancy of any single group or canton and promoted internal, as well as external, peace. Applied at the global level, it would preclude the ascendancy of any single region, political bloc or nation.

How many members a global Executive Council might optimally have is debatable; and there are many possible ways by which those councillors might be chosen and function. I here offer but one set of recommendations to demonstrate that the problem of creating a plural executive is not insoluble.[12]

With regard to composition and terms of office I recommend 12 councillors, nominated by 12 regional caucuses generally conforming to the broad regional divisions of the world discussed in Chapter 4 and plotted in Figure 4.3. While every region would have an opportunity to have one of its candidates elected, several regions with relatively small populations might fail to obtain the requisite support. In such a case the most populous regions might be able to have two council members. The specific set of countries within each region could, however, vary over time. While most regions would be multinational, a few individual nations – China, India and the United States – would be sufficiently populous to be regarded as regions in their own right.[13]

Councillors would serve four-year terms. None would be allowed to serve more than two consecutive terms; and no more than six could be re-elected at the conclusion of a four-year election cycle. All councillors would cast an equal (i.e. unweighted) vote.

In the interest of democratic government, representation would be partially based on population. Merit, however, would normally determine the choice among competing candidates. Since it is improbable that an Executive Council will be created in the near future, I have used in Table 14.1 a set of projected national population data, as of the year 2050, aggregated by region, to help illustrate what I deem a fair and workable method.[14]

Nominations for council seats would be made by each of 12 regions according to methods of their own choosing, but subject to certain constraints. To fill each vacancy there must be no fewer than two nor more than nine candidates. To promote gender balance the number of candidates of either sex must be not less than one-third nor more than two-thirds the total. Thus if only two candidates were proposed they would necessarily be one male and one female. With nine candidates, at least three but no more than six would be of each sex.

Elections, possibly involving two rounds of voting, would be carried out jointly by both legislative chambers. To win a seat a candidate would have to obtain a simple majority of the *average* of the percentages of votes cast in the two legislative chambers. In the first round of voting, balloting would be sequenced in accordance with population rankings, as indicated in Table 14.1. *One* winner would then be declared for all regions with populations exceeding some agreed threshold, say 4 per cent (there would be nine such seats based on the 2050 population projections). For these seats a ranked-choice system of vote counting would be

Table 14.1 Projected 2050 populations and seat entitlements in a proposed UN Executive Council

Rank	Region	Population (millions)	% of total	Seat entitlement
1	India	1,747	18.8	1 or 2
2	Africa (excluding Arab League)	1,616	17.4	1 or 2
3	China	1,465	15.8	1 or 2
4	West Asia (excluding Arab League)	880	9.5	1
5	Southeast Asia	798	8.6	1
6	Latin America	772	8.3	1
7	Arab League	585	6.3	1
8	Europe	528	5.7	1
9	United States	420	4.5	1
10	East Asia (excluding China)	211	2.3	0 or 1
11	Russia (including five neighbouring states)	169	1.8	0 or 1
12	Westminster League	104	1.1	0 or 1
	World	9,294	100.0	12

used wherever there were more than two candidates.[15] Seats from the three regions with less than 4 per cent of the total world population would be filled only by candidates receiving more than 50 per cent of all votes on a *non*-ranked-choice ballot, thereby making election somewhat more difficult than for more populous regions.

Regions with over 12 per cent of the total world population – India, Africa (excluding the Arab League) and China – would have a chance to have two of their nominees elected. If the number of remaining vacancies after the initial round of voting were three, one seat each would automatically go to the first runner-up candidates of the regions ranked 1–3. If the number of remaining vacancies were one or two, a ranked-choice second selection process would be employed, but with candidates limited to the first runners-up of regions 1–3.

It would be in the interests of all regions to nominate meritorious candidates since, with multiple candidates, unworthy nominees would have little chance of being elected by the global legislature, Similarly, within the multinational regional caucuses it would make sense for member nations to promote the candidacy only of worthy individuals, since those lacking in merit would have little chance of selection.

Once elected, councillors would serve in an *individual* capacity, without direction from their home regions or countries in carrying out the functions noted earlier. They would take an oath to act in accordance with what they believe would best serve *the interest of the world as a whole*, and would be guaranteed immunity from sanctions by their respective national governments or regional organizations for any legal actions taken in pursuit of their executive duties.

Linkages from global to regional and lower levels

Federal systems of government are predicated on establishing a set of constitutional linkages and a division of power between central (federal) and lower-level authorities. At the global level this would work no differently in principle from federalism at the national level in countries such as Australia, Brazil, Germany, India, Nigeria, the United States or any other of the two dozen or so federations in the contemporary world. A problem arises, however, from the fact that the present number of constituent units in the United Nations, namely its 193 member nations – with the prospect of a significant increase in coming generations – is far higher than in any existing national federation.[16] The United States, which began its existence with only 13 such units, now has 50. All other federations have considerably fewer.[17] While there would be no legal impediment to a UN federation dealing effectively with 193 or more members, doing so would put considerable stress on the system's financial and personnel resources and be costly and inefficient. It would make greater sense, I believe, to act where possible through regional organizations.

Another practical problem is that the demographic, territorial and economic disparities among UN members are vastly greater than among the highest-order constituent units of individual nations. As noted in Chapter 1, the ratio of the present populations of China and Nauru is roughly 145.000:1, which is more than two orders of magnitude greater than in any national federation. The maximum ratio in India (between the states of Uttar Pradesh and Goa) is about 1,175:1 (probably greater than in any other federation). In the United States the maximum ratio (between California and Wyoming) is only 66:1.[18] Thus for a prospective world federation to adhere to the legal fiction that all member nations should be treated as if they were sovereign *equals* (sovereignty now being divided between the centre and the states) would require far greater political accommodation than in any other federation to date.

Several ways of dealing with these problems suggest themselves. One would be to redraw the world political map substantially so as to create a set of nations that would be more or less comparable in population, with differences falling, let us say, within two orders of magnitude and with all states large enough to be viable. While such a radical approach might seem appealing in the abstract, its disregard of the historical antecedents of the areas in question, their existing governmental infrastructure and citizen sentiment argue strongly against it. Also, who would wield the carving knife and by what authority?

It would not be unreasonable, however, to stipulate that membership in the world federation would be open only to states with more than some threshold[19] population (say 5 million). States with smaller populations would then choose either not to be admitted into the system or to be aggregated with one or more neighbours so as collectively to pass the population threshold. Possibly some small states would opt, for a time, to be holdouts and try to go it alone (as did four American states briefly between the adoption of the US Constitution in June 1789 and the decisive ratification – by Rhode Island – in May 1790). However, the total population of all the 85 or so states likely to have fewer than 5 million people in the late twenty-first century would only be in the order of 175–200 million, roughly 2 per cent of the world's then projected total of 9.5 billion.[20] The likelihood of the holdouts being able to function well outside the UN system would be small. But if some chose to do so, whom but themselves would they hurt?

Fortunately, there is a worldwide trend towards the development of increasingly robust regional organizations. This is particularly true of the European Union (notwithstanding occasional retrograde parochial movements). And Europe has provided models which Africa, Latin America and, arguably, the ASEAN bloc are seeking gradually to emulate. The Arab League should also be able to do so, despite little recent movement in that direction. Elsewhere regional organizations do exist, but – as in the case of SAARC and the CIS, among others – they have yet to demonstrate much political efficacy.

In addition to possible *future* unions, a number of large and important nations, including India, the United States, Pakistan, Brazil, Nigeria, Russia, Mexico, Canada and Australia, already constitute territorially vast federal states. Thus, in terms of both area and population, most of the world *already* consists of either federal polities or leagues in various stages of progress on the road to federalism. One can likely anticipate continuation of the trend towards closer regional union, driven by the same logic as was indicated by Wendt for the world as a whole.

Wherever possible, the United Nations should work through existing unions. This book has repeatedly indicated ways by which this might be accomplished. To promote efficient interaction, it would often behoove regions to establish agencies of governance mirroring some of those indicated in Figure 14.1. But working increasingly through regional organizations should not diminish UN concern for needy nations that are inadequately integrated within their respective regional organizations or located in parts of the world where such organizations are ineffective.

With respect to a division of labour between the United Nations and lower tiers of government, one may anticipate that it will take many years – perhaps generations – before the United Nations can provide all the centralized services presently performed by most stable democratic federations. What the central institutions can and should promote would, minimally, include enhanced respect for the rule of law, increasingly democratic and transparent decision-making, major advances in promoting human rights, effective agencies for peacekeeping and peacemaking, better models for economic and social development, a deeper sense of stewardship for our common planetary heritage and greater allegiance to the whole of humanity.

In working towards these ends, the United Nations would interact mainly with regional organizations and established national governments. It would differ from existing federations in having relatively little contact with individual citizens. Its revenues would come mainly from assessments levied on member nations (including regional federations) and voluntary contributions from public and private actors. But other sources of funding (discussed in Chapter 11) would be utilized. However, it is hard to imagine in the foreseeable future imposing a global system of taxation of individual – or even corporate – income, of real estate or of inheritances. And even in a federated United Nations, responsibility for promoting the general welfare of citizens would remain primarily in the hands of national and lower-level governments. A UN Bill of Rights for *Nations* should be drafted to stipulate limits for the UN's fiscal powers *vis-à-vis* member nations and specify domains of governance into which the United Nations may not enter (unless specifically invited by states to do so).

Conclusion

While not predetermined, our future will largely be of our own devising. However, human capacity for serious error and unforeseeable environmental events are such that they can undermine functioning political systems and frustrate the designs of would-be reformers. Thus, despite my personal preferences, I cannot agree with those who assume that a world government is historically inevitable. On the other hand, I firmly believe that a democratic, federal world government with a built-in constitutional system of checks and balances provides the best of the many conceivable future ways of governing our increasingly interconnected world. Given the existential environmental threats confronting our society, as well as long-recognized threats from our presently anarchic "war system", we must now plan for and seek to create an essentially new global political order as quickly as possible, perhaps even within the next generation.

Building on analyses and recommendations in Chapters 2–13, this chapter proposes numerous new institutions that a reformed system of global government will need to strengthen or establish, and indicates the functions they will have to undertake. It bears repeating, however, that the schema described here is open to debate. The proposals put forward form but one workable system among a virtually limitless set of possibilities.

Notes

1. For Einstein's views on world government, see Otto Nathan and Heinz Norden (eds), *Einstein on Peace*, New York: Schocken, 1960, especially pp. 400–508. A thorough and persuasive case for democratic, federal world government is Ronald Glossop, *World Federation? A Critical Analysis of Federal World Government,* Jefferson, NC, and London: McFarland & Company, 1993. An excellent two-volume history of the world government movement is provided by Joseph P. Baratta, *The Politics of World Federalism,* Westport, CT: Praeger, 2004. Also very useful is Joseph P. Baratta, *Strengthening the United Nations: A Bibliography on U.N. Reform and World Federalism,* New York: Greenwood, 1987. Numerous constitutional proposals for world government have been published, of which several are noted elsewhere in this work.
2. Alexander Wendt, "Why a World State Is Inevitable", *European Journal of International Relations* 9(4), 2003, pp. 491–541. See also Vaughan P. Shannon, "Wendt's Violation of

the Constructivist Project: Agency and Why a World State Is *Not* Inevitable", *European Journal of International Relations* 11(4), 2005, pp. 581–587; Alexander Wendt, "Agency, Teleology and the World State: A Reply to Shannon", *European Journal of International Relations* 11(4), 2005, pp. 589–598. For additional statements on the presumed inevitability of world government see Glossop, note 1 above, p. viii. Evidence of a shift in scholarly discourse towards the belief that global government is in fact possible, even if not inevitable, is provided by John E. Trent, "Once Again the Spotlight Focuses on the Idea of World Government", *Minerva* 38, April 2011, pp. 36–41, a review essay on important papers by Campbell Craig, Catherine Lu and Thomas Weiss. Thomas Weiss, "What Happened to the Idea of World Government?", *International Relations Quarterly* 53, 2009, pp. 254–271 is an excellent summary of recent thinking on the issue.

3. Wendt (2003), ibid., fn. 34. p. 532.
4. Ibid.
5. Ibid., pp. 491–492.
6. Supporting evidence in ecological literature is voluminous. For a good summary in layman's language see Lester R. Brown, *Plan B 3.0: Mobilizing to Save Civilization*, New York and London: W. W. Norton & Company, c. 2008.
7. The inspiration for this diagram came from Mathias Koenig-Archibugi, "Mapping Global Governance", in David Held and Anthony McGrew (eds), *Governing Globalization: Power, Authority and Global Governance*, Cambridge: Polity, 2002, pp. 46–69, especially Figure 2.3. My layout of fields of action, however, differs substantially from that of Koenig-Archibugi. Additionally, his schema relates to the present, whereas Figure 14.1 is for some indeterminate future period. Finally, Koenig-Archibugi includes many more agencies than those indicated in this work and does not differentiate among agencies regarding whether the decision-makers are regions and/or states as opposed to individuals.
8. Koenig-Archibugi, ibid., indicates an innermost field of "Main UN organs", a surrounding field of "UN programmes", a peripheral field of "UN specialized agencies" and an external field "outside the UN system". The second and third of these, taken together, are essentially the equivalent of field III of Figure 14.1.
9. For an extensive analysis of the problem see Morrison Bonpasse, *The Single Global Currency, Common Cents for the World*, Newcastle, ME: Single Global Currency Association, 2006. The association's web homepage quotes no less a figure than Paul Volcker, former chair of the US Federal Reserve, as follows: "A global economy requires a global currency." In contrast to those who envisage a common global currency as a medium of economic exchange comparable to the euro in Europe are those who, like former World Bank chief economist and Nobel Laureate Joseph Stiglitz (and before him John Maynard Keynes), advocate creation of a world common *reserve* currency pegged to a basket of leading national currencies, rather than to the US dollar. For an overview of needed global financial reforms see Alfonso Iozzo and Antonio Mosconi, "The Foundation of a Cooperative Global Financial System: A New Bretton Woods to Confront the Crisis of the International Role of the US Dollar", *The Federalist Debate* 19(2), 2006, pp. 6–10.
10. While I know of no published statistics to substantiate these claims, they are based on the reactions of audiences to scores of talks on world government that I have presented over a period of more than half a century.
11. Edgar Bonjour, H. S. Offler and G. R. Potter, *A Short History of Switzerland*, Oxford: Clarendon Press, 1952, pp. 257–301.
12. For alternative recommendations relative to a plural executive see Glossop, note 1 above, p. 159.
13. Should Europe federate, it would qualify for a single-nation seat. So too might Africa south of the Sahara or Latin America should they become unified federal states.

14. "2007 World Population Data Sheet", Population Reference Bureau, Washington, DC, 2007.
15. In such a system the *second*-place votes of the candidate with the lowest *first*-place total would be transferred to the remaining candidates. This process would be repeated for the successively lowest-ranking remaining candidates until such time as one had garnered at least 50 per cent.
16. Factors that would contribute to an increase include continuation of the decolonization process, which alone could add dozens of new UN members, as well as successful secessionist struggles, especially in Africa, which could lead to scores of additional states. On the other hand, absorption of nations into new federations in Europe, Africa or other regions could greatly reduce UN membership. Which trend will prove more influential is uncertain.
17. For example, excluding specially administered territories, Australia has 6 second-order units, Brazil 26, Canada 10, Germany 16, India 28, Nigeria 36, Pakistan 4 and Russia 19. Figures are derived from *Encyclopaedia Britannica 2011 Book of the Year*, Chicago, IL: Encyclopaedia Britannica, 2011, individual country entries.
18. When the US Constitution was adopted the ratio between the most and least populous states, Virginia and Delaware respectively, was roughly 12:1. Carl Van Doren, *The Great Rehearsal: The Story of the Making and Ratifying of the Constitution of the United States*, New York: Viking Press, 1948, pp. 216–238.
19. "2010 World Population Data Sheet", Population Reference Bureau, Washington, DC, 2010.
20. These numbers are based on a set of rough calculations by the author.

15

Getting there

The world is my country, all mankind are my brethren, and to do good is my religion.
Thomas Paine

Nothing is as powerful as an idea whose time has come.
Victor Hugo

It is not because it is difficult that we are afraid to act; it is because we are afraid to act that it is difficult.
Seneca

Where there's a will, there's a way.
Old English proverb

Introduction

In Chapter 14 I observed that our future is not pre-ordained. While no one is in complete control of her/his destiny, our individual and collective actions do matter and are often decisive in determining whether or not we reach our goals. But political goals that are not widely shared are seldom reached. In regard to our planetary society, it cannot yet be said that there is broad agreement as to where we ought to be going, much less on how to proceed. Although we do largely agree in desiring freedom from the scourges of war, terrorism, poverty and eco-catastrophe, there is still

Transforming the United Nations system: Designs for a workable world, Schwartzberg, United Nations University Press, 2013, ISBN 978-92-808-1230-5

little commitment to *working* for those causes. A widely shared sense of urgency is lacking. Thus we drift ever closer to collective disaster. This can and must be reversed. We must muster the requisite *will, wisdom* and *cooperative spirit* to do so. And we must do so *soon*.

Many approaches are possible. Some will yield greater dividends than others; but all promising peaceful tactics should be utilized. A well-integrated, broadly based and sustained strategy is needed. Civil society networks will have to assume a major role. So, too, will forward-looking national governments and regional organizations from the global North and South. Good leadership will be of the utmost importance.

Chapter 14 set forth a vision for a constitutionally based, democratic, federal world government. While I am convinced that such a workable and economically affordable government *could* be established by the year 2050, I do not suppose that a majority of my readers would presently accept my radical views. This does not mean, however, that advocates of major transformation of the UN system cannot work cooperatively for fundamental change. Those with visions of the future less far-reaching than my own can still cooperate on achieving needed initial goals. And with even modest successes, activists will be inclined to work to attain additional goals previously considered beyond reach.

In this chapter, the following aspects of a multipronged, long-term strategy for change will be considered.

- Improving the domestic political and economic climate to facilitate working for reform.
- Establishing a system of global education and encouraging development of a cosmopolitan ethos.
- Creating effective civil society networks dedicated to promoting fundamental change.
- Effecting key changes in the present UN system, especially in decision-making and funding, to promote confidence that additional changes are indeed attainable.
- Forging strategic alliances between civil society and progressive UN member nations and/or regional organizations committed to transforming the UN system.

I conclude with a note of hope for building a workable world.

Improving the domestic climate for change

Despite repeated lofty pronouncements about the importance of the United Nations, most member states do little to back up their rhetoric with support for Charter reform or major increases in the organization's budget. Additionally, since the UN's decisions – those of the SC excepted – are not binding, they are often ignored with impunity. State sovereignty is safeguarded and most of the myriad problems remain unresolved.

Increasingly, when action on pressing global issues is deemed necessary by major global powers, they bypass the United Nations and work instead through the undemocratic Bretton Woods institutions or the self-selected G-8 or G-20, which better reflect the real distribution of power in the world than does the one-nation-one-vote system followed by the United Nations since its inception. The accusation that the United Nations has become irrelevant no longer seems as unwarranted as the organization's supporters assert. Most medium and small powers are also guilty of excessive zeal in protecting their sovereignty and of putting their parochial interests ahead of those of the global community. Political considerations persistently trump morality in formulating UN policy. Thus in most countries it is difficult to maintain effective civil society constituencies in support of the UN system.

It is widely asserted that without US support serious UN reform will not be possible. While that may now be true, it does not follow that support unthinkable today might not become acceptable a decade hence. Sea changes in public sentiment do occur. Nor does it follow that support for reform must *begin* with the US government. Rather, in light of recent history and the increasingly widespread perception of the United States as a predatory imperial power, a case can be made that reform initiatives emanating from the US State Department, even if well intentioned, might – in the near term – do more harm than good.

In any event, the State Department is one thing and American civil society quite another. The latter has enormous, though still little realized, potential to influence global thinking and advocacy. On the one hand civil society can bring pressure on government to curb its propensity for unilateral interventions and its tendency to address problems by means of military force. On the other it can promote a longer-term agenda of reforming aspects of the American governance system that foster a regressive foreign policy. Some specifics are suggested below.

Perhaps the most pernicious aspect of contemporary US governance is the influence exerted by powerful corporations, especially those associated with what President Eisenhower presciently described as the "military-industrial complex".[1] Corporate financial contributions – now without legal limits – to the electoral campaigns of candidates for both houses of Congress have become scandalously influential.[2] So too have political lobbies, many employing retired generals, admirals and legislators. The resultant web of defence-related industries and military bases in all 50 states (mainly in those with a strong conservative base) makes it difficult for members of Congress to support diplomatic – rather than militaristic

– responses to political problems around the world that supposedly might threaten American overseas interests.[3]

More generally, the belief that an empowered United Nations might constrain the freedom of action of US firms outside the legal limits of the United States may lead corporations to oppose UN reform. For example, conventional energy industries (coal, petroleum and natural gas) are leery of international regulation to mitigate climate change; their influence was largely responsible for the US refusal to accept the Kyoto Protocol limiting CO_2 emissions. Additionally, US military and financial support for corrupt dictatorships in oil-rich countries perpetuates regimes opposed to political reform. This calls into question America's professed concern for human rights and democratic governance.

The mass media are increasingly complicit in supporting the inordinate power of corporations in US politics.[4] They depend on advertising to stay in business, and the implicit threat of losing advertising revenue from corporate giants leads to circumspection, if not to utter silence, in coverage of dubious corporate behaviour. The media have increasingly become dispensers of vacuous "infotainment", either for its own sake or in the guise of news. Some – generally small – independent outlets do survive, however, and new independent internet bloggers brighten the media landscape. Indeed, the internet has become a major change agent. Evidence of its political potential is provided by the dramatic events of the so-called "Arab Spring".

Aspects of the US electoral system favour federal and state governments with conservative agendas that do not reflect the views on the United Nations held by a majority of voters.[5] The first-past-the-post system for choosing winners in US elections reinforces a two-party system in which candidates from both major parties gravitate towards the political centre as campaigns unfold, hoping to win the support of uncommitted voters. What often results is political apathy, with many voters concluding that there are no meaningful differences between Democrats and Republicans. Thus voter turnout is low in comparison to other democracies. The system inhibits support for bold initiatives in both domestic and foreign affairs. A reformed system of instant run-off (ranked-choice) voting or, alternatively, proportional representation would enable additional parties to enter the political arena with some hope of success and lead to a more nuanced range of choices.[6] Proportional representation with multiseat electoral districts would also preclude the mainly conservative gerrymandering of legislative districts.

The distribution of powers in the US Congress further favours a conservative perspective. The Senate, which tends to be slightly more conservative than the House of Representatives, is responsible for ratifying treaties (by a two-thirds majority, which is seldom easy to obtain) and approving ambassadorial appointments and nominees to cabinet positions. Its conservative bias stems largely from America's demographic make-up. All 50 states, irrespective of population, have two senators. But most of the 33 states with below-average populations are relatively rural and have proportionally fewer foreign-born, non-anglophone citizens among their population. In appealing for votes in these states, aspirants for Senate seats characteristically promote conservative, inward-looking "American" values and eschew internationalist positions. This is unlikely to change without a substantial shift in the world-view of the US electorate.

Finally, the decentralized American educational system is, on the whole, remarkably cautious in advancing an international agenda, especially at pre-collegiate levels. A Congressional proposal to establish a US Department of Peace (USDP) might, if implemented, do much to ameliorate this situation. Introduced in 2001, the bill has since been put forward every two years, and has had scores of co-sponsors (72 in 2011) and abundant support from civil society. The USDP would address issues such as violence prevention, conflict resolution and mediation in schools; peacemaking among conflicting cultures; monitoring domestic arms production; promotion of international dialogue; establishment of a US Peace Academy (to train personnel for peacekeeping missions); monitoring human rights observance; expansion of the Sister City programme; and establishing a national "Peace Day". The department would be headed by a cabinet-level secretary of peace, who would serve on the National Security Council, and have a budget not less than 1 per cent of the national discretionary budget.[7]

I have focused on the United States because of its unrivalled influence in world affairs. But other important countries have their own equivalents of the military-industrial complex and are also excessively influenced by jingoistic and xenophobic sentiment. Although political and economic impediments to UN reform differ from nation to nation, citizen action – especially through civil society organizations – can do much to smooth the path. This is increasingly true in an electronically interconnected world. Whether or not a critical mass of civil society eventually supports reform initiatives will depend largely on the educational and cultural milieux shaping its world-view. I turn now to consideration of that matter.

Global education and the promotion of a cosmopolitan ethos

A virtually universal objective of public educational systems is promoting loyalty to the state. In school assemblies and public gatherings it is customary to sing the national anthem, pledge allegiance to the nation's flag, honour those who have died in the nation's wars and express reverence for the iconic places and events that help define the nation and its people. Within limits, this is laudable. It gives students and adult citizens a feeling of belonging and imbues in them a sense of duty to promote the nation's welfare. There is, however, danger that patriotism can become excessive. When it does, it often leads to the stifling of dissent and accusations that dissenters are lacking in patriotism, if not outright traitors. Such chauvinism can threaten international peace.

But let us assume that the patriotic acculturation of students remains essentially benign. Would that preclude a sense of allegiance to something even more inclusive than one's own nation? Might not students also recognize their membership in a larger community comprising the entire human family? Might they not then regard the earth as that family's shared home? Would that not increase their willingness to act for the common good of all human beings? Finally, would that not facilitate the establishment of a political climate conducive to UN reform?

Many of the foregoing considerations were put forward in 1975 by a former US ambassador to Japan, the historian Edwin O. Reischauer, in *Towards the 21st Century, Education for a Changing World.* Reischauer argued the necessity of educating youth, beginning as early as kindergarten, to think like global citizens.[8] His conclusions should be even more persuasive in today's tightly interconnected world than when they were initially advanced.

In 1976, with Reischauer's admonition in mind, I composed a creed that I have sought to live by ever since. I subsequently modified the text slightly on several occasions, and present the current version below.

An Affirmation of Human Oneness

I am a member of the human family, a citizen of the world.
The achievements of men and women throughout the ages are my heritage.
My destiny is bound to that of all my fellow human beings.
What we jointly create forms our bequest to future generations.
May my life serve the good of my family.
May our use of the earth preserve it for those yet to come.

My intention was that the affirmation would be used not only in school assemblies to supplement more narrowly nationalistic observations but also in civic gatherings, including church services, public observances on national holidays and other fitting occasions such as Earth Day (22 April), UN Day (24 October) and Human Rights Day (10 December).

This wish has been fulfilled to a modest degree in my home state, Minnesota; but I dare hope that the affirmation – or some comparable statement – will eventually gain worldwide acceptance. Towards that end, I have had the affirmation translated into 44 languages in addition to English.[9] I would estimate that at least one of these 45 languages is spoken as either the mother tongue or an ancillary language by at least 95 per cent of all people living today.

The discussion to this point has dealt largely with *values*. But education relates to *substantive knowledge* as well. It is important that youth be made more aware of how the world works; of the unconscionable economic disparities between the global North and South and the reasons why those disparities persist; of the history, geography and culture not only of their own country but of other parts of the world; and of existential environmental threats such as global warming. They must be made aware of the enormous cost and inherent shortcomings of the "war system". They need to know more about the workings of government from the local level up, and gain a basic understanding of how the United Nations functions. They must become more sophisticated critical thinkers so as not to become unwitting believers in the propaganda of self-serving political actors or the slick flim-flam of many big corporations. And – returning to values and attitudes – they must learn how to get along with one another respectfully and cooperatively. While this is all more easily said than done, the task is not beyond our capability. Institutions along the lines of the previously discussed USDP could help greatly in the endeavour. Schools, religious organizations, think-tanks and other components of civil society must all play a role. Happily, some excellent beginnings have been made.[10]

Education ought not end with the granting of a diploma or the conferring of a terminal degree, but should be a lifelong enterprise. Over much of the world, even in times of economic stagnation or depression, tens of millions of citizens can now avail themselves of opportunities for continued learning scarcely conceivable only a generation ago: through free online college courses, in community centres, libraries, museums, clubs, informal learning programmes, Great Decisions discussion groups, elderhostels and so forth. Much of this learning will have an international dimension.

Programmes such as the US Peace Corps, Service Civil International, UN Volunteers (discussed in Chapter 12), Rotary International (among other fraternal organizations), sister city partnerships and university-sponsored, service-oriented foreign internships also provide vehicles for enhancing international understanding, establishing meaningful contacts and bonds of affection between programme participants and other citizens over much of the world. Also valuable are study-abroad programmes focusing on language and culture, especially those entailing reciprocal exchanges and periods of residence with host families.

International tourism, which accounted for 922 million country-arrivals in 2008 and generated nearly a trillion dollars in revenue, also breaks down parochialism.[11] While much foreign travel is solely for relaxation and pleasure, a rapidly growing proportion is devoted to alternative ends such as ecotourism, focused learning programmes (relating, for example, to cooking, music, art or urban planning), low-budget backpacking and service tours (often sponsored by churches or NGOs). Brief though such tours usually are, they expand the traveller's horizons and contribute to better appreciation of what is worthwhile in cultures different from one's own and deeper, lifelong understanding of problems faced by the peoples of countries visited. Visits to UNESCO-certified natural and cultural heritage sites are especially recommended.

Even for stay-at-homes, the world is drawing closer together. Foreign cuisine, clothing styles, music, movies and literature form increasingly large components of our patterns of consumption. So too do foreign manufactures, especially in the automotive, electronics and apparel industries. Sporting events occasionally attract international TV audiences in the hundreds of millions. Finally, we may note the rapid dissemination of relatively new faiths stressing human community, for example the Baha'i religion (founded in the late nineteenth century), one of whose tenets is advocacy of world government, or the Soka Gakkai, an offshoot of Japanese Nichiren Buddhism (dating only from the mid-twentieth century).

The activities and trends noted above are powerful change agents. While they do not form part of any master plan to unify the world, they collectively foster a social and political climate conducive to changing our system of global governance. In short, our expanding horizons are making the world much more cosmopolitan than it was when the United Nations was established. That ever-increasing numbers of the world's people should now think of themselves as world citizens is hardly surprising.

Nor is it surprising that political commentators should now resurrect old truths and espouse cosmopolitanism as a needed political ethos: John Donne's observation that "No man is an island, entire of itself" and each of us is "a part of the main";[12] Thomas Paine's declaration that "The world is my country, all mankind are my brethren";[13] and Immanuel Kant's conclusion that "All men who have a mutual influence over one another ought to have a civil constitution."[14] To many observers, such declarations no longer appear to be flights of utopian fancy. The roster of scholars taking a cosmopolitan position and the body of literature they have generated within recent decades are truly remarkable.[15]

Establishing effective civil society networks

Although it is easy to agree in principle that major changes in the system of global governance are necessary, it is not immediately apparent who should assume the lead responsibility for so huge an undertaking. That question provides a *leitmotif* for a detailed and trenchant study of *how* to achieve UN reform – as opposed to *what* reforms are needed – by the Canadian political scientist John E. Trent.[16] In seeking an answer, Trent proceeds by a process of elimination. He demonstrates successively why significant initiatives will not come from the great powers; nor from other UN members, which for now wish to do nothing that might threaten their sovereignty; nor from the sclerotic UN Secretariat; nor from the corporate world, whose motives would be suspect; nor from the academic community, who by and large have little practical political experience (they can "be of the game," Trent opines, "But they cannot be the game"); nor, finally, from foundations, which do much good work but "do not have a mandate to spearhead political action" and tend to be too closely identified with affluent Western interests.[17] What remains, as the best candidates, Trent concludes, are NGOs and – especially – INGOs. Trent quotes the Hungarian economist Mihaly Simai, an old UN hand, as follows:

> NGOs are increasingly needed as forces of independent and innovative political thinking and as champions of pluralism and democracy. The future vitality of international multilateralism depends on NGOs continuing to place critical issues on the global agenda and mobilizing national publics to ensure that collective action is taken and programs implemented.[18]

On the whole I concur with Trent's conclusion, though I am more sanguine in respect to potential contributions from academics and foundations.

As documented in Chapter 10, civil society has expanded in recent decades to a mind-boggling extent and continues to grow exponentially. More than a million NGOs and well above 250,000 INGOs already exist. Of these, well over 3,000 enjoy consultative status with ECOSOC. But if so fragmented a group of organizations are to become effective change agents, they must establish efficient and sustainable networks and coalitions. This will not be easy. Recent improvements in telecommunications

and transportation technology, however, make the task much more do-
able today than previously.

Among existing coalitions of civil society organizations, three merit
special notice: Parliamentarians for Global Action (www.pgaction.org)
and the World Federalist Movement (www.wfm.org), both with headquarters in New York and The Hague, and the World Federation of
United Nations Associations (www.wfuna.org), with headquarters in New
York and Geneva, are particularly well connected for assuming positions
of leadership.[19]

Trent provides several reasons why civil society leaders are well suited
to be change agents:

> First, while politicians are generally activated by power and executives by
> profit, association leaders normally are motivated by doing good. Second, over
> time, they have become highly knowledgeable in their international field of in-
> terest. They not only have a deep understanding of their special domain, say
> the environment or human rights, but they also develop expertise in operating
> within the international system. Third, while NGOs must learn to deal with
> "real politick," [sic] they must also be responsible to their very morally ori-
> ented members. Thus, as leaders, they are not foreign to the use of power and
> profit . . .[20]

But there are potential dangers to reliance on NGOs. First, when many
organizations focus on a given problem, there is likely to be harmful conflict and disorder, "anarchy rather than accommodation". Second, "interest groups tend to be inherently undemocratic in their internal working",
granting excessive power to "elites" within the group, in which case accommodation could lead to oligopoly, clientism, patronage and/or greater
inequality among groups. Third, there is a danger that coalitions will
coopt "loonies", paranoids and unrepresentative, unaccountable, self-
aggrandizing entities. Fourth, there is the parallel danger of NGOs allowing themselves to be coopted by governments in their quest for
recognition. Fifth, getting many organizations to agree on a common
front may create an impression of amorphousness in the international
community. Finally, the dominance of relatively wealthy Western/Northern
NGOs in virtually all fields impedes the generation of mutual trust among
advocates of change.[21]

Many of the problems alluded to above would be substantially mitigated if the world were able to establish the system of UN-linked civil
society coordination councils discussed in Chapter 10 and illustrated in
Figures 10.1 and 14.1. The proposed councils would institutionalize, regu-
larize and legitimize contacts between NGOs and key components of the
UN system and make civil society as a whole more open, transparent,

representative, accountable and predictable. In particular it would minimize the East-West/North-South gap among NGOs and INGOs. But even
if the recommended CSCCs were in place, that would not preclude NGOs
from acting independently, either alone or in strategic alliances, when and
if they so wished. If agencies within the UN system were to deny the
CSCCs a respectful hearing, civil society would then be altogether justified in making its case before the bar of global public opinion.

Effecting catalytic changes in the UN system

Whether coming about as a result of civil society activism or through
some combination of methods, several key reforms of the present UN
system appear especially likely to become catalysts for additional change.
In my judgement, those catalysts are in the domains of funding, decision-
making and peacekeeping. Let us consider them in that order.

In many contexts throughout this work I have noted the pitiful inadequacy of funding for complex tasks the UN system is called upon to
address. For the United Nations to be blamed for its inability to deal effectively with problems is both unfair and unwarranted. Much of the fault
lies not with the organization but, as discussed, with its parsimonious
members, especially those of the global North.

Additionally, the problem derives from a revenue assessment system
that is excessively fragmented, complex and arbitrary. The proposal put
forward in Chapter 11 for a uniformly applied system wherein all countries were assessed an equal, but very low, percentage of their GNI – say
a mere 0.1 per cent initially – could yield revenues at least twice as great
as the total for the entire UN system (excluding the Bretton Woods agencies), eliminate reliance on undependable and earmarked voluntary contributions, and yet leave a substantial remainder for an escrow fund for
addressing unforeseeable security threats and other emergencies. This
change would greatly strengthen numerous agencies within the UN
system and could yield sufficient benefits to galvanize the UN reform
movement.

Changes that would alter the decision-making system of major UN
agencies, replacing the present one-nation-one-vote rule with weighted
voting according to uniformly applied, objective mathematical formulae,
are more problematic in that some would require Charter amendment.
(Paradoxically, the creation of a WPA under the aegis of the GA would
be allowable under Article 22.) Nevertheless, the world must, before long,
recognize the necessity of enabling the GA to make *binding decisions*.
But the only circumstances under which major powers would agree to
this would be to adopt a weighted voting system in which voting weights

more closely reflected the actual distribution of power in the world outside the United Nations itself. Giving the United Nations the legal ability to deal effectively with serious global problems through binding legislation would complement the proposed increase in financial resources in making the organization an effective catalyst for vitally needed change.

With respect to the presently unfair, anachronistic and all-too-often ineffective Security Council, making that body universally inclusive, with weighted *regional* voting and no single-nation veto, as discussed in Chapter 4, would go far in generating respect for the body and enhancing its effectiveness. This, too, would surely strengthen the UN-reform constituency.

With regard to peacekeeping, the spotty record of SC-mandated missions provides powerful reasons to establish a robust, standing, all-volunteer, elite peace force under direct UN command, as discussed in Chapter 11. Lacking such an agency, powerful nations or coalitions – especially the United States and/or NATO – are often employed, without UN authorization, to fill the breach. Alternatively, as in the 2011 Libyan civil war, such coalitions might undertake actions that go well beyond what the SC actually called for. Thus despite widespread and understandable reluctance to institute a reform that might infringe upon the sovereignty of many strife-torn states, the time has arrived to provide the United Nations with a rapid-response capability and much better prospects for success; in short, with a standing and robust UN Peace Corps.

Additionally, future peacekeeping missions should incorporate expert civilian assistance from a culturally diverse, rapidly deployable UN Administrative Reserve Corps. Major successes brought about by a thoroughly reformed peacekeeping system would do much to promote support for UN reform, especially if the reforms were to lead to a substantial peace dividend in the form of lowered taxes for national military establishments.

Although only a few key areas for reform are touched on here, any successful measure will stimulate demand for further change. Whether this will eventually lead to a cascade of reform initiatives remains to be seen.

Forging strategic alliances

Civil society coalitions and networks can set the UN reform train in motion; but they cannot make it reach their desired destination alone. Sooner or later progressive states must get aboard. Fortunately, in much of the world – North and South, East and West – there exist responsible small and medium-sized states whose international record and policies are highly regarded. The Nordic nations, Canada, Costa Rica, Uruguay,

Senegal, Singapore and New Zealand are among those that come to mind. These trusted states are well led, do not aspire to become major powers and are not feared by their regional neighbours. Other such nations will undoubtedly emerge. While collectively they will not command a large share of GA votes or SC representation, they may make up in moral authority what they lack in voting power. The power of ideas still matters.

Endorsement of reform initiatives by regional organizations, which do not have the same concerns about sovereignty as their individual members, may also play a major role. Presently, the European Union is in the forefront in devising new modes of supranational cooperation. Any global initiatives that it chooses to back benefit appreciably from EU support. Latin America and the African Union are endeavouring to establish organizational reforms similar to those achieved in Europe. The Southeast Asia Treaty Organization (SEATO), too, is on a reform trajectory. Support for UN reform by any of these regions – and others as well – will become increasingly important.

Global governance reforms can come about in several ways. Within the United Nations itself, some reforms (e.g. of the budget) would require no more than a two-thirds vote in the GA. Further, since the GA has the authority (under Article 22 of the UN Charter) to "establish such subsidiary organs as it deems necessary for the performance of its functions", it could even create a WPA or other key governance agencies if it wished. The WPA in particular might energize the presently somnolent global community.

Charter amendments can come about in two ways. Article 108 – the only way thus far employed – stipulates that an amendment will require approval by a vote of two-thirds of member nations and subsequent ratification by two-thirds of member nations, including all five permanent members of the SC "in accordance with their respective constitutional processes". This is not an easy process. To date only two amendments have been ratified. The first enlarged the SC and ECOSOC in 1965 (two years after passage in the GA). The second, in 1973, further enlarged ECOSOC. This, admittedly, does not augur well for the sweeping changes advocated in this work. But a few key changes could set a more ambitious reform process in motion, especially if they were regarded as resulting in significant successes.

The second way by which Charter reform can come about is prescribed in Article 109, which stipulates that "A General Conference of the Members of the UN for the purposes of reviewing the present Charter may be held at a date and place to be fixed by a two-thirds vote of the Members of the General Assembly and by a vote of any nine members of the Security Council." It states, further: "Any alteration of the present Charter recommended by a two-thirds vote of the conference shall take effect when ratified in accordance with their respective constitutional processes by two-thirds of the Members of the UN including all five permanent members of the Security Council."

Thus while there can be no veto of a decision to hold a Charter review conference, the veto would apply to whatever the conference agreed to. While this may appear to present an insuperable obstacle to change, assuming a review conference were actually held, there are grounds to believe otherwise. When the idea of expanding the SC was first put forward and approved by a 97-11-4 vote in the GA, four of the P-5 opposed it. Only China (i.e. the then rump Nationalist regime in Taiwan) was amenable to change. But once the process was set in motion, the Soviet Union was the first of the P-5 to ratify the GA's decision. It assumed at the time continued opposition from the United States and sought with its vote to curry favour among the expanding number of developing member nations. China, France and the United Kingdom soon followed suit. And it was not long thereafter before the Johnson administration in Washington decided against the United States being the odd man out and that a council of 15 members would not be such a bad idea after all.[22]

Although one cannot take decisions made in the context of the Cold War as precedents for what might transpire a decade or so hence, these events do indicate that even great powers are loath to ignore global opinion. That will undoubtedly remain true in the future. If, then, the United States chooses to flout the wishes of the vast majority of the world's states and peoples, one may reasonably assume that China or some other rising power such as India or Brazil will seek to play the needed leadership role.

Around the world, increasing numbers of activists now demand a more just global order. More and more are calling attention to a broad range of existential threats to life on our planet, including the insupportably high costs of maintaining our anarchic "war system". Civil society organizations, think-tanks, foundations, individual academics, wealthy and influential individuals and even some national governments are demonstrating increasing interest in systemic reform.

Further, the number of individuals who have given *more than a billion dollars* each to charities or foundations has risen dramatically in the past few years; as of mid-2011 there were 19. Leading the list, with contributions totalling $28 billion, was Microsoft founder Bill Gates. Other well-known names include runner-up Warren Buffett ($8 billion), George Soros and Ted Turner. Additionally, 69 of America's wealthiest individuals have pledged to give away a majority of their wealth to charity. Non-American philanthropists include the Indian business tycoon Azim Premji, founder of the global information technology firm WIPRO, and the world's richest man, Mexican telecommunications magnate Carlos Slim (with donations of $4 billion each).[23]

It is arguably only a matter of time before a multitude of actors coalesce into a powerful global governance reform movement. Whether that movement will bring about an Article 109 UN reform conference or choose some other route remains to be seen. But the Article 109 route is not really necessary. If enough powerful actors so decide, a *completely new beginning* may prove to be the preferred avenue for change. And there is much to be said for a completely new approach, given the many inadequacies of the existing Charter.

Whichever reform strategy eventually prevails, it will likely come in the wake of some major global catastrophe, as was the case for the League of Nations and the United Nations following the First and Second World Wars respectively. Given the destructive power of modern weapons systems, it seems improbable that any political leader will be foolish enough to embark deliberately upon a third world war, though war by accidental misinterpretation of the security environment cannot be ruled out. More likely, in light of recent experience, would be a terrorist attack on a scale even greater than that of 9/11 2001.

There is no shortage of additional horrendous scenarios, mainly in the ecological domain. The most likely would result from global warming. All over the world mountain glaciers are melting at alarming rates, as are Arctic and Antarctic ice-caps and sea ice. While melting ice at high latitudes is particularly dramatic (giving rise, for example, to an iceberg four times the size of Manhattan breaking away from Greenland in 2010),[24] the likelihood of large-scale catastrophe from the disappearance of mountain glaciers is more immediate. In particular, the glaciers of the Himalayan and Karakoram mountain ranges are major sources of water for many hundreds of millions of people in India, Pakistan, Bangladesh, Nepal and China. By the time they vanish, not many generations hence, the amount of water available to farmers and urban dwellers in the already water-short plains of South and East Asia will have been dramatically reduced. Prolonged drought and severe food scarcity will ensue, as will political unrest. Whether growth of the Chinese and Indian economies can then continue is problematic.

A possibly greater threat, though on a longer time scale, is rising sea levels due to the melting of high-latitude ice-caps. Estimates on rates of change vary, but recent dramatic increases in melting rates are a major cause for concern given the expectation that climatic feedback loops, once certain atmospheric thresholds are passed, might accelerate the change process.[25] The threat to broad, exceedingly flat and densely settled deltaic regions, especially in Bangladesh, adjacent regions of India and the Hwang Ho and Yangtze Deltas of China, is enormous and would give rise to refugee flows in the tens of millions. The ensuing social unrest and international tension may well prove to be unmanageable.

While the less dense coastal populations of wealthy countries are unlikely to experience disruptions on the scale indicated for Asia, they will hardly be immune from the economic impact of rising sea levels. Merely maintaining port facilities will impose a tremendous financial burden, and in locales below sea level, including substantial areas in Louisiana and the Netherlands, the risks – and insurance costs – will be commensurately greater.

Dozens of small island states will also be severely affected. Two that could disappear altogether are the Republic of Maldives, whose highest elevation barely exceeds two metres, and Nauru, where phosphate mining is destroying the environment even in the absence of rising seas. Imagine the dramatic effect of a video showing the last boatload of Maldivians leaving their vanishing atoll homes for a new life in Sri Lanka, Australia or whatever other country will accept them. And what would then become of their UN seat?

With or without climate change, population growth, combined with increasing levels of consumption among the economically well endowed, will also lead to periodic crises and civil unrest. Resource wars, especially in regard to dwindling supplies of petroleum, pose an increasing threat. Although the world's population will almost certainly stabilize in the next half-century or so, that will not suffice to safeguard vast areas subject to chronic economic stress.

The foregoing account touches on only a handful of obvious threats to civilization. A comprehensive account would greatly extend this chapter. But even this broad sketch should make it apparent that failure to plan for dangers ahead will exact a high price. Among other effects, it will contribute to the rise of revolutionary movements (such as the already serious Naxalite/Maoist movement over much of India), mafia-like criminal syndicates and terrorist networks. Many of these will operate transnationally. Countries will have no alternative but to deal collectively with such groups and the political and environmental factors that helped create them. This will require a greatly strengthened system of global governance.

Conclusion

The future of our species is fraught with danger. But humankind possesses many resources with which to deal with the challenges ahead. New technology and skills will be needed, and many presently unforeseeable scientific and engineering innovations will surely be forthcoming. But that, arguably, will be the easy part. More challenging, though well within our power, will be the development of an appropriate global ethos. It will probably take several generations before such an ethos becomes the global norm. But it is already growing apace and will eventually take root among a critical mass of citizen activists. This new cosmopolitan ethos will emphasize inclusiveness and equality of opportunity. It will promote social and economic systems marked by mutual concern and respect, fairness and cooperation. It will foster a sense of shared stewardship of our endangered planet.

Humankind will also have to transform its systems of *government* (not merely *governance*) at the global, regional, national and local levels, strengthening some existing agencies, doing away with others and inventing still more needed to address mounting existential dangers and evolving human needs. Difficult though the task will be, we have it within our power to build a workable world. The present volume provides numerous designs to help bring that world to fruition.

Notes

1. Office of the Federal Register, National Archives and Records Administration, *The Public Papers of the Presidents, Dwight D. Eisenhower, 1960*, Ann Arbor, MI: University of Michigan Digital Library, quod.lib.umich.edu/p/ppotpus, pp. 1035–1040.
2. A five-to-four US Supreme Court decision in the case of *Citizens United v. Federal Election Commission* ruled in 2010 that corporations, being regarded as "legal persons", were entitled to free speech under the First Amendment to the US Constitution, and held that contributing financially to political campaigns was an expression of that right. *New York Times*, "Justices, 5–4, Reject Corporate Spending Limit", *New York Times*, 21 January 2010.
3. The ideas addressed here are documented in virtually every issue of *Defense Monitor*, published by the Center for Defense Information, www.cdi.otg. Also quite useful is the newsletter of Economists for Peace and Security (originally Economists Allied for Arms Reduction), http://epsusa.org.
4. Robert W. McChesney and John Nichols, *The Death and Life of American Journalism: The Media Revolution That Will Begin the World Again*, New York: Nation Books, 2010.
5. Year after year, according to World Public Opinion Org (www.americans-world.org/digest/global_issues/un/un1.cfm), polls demonstrate overwhelming support for the United Nations among the US public. In February 2005, for example, a Gallup poll indicated 64 per cent of Americans believed that "The UN plays a necessary role in the world." In May 2005 a Group Managers Forum poll found 56 per cent agreed that the United Nations "can manage most of the world's most pressing problems better than any single country". A Program on International Policy Attitudes poll in November 2003 found that 72 per cent of Americans believed the United Nations should play "a greater role in ... dealing with world problems". A Chicago Council poll in July 2006 found that 79 per cent felt strengthening the United Nations should be a "very important" (40 per cent) or "important" (39 per cent) goal, as opposed to only 19 per cent who felt otherwise.

6. A broad spectrum of voting reform measures is offered by Fair Vote (formerly the Center for Voting and Democracy), www.fairvote.org. For recommendations focusing on campaign financing see Common Cause, www.commoncause.org.

7. Wikipedia, "Department of Peace", http://en.wikipedia.org/wiki/Department_of_Peace.

8. Edwin O. Reischauer, *Towards the 21st Century: Education for a Changing World*, New York: Alfred A. Knopf, 1973.

9. Translations are presently available in Arabic, Bahasa Indonesia/Malay, Bengali, Chinese, Czech, Danish, Dutch, Esperanto, Farsi (Persian), Finnish, French, German, Greek, Gujarati, Hausa, Hebrew, Hindi, Hmong, Italian, Japanese, Kannada, Kashmiri, Khmer (Cambodian), Korean, Marathi, Norwegian, Ojibway, Polish, Portuguese, Punjabi, Russian, Sanskrit, Sinhala, Somali, Spanish, Swahili, Swedish, Tamil, Telugu, Thai, Turkish, Urdu and Vietnamese. All translations are available in the roman script and, wherever appropriate, in other scripts as well.

10. Among numerous worthy initiatives, I would single out the International Peace Research Association, www.iprafoundation.org, founded in 1964 and operating through five regional groups: Africa, Asia-Pacific, Latin America, Europe and North America. The North American affiliate is the Peace and Justice Studies Association (PJSA), www.peacejusticestudies.org, formed in 2001 through merger of the Consortium on Peace Research, Education and Development and the Peace Studies Association. The PJSA works mainly with academics, K-12 teachers and grassroots activists to explore alternatives to violence and promote strategies for peacebuilding, social justice and social change.

11. The figure 922 million should not be taken as an indication of the actual number of tourists, since many tourists visit multiple countries on a single trip abroad. Additionally, some tourists make multiple trips during a single year. Figures provided by UN World Tourism Organization, cited in Wikipedia, "Tourism", http://en.wikipedia.org/wiki/Tourism.

12. John Donne, "No Man Is an Island", Meditation XVII, Devotions from Emergent Occasions [1620], in M. H. Abrams (ed.), *The Norton Anthology of English Literature*, Vol. 1, 4th edn, New York: W. W. Norton, 1979, pp. 1108–1109.

13. Quotation varies from one commentator to another; source and date are in dispute.

14. Immanuel Kant, *Perpetual Peace*, New York: Columbia University Press, 1939 (translation of 1796 edition), p. 11.

15. Prominent among modern advocates of cosmopolitanism is David Held of the London School of Economics and Political Science. Among his works are *Global Covenant, The Social Democratic Alternative to the Washington Consensus*, Cambridge: Polity Press, 2004; *Cosmopolitanism: Ideals and Reality*, Cambridge: Polity Press, 2010. See also David Held and Anthony McGrew (eds), *Governing Globalization: Power, Authority and Global Governance*, Cambridge: Polity Press, 2002; David Held and Garrett Wallace Brown (eds), *The Cosmopolitanism Reader*, Cambridge: Polity Press, 2010. The 26 essays in this reader include four by or about Kant, including Kant's "The Idea of a Universal History with a Cosmopolitan Purpose". Apart from the editors, other prominent authors include Daniele Archibugi, Brian Barry, Jacques Derrida, Jürgen Habermas and Mary Kaldor. A variant of the concept of cosmopolitanism is "communitarianism", an approach that lays relatively greater stress on responsibility (in addition to rights), and is championed by Amitai Etzioni, a professor of sociology at George Washington University and founder and director of the Communitarian Network. Among his many books are *The New Golden Rule: Community and Morality in a Democratic Society*, New York: Basic Books, 1997; *Political Unification Revisited: On Building Supernational Communites*, Lanham, MD: Lexington Books, 2001; *From Empire to Community, A New Approach to International Relations*, New York: Palgrave Macmillan, 2004.

16. John E. Trent, *Modernizing the United Nations System: Civil Society's Role in Moving from International Relations to Global Governance*, Opladen and Farmington Hills, MI: Barbara Budrich Publishers, 2007.
17. Ibid., pp. 240–241.
18. Ibid., p. 241, citing Mihaly Simai, *The Future of Global Governance*, Washington, DC: US Institute of Peace Press, 1994, p. 348.
19. Trent, ibid., pp. 199–215, succinctly describes 59 coalitions, organizations and prominent individual reform activists and provides their internet addresses.
20. Ibid., pp. 242–243.
21. Ibid., pp. 243–245. In the foregoing paragraph, I have simplified a rather nuanced discussion.
22. Edward C. Luck, "Principal Organs", in Thomas G. Weiss and Sam Daws (eds), *The Oxford Handbook on the United Nations*, New York and Oxford: Oxford University Press, 2007, pp. 660–661.
23. Luisa Kroll, "The World's Biggest Givers", *Forbes*, http://blogs.forbes.co/luisakroll//2011/05/19/the-world's-biggest-givers.
24. See www/bloomberg.com/news/2010-08-11/biggest-iceberg-in-half-a-century-flows-toward-atlantic-shipping-lanes.html.
25. Climate Institute, www.climate.org/topics/sea-level/index.html.

Appendix 1

Selected data for UN members

By column

1. **Current name.**
2. **Date of admission to United Nations** (where two dates are given, the first indicates admission as part of another nation from which the nation named was later separated; the second indicates when the nation was admitted in its own right).
3. **Population** (in 000s, 2010).
4. **Population as percentage of total.**
5. **UN assessment** (percentage of regular budget).
6. **GNI** (gross national income, US$ billion, 2009).
7. **GNI as percentage of total.**
8. **Weighted vote** in proposed General Assembly (based on 2009–2010 data); GNI data used for assessment term in weighted voting formula.
9. **Economic bloc:** OECD, G-77 or neither (N).
10. **Freedom House rating** (based on average scores for political liberties and civil liberties, 2010; F, Free; PF, Partly free; and NF, Not free).
11. **Proposed Security Council regions: AF,** Africa South of the Sahara; **AL,** Arab League; **CH,** China; **EA,** East Asia; **EU,** Europe; **IN,** India; **LA,** Latin America and Caribbean; **RU,** Russia and certain neighbouring republics; **SE,** Southeast Asia; **US**, United States; **WA,** West Asia, **WL,** Westminster League.

Transforming the United Nations system: Designs for a workable world, Schwartzberg, United Nations University Press, 2013, ISBN 978-92-808-1230-5

Nation 1	Date of UN admission 2	Population (thousands) 3	Population (%) 4	UN assessment (%) 5	GNI ($ billion) 6	GNI (%) 7	Weighted vote, GA 8	Economic bloc 9	FH class 10	Proposed SC region 11
Afghanistan	1946	26,290	0.386	0.004	10.60	0.018	0.308	G-77	NF	WA
Albania	1955	3,205	0.047	0.010	12.50	0.021	0.196	N	PF	EU
Algeria	1961	35,866	0.527	0.128	154.20	0.263	0.437	G-77	NF	AL
Andorra	1993	83	0.001	0.007	3.40	0.006	0.176	N	F	EU
Angola	1976	18,993	0.279	0.010	64.50	0.110	0.303	G-77	NF	AF
Antigua & Barbuda	1981	90	0.001	0.002	1.10	0.002	0.175	G-77	F	LA
Argentina	1945	40,666	0.598	0.287	304.70	0.520	0.546	G-77	F	LA
Armenia	1945/1992	3,090	0.045	0.005	9.50	0.016	0.194	N	PF	RU
Australia	1945	22,403	0.329	1.933	957.50	1.633	0.828	OECD	F	WL
Austria	1955	8,382	0.123	0.851	391.80	0.668	0.437	OECD	F	EU
Azerbaijan	1945/1992	9,063	0.133	0.015	42.50	0.072	0.242	N	NF	WA
Bahamas	1973	347	0.005	0.018	7.10	0.012	0.179	G-77	F	LA
Bahrain	1971	1,216	0.018	0.039	19.70	0.034	0.191	G-77	NF	AL
Bangladesh	1945/1974	158,066	2.324	0.010	95.40	0.163	1.002	G-77	PF	WA
Barbados	1966	276	0.004	0.008	3.30	0.006	0.177	G-77	F	LA
Belarus	1945	9,457	0.139	0.042	53.50	0.091	0.250	N	NF	RU
Belgium	1945	10,868	0.160	1.075	488.80	0.833	0.505	OECD	F	EU
Belize	1961	345	0.005	0.001	1.20	0.002	0.176	G-77	F	LA
Benin	1960	9,050	0.133	0.003	6.70	0.011	0.222	G-77	F	AF
Bhutan	1971	721	0.011	0.001	1.40	0.002	0.178	G-77	PF	EA
Bolivia	1945	9,947	0.146	0.007	16.00	0.027	0.231	G-77	PF	LA
Bosnia & Herzegovina	1945/1992	3,859	0.057	0.014	17.70	0.030	0.203	G-77	PF	EU
Botswana	1966	2,029	0.030	0.018	12.20	0.021	0.190	G-77	F	AF
Brazil	1945	193,253	2.841	1.611	1,557.20	2.655	2.006	G-77	F	LA
Brunei	1964	414	0.006	0.028	10.20	0.017	0.181	G-77	NF	SE

Nation 1	Date of UN admission 2	Population (thousands) 3	Population (%) 4	UN assessment (%) 5	GNI ($ billion) 6	GNI (%) 7	Weighted vote, GA 8	Economic bloc 9	FH class 10	Proposed SC region 11
Bulgaria	1955	7,562	0.111	0.038	43.70	0.075	0.236	N	F	EU
Burkina Faso	1960	16,287	0.239	0.003	8.00	0.014	0.258	G-77	PF	AF
Burundi	1962	8,519	0.125	0.001	1.20	0.002	0.216	G-77	PF	AF
Cambodia	1955	14,414	0.212	0.003	9.70	0.017	0.250	G-77	NF	SE
Cameroon	1960	19,640	0.289	0.011	22.80	0.039	0.283	G-77	NF	AF
Canada	1945	34,132	0.502	3.207	1,423.00	2.426	1.150	OECD	F	WL
Cape Verde	1975	509	0.007	0.001	1.50	0.003	0.177	G-77	F	AF
Central African Republic	1960	4,845	0.071	0.001	2.00	0.003	0.198	G-77	PF	AF
Chad	1960	11,594	0.170	0.002	6.90	0.012	0.234	G-77	NF	AF
Chile	1945	16,746	0.246	0.236	159.90	0.273	0.347	OECD	F	LA
China	1945	1,345,672	19.783	3.189	5,053.10	8.616	9.640	G-77	NF	CH
Colombia	1945	44,205	0.650	0.144	225.20	0.384	0.518	G-77	PF	LA
Comoros	1975	691	0.010	0.001	0.60	0.001	0.177	G-77	PF	LA
Congo, Democratic Republic of	1960	67,827	0.997	0.003	6.70	0.011	0.197	G-77	NF	AF
Congo, Republic of	1960	3,936	0.058	0.003	10.70	0.018	0.512	G-77	NF	AF
Costa Rica	1945	4,516	0.066	0.034	28.50	0.049	0.212	G-77	F	LA
Côte d'Ivoire	1960	21,059	0.310	0.010	22.40	0.038	0.290	G-77	NF	AF
Croatia	1945/1992	4,426	0.065	0.097	61.20	0.104	0.230	N	F	EU
Cuba	1945	11,239	0.165	0.071	51.50	0.088	0.258	G-77	NF	LA
Cyprus	1960	1,085	0.016	0.046	21.40	0.036	0.191	N	F	EU
Czech Republic	1945	10,526	0.155	0.349	181.50	0.309	0.328	OECD	F	EU
Denmark	1945	5,546	0.082	0.736	325.80	0.556	0.386	OECD	F	EU
Djibouti	1977	833	0.012	0.001	1.10	0.002	0.178	G-77	PF	AL
Dominica	1978	72	0.001	0.001	0.40	0.001	0.174	G-77	F	LA

	1945	9,864	0.145	0.042	45.50	0.078	0.248	G-77	F	LA
Dominican Republic	1945	9,864	0.145	0.042	45.50	0.078	0.248	G-77	PF	LA
Ecuador	1945	14,219	0.209	0.040	53.40	0.091	0.274	G-77	PF	LA
Egypt	1945	84,474	1.242	0.094	172.00	0.293	0.685	G-77	NF	AL
El Salvador	1945	6,052	0.089	0.019	20.80	0.035	0.215	G-77	F	LA
Equatorial Guinea	1968	651	0.010	0.008	8.40	0.014	0.182	G-77	NF	AF
Eritrea	1952/1993	5,224	0.077	0.001	1.50	0.003	0.200	G-77	NF	AF
Estonia	1945/1991	1,348	0.020	0.040	18.80	0.032	0.191	N	F	EU
Ethiopia	1945	79,456	1.168	0.008	27.00	0.046	0.578	G-77	PF	AF
Fiji	1970	844	0.012	0.004	3.40	0.006	0.180	G-77	PF	WL
Finland	1955	5,364	0.079	0.566	243.90	0.416	0.339	OECD	F	EU
France	1945	62,762	0.923	6.123	2,754.60	4.697	2.047	OECD	F	EU
Gabon	1960	1,501	0.022	0.014	10.90	0.019	0.187	G-77	NF	AF
The Gambia	1965	1,751	0.026	0.001	0.70	0.001	0.183	G-77	PF	AF
Georgia	1945/1992	4,356	0.064	0.006	11.10	0.019	0.201	N	PF	RU
Germany	1973	81,644	1.200	8.018	3,484.70	5.942	2.554	OECD	F	EU
Ghana	1957	24,340	0.358	0.006	16.60	0.028	0.302	G-77	F	AF
Greece	1945	11,329	0.167	0.691	323.10	0.551	0.413	OECD	F	EU
Grenada	1974	108	0.002	0.001	0.60	0.001	0.174	G-77	F	LA
Guatemala	1945	14,377	0.211	0.028	36.80	0.063	0.265	G-77	PF	LA
Guinea	1958	10,324	0.152	0.002	3.80	0.006	0.226	G-77	NF	AF
Guinea-Bissau	1974	1,593	0.023	0.001	0.80	0.001	0.182	G-77	PF	AF
Guyana	1966	748	0.011	0.001	1.10	0.002	0.178	G-77	F	LA
Haiti	1945	9,649	0.142	0.003	4.60	0.008	0.224	G-77	PF	LA
Honduras	1945	7,616	0.112	0.008	13.60	0.023	0.219	G-77	PF	LA
Hungary	1955	10,005	0.147	0.291	130.10	0.222	0.297	G-77	F	EU
Iceland	1946	317	0.005	0.042	13.80	0.024	0.183	OECD	F	EU
India	1945	1,173,108	17.246	0.534	1,368.70	2.334	6.700	G-77	F	IN
Indonesia	1950	232,517	3.418	0.238	513.40	0.875	1.605	G-77	F	SE
Iran	1945	73,887	1.086	0.233	330.60	0.564	0.724	G-77	NF	WA
Iraq	1945	31,467	0.463	0.020	69.70	0.119	0.367	G-77	NF	AL
Ireland	1955	4,451	0.065	0.498	197.20	0.336	0.308	OECD	F	EU

Nation 1	Date of UN admission 2	Population (thousands) 3	Population (%) 4	UN assessment (%) 5	GNI ($ billion) 6	GNI (%) 7	Weighted vote, GA 8	Economic bloc 9	FH class 10	Proposed SC region 11
Israel	1949	7,302	0.107	0.384	191.60	0.327	0.318	OECD	F	EU
Italy	1955	60,487	0.889	4.999	2,112.50	3.602	1.671	OECD	F	EU
Jamaica	1962	2,702	0.040	0.014	13.50	0.023	0.195	G-77	F	LA
Japan	1956	127,320	1.872	12.530	4,830.30	8.236	3.543	OECD	F	EA
Jordan	1955	6,046	0.089	0.014	22.30	0.038	0.216	G-77	NF	AL
Kazakhstan	1945/1992	16,310	0.240	0.076	107.10	0.183	0.314	N	NF	WA
Kenya	1963	40,863	0.601	0.012	30.70	0.052	0.391	G-77	PF	AF
Kiribati	1999	99	0.001	0.001	0.20	0.000	0.174	N	F	WL
Korea, Democratic People's Republic of	1991	24,247	0.356	0.007	25.60	0.044	0.307	G-77	NF	EA
Korea, Republic of	1991	49,169	0.723	2.260	966.60	1.648	0.964	OECD	F	EA
Kuwait	1963	3,529	0.052	0.263	117.00	0.199	0.257	G-77	PF	AL
Kyrgyzstan	1945/1992	5,141	0.076	0.001	4.60	0.008	0.201	N	NF	WA
Laos	1955	6,258	0.092	0.001	5.60	0.010	0.207	G-77	NF	SE
Latvia	1945/1991	2,238	0.033	0.038	27.90	0.048	0.200	N	F	EU
Lebanon	1945	4,125	0.061	0.033	33.60	0.057	0.213	G-77	PF	AL
Lesotho	1966	1,920	0.028	0.001	2.10	0.004	0.184	G-77	PF	AF
Liberia	1945	3,763	0.055	0.001	0.60	0.001	0.192	G-77	PF	AF
Libya	1955	6,546	0.096	0.129	77.20	0.132	0.250	G-77	NF	AL
Liechtenstein	1990	36	0.001	0.009	4.00	0.007	0.176	N	F	EU
Lithuania	1945/1991	3,297	0.048	0.065	38.10	0.065	0.211	N	F	EU
Luxembourg	1945	506	0.007	0.090	37.10	0.063	0.197	OECD	F	EU
Macedonia	1945/1993	2,051	0.030	0.007	9.00	0.015	0.189	G-77	PF	EU
Madagascar	1960	20,146	0.296	0.003	7.90	0.013	0.277	G-77	PF	AF
Malawi	1964	15,448	0.227	0.001	4.20	0.007	0.252	G-77	PF	AF

Country	Year									
Malaysia	1957	28,275	0.416	0.253	198.70	0.339	0.425	G-77	PF	SE
Maldives	1965	320	0.005	0.001	1.20	0.002	0.176	G-77	PF	WA
Mali	1960	15,022	0.221	0.003	8.90	0.015	0.252	G-77	F	AF
Malta	1964	413	0.006	0.017	6.80	0.012	0.179	N	F	EU
Marshall Islands	1991	54	0.001	0.001	0.20	0.000	0.174	G-77	F	WL
Mauritania	1961	3,205	0.047	0.001	3.20	0.005	0.191	G-77	NF	AL
Mauritius	1968	1,282	0.019	0.011	9.20	0.016	0.185	G-77	F	AF
Mexico	1945	108,396	1.594	2.356	958.80	1.635	1.250	OECD	F	LA
Micronesia	1991	111	0.002	0.001	0.20	0.000	0.174	G-77	F	WL
Moldova	1945/1992	3,941	0.058	0.002	5.70	0.010	0.196	N	PF	RU
Monaco	1993	35	0.001	0.003	6.70	0.011	0.178	N	F	EU
Mongolia	1961	2,763	0.041	0.002	4.40	0.008	0.190	N	F	EA
Montenegro	1945/2006	633	0.009	0.004	4.10	0.007	0.179	N	F	EU
Morocco	1956	31,627	0.465	0.058	90.70	0.155	0.380	G-77	PF	AL
Mozambique	1975	22,426	0.330	0.003	10.00	0.017	0.289	G-77	PF	AF
Myanmar (Burma)	1948	53,414	0.785	0.006	13.60	0.023	0.443	G-77	NF	SE
Namibia	1990	2,212	0.033	0.008	9.30	0.016	0.190	G-77	F	AF
Nauru	1999	0	0.000	0.001	0.80	0.001	0.174	N	F	WL
Nepal	1955	28,952	0.426	0.006	13.00	0.022	0.323	G-77	PF	EA
Netherlands	1945	16,602	0.244	1.855	815.80	1.391	0.719	OECD	F	EU
New Zealand	1945	4,367	0.064	0.273	114.50	0.195	0.260	OECD	F	WL
Nicaragua	1945	5,822	0.086	0.003	5.80	0.010	0.205	G-77	PF	LA
Niger	1960	15,678	0.230	0.002	5.20	0.009	0.253	G-77	PF	AF
Nigeria	1960	158,259	2.327	0.078	175.80	0.300	1.049	G-77	PF	AF
Norway	1945	4,888	0.072	0.871	417.30	0.712	0.435	OECD	F	EU
Oman	1971	2,968	0.044	0.086	49.80	0.085	0.216	G-77	NF	AL
Pakistan	1945/1947	184,405	2.711	0.082	172.90	0.295	1.176	G-77	PF	WA
Palau	1994	21	0.000	0.001	0.20	0.000	0.174	N	F	WL
Panama	1945	3,328	0.049	0.022	23.20	0.040	0.203	G-77	F	LA
Papua New Guinea	1975	6,065	0.089	0.002	7.90	0.013	0.208	G-77	PF	WL
Paraguay	1945	6,376	0.094	0.007	14.40	0.025	0.213	G-77	PF	LA
Peru	1945	29,244	0.430	0.090	120.90	0.206	0.386	G-77	F	LA

Nation 1	Date of UN admission 2	Population (thousands) 3	Population (%) 4	UN assessment (%) 5	GNI ($ billion) 6	GNI (%) 7	Weighted vote, GA 8	Economic bloc 9	FH class 10	Proposed SC region 11
Philippines	1945	93,617	1.376	0.090	164.50	0.280	0.726	G-77	PF	SE
Poland	1945	38,183	0.561	0.828	467.50	0.797	0.626	OECD	F	EU
Portugal	1955	10,643	0.156	0.511	222.60	0.380	0.352	OECD	F	EU
Qatar	1971	1,697	0.025	0.135	54.30	0.093	0.213	G-77	NF	AL
Romania	1955	21,444	0.315	0.177	178.90	0.305	0.380	N	F	EU
Russia	1945	141,892	2.086	1.602	1,329.70	2.267	1.625	N	NF	RU
Rwanda	1962	10,277	0.151	0.001	4.60	0.008	0.227	G-77	NF	AF
Samoa	1976	183	0.003	0.001	0.50	0.001	0.175	G-77	F	WL
San Marino	1992	31	0.000	0.003	1.60	0.003	0.175	N	F	EU
São Tomé & Príncipe	1975	176	0.003	0.001	0.20	0.000	0.175	G-77	F	AF
Saudi Arabia	1945	25,732	0.378	0.830	439.00	0.749	0.549	G-77	NF	AL
Senegal	1960	12,323	0.181	0.006	12.90	0.022	0.241	G-77	PF	AF
Serbia	1945/2000	7,293	0.107	0.037	43.80	0.075	0.234	N	F	EU
Seychelles	1976	88	0.001	0.002	0.70	0.001	0.174	G-77	PF	AF
Sierra Leone	1961	5,836	0.086	0.001	1.90	0.003	0.203	G-77	PF	AF
Singapore	1963/1965	5,093	0.075	0.335	185.70	0.317	0.304	G-77	PF	SE
Slovakia	1945/1993	5,431	0.080	0.142	87.40	0.149	0.250	OECD	F	EU
Slovenia	1992	2,051	0.030	0.103	48.10	0.082	0.211	OECD	F	EU
Solomon Islands	1978	536	0.008	0.001	0.50	0.001	0.177	G-77	PF	WL
Somalia	1960	9,359	0.138	0.001	2.30	0.004	0.221	G-77	NF	AL
South Africa	1945	49,991	0.735	0.385	284.50	0.485	0.580	G-77	F	AF
Spain	1955	46,508	0.684	3.177	1,464.70	2.497	1.234	OECD	F	EU
Sri Lanka	1955	20,410	0.300	0.019	40.40	0.069	0.297	G-77	PF	SE
St Kitts & Nevis	1983	50	0.001	0.001	0.50	0.001	0.174	G-77	F	LA
St Lucia	1979	174	0.003	0.001	0.90	0.002	0.175	G-77	F	LA
St Vincent & Grenadines	1980	101	0.001	0.001	0.60	0.001	0.174	G-77	F	LA

Country										
Sudan	1956	43,940	0.646	0.010	51.60	0.088	0.418	G-77	NF	AL
Suriname	1975	524	0.008	0.003	2.50	0.004	0.178	G-77	F	LA
Swaziland	1968	1,354	0.020	0.003	2.80	0.005	0.182	G-77	NF	AF
Sweden	1946	9,380	0.138	1.064	455.20	0.776	0.478	OECD	F	EU
Switzerland	2002	7,807	0.115	1.130	431.10	0.735	0.457	OECD	F	EU
Syria	1945	22,141	0.325	0.025	50.90	0.087	0.311	G-77	NF	AL
Tajikistan	1945/1992	7,075	0.104	0.002	4.80	0.008	0.211	G-77	NF	WA
Tanzania	1961	41,893	0.616	0.008	21.30	0.036	0.391	G-77	PF	AF
Thailand	1946	67,090	0.986	0.209	254.70	0.434	0.647	G-77	PF	SE
Timor-Leste	2002	1,143	0.017	0.001	2.70	0.005	0.181	G-77	PF	SE
Togo	1960	6,587	0.097	0.001	2.90	0.005	0.208	G-77	PF	AF
Tonga	1999	103	0.002	0.001	0.30	0.001	0.174	G-77	PF	WL
Trinidad & Tobago	1962	1,312	0.019	0.044	22.10	0.038	0.193	G-77	F	LA
Tunisia	1956	10,374	0.153	0.030	38.80	0.066	0.247	G-77	NF	AL
Turkey	1945	73,085	1.074	0.617	653.10	1.114	0.903	OECD	PF	WA
Turkmenistan	1945/1992	4,941	0.073	0.026	17.50	0.030	0.208	G-77	NF	WA
Tuvalu	2000	11	0.000	0.001	0.03	0.000	0.174	N	F	WL
Uganda	1962	33,793	0.497	0.006	15.00	0.026	0.348	G-77	PF	AF
Ukraine	1945	45,858	0.674	0.087	128.80	0.220	0.472	N	F	RU
United Arab Emirates	1971	5,188	0.076	0.391	174.50	0.298	0.298	G-77	PF	AL
United Kingdom	1945	62,227	0.915	6.604	2,567.50	4.378	1.938	OECD	F	EU
United States	1945	310,062	4.558	22.000	14,502.60	24.728	9.936	OECD	F	US
Uruguay	1945	3,372	0.050	0.027	31.30	0.053	0.208	G-77	F	LA
Uzbekistan	1945/1992	27,866	0.410	0.010	30.50	0.052	0.328	N	NF	WA
Vanuatu	1981	251	0.004	0.001	0.60	0.001	0.175	G-77	F	WL
Venezuela	1945	29,094	0.428	0.314	288.10	0.491	0.480	G-77	PF	LA
Viet Nam	1977	87,117	1.281	0.033	88.00	0.150	0.651	G-77	NF	SE
Yemen	1947	23,494	0.345	0.010	25.00	0.043	0.303	G-77	NF	AL
Zambia	1964	13,460	0.198	0.004	12.60	0.021	0.247	G-77	PF	AF
Zimbabwe	1980	12,644	0.186	0.003	1.70	0.003	0.237	G-77	NF	AF
		6,802,164	100.000	100.000	58,648.03	100.000	100.000			

Appendix 2

Composition of proposed Security Council regions

Notes: Population in thousands as of 2010; GNI in US$ billions as of 2009.

Africa South of the Sahara

Angola, Benin, Botswana, Burkina Faso, Burundi, Cameroon, Cape Verde, Central African Republic, Chad, Democratic Republic of the Congo, Republic of Congo, Côte d'Ivoire, Equatorial Guinea, Eritrea, Ethiopia, Gabon, The Gambia, Guinea, Guinea-Bissau, Kenya, Lesotho, Liberia, Madagascar, Malawi, Mali, Mauritius, Mozambique, Namibia, Niger, Nigeria, Rwanda, São Tomé & Príncipe, Senegal, Seychelles, Sierra Leone, South Africa, Swaziland, Tanzania, Togo, Uganda, Zambia, Zimbabwe
Number of countries: 42 – 21.88 per cent
Population: 794,569 – 11.68 per cent
GNI: 860.30 – 1.49 per cent
Voting weight: 7.16 per cent

Arab League

Algeria, Bahrain, Comoros, Djibouti, Egypt, Iraq, Jordan, Kuwait, Lebanon, Libya, Mauritania, Morocco, Oman, Qatar, Saudi Arabia, Somalia, Sudan, Syria, Tunisia, United Arab Emirates, Yemen

Transforming the United Nations system: Designs for a workable world, Schwartzberg,
United Nations University Press, 2013, ISBN 978-92-808-1230-5

Number of countries: 21 – 10.42 per cent
Population: 353,827 – 5.20 per cent
GNI: 1,646.9 – 2.82 per cent
Voting weight: 5.45 per cent

China

Number of countries: 1 – 0.52 per cent
Population: 1,345,672 – 19.78 per cent
GNI: 5,053.1 – 8.62 per cent
Voting weight: 12.24 per cent

East Asia

Bhutan, Japan, Democratic People's Republic of Korea, Republic of Korea, Mongolia, Nepal
Number of countries: 6 – 3.13 per cent
Population: 233,172 – 3.43 per cent
GNI: 5,841.3 – 9.96 per cent
Voting weight: 7.24 per cent

Europe

Albania, Andorra, Austria, Belgium, Bosnia & Herzegovina, Bulgaria, Croatia, Cyprus, Czech Republic, Denmark, Estonia, Finland, France, Germany, Greece, Hungary, Iceland, Ireland, Israel, Italy, Latvia, Liechtenstein, Lithuania, Luxembourg, Macedonia, Malta, Monaco, Montenegro, The Netherlands, Norway, Poland, Portugal, Romania, San Marino, Serbia, Slovakia, Slovenia, Spain, Sweden, Switzerland, United Kingdom
Number of countries: 41 – 21.35 per cent
Population: 542,248 – 7.97 per cent
GNI: 18,353.3 – 31.29 per cent
Voting weight: 15.86 per cent

India

Number of countries: 1
Population: 1,173,108 – 17.25 per cent

GNI: 1,368.7 – 2.33 per cent
Voting weight: 9.30 per cent

Latin America and the Caribbean

Antigua & Barbuda, Argentina, Bahamas, Barbados, Belize, Bolivia, Brazil, Chile, Colombia, Costa Rica, Cuba, Dominica, Dominican Republic, Ecuador, El Salvador, Grenada, Guatemala, Guyana, Haiti, Honduras, Jamaica, Mexico, Nicaragua, Panama, Paraguay, Peru, St Kitts & Nevis, St Lucia, St Vincent & Grenadines, Suriname, Trinidad & Tobago, Uruguay, Venezuela
Number of countries: 33 – 17.19 per cent
Population: 574,830 – 8.46 per cent
GNI: 4,015.1 – 6.92 per cent
Voting weight: 7.90 per cent

Russia and Neighbours

Armenia, Belarus, Georgia, Moldova, Russia, Ukraine
Number of countries: 6 – 3.13 per cent
Population: 208,594 – 3.07 per cent
GNI: 1,538.3 – 2.62 per cent
Voting weight: 4.67 per cent

Southeast Asia

Brunei, Cambodia, Indonesia, Laos, Malaysia, Myanmar (Burma), Philippines, Singapore, Sri Lanka, Thailand, Timor-Leste, Viet Nam
Number of countries: 12 – 6.25 per cent
Population: 609,762 – 8.96 per cent
GNI: 1,487.2 – 2.54 per cent
Voting weight: 6.61 per cent

United States

Number of countries: 1 – 0.52 per cent
Population: 310,062 – 4.56 per cent
GNI: 14,502.6 – 24.73 per cent
Voting weight: 12.53 per cent

West Asia

Afghanistan, Azerbaijan, Bangladesh, Iran, Kazakhstan, Kyrgyzstan, Maldives, Pakistan, Tajikistan, Turkey, Turkmenistan, Uzbekistan
Number of countries: 12 – 6.25 per cent
Population: 586,449 – 8.62 per cent
GNI: 1,470.8 – 2.51 per cent
Voting weight: 6.49 per cent

Westminster League

Australia, Canada, Fiji, Kiribati, Marshall Islands, Micronesia, Nauru, New Zealand, Palau, Papua New Guinea, Samoa, Solomon Islands, Tonga, Tuvalu, Vanuatu
Number of countries: 15 – 7.81 per cent
Population: 69,180 – 1.02 per cent
GNI: 2,509.83 – 4.28 per cent
Voting weight: 4.53 per cent

Index